MEDIA IN
AMERICA

MEDIA IN

THE WILSON QUARTERLY READER

AMERICA

Revised Edition

edited by

DOUGLAS GOMERY

Published by the

WOODROW WILSON CENTER PRESS

Distributed by the

JOHNS HOPKINS UNIVERSITY PRESS

The Woodrow Wilson Center Press
Editorial Offices
370 L'Enfant Promenade, S.W.
Suite 704
Washington, D.C. 20024-2518 U.S.A.
telephone 202-287-3000, ext. 218

Distributed by
The Johns Hopkins University Press
Hampden Station
Baltimore, Maryland 21211
order department telephone 1-800-537-5487

Printed in the United States of America

♾ Printed on acid-free paper.

9 8 7 6 5 4 3 2 1

Library of Congress Cataloging-in-Publication Data
Media in America : the Wilson quarterly reader / edited by Douglas
    Gomery.—Rev. ed.
        p.   cm
    Rev. ed. of: American media / edited by Philip S. Cook. 1989.
    Includes bibliographical references.
    ISBN 0-943875-86-2 (alk. paper).—ISBN 0-943875-87-0 (pbk.
alk. paper)
    1. Mass media—United States.   2. Popular culture—United States.
I. Gomery, Douglas.   II. Wilson quarterly.   III. American media.
P92.U5A49   1998
302.23'097—dc21   98-13340
                                                                CIP

CONTENTS

TELEVISION AND NEW TECHNOLOGIES

FOREWORD

LAWRENCE W. LICHTY

This book is dedicated to Peter Braestrup, 1929–1997. In his "Editor's Comment" of the first issue of *The Wilson Quarterly,* autumn 1976, Peter Braestrup wrote: "Our aim is to provide an authoritative overview of current ideas and research on matters of public policy and general intellectual interest." I think Peter would agree that the articles of this volume are a very fine example of what he had in mind at that time.

From the beginning, the *Quarterly* has presented thoughtful and balanced accounts of the impact of media on American life. A cluster of articles on TV news and politics in winter 1998 provided a criticism of the coverage of the 1976 election with responses from TV network news executives. It was based on a Woodrow Wilson Center conference held January 18, 1997. The *Quarterly's* review of periodicals includes a section on Press and Television. Besides his years as a reporter, Peter's deep interest in evaluating press performance stemmed from his massive analysis of the Tet offensive in *The Big Story.*

I met Peter at the Da Nang airport in July 1968. He was a correspondent for the *Washington Post,* having just recently moved from the *New York Times.* I was visiting Vietnam trying to learn more about the TV coverage of the war. We were sitting back to back trying to sleep while waiting for a flight north to I Corps when he introduced himself to me.

In 1977 while I was fellow at the Woodrow Wilson Center, and just after Peter had founded the *Quarterly,* I proposed that we collaborate to try to establish a small unit within the Center to study the media. Peter was the promoter, organizer, and tireless fundraiser. By 1988, he had secured enough money to support the Center's new Media Studies Project for five years of operation. By 1992, the Media Studies Project had produced more than a score of monographs, articles, and book chapters by a nearly equal mix of journalists and academics. There were also contributions to a number of books—listed at the end of this volume. Most were evaluations of press performance based on careful case studies. But it was the mix of fellows that most interested Peter. His fervent belief was that journalists and academics had much to learn from each other. It is self-centered, of course, but I always believed that part of this came from the constant dialogue we had about television and newspapers. More realistically, I know it was from his own education—his father was a distinguished scientist and professor, and he was a Nieman fellow—and careful reading.

Few things pleased Peter more than the idea that time at the Media Studies Project could convince an academic to pick up the phone or trot across town to talk with a source with first-hand experience on reporting a story. Yet he was just as pleased when journalists would seek the aid of scholars or bury themselves in books. Again, as he stated in that first issue of the *Quarterly:* "As a group, of course, scholars have no monopoly on wisdom or even rational analysis."

Phil Cook directed the Project for half its time, I followed him. Douglas Gomery, editor of this volume, was the senior researcher during the life of the Media Studies Project and was the single most important influence on virtually all of the work done there. Doug's fine hand was never more in evidence than in this book. Peter always intended that there be very close cooperation between the Project and the *Quarterly.* The prodding, questioning, and editing of Steve Lagerfeld, Jay Tolson, and others greatly benefited most of the articles contained herein.

After you have read the articles gathered here, I think you will agree that what Peter said in 1976 of scholars applies equally to this collection:

"They refresh our thinking, surprise us with new data, occasionally remind us of old truths and new paradoxes lost in the daily hubbub of the press and television. Their more powerful ideas eventually help shape our perceptions, our politics, and our lives."

INTRODUCTION

Since *The Wilson Quarterly* first appeared in autumn of 1976 as a "national review of ideas," this influential magazine, based at the Woodrow Wilson International Center for Scholars in Washington, D.C., has published essays on everything from the changes in American agriculture to the destiny of biology. In analyzing these complex concerns, the *Quarterly* has brought, to quote its mission statement, "the world of scholars and specialists to the intelligent lay reader" and has provided "an authoritative overview of current ideas and research on matters of public policy and general intellectual interest."

For more than two decades the *Quarterly* has included examinations of the mass media as part of its project. *Media in America: The Wilson Quarterly Reader* has collected the best of this writing in one volume. The insights of the articles remain fresh, their lessons profound. The lone exception is a new contribution that never appeared in the *Quarterly:* an essay on country music, a companion piece to Martha Bayles's piece on rock music.

The articles on media that have appeared in the *Quarterly* over the years have been written most often by historians, but *Media in America* also contains sociological, critical, and economic analysis. All contributors take a broad brush to their subjects, to illustrate how the mass media have influenced both our vision of ourselves and our enjoyment of the world. Organized under the general headings of "Literacy, Popular Culture, and Advertising," "News and Politics," "Movies and Music," and "Television and New Technologies," each cluster of articles ends with an up-to-date discussion of "Further Reading," selected by me, but inspired by various "Background Books" essays which have appeared in the *Quarterly* over the years. *Media in America* does not seek to provide a complete primer on all the mass media in the United States. Nevertheless, these essays, written by noted authorities in their fields from telling points of view, contribute to our understanding of the American mass media—how these institutions came to be, how they operate, and what might lie in their future.

Media in America begins, logically enough, with issues of literacy and the written word. Reading is reading is reading, as Gertrude Stein might have said. Medieval monks read the Bible aloud; today's subway commuters scan the *New York Post*. All, it may seem, are engaged in the same activity, but historian Robert Darnton thinks not. In our first essay Darnton examines the history of the act of reading. Frequently, he argues, *how* people read can be more revealing than *what* they read. By showing how readers variously approached the written word, Darnton opens up a new window on the ways our ancestors made sense of their changing world.

Reading led to shared ideas and beliefs. Today the hegemony of public opinion is taken more or less for granted. Presidents conduct polls before announcing new policies, legislators invoke their constituents' desires to justify their votes, television network executives worship the Nielsen ratings. What we today think of as "public opinion" is far different from what it meant in the eighteenth century. The idea of a public with a defined will that can be expressed is a relatively modern concept, born of the Age of Enlightenment. Historian Anthony La Vopa examines how the idea of a collectively shared belief came to play such an important role in modern mass media.

The advent of reading and public opinion means more than the transmission of ideas and mass will, however. It also connotes shared entertainment, a vast array of popular culture from sporting spectaculars to pop music melodies. Hawking and exploiting mass culture began more than one hundred years ago, pioneered by P. T. Barnum, who proudly called himself the "Prince of Humbugs." Today, most remember Barnum for his circus and for one cynical observation ("There's a sucker born every minute") that in fact he never made. It is less well known that Barnum first made his mark as the proprietor of the American Museum in New York City. There, from 1841 to 1868, he combined freak shows and serious scientific exhibits, entertainment and edification, to amuse a remarkably diverse audience then filling the boroughs of what was becoming the nation's largest city. Historian A. H. Saxon analyzes Barnum's role in shaping the popular culture that envelops us today.

T. J. Jackson Lears provides the finale to the first section as he describes and analyzes the historical development of advertising, the most pervasive of mass cultural forms. From the earliest painted brick walls to the "psychological" targeting techniques now used to promote politicians as well as move cars, perfume, and razor blades, advertising touches all of today's mass media, often providing sustaining revenues. Thus it is fitting that a survey of the rise of advertising completes the first unit of *Media in America,* preparing the way for the discussions of current media practices that follow.

The next section, collecting articles on "News and Politics," begins with a consideration of the impact and importance of newspapers in the United States. The newspaper business has been undergoing a process of consolidation since the end of World War II, leading to a decline in the number of daily newspapers and the creation of increasingly powerful chains, most of which are also major players in television, radio, and on-line offerings. But while these "newspaper companies" have more resources to allocate to news gathering, and offer analysis superior to other media, their role in society in general and in the political process in particular has been subjected to widening criticism. Fewer and fewer vote; more and more seem content to sit back and criticize. Is poor news coverage to blame? These and other matters are explored by sociologist Leo Bogart and historian James Boylan. The trends they identified a decade ago are still in play; their probing and penetrating analyses still pinpoint the key issues.

There was no more famous newspaperman during the first half of the twentieth century than H. L. Mencken. During the 1920s in particular, Mencken, from his base at the *Baltimore Sun,* represented the voice of the educated and sophisticated urban dweller. His criticism of presidents and his characterization of Main Street Americans as the "booboisie" made Mencken a nationally known communicator. But during the 1930s, when he directed his anti-Establishment ferocity at President Franklin D. Roosevelt and the social welfare programs of the New Deal, Mencken found himself rejected as an anachronism. Yet today, a "Mencken revival" indicates that many Americans find a new appreciation for and sympathy with this newspaper writer. In his essay, historian T. J. Jackson Lears explores the contradictions that made Mencken one of the most important voices in the annals of America's newspapers.

If the presidential campaigns of the 1990s are any measure, Americans are becoming more and more critical of news coverage. They know (and detest) "spin control"—is this what politics is supposed to be about? The villain seems to be television, not newspapers. Exploring the evolution of television's influence on newspapers, the odd history of the sound bite, and the mass media formulae that govern today's political reporting, historians Robert Donovan and Ray Scherer and political scientist Michael Cornfield show how far the media have taken us from the real and important business of democratic politics—and what it might require to take us back closer to the ideal.

The third section of *Media in America* considers the pure fun found in movies and popular music. American movies and music project the image of the nation throughout the world, conveying the hopes, dreams, fears, and preoccupations that ripple across the entire planet. Today's movies, seen on screen, on TV, and more and more by way of home video, reach millions on a daily basis. In the essay beginning this cluster I explain, using economic and historical methods, how Hollywood has changed since Universal's *Jaws* (1975) reoriented the film industry into its current blockbuster mode. The *Quarterly* article on which this essay is based, "Hollywood's Business," was published in 1986. For this volume, it has been updated.

Crafting the history of the movies, dealing with such a myth-making, self-promoting, skilled industry, can prove tricky. One small chunk of this history is tackled in a retitled chapter; the original, published in 1991, was called "Who Killed Hollywood?" If it were a movie, it would go like this: "During the 'Golden Age' of the 1930s and 1940s Hollywood was a fabulous city of dreams that dazzled the world with its mighty studios and captivating images and sounds, its beautiful stars and its glitz and glamour. But then in the 1950s TV came along and, like some cheap hood in a 'B' movie, killed the fabled studio factories. Hollywood has never been the same." Historical change is rarely that simple, and moviemaking and promotion were affected by the same forces that shaped America at mid-century: suburbanization, a "baby boom," a new plethora of lifestyle choices.

In the first of two accompanying articles, critic Frank McConnell asserts that "we are not alone because we speak to one another—and nowhere at a deeper level than through the mythology of film." Historian Nathan Reingold looks at a specific case, the birth pains of Hollywood struggling to make stories concerning the first atomic bomb. Reingold offers a curious tale that helps explain why Hollywood art has such trouble holding a steady mirror to life.

Popular music has a fascinating and important history as well. Critic Martha Bayles finds the 1950s transformation of rock 'n' roll did alter pop music for the masses, but in the long run not for the good. By the 1990s, she argues, rock has lost its soul. While the blame is often placed on the lures of crude commerce and expert exploitation, she finds that American music went astray when it lost touch with one of its taproots—the blues tradition that moved up from the American South during the first half of the twentieth century. In a companion article written for this book, I trace the history of another form of pop music—country. Until the 1950s the songs of plain white Southerners were labeled "hillbilly music"; now, repackaged, the melodies that filled the hills of Virginia, Kentucky, and Tennessee are beloved in Africa, Asia, and Europe—indeed throughout the world.

Watching television is the one thing virtually all Americans do, and its history, contemporary practice, and possible future are considered in the final section of *Media in America*. As Todd Gitlin, Frank McConnell, and I demonstrate, no new social and cultural force since the end of World War II has done more to reshape the United States than TV. Today television is so pervasive that defining its influence is as difficult as drawing a circle around the air we breathe. The first essay lays out the history and current operation of a TV industry that occupies viewers for almost as much time each day as work or sleep. Sociologist Gitlin proposes that television is America's school for morals and manners, one that has re-educated our national character into something far different than it was a half-century ago. Critic McConnell, in a cautious defense of television, suggests that its opponents, more often than not, make too much of the hazards of the medium in order to advance their own social agendas.

The final three essays in *Media in America* take up the trickiest territory: the future. The dominant methodology in the essays preceding these final three has been historical—learning about the present by understanding the past. This final section tackles the future directly. In the mid-1990s, the race seems to be toward an information and entertainment superhighway. From business, government, and the computer industry around the world came promising talk of empowering all of us with instantaneous, free information, launching a new digital age. Edward Tenner, Tom Maddox, and I look to past technological changes—from the printing press to the telegraph to the space satellite—and warn that the new world of media might look a lot like present-day television: dozens of channels showing only reruns. Together we try to seek criteria by which society might ask, what do we want from the media we get?

As editor and multiple contributor, I take responsibility not only for the articles I have written and selected, but also for all the "Further Reading" units at the end of each section. Yet surely *Media in America,* as can be seen from "About the Authors," is the product of many talents. I wish to thank not only each contributor, but also Phil Cook and his successor Larry Lichty, directors of the Woodrow Wilson International Center for Scholars Media Studies Project, for which I was senior researcher from 1988 to 1992.

The current editor of *The Wilson Quarterly,* Jay Tolson, its longtime deputy editor, Steven Lagerfeld, and other members of the staff conceive and shape the original work that regularly appears in the *Quarterly.* For this, on behalf of millions of readers and the many who will read this anthology, I thank them.

At the Wilson Center Press I thank Joseph Brinley for saying "let's do it," and Joe and his great staff for making a pile of paper into a handsome book.

And I thank Marilyn Moon, who, by her commitment to public service and research, provides daily inspiration.

Finally, this volume is dedicated to Peter Braestrup, for initiating this project and for being godfather to the Media Studies Project.

Douglas Gomery

LITERACY, POPULAR CULTURE, AND ADVERTISING

ROBERT DARNTON

In *The Art of Love,* the Roman poet Ovid offers advice on how to read a love letter: "If your lover should make overtures by means of some words inscribed on
tablets delivered to you by a clever servant, meditate on them carefully, weigh his
phrases, and try to divine whether his love is only feigned or whether his prayers
really come sincerely in love." It is extraordinary. This poet of the first century B.C.
might be one of us. He speaks to a problem that could arise in any age, that appears
to exist outside of time. In reading about reading in *The Art of Love,* we seem to
hear a voice that speaks directly to us across a distance of two thousand years.

But as we listen further, the voice sounds stranger. Ovid goes on to prescribe
techniques for communicating with a lover behind a husband's back:

> It is consonant with morality and the law that an upright woman should fear her
> husband and be surrounded by a strict guard. . . . But should you have as many
> guardians as Argus has eyes, you can dupe them all if your will is firm enough. For
> example, can anyone stop your servant and accomplice from carrying your notes in
> her bodice or between her foot and the sole of her sandal? Let us suppose that your
> guardian can see through all these ruses. Then have your confidante offer her back in
> place of the tablets and let her body become a living letter.

The lover is expected to strip the servant girl and read her body—not exactly the
kind of communication that we associate with letter writing today.

Despite its air of beguiling contemporaneity, *The Art of Love* catapults us into
a world we can barely imagine. To get the message, we must know something

---

Reprinted from the autumn 1989 issue of *The Wilson Quarterly.*

about Roman mythology, writing techniques, and domestic life. We must be able to picture ourselves as the wife of a Roman patrician and to appreciate the contrast between formal morality and the ways of a world given over to sophistication and cynicism at a time when the Sermon on the Mount was in a barbarian tongue far beyond the Romans' range of hearing.

To read Ovid is to confront the mystery of reading itself. Both familiar and foreign, it is an activity that we share with our ancestors yet one that never can be the same as what they experienced. We may enjoy the illusion of stepping outside of time in order to make contact with authors who lived centuries ago. But even if their texts have come down to us unchanged—a virtual impossibility, considering the evolution of layout and of books as physical objects—our relation to those texts cannot be the same as that of readers in the past. Reading has a history. But how can we recover it?

We could begin by searching the record for readers. The Italian historian Carlo Ginzburg found one, a humble miller from sixteenth-century Friuli, in the papers of the Inquisition. Probing for heresy, the inquisitor asked his victim about his reading. Menocchio replied with a string of titles and elaborate comments on each of them. He had read a great number of biblical stories, chronicles, and travel books of the kind that existed in many patrician libraries. By comparing the texts and the commentary, Ginzburg discovered that Menocchio did not simply receive messages transmitted down through the social order. He read aggressively, transforming the contents of the material at his disposition into a radically non-Christian view of the world. Whether that view can be traced to an ancient popular tradition, as Ginzburg claims, is a matter of debate. But Ginzburg certainly demonstrated the possibility of studying reading as an activity among the common people four centuries ago.

I ran across a solidly middle-class reader in my own research on eighteenth-century France. He was a merchant from La Rochelle named Jean Ranson and an impassioned Rousseauist. Ranson did not merely read Rousseau and weep; he incorporated Rousseau's ideas into the fabric of his life as he set up business, fell in love, married, and raised his children. Reading and living run parallel as leitmotifs in a rich series of letters that Ranson wrote between 1774 and 1785. These letters show how Rousseauism became absorbed in the way of life of the provincial bourgeoisie under the Old Regime. Rousseau had received a flood of letters from readers like Ranson after the publication of *The New Eloise* (1761). It was, I believe, the first tidal wave of fan mail in the history of literature, although the novelist Samuel Richardson had already produced some impressive ripples in England. The mail reveals that readers responded as Ranson did everywhere in France and, furthermore, that their responses conformed to those Rousseau had called for in the two prefaces to his novel. He had instructed his readers how to read him. He had assigned them roles and provided them with a strategy for taking in his novel. The new way of reading worked so well that *The New Eloise* became the greatest best-seller of the century, the most important single source of romantic sensibility. That sensibility is now extinct. No modern reader can weep his way through the six volumes of *The New Eloise* as his predecessors did two centuries ago. But in his day, Rousseau captivated a generation of readers by revolutionizing reading itself.

The examples of Menocchio and Ranson suggest that reading and living, construing texts and making sense of life, were much more closely related in the early modern period than they are today. But before jumping to conclusions, we need to work through more archives, comparing readers' accounts of their experience with the protocols of reading in their books and, when possible, with their behavior. It was believed that Johann Wolfgang von Goethe's *Sorrows of Young Werther* (1774) touched off a wave of suicides in Germany. Is not the *Wertherfieber* ripe for fresh examination? The pre-Raphaelites in England provide similar instances of life imitating art, a theme that can be traced from *Don Quixote* to *Madame Bovary* and *Miss Lonelyhearts*. In each case the fiction could be fleshed out and compared with documents—actual suicide notes, diaries, and letters to the editor. The correspondence of authors and the papers of publishers are ideal sources of information about real readers. There are dozens of letters from readers in the published correspondence of Voltaire and Jean-Jacques Rousseau, and hundreds in the unpublished papers of Honoré de Balzac and Émile Zola.

In short, it should be possible to develop a history as well as a theory of reader response. Possible, but not easy.

The documents rarely show readers at work, fashioning meaning from texts, and the documents are texts themselves, which also require interpretation. Few of them are rich enough to provide even indirect access to the cognitive and affective elements of reading, and a few exceptional cases may not be enough for one to reconstruct the inner dimensions of that experience. But historians of the book have already turned up a great deal of information about the external history of reading. Having studied it as a social phenomenon, they can answer many of the "who," the "what," the "where," and the "when" questions, which can be of great help in attacking the more difficult "whys" and "hows."

THE INSTITUTIONAL BASES OF READING

Studies of who reads what at different times fall into two main types: the macro- and the microanalytical. Macroanalysis has flourished above all in France, where it has traced the evolution of reading habits from the sixteenth century to the present. One can follow in these studies many intriguing phenomena: the decline of Latin, the rise of the novel, the general fascination with the immediate world of nature and the remote worlds of exotic countries that spread throughout the educated public between the time of René Descartes and that of Louis-Antoine de Bougainville.

By the late nineteenth century, borrowing patterns in German, English, and American libraries had fallen into a strikingly similar pattern: 70 to 80 percent of the books came from the category of light fiction (mostly novels); 10 percent came from history, biography, and travel; and less than 1 percent came from religion. In little more than two hundred years, the world of reading had been transformed. The rise of the novel had balanced a decline in religious literature, and in almost every case the turning point could be located in the second half of the eighteenth century, especially the 1770s, the years of the *Wertherfieber*. *The Sorrows of Young Werther* produced an even more spectacular response in Germany than *The New Eloise* had done in France or *Pamela* in England. All three novels marked the triumph of a new literary sensitivity, and the last sentences of *Werther* seemed to announce the advent of a new reading public along with the death of a traditional Christian culture: "Artisans bore him. No minister accompanied him."

Thus for all their variety and occasional contradictions, the macroanalytical studies suggest some general conclusions, something akin to what Max Weber described as the "demystification of the world." That may seem too cosmic for comfort. Those who prefer precision may turn to microanalysis, although it usually goes to the opposite extreme—excessive detail. We have hundreds of lists of books in libraries from the Middle Ages to the present, and most of us would agree that a catalogue of a private library can serve as a profile of a reader. To scan the catalogue of the library in Monticello is to inspect the furnishings of Thomas Jefferson's mind. And the study of private libraries has the advantage of linking the "what" with the "who" of reading.

The French have taken the lead in this area, too. Daniel Mornet's essay of 1910, *"Les bibliothèques privées"* (The private libraries) demonstrated that the study of library catalogues could produce conclusions that challenged some of the commonplaces of literary history. After tabulating titles from 500 eighteenth-century catalogues, he found only one copy of the book that was to be the bible of the French Revolution, Rousseau's *Social Contract* (1762). The libraries provided no basis for connecting certain kinds of literature (the work of the philosophes, for example) with certain classes of readers (the bourgeoisie).

Seventy years later, we now have statistics on the libraries of noblemen, magistrates, priests, academicians, burghers, artisans, and even some domestic servants. Parisians were readers: before 1789, Paris had 500 primary schools, one for every 1,000 inhabitants, all more or less free. But for artisans, reading did not take the form of the books that show up in inventories. It involved chap-books, broadsides, posters, personal letters, and the signs on the streets. Parisians read their way through the city and through their lives, but their ways of read-ing did not leave enough archival evidence for the historian to follow closely on their heels.

Subscription lists and the records of lending libraries offer an opportunity to make connections between literary genres and social classes. The most remark-able are the registers of borrowings from the ducal library of Wolfenbüttel, which extend from 1666 to 1928. They show a significant "democratization" of read-ing in the 1760s: The number of books borrowed doubled; the borrowers came from lower social strata; and the reading matter became lighter, shifting from learned tomes to sentimental novels (imitations of *Robinson Crusoe* went over especially well). Curiously, the registers of the *Bibliothèque du Roi* in Paris show that it had the same number of users at this time—about 50 a year, including one Denis Diderot. The Parisians could not take the books home, but they enjoyed the hospitality of a more leisurely age. Although the librarian opened his doors to them only two mornings a week, he gave them a meal before he turned them out. Conditions are different in the *Bibliothèque Nationale* today. Librarians have had to accept a basic law of economics: There is no such thing as a free lunch.

The microanalysts have come up with many other discoveries—so many, in fact, that they face the same problem as the macroquantifiers: how to put it all together? The disparity of the documentation—auction catalogues, notarial records, subscription lists, library registers—does not make the task easier.

So far only one book historian has been hardy enough to propose a general model. Rolf Engelsing has argued that a "reading revolution" (*Leserevolution*) took place at the end of the eighteenth century. From the Middle Ages until sometime after 1750, according to Engelsing, men read "intensively." They had only a few books—the Bible, an almanac, a devotional work or two—and they read them over and over again, usually aloud and in groups, so that a narrow range of traditional literature became deeply impressed on their consciousness. By 1800 people were reading "extensively." They read all kinds of material, espe-cially periodicals and newspapers, and read things only once before racing on to the next item. Engelsing does not produce much evidence for his hypothesis: Most of his research concerns only a small sampling of burghers in Bremen. But it has an attractive before-and-after simplicity, and it provides a handy formula for contrasting modes of reading very early and very late in European history. Its main drawback, as I see it, is its unilinear character.

Reading did not evolve in one direction, toward extensiveness. It assumed many different forms among different social groups during different eras. Men and women have read in order to save their souls, to improve their manners, to repair their machinery, to seduce their sweethearts, to learn about current events, and simply to have fun. In many cases, especially among the publics of Richardson, Rousseau, and Goethe, the reading became more intensive, not less. But the late eighteenth century does seem to represent a turning point, a time when more reading matter became available to a wider readership that in the nineteenth century would grow to giant proportions with the development of machine-made paper, steam-powered presses, linotype, and, in the Western world, nearly universal literacy. All these changes opened up new possibilities, not by decreasing intensity but by increasing variety.

I must therefore confess to some skepticism about the "reading revolution." Yet an American historian of the book, David Hall, has described a transformation in the reading habits of New Englanders between 1600 and 1850 in almost exactly the same terms as those used by Engelsing. Before 1800, New Englanders read a small corpus of venerable "steady sellers"—the Bible, almanacs, the *New England Primer,* Philip Doddridge's *Rise and Progress of Religion,* Richard Baxter's *Call to the Unconverted*—and read them over and over again, aloud, in groups, and with exceptional intensity. After 1800 they were swamped with new kinds of books—novels, newspapers, fresh and sunny varieties of children's literature—and they read through them ravenously, discarding one thing as soon as they could find another. Although Hall and Engelsing had never heard of one another, they discovered a similar pattern in two quite different areas of the Western world. Perhaps a fundamental shift in reading took place at the end of the eighteenth century. It may not have been a revolution, but it marked the end of an Old Regime—the reign of Thomas à Kempis, Johann Arndt, and John Bunyan.

The "where" of reading is more important than one might think, because by placing the reader in his setting one might find hints about the nature of his experience. In the University of Leiden there hangs a print of the university library, dated 1610. It shows the books, heavy folio volumes, chained on high shelves jutting out from the walls in a sequence determined by the rubrics of classical bibliography: *Jurisconsulti, Medici, Historici,* and so on. Students are scattered about the room, reading the books on counters built at shoulder level below the shelves. They read standing up, protected against the cold by thick cloaks and hats, one foot perched on a rail to ease the pressure on their bodies. Reading can not have been comfortable in the age of classical humanism.

In pictures done a century and a half later, "La Lecture" and "La Liseuse" by Jean-Honoré Fragonard, for example, readers recline in chaise longues or well-padded armchairs with their legs propped on footstools. They are often women, wearing loose-fitting gowns known at the time as *liseuses.* They usually hold a dainty duodecimo volume in their fingers and have a faraway look in their eyes.

From Fragonard to Claude Monet, who also painted a "Liseuse," reading moves from the boudoir to the outdoors. The reader backpacks books to fields and mountaintops, where, like Rousseau and Heinrich Heine, he can commune with nature.

The human element in the setting must have affected the understanding of the texts. No doubt Jean-Baptiste Greuze (1725–1805) sentimentalized the collective character of reading in his painting of *A Father of the Family Reads the Bible to his Children*. Restif de la Bretonne (1734–1806) probably did the same in the family Bible readings described in *The Life of My Father* (1779): "I could only remember with emotion the interest with which this reading was heard; how it conveyed to everybody in our numerous family a tone of goodheartedness and brotherhood (in the family I include the servants). My father always started with these words: 'Let us gather my children; it is the Holy Spirit that is going to speak.' " But for all their sentimentality, such descriptions proceed from a common assumption: For the common people in early modern Europe, reading was a social activity. It took place in workshops, barns, and taverns. It was almost always oral but not necessarily edifying. Thus it was for the peasant in the country inn described, with some rose tinting around the edges, by Christian Schubart in 1786:

And when the evening breaks in,
I just drink my cup of wine;
Then the Schoolmaster reads to me
From the newspaper what news there is.

The most important institution of popular reading under the Old Regime was a fireside gathering known as the *veillée* in France and the *Spinnstube* in Germany. While children played, women sewed, and men repaired tools, one of the company who could decipher a text would regale them with the adventures of *Les quatre fils Aymon, Till Eulenspiegel,* or some other favorite from the standard repertory of the cheap, popular chapbooks. Some of these primitive paperbacks indicated that they were meant to be taken in through the ears by beginning with phrases such as, "What you are about to hear. . . ." During the nineteenth century groups of artisans, especially cigar makers and tailors, took turns reading or hired a reader to keep themselves entertained while they worked. Even today many people get their news by being read to by a telecaster. Television may be less of a break with the past than is generally assumed. In any case, for most people throughout most of history, books had audiences rather than readers. They were better heard than seen.

Reading was a more private experience for the minority of educated persons who could afford to buy books. But many joined reading clubs, *cabinets littéraires*, or *Lesegesellschaften,* where they could read almost anything they wanted, in a sociable atmosphere, for a small monthly payment. Françoise Parent-Lardeur has traced the proliferation of these clubs in Paris under the Restoration, but they went back well into the eighteenth century. Provincial booksellers often turned their stock into a library and charged dues for the right to frequent it. Good light, some comfortable chairs, a few pictures on the wall, and subscriptions to a half-dozen newspapers were enough to make a club out of almost any bookshop. Thus the *cabinet littéraire* advertised by P. J. Bernard, a minor bookseller in Lunéville: "A commodious establishment, large, well illuminated and heated, which will be open every day, from nine o'clock in the morning until noon and from one until 10, will offer starting now to booklovers 2,000 volumes which will increase by 400 volumes annually." By November 1779, the club had 200 members, mostly officers from the local *gendarmérie.* For the modest sum of three livres a year, they had access to 5,000 books, 13 journals, and special rooms set aside for conversation and writing.

German reading clubs provided the social foundation for a distinct variety of bourgeois culture in the eighteenth century. They sprang up at an astounding rate, especially in the northern cities. Perhaps one of every five hundred adult Germans belonged to a *Lesegesellschaft* by 1800. All of these reading clubs had a basic supply of periodicals supplemented by uneven runs of books, usually on fairly weighty subjects like history and politics. They seem to have been a more serious version of the coffeehouse, itself an important institution for reading, which spread through Germany from the late seventeenth century. By 1760, Vienna had at least sixty coffeehouses. They provided newspapers, journals, and endless occasions for political discussions, just as they had done in London and Amsterdam for over a century.

CHANGES IN READING HABITS

Thus we already know a good deal about the institutional bases of reading. We have some answers to the "who," "what," "where," and "when" questions. But the "whys" and "hows" elude us. We have not yet devised a strategy for understanding the inner process by which readers made sense of words. We do not even understand the way we read ourselves, despite the efforts of psychologists and neurologists to trace eye movements and to map the hemispheres of the brain.

Is the cognitive process different for Chinese, who read pictographs, and for Westerners, who scan lines? For Israelis, who read words without vowels moving from right to left, and for blind people, who transmit stimuli through their fingers? For Southeast Asians, whose languages lack tenses and who order reality spatially, and for American Indians, whose languages have been put into writing only recently by alien scholars? For the holy man in the presence of the Word and for the consumer studying labels in a supermarket?

The differences seem endless, for reading is not simply a skill but a way of making meaning, which must vary from culture to culture. We could not expect to find a formula that could account for all those variations. But it should be possible to develop a way to study the changes in reading within our own culture. I would like to suggest five approaches to the problem.

First, I think it should be possible to learn more about the ideals and assumptions underlying reading in the past. We could study contemporary depictions of reading in fiction, autobiographies, polemical writings, letters, paintings, and prints in order to uncover some notions of what people thought took place when they read. Consider, for example, the great debate about the craze for reading in late-eighteenth-century Germany. Those who deplored the reading mania did not simply condemn its effects on morals and politics. They feared it would damage public health. In a tract of 1795, J. G. Heinzmann listed the physical consequences of excessive reading: "susceptibility to colds, headaches, weakening of the eyes, heat rashes, gout, arthritis, hemorrhoids, asthma, apoplexy, pulmonary disease, indigestion, blocking of the bowels, nervous disorder, migraines, epilepsy, hypochondria, and melancholy."

On the positive side of the debate, Johann Adam Bergk, author of *The Art of Reading Books* (1799), accepted the premises of his opponents but disagreed with their conclusions. He took it as established that one should never read immediately after eating or while standing up. But by correct disposition of the body, one could make reading a force for good. The "art of reading" involved washing the face with cold water and taking walks in fresh air as well as concentration and meditation. No one challenged the notion that there was a physical element in reading, because no one drew a clear distinction between the physical and the moral world. Eighteenth-century readers attempted to "digest" books, to absorb them in their whole being, body and soul. The physicality of the process sometimes shows on the pages. The books in Samuel Johnson's library, now owned by Mrs. Donald F. Hyde, are bent and battered, as if Johnson had wrestled his way through them.

Throughout most of Western history, and especially in the sixteenth and seventeenth centuries, reading was seen above all as a spiritual exercise. But how was it performed? One could look for guidance in the manuals of Jesuits and the hermeneutical treatises of Protestants. Family Bible readings took place on both sides of the great religious divide. And as the example of Restif de la Bretonne indicates, the Bible was approached with awe, even among some Catholic peasants. Of course Giovanni Boccaccio, Baldassare Castiglione, Miguel de Cervantes, and François Rabelais had developed other uses of literacy for the elite. But for most people, reading remained a sacred activity. It put you in the presence of the Word and unlocked holy mysteries. As a working hypothesis, it seems valid to assert that the farther back in time you go the farther away you move from instrumental reading. Not only does the "how-to" book become rarer and the religious book more common, reading itself is different. In the age of Martin Luther and St. Ignatius Loyola, it provided access to absolute truth.

On a more mundane level, assumptions about reading could be traced through advertisements and prospectuses for books. Thus some typical remarks from an eighteenth-century prospectus taken at random from the rich collection in the Newberry Library in Chicago: A bookseller is offering a quarto edition of the *Commentary on the Customs of the Residents of Angoumois,* an excellent work, he insists, for its typography as much as its content—"The text of the *Commentary* is printed in *grosromain* type; the summaries that precede the commentaries are printed in *cicéro;* and the commentaries are printed in *Saint-Augustin.* The whole work is made from very beautiful paper manufactured in Angoulême."

No publisher would dream of mentioning paper and type in advertising a law book today. During the eighteenth century advertisers assumed that their clients cared about the physical quality of books. Buyers and sellers alike shared a typographical consciousness that is now nearly extinct.

The reports of censors also can be revealing, at least in the case of books from early modern France, where censorship was highly developed if not enormously effective. A typical travel book, *New Voyage to the American Islands* (Paris, 1722) by J.-B. Labat, contains four "approbations" printed out in full next to the imprimatur. One censor explains that the manuscript piqued his curiosity: "It is difficult to begin reading it without feeling that mild but avid curiosity that impels us to read further." Another recommends it for its "simple and concise style" and also for its utility: "Nothing in my opinion is so useful to travellers, to the inhabitants of that country, to tradesmen, and to those who study natural history." And a third simply found it a good read: "I had great pleasure in reading it. It contains a multitude of curious things."

Censors did not simply hound out heretics and revolutionaries, as we tend to assume in looking back at the Inquisition and the Enlightenment. They gave the royal stamp of approval to a work, and in doing so they provided clues as to how it might be read. Their values constituted an official standard against which ordinary readings might be measured.

But how did ordinary readers read? My second suggestion for attacking that problem concerns the ways reading was learned. In seventeenth-century England, a great deal of learning took place outside the schoolroom, in workshops and fields where laborers taught themselves and one another. Inside the school, English children learned to read before they learned to write, instead of acquiring the two skills together at the beginning of their education as they do today. They often joined the workforce before the age of seven, when instruction in writing began. So literacy estimates based on the ability to write may be much too low, and the reading public may have included a great many people who could not sign their names.

But "reading" for such people probably meant something quite different from what it means today. In early modern France the three R's were learned in sequence—first reading, then writing, then arithmetic—just as in England and, it seems, all other countries in the West. The most common primers from the Old Regime—ABCs like the *Croix de Jésus* and the *Croix de par Dieu*—begin as modern manuals do, with the alphabet. But the letters had different sounds. The pupil pronounced a flat vowel before each consonant, so that *p* came out as "ehp" rather than "pé" as it is today. When said aloud, the letters did not link together phonetically in combinations that could be recognized by the ear as syllables of a word. Thus *p-a-t* in *pater* sounded like "ehp-ah-eht." But the phonetic fuzziness did not really matter, because the letters were meant as a visual stimulus to trigger the memory of a text that had already been learned by heart—and the text was always in Latin. The whole system was built on the premise that French children should not begin to read in French. They passed directly from the alphabet to simple syllables and then to the *Pater Noster, Ave Maria, Credo,* and *Benedicite.* Having learned to recognize these common prayers, they worked through liturgical responses printed in standard chapbooks. At this point many of them left school. They had acquired enough mastery of the printed word to fulfill the functions expected of them by the Church—that is, to participate in its rituals. But they had never read a text in a language they could understand.

Some children—we don't know how many; perhaps a minority in the seventeenth century and a majority in the eighteenth—remained in school long enough to learn to read in French. Even then, however, reading was often a matter of recognizing something already known rather than a process of acquiring new knowledge. Nearly all of the schools were run by the Church, and nearly all of the schoolbooks were religious, usually catechisms and pious textbooks like *The Parish School* by Jacques de Batencour. In the early eighteenth century the Brothers of Christian Schools began to provide the same text to several pupils and to teach them as a group—a first step toward standardized instruction, which was to become the rule a hundred years later. At the same time, a few tutors in aristocratic households began to teach reading directly in French. They developed phonetic techniques and audiovisual aids like the pictorial flash cards of the abbé Berthaud and the *bureau typographique* of Louis Dumas. By 1789 their example had spread to some progressive primary schools.

But most children still learned to read by standing before the master and reciting passages from whatever text they could get their hands on while their classmates struggled with a motley collection of booklets on the back benches. Some of these "schoolbooks" would reappear in the evening at the *veillée*, because they were popular "best-sellers" retelling old tales of chivalry. So reading around the fireside had something in common with reading in the classroom: It was a recital of a text that everyone already knew. Instead of opening up limitless vistas of new ideas, it probably remained within a closed circuit, exactly where the post-Tridentine Church wanted to keep it. "Probably," however, is the governing word in that proposition. We can only guess at the nature of early modern pedagogy by reading the few primers and the still fewer memoirs that have survived from that era. We don't know what really happened in the classroom. The peasant reader-listeners may have construed their catechism as well as their adventure stories in ways that escape us.

If the experience of the great mass of readers lies beyond the range of historical research, historians should be able to capture something of what reading meant for the few persons who left a record of it. A third approach could begin with the best known autobiographical accounts—those of Saint Augustine, Saint Theresa of Avila, Michel de Montaigne, Rousseau, and Stendhal, for example—and move on to less familiar sources.

J.-M. Goulemot has used the autobiography of Jamerey-Duval to show how a peasant could read and write his way up through the ranks of the Old Regime, and Daniel Roche discovered an eighteenth-century glazier, Jacques-Louis Ménétra, who read his way around a typical tour de France. Although he did not carry many books in the sack slung over his back, Ménétra constantly exchanged letters with fellow travelers and sweethearts. He squandered a few sous on broadsides at public executions and even composed doggerel verse for the ceremonies and farces that he staged with the other workers. When he told the story of his life, he organized his narrative in picaresque fashion, combining oral tradition (folk tales and the stylized braggadocio of male bull sessions) with genres of popular literature (such as the novelettes of chivalry). Unlike other plebeian authors—Restif, Mercier, Rousseau, Diderot, and Marmontel—Ménétra never won a place in the Republic of Letters. But he showed that letters had a place in the culture of the common man.

That place may have been marginal, but margins themselves provide clues to the experience of ordinary readers. During the sixteenth century marginal notes appeared in print in the form of glosses, which steered the reader through humanist texts. In the eighteenth century the gloss gave way to the footnote. How did the reader follow the play between text and para-text at the bottom or side of the page? The historian Edward Gibbon created ironic distance by masterful deployment of footnotes. A careful study of annotated eighteenth-century copies of *The Decline and Fall of the Roman Empire* might reveal the way such distance was perceived by Gibbon's contemporaries. John Adams covered his books with scribbling. By following him through his copy of Rousseau's *Discourse on the Origin of Inequality,* one can see how radical Enlightenment philosophy looked to a retired revolutionary in the sober climate of Quincy, Massachusetts. Thus Rousseau, in the first English edition:

> There was no kind of moral relation between men in this state [the state of nature]; they could not be either good or bad, and had neither vices nor virtues. It is proper, therefore, to suspend judgment about their situation . . . until we have examined whether there are more virtues or vices among civilized men. . . .

And Adams, in the margin:

> Wonders upon wonders. Paradox upon paradox. What astonishing sagacity had Mr. Rousseau! Yet this eloquent coxcomb has with his affectation of singularity made men discontented with superstition and tyranny.

Scholars have charted the currents of literary history by trying to reread great books as great writers have read them, using the annotations in collectors' items such as Diderot's copy of the *Encyclopédie* and Herman Melville's copy of Ralph Waldo Emerson's essays.

But the inquiry needn't be limited to great books or to books at all. Peter Burke is currently studying the graffiti of Renaissance Italy. When scribbled on the door of an enemy, they often functioned as ritual insults, which defined the lines of social conflict dividing neighborhoods and clans. When attached to the famous statue of Pasquino in Rome, this public scribbling set the tone of a rich and intensely political street culture. A history of reading might be able to advance by great leaps from the Pasquinade and the commedia dell'arte to Molière, from Molière to Rousseau, and from Rousseau to Robespierre.

My fourth suggestion concerns literary theory. It can, I agree, look daunting, especially to the outsider. It comes wrapped in imposing labels—structuralism, deconstruction, hermeneutics, semiotics, phenomenology—and it goes as rapidly as it comes, for the trends displace one another with bewildering speed. Through them all, however, runs a concern that could lead to some collaboration between literary critics and historians of the book—the concern for reading. Whether they unearth deep structures or tear down systems of signs, critics have increasingly treated literature as an activity rather than an established body of texts. They insist that a book's meaning is not fixed on its pages; it is construed by its readers. So reader response has become the key point around which literary analysis turns.

In Germany, this approach has led to a revival of literary history as "reader response aesthetics" under the leadership of Hans Robert Jauss and Wolfgang Iser. In France, it has taken a philosophical turn in the work of Roland Barthes, Paul Ricoeur, Tzvetan Todorov, and Georges Poulet. In the United States, it is still in the melting-pot stage. Wayne Booth, Paul de Man, Jonathan Culler, Geoffrey Hartman, J. Hillis Miller, and Stanley Fish have supplied ingredients for a general theory, but no consensus has emerged from their debates. Nonetheless, all this critical activity points toward a new textology, and all the critics share a way of working when they interpret specific texts.

Consider, for example, Walter Ong's analysis of the first sentences in Ernest Hemingway's *A Farewell to Arms:*

> In the late summer of that year we lived in a house in a village that looked across the river and the plain to the mountains. In the bed of the river there were pebbles and boulders, dry and white in the sun, and the water was clear and swiftly moving and blue in the channels.

What year? What river? Ong asks. Hemingway does not say. By unorthodox use of the definite article—the river instead of "a river"—and sparse deployment of adjectives, he implies that the reader does not need a detailed description of the scene. A reminder will be enough, because the reader is deemed to have been there already. He is addressed as if he were a confidant and fellow traveler, who merely needs to be reminded in order to recollect the hard glint of the sun, the coarse taste of the wine, and the stench of the dead in World War I Italy. Should the reader object—and one can imagine many responses such as, "I am a sixty-year-old grandmother and I don't know anything about rivers in Italy"—he won't be able to "get" the book. But if he accepts the role imposed on him by the rhetoric, his fictionalized self can swell to the dimensions of the Hemingway hero; and he can go through the narrative as the author's companion in arms.

Earlier rhetoric usually operated in the opposite manner. It assumed that the reader knew nothing about the story and needed to be oriented by rich descriptive passages or introductory observations. Thus the opening of *Pride and Prejudice:*

> It is a truth universally acknowledged, that a single man in possession of a good fortune must be in want of a wife.
>
> However little known the feelings or views of such a man may be on his first entering a neighborhood, this truth is so well fixed in the minds of the surrounding families that he is considered as the rightful property of some one or other of their daughters.
>
> "My dear Mr. Bennett," said his lady to him one day, "have you heard that Netherfield Park is let at last?"

This kind of narrative moves from the general to the particular. It places the indefinite article first, and helps the reader get his bearing by degrees. But it always keeps him at a distance, because he is presumed to enter the story as an outsider and to be reading for instruction, amusement, or some high moral purpose. As in the case of the Hemingway novel, he must play his role for the rhetoric to work; but the role is completely different.

Writers have devised many other ways to initiate readers into stories. A vast distance separates Melville's "Call me Ishmael" from John Milton's prayer for help to "justify the ways of God to men." But every narrative presupposes a reader, and every reading begins from a protocol inscribed within the text. The text may undercut itself, and the reader may work against the grain or wring new meaning from familiar words: hence the endless possibilities of interpretation proposed by the deconstructionists and the original readings that have shaped cultural history—Rousseau's reading of Molière's *Le Misanthrope,* for example, or Søren Kierkegaard's reading of Genesis 22. But whatever one makes of it, reading has re-emerged as the central fact of literature.

If so, the time is ripe for making a juncture between literary theory and the history of books. The theory can reveal the range in potential responses to a text—that is, to the rhetorical constraints that direct reading without determining it. The history can show what readings actually took place—that is, within the limits of an imperfect body of evidence. By paying heed to history, the literary critics may avoid the danger of anachronism.

By taking account of rhetoric, the historians may find clues to behavior that would otherwise be baffling, such as the passions aroused from *Clarissa* to *The New Eloise* and from *Werther* to *René.* I would therefore argue for a dual strategy, which would combine textual analysis with empirical research. In this way it should be possible to compare the implicit readers of the texts with the actual readers of the past and thus to develop a history as well as a theory of reader response.

Such a history could be reinforced by a fifth mode of analysis, one based on analytical bibliography. By studying books as physical objects, bibliographers have demonstrated that the typographical disposition of a text can to a considerable extent determine its meaning and the way it was read. In a remarkable study of Congreve, D. F. McKenzie has shown that the bawdy, neo-Elizabethan playwright known to us from the quarto editions of the late seventeenth century underwent a typographical rebirth in his old age and emerged as the stately, neoclassical author of the three-volume octavo *Works* published in 1710. Individual words rarely changed from one edition to another, but a transformation in the design of the books gave the plays a new flavor. By adding scene divisions, grouping characters, relocating lines, and bringing out *liaisons des scènes,* Congreve fit his old texts into the new classical model derived from the French stage. To go from the quarto to the octavo volumes is to move from Elizabethan to Georgian England.

Roger Chartier has found similar but more sociological implications in the metamorphoses of a Spanish classic, *Study of the Life of Buscón* by Francisco de Quevedo. The novel was originally intended for a sophisticated public, both in Spain where it was first published in 1626 and in France where it came out in an elegant translation in 1633. But in the mid–seventeenth century the Oudot and Garnier houses of Troyes began to publish a series of cheap paperback editions, which made *Buscón* a staple of a variety of popular literature known as the *bibliothèque bleue* for two hundred years. The popular publishers did not hesitate to tinker with the text, but they concentrated primarily on book design, what Chartier calls the "mise en livre." They broke the story into simple units, shortening sentences, subdividing paragraphs, and multiplying the number of chapters.

The new typographical structure implied a new kind of reading and a new public: humble people, who lacked the facility and the time to take in lengthy stretches of narrative. The short episodes were autonomous. They did not need to be linked by complex sub-themes and character development, because they provided just enough material to fill a *veillée.* So the book itself became a collection of fragments rather than a continuous story, and it could be put together by each reader-listener in his own way. Just how this "appropriation" took place is a mystery, because Chartier limits his analysis to the book as a physical object. But he shows how typography opens onto sociology, how the implicit reader of the author became the implicit reader of the publisher, moving down the social ladder of the Old Regime and into the world that would be recognized in the nineteenth century as "le grand public."

A few adventuresome bibliographers and book historians have begun to speculate about long-term trends in the evolution of the book. They argue that readers respond more directly to the physical organization of texts than to their surrounding social environment. So it may be possible to learn something about the remote history of reading by practicing a kind of textual archeology. If we cannot know precisely how the Romans read Ovid, we can assume that like most Roman inscriptions, the verse contained no punctuation, paragraphing, or spaces between words. The units of sound and meaning probably were closer to the rhythms of speech than to the typographical units—the letters, words, and lines—of the printed page.

The page as a book unit dates only from the third or fourth century A.D. Before then, one unrolled a book to read it. When gathered pages (the *codex*) replaced the scroll (*volumen*), readers could move backwards and forwards through books. Texts became divided into segments that could be marked off and indexed. Yet long after books acquired their modern form, reading continued to be an oral experience, performed in public. At some point, perhaps in monasteries in the seventh century and certainly in the universities of the thirteenth century, men began to read silently and alone. The shift to silent reading might have involved a greater adjustment than the shift to the printed text, for it made reading an individual, interior experience.

Printing made a difference, of course, but it probably was less revolutionary than is commonly believed. Some books had title pages, tables of contents, indexes, pagination, and publishers who produced multiple copies from scriptoria for a large reading public before the invention of movable type. For the first half-century of its existence, the printed book continued to be an imitation of the manuscript book. No doubt it was read by the same public in the same way. But after 1500 the printed book, pamphlet, broadside, map, and poster reached new kinds of readers and stimulated new kinds of reading. Increasingly standardized in its design, cheaper in its price, and widespread in its distribution, the new book transformed the world. It did not simply supply more information. It provided a mode of understanding, a basic metaphor of making sense of life.

So it was that during the sixteenth century men took possession of the Word. During the seventeenth century they began to decode the "book of nature." And in the eighteenth century they learned to read themselves. With the help of books, John Locke and Étienne de Condillac studied the mind as a tabula rasa, and Benjamin Franklin formulated an epitaph for himself:

The Body of
    B. Franklin, Printer,
    Like the cover of an old Book,
    Its Contents torn out,
    And stript of its Lettering & Gilding
    Lies here, Food for Worms.
    But the Work shall not be lost;
    For it will, as he believ'd,
    Appear once more
    In a new and more elegant Edition
    Corrected and improved
    By the Author.

I don't want to make too much of the metaphor, since Franklin has already flogged it to death, but rather to return to a point so simple that it may escape our notice. Reading has a history. It was not always and everywhere the same. We may think of it as a straightforward process of lifting information from a page; but if we considered it further, we would agree that information must be sifted, sorted, and interpreted. Interpretive schemes belong to cultural configurations, which have varied enormously over time. As our ancestors lived in different mental worlds, they must have read differently, and the history of reading could be as complex as the history of thinking. Although readers and texts have varied according to social and technological circumstances, the history of reading should not be reduced to a chronology of those variations. It should go beyond them to confront the relational element at the heart of the matter: How did changing readerships construe shifting texts?

The question sounds abstruse, but a great deal hangs on it. Think how often reading has changed the course of history—Luther's reading of Paul, Marx's reading of Hegel, Mao's reading of Marx. Those points stand out in a deeper process—man's unending effort to find meaning in the world around him and within himself. If we could understand how he has read, we could come closer to understanding how he made sense of life; and in that way, the historical way, we might even satisfy some of our own craving for meaning.

2 | THE BIRTH OF PUBLIC OPINION

ANTHONY J. LA VOPA

In the liberal democracies of the West, and in a growing number of other nations, the "public" and its "opinion" are fixtures of modern life. Indeed, it is hard to imagine how culture and politics ever managed without them. The highbrow poet, the pulp novelist, the classical musician, the rock star, the avant-garde film-maker, the director of TV sitcoms: all of these producers of "culture" need an image of the "public" and its expected reaction, whether they aim to please or to antagonize their audience. Without a "public," government has no way of entering into a dialogue with society; it relies instead on a barrage of propaganda. Unable to express its opinion publicly, society has no way (short of the threat of violent upheaval) of making government responsive to its changing needs.

The ancient *polis,* of course, had its public forum and its *vox populi.* But "public opinion" is, as historians measure such things, a recent innovation. It was in the course of the eighteenth century that "public" joined "opinion" in a new pairing—and the result was a dramatic change in the meaning of the latter word. At the beginning of the eighteenth century, "opinion" had generally connoted blinkered vision and fickleness, in contrast to the unchanging universality of Truth. By the end of the century, opinion in its "public" guise was endowed with a rational objectivity. Public opinion was the authoritative judgment of a collective conscience, the ruling of a tribunal to which even the state was subject. It was to be confused neither with blind adherence to traditional authority nor with the mob loyalty that modern political demagoguery seemed to command.

The timing of this semantic shift was no accident. The eighteenth century was the Age of Enlightenment in Europe, and "public opinion" was one of its

Reprinted from the winter 1991 issue of *The Wilson Quarterly.*

characteristic products. It was not simply that the "public," in the ideal, embodied the Enlightenment's aspiration to construct a truly rational polity, able to criticize itself objectively. The new pairing distilled the values, aspirations, and misgivings of the educated and propertied elite that gave the Enlightenment its social profile.

As historian Keith Baker and several other scholars have demonstrated, "public opinion" exercised its strongest appeal and exhibited its ironies most dramatically in *ancien régime* France. That, too, is no accident. As the sacred authority of the Bourbon monarchy was eroded beyond recovery, the need for a secular replacement—a single, undivided source of political legitimacy—seemed increasingly urgent. An arena of open political conflict was forming, but to many in France it seemed to portend chaos rather than progress. Hence the duality that marked eighteenth-century appeals to public opinion everywhere in continental Europe and the Anglo-American world was heightened in France. "Public opinion" *did* loom as a workable alternative to traditional authority, and in that sense it was eminently modern from birth. And yet there is also a sense in which the concept, in its original state of innocence, was an antidote to the onset of modern politics. In our own era, as politics takes the form of photo opportunities and sound bites, that antidote can seem at once all the more appealing and all the less likely to work.

Who appealed to the tribunal of public opinion in the eighteenth century? A complete list would include Voltaire, Immanuel Kant, Denis Diderot, and other familiar figures from the Enlightenment's pantheon, but it would also take us deep into the lower tiers of thinkers. By the close of the eighteenth century, reverence for the public's judgment had become obligatory among progressive members of the clergy as well as among the skeptics who dismissed Christianity as mere "superstition." It was shared—or at least seemed to be shared—by opposing camps of scholars; by novelists and by their critics; by government ministers and by opposition journalists.

Whether "public opinion" was already a "preponderant force" in Europe by the 1780s, as playwright Louis-Sébastien Mercier claimed at the time, is open to question. The historical record leaves no doubt, however, that the concept was gaining currency and winning credibility. It became credible in part because an actual "public" was forming. Historians are now in a position to explain this phenomenon, since they have ceased to approach the Enlightenment simply as a March of Ideas and have studied it as a process of social communication and social change. Public opinion—in the broadest sense of the term—was an intricate circuit of writing, reading, and talking. Its jurisdiction lay within the expanding universe of print. Full-fledged membership in the true "public"—the "enlightened" tribunal—required a measure of affluence and education that the majority of Europeans, including many of the literate, did not enjoy. Within that limitation, however, the public was to be found in microcosm wherever men gathered to discuss the ideas circulated in print. Its locales ranged from elegant salons to modest coffeehouses. It might be said, in fact, that a network of "enlightened" communities, peopled by only a few thousand souls, invented public opinion as a way of talking about and validating itself.

This is also a way of saying, of course, that the tribunal of public opinion was a weapon in the Enlightenment's large arsenal of abstractions. It figures as such in Voltaire's campaign against Christian intolerance; in the mounting attacks on royal despotism and aristocratic corruption in France; in the rationales of reform-minded government officials throughout Europe; in the efforts to liberate literature and the arts from conventional rules. The point is not that public opinion was an empty abstraction from the start but that it was so appealing precisely because it was a highly serviceable fiction.

Napoleon once remarked that "cannon killed feudalism," but "ink will kill modern society." The eighteenth-century men of letters were more likely to observe that ink—or, more precisely, printer's ink—was *creating* modern society. Its most obvious creation was "the public."

This is not to suggest that print was being produced on a modern scale. Until the steam engine was harnessed to movable type in the early nineteenth century, there was little improvement in the hand-operated wooden press Johann Gutenberg had invented in 1450. Even if the technology had been better, the market for print would have remained pitifully small by modern commercial standards. The majority of the European population still lacked the excess cash and the sophisticated reading skills that most books and periodicals required. In 1785 the Netherlands' *Gazette de Leyde,* a French-language newspaper with a press run of just over four thousand, was one of the most widely read in Europe.

And yet historians speak of an eighteenth-century "revolution" in print, and not simply because the century witnessed a proliferation of printing shops, booksellers, reading clubs, and circulating libraries. On the eve of the French Revolution print offered Europeans far more information, a much greater variety of ideas, and incomparably more entertainment than it had offered a century earlier. In most educated homes reading was no longer primarily an act of religious devotion; the Bible and the devotional tract had been displaced by the novel and the entertaining journal. Government had become a newsworthy subject, and often an object of controversy, in a variety of newspapers available along the main commercial and postal routes.

The demand for print was growing, though it remained narrowly restricted by modern standards. In aristocratic circles "pedantry" still provoked disdain but illiteracy had become an embarrassment. If reading had become a habit among the well-born, there was a veritable craving for print among the much larger population Samuel Johnson classified as "that middle race . . . who read for pleasure or accomplishment." Bourgeois government officials, clergymen, lawyers and other professionals, merchants, affluent artisans, and shopkeepers—these educated and propertied commoners, along with their wives and children, were the typical consumers in the new print market.

If alarmed government officials and clerics had had their way, the range of consumer choices would have been considerably narrower. Even in "absolutist" France, however, official censorship was held in check by its own inconsistencies and the behind-the-scenes mediation of liberal-minded officials. The royal law courts (the *parlement*) in Paris still ordered the hangman to burn books publicly, and among the works consumed by the flames were Voltaire's *Philosophical Letters* (1734) and Jean-Jacques Rousseau's *Émile* (1762). But these acts of official censure likely whetted the reading public's appetite for risqué literature, and in any case they were not necessarily followed by a royal ban. Many publishers— the publication of the last ten volumes of the *Encyclopédie* may offer the most striking example—simply sidestepped the director of the Library and his small army of censors by not applying for the royal *privilège*. More often the government allowed questionable material to pass through the quasi-legal loophole of "tacit" permission. Even that was not required for legal briefs. In the scandal trials of the 1780s barristers used these briefs to portray their clients as hapless victims of aristocratic arrogance and royal despotism. Printed in thousands of copies, these *mémoires* did much to create the impression that the entire establishment was hopelessly corrupt.

There was also a heavy flow of illegal literature, most of which was supplied by Dutch and Swiss publishers on the borders of the Bourbon kingdom. Contraband in print was smuggled in crates past bribed customs officials, or hidden in men's breeches and under women's skirts. French booksellers tempted their customers with anti-Christian tracts and with pornography; with pamphlets detailing the sufferings of dissident writers in royal dungeons; with scabrous "libels" of prominent figures in the royal family, at court, and in the government. *Les Fastes de Louis XV* (1782) was perhaps the most widely read clandestine book in France on the eve of the Revolution. It included a lurid inventory of the depravities of Madame du Barry, the court mistress of Louis XV, who, in the words of its anonymous author, "had ascended in one leap from the brothel to the throne."

The modern "public" owed its origins and its growth to this cornucopia of print. In its broadest contours, however, the new public was as much a product of talk as it was of reading. As print entered symbiosis with new kinds of conversation in new social settings, it produced myriad ripple effects that cannot be measured by press runs and sales figures. Novel-reading, for example, was central to a new kind of domestic privacy in many educated bourgeois households.

Among the best-sellers were epistolary novels such as Samuel Richardson's *Pamela* (1741) and Rousseau's *La Nouvelle Héloise* (1761), which spun their plots around the joys and perils of courtship and marital life and were well suited to filling the idle hours of mothers and daughters. Even when such novels were not read aloud in the family circle, as they often were, they helped create a new, emotion-charged language of family intimacy.

As the bourgeois family circumscribed its private space, developing its own moral standards, it also examined itself obsessively in the printed pages of the novel. This self-examination was critical to the emergence of a modern public. It helps explain, in fact, why the public eventually assumed a critical posture toward government.

By the early eighteenth century, reading and conversation were nourishing each other in a variety of new public and quasi-public spaces. These spaces formed as the center of public life shifted from the royal courts of Europe to the cities, and as pedigrees and titles ceased to be the exclusive requirements for admission. Versailles and the courts modeled on it embodied the principle that the king was the only "public" figure, since his person was the single and indivisible source of all public authority. Royal splendor radiated outward through a court aristocracy displaying itself in relentless rounds of ceremony and theatrical festivity.

Since the early seventeenth century, Paris had witnessed the emergence of a new kind of public society that would eventually displace Versailles. Originally an overwhelming aristocratic milieu, it called itself "the world" (*le monde*) as a way of saying that it encompassed everyone who counted. *Le monde* gathered regularly in the capital's salons, under the guidance of highborn women in need of amusement and intellectual sustenance. In the highly mannered conversational art of the salon, gossip and scandal shaded naturally into literary discussion. In the eighteenth century, as the market for literature expanded, *le monde* opened its doors to the well-known as well as to the well-born and the well-heeled. For the bourgeois man of letters regular appearances on the salon circuit, perhaps at the cost of literary effort, had become a requirement of literary celebrity.

By the mid–eighteenth century the salon was one of several European institutions that brought together noblemen and educated and propertied commoners in new rituals of sociability and intellectual exchange. The royal academies founded in the seventeenth century by Louis XIV in Paris had counterparts throughout provincial France. The "academicians" were appointed from the ranks of the educated bourgeoisie and the clergy as well as from the office-holding aristocracy. While their public ceremonies paid homage to the monarchy, they formed what one member in Dijon called a "republic" of "citizen-spirits" behind closed doors. The monarchy had no reason to question this arrangement; by promoting a frank exchange of ideas, the academies were able to clarify vital public issues. The same purpose was served by the academies' many essay contests, which were open to all men of wit and literary talent. The typical winner may have been a mediocrity mouthing conventional wisdom, but there were stunning exceptions. In 1750 the Dijon Academy awarded first prize to a watchmaker's son and former vagabond named Jean-Jacques Rousseau. A misfit in *le monde,* paralyzed in the face of salon politesse and wit, Rousseau had used the occasion of the essay contest to launch his attack on the falseness of modern civilization.

Most European universities suffered by comparison with the new academies. Stereotyped as bastions of tradition-bound, boorish pedantry, they were crowded with obscure commoners who survived hand-to-mouth while preparing for the clergy. They were not the kind of places aristocratic scions were likely to visit on the Grand Tour. But several universities were anything but academic ghettos. Tounis College in Edinburgh entered the eighteenth century as little more than a stodgy Presbyterian seminary, but in the middle decades of the century, under the leadership of the town council and several reform-minded professors, it introduced a modern curriculum in the liberal arts. The new offerings catered to sons of gentlemen as well as to future clergymen, since they blended a "godliness" free of zealotry with the urbane "politeness" that the weekly *Spectator* had begun to propagate from London several decades earlier. Thanks to its university, Edinburgh, a provincial city in London's orbit, became known as a modern Athens.

On the continent, the closest equivalent was the Georg-August-Universität, Göttingen, founded by the Hanoverian government in 1737. Attracting first-rate scholars with its generous salaries and well-endowed library, and frowning on the theological polemics that soured life at other universities, the Georg-August was soon an innovative center in the fields of law, politics, history, and classical studies. Again commoners mixed with noblemen, who came to Göttingen from across Europe to groom themselves for government service or simply for a life of leisured refinement. In the space of a few decades a sleepy provincial town became one of the intellectual entrepôts of Europe.

Another refuge from social convention was the new "brotherhood" of Freemasonry, which crossed the Channel from London in the 1730s and spread across the urban landscape of France and the German states. Outside the lodge "brothers" might face each other across the barriers of rank and wealth, or might find themselves on opposite sides of volatile confessional and "political" issues. But within its artificially segregated space they could shed their social skins and inherited prejudices and discuss ideas (or at least some ideas) as one "human being" to another.

If Freemasonry formed a micropublic, it was also paradoxically a cult movement that shut out the public at large. More typical of the new sociability was the coffeehouse. In the course of the eighteenth century, as coffee drinking became a daily habit for millions of Europeans, the café became a fixture of urban life. London may have remained the world's caffeine capital, but Vienna, with 48 coffeehouses by 1770, was a formidable rival. The visitor to any provincial capital, court town, or university town could expect to find at least one or two such establishments. Most did not aspire to the elegance of Vienna's café Milani, whose mirrored hallways, marble façades, and chandeliers were reminiscent of Versailles. Instead they offered an atmosphere of intimacy to be found nowhere else outside the home. Friends and colleagues could gather regularly to enjoy a cup of coffee or tea, perhaps accompanied by a pastry; to play cards or billiards; to read the newspapers and other periodicals; to discuss the affairs of the day.

"You can meet half the world in Richter's café," Friedrich Schiller observed from Leipzig in 1785. This was still an exclusive "world," requiring affluence and leisure, but it was far more open than the Parisian salons of a century earlier. The openness and the informality made for intense, sometimes volatile discussion of the latest novel or review, of changes in government policy, of rumors of war and prospects for peace. The vibrant coffeehouse, a German observer remarked with understandable exaggeration, was a "political stock exchange where the most daring and clever heads from all social stations gather."

Ironically, women were not among the assembled heads, just as they were largely absent from the academies, the lodges, and the university lecture halls. As the presiding figures at salons, and as authors and readers of fiction, women had played a critical role in the formation of a "public." But political scientist Joan Landes is probably correct in arguing that, the more bourgeois the public became, the less room and tolerance it had for women. Bourgeois resentment of aristocratic privilege often focused on the intellectual pretensions and the political intrigues of highborn salon women. The *salonnière* became the foil to the ideal wife and mother, who shunned public life in the conviction that her "natural" role was to rear her children and to support her husband with modest intellectual companionship at home. If the novel kept women involved in the literary public as readers, it also directed their search for self-fulfillment to an idealized world of domestic happiness, insulated from the hurly-burly of professional life and politics.

This fictional dichotomy at once reflected and sanctioned a new kind of social segregation. As educated men found a refuge from the rigors of public life in the new domesticity, they found a respite from domesticity in their lodges, their clubs, and their coffeehouses.

But while the eighteenth-century public had its visible locales, there was also a sense in which it remained invisible. To some, its invisibility was the key to its power. The true public had to have a single will or conscience, and that evoked something greater than a mere aggregate of institutions or communities. This is not to say that the public was a fiction; there *was* a circuitry of written and spoken words out there, and somehow something called "opinion" formed in it and flowed through it.

When authors appealed to this invisible tribunal of public opinion, however, they were evoking an *ideal* rather than a measurable force. It requires a strenuous leap of historical imagination to grasp the ideal in its original state of innocence and to make sense of expectations that may seem hopelessly naive today.

At the core of the ideal was the principle of "publicity." Today this term makes us think of the corporate PR person, with smokescreens of apparent candor, or of *paparazzi* appealing to the public's "right to know" as their cameras follow celebrities into bedrooms. What struck eighteenth-century observers was not the abuse of publicity in an open society, but its vast potential to open up a closed society. In Old Regime Europe, secrecy was one of the guiding principles of life. Government set an example by regarding the practice of statecraft as an *arcanum,* a secret expertise that ordinary subjects were not in a position to understand and had no right to know. When the French *parlements* began to "go public" by publishing their remonstrances, the Crown stubbornly insisted that it alone decided what was fit for public consumption. England was considered an excessively open polity by French standards, but until at least the 1770s London newspapers risked prosecution when they published reports on the debates of the House of Commons.

Government policy reflected the tenacity of traditional norms. In the political arena formed by the ruler's court, intrigue was the stuff of politics; behind the court's elaborate façade of public ceremony, ministers competed with courtiers and mistresses to win favor and to carry the day. In their very different social settings, guilds of skilled craftsmen jealously guarded trade secrets.

"Publicity" meant a new openness, with its promise of a new civic spirit. The expectation was not, of course, that closed governments would suddenly throw open their doors to public scrutiny. Government would follow the example of society, as people became more transparent to each other in all walks of life. In the intricate pecking order of Old Regime corporatism, everyone was expected to command the authority and render the deference appropriate to his station. Confined to their social personae, people never interacted simply as persons or, in eighteenth-century parlance, in the purity of their shared "humanity." It was this kind of purely human communication that Masonic lodges aspired to achieve, and that the eighteenth-century cult of friendship idealized.

Print had even greater potential to effect the same egalitarian transparency. Print did not bring author and reader face to face, and that was its paradoxical advantage. Its impersonality made for a kind of "human" intimacy, free of domination and subservience, that face-to-face social relations rarely admitted. Eighteenth-century authors were fond of evoking this paradox; the faceless mass of readers was, or at least could be, their "friends" and their "confidantes."

With its call for public scrutiny and, at a deeper level, its new spirit of open and egalitarian exchange, the Enlightenment developed a strikingly modern strategy for reform. If government was to be accountable to public opinion, it had to be open to the public gaze. If abuses were to be remedied, they had to be brought to the light of day and discussed without inhibition in the public forum. All this sounds sensible enough, but we are likely to be brought up short by the eighteenth-century corollary: that the new openness would somehow generate a moral consensus about the direction reform ought to take. In our age of election polls and marketing surveys, the "public" tends to break down into groups with "interests" and corresponding "opinions," some coalescing into larger coalitions, others colliding head-on. Public opinion is a statistical aggregate, not the judgment of a single ethical voice.

There was a strain of eighteenth-century thought that regarded the pursuit of self-interest as a positive force for change, although it saw the individual, and not the group, as its proper agent. It was precisely because public opinion promised to transcend self-interest, however, that it was hailed as the moral arbiter for the entire society and polity. Inspired by their roseate image of Periclean Athens and the Roman Republic, eighteenth-century rationalists sought a modern collective expression of the classical ideal of civic virtue. Now that "each citizen is able to speak to the entire nation through the medium of print," the French Academy was informed by one of its new members in 1755, "the men of letters are for a dispersed public what the orators of Rome and Athens were in the midst of an assembled public."

In a rational society, public goals would be established by men who had an unobstructed view of the public welfare and hence could form disinterested judgments. Their consensus was, to be sure, an "opinion," which was to say that it was less than a definitive grasp of Truth. If the consensus was nonetheless authoritative, that was because the myriad judgments that constituted it had been made in splendid moral isolation. The crux of the matter—the axiomatic assumption—was that public opinion ought to be grounded in, and ought to draw its moral force from, the inviolable privacy of the individual conscience.

Like the ancient assembly, public discussion in print was a collective enterprise; but, as the German philosopher Christian Garve (1742–98) reminded his readers, in the end each member of the public "must judge for himself," as though from a position of unconditional moral autonomy. The point was not simply that open coercion was intolerable; even subtler forms of power—the authority of tradition, for example, or the seductive force of rhetoric—threatened to violate the purity of this ideal.

The formation of public opinion was seen as a process of purification. As the warring "passions" were strained out, the authoritative consensus of "reason" emerged.

We tend to smile patronizingly at the naiveté of this expectation. The assumption of a universal "reason" seems highly dubious in the light of modern cultural relativism and philosophical agnosticism, and in any case the need for consensus now seems less urgent. The ascendancy of interest-group politics, after all, has not shattered most Western polities; nor has a pluralistic culture, with its incessant clash of opinions, torn them apart.

To reform-minded men in the eighteenth century, however, the term "interests" often evoked caste prejudices and the abuse of legal privileges. Group self-interest meant corporate selfishness, which seemed incompatible with rational progress. The prospect of open conflict raised the specter of chaos, probably in the form of civil war. In the sixteenth and seventeenth centuries, Europeans had been plagued by religious war between Catholics and Protestants (as in France, the Netherlands, and Germany) and between a Protestant Establishment and radical dissenters (as in England). Skeptical rationalists wanted to tame religious beliefs by reducing them to one more species of "opinion," but they were acutely aware that in matters of faith, opinions easily hardened into prejudices.

The eighteenth century was "an age of *enlightenment*," Immanuel Kant reminded his readers in 1784, but it was not "an *enlightened* age." There was ample reason to fear that religious fanaticism and intolerance were alive and well. In England and Germany, Protestantism proved receptive to Enlightenment rationalism, but it also spawned movements like Pietism and Methodism, which sought to rekindle the evangelical fire. In France, Jansenism had similar aspirations, as its cult of miracles and the ecstasies of its "convulsionaries" demonstrated. As late as 1766, following an unsuccessful appeal to the *parlement* in Paris, the young Chevalier de la Barre was tortured, beheaded, and burned on suspicion of having mutilated crucifixes. The case prompted one of Voltaire's most impassioned appeals to "the public."

In modern democracies, political parties are supposed to play a central role in generating public opinion. But most eighteenth-century observers would have agreed with Christian Garve that "public opinion ceases to exist as soon as parties occur." The spirit of "party" meant fierce loyalty to a "particular" cause, without regard for the common welfare, and the history of sectarian fanaticism left no doubt that the spirit was pernicious. This was the lesson that accompanied the application of the word "party" to an emerging arena of modern political conflict. Political partisanship joined religious zealotry as a threat to the reasoned, tolerant consensus that public opinion promised to articulate.

Both varieties of "party" threatened to fracture the body politic—or, as Garve might have put it, both kinds of opinion were incompatible with a truly public opinion. Whether the leader was a religious zealot or a political demagogue, he won the blind following of the "mob" rather than the reasoned consent of autonomous individuals. In both cases mass mobilization was a kind of contagion, an epidemic of "enthusiasm." And in both cases "enthusiasm" meant the kind of self-delusion that precluded rational judgment. The religious enthusiast mistook his neurotic obsessions for the voice of the Lord. Likewise, the political enthusiast mistook his "metaphysical" fantasies for universal truths about man and his "natural" rights.

By the eve of the French Revolution, the tribunal of public opinion was expected to fill a plethora of needs, and it was beginning to register the tensions among them. When the public censured the authoritarian government, the tunnel-visioned corporatism, and the overzealous confessionalism of the Old Regime, it was the voice of a modern polity in the making. But public opinion also promised to preclude new, secular outbreaks of the party spirit. In that capacity it was an antidote to modernity, embodying the rationalist's fear that the polity was entering a chronic condition of partisan conflict. Even as French critics of the monarchy assumed an openly confrontational stance, they sought to dispel the specter of open contestation with their appeals to an authoritative consensus. Still "absolutist" in theory, the government had little choice but to respond in kind.

The final irony is that public opinion had become a kind of absolute in its own right. Precisely because the public will was no longer embodied in the person of the king, it had to find expression in a collective unity. It expressed itself in "opinion," and not in the transcendent truths that religious believers claimed to find in Revelation or in the depths of their own souls. But as a collective conscience hovering above mere "interests," and as a consensus purified of passions, public opinion had its own claim to transcendence.

The "people of intellect govern, because in the long run they form public opinion, which sooner or later subjugates or reverses every kind of despotism." This dictum was published by the royal historiographer of France in 1767, but it would not have been a bad guess to attribute it to a Czech intellectual celebrating the recent Velvet Revolution. When we speak of the former East Bloc countries joining (or returning to) the "free" West, we mean, among other things, that their governments have at last abandoned the pretext of embodying the Will of the Proletariat and have become accountable to public opinion.

As the recent thaw in Eastern Europe advanced, in fact, some historians had the eerie feeling that they were listening to a telescoped replay of an eighteenth-century script. Once again intellectuals were orchestrating a verbal assault on authoritarian government, often couched in the morally charged languages of fiction and philosophy. There was the same evocation of the public as a collective conscience, of public opinion as the record of its judgment, and of the principle of openness, or publicity, as the crux of reform. We seemed to have entered a time warp and to have recovered the original innocence invested in the concept of public opinion.

But the script has also been telescoped in another sense. The former Stalinist satellites are leaping headlong into the world of political parties, election campaigns, interest-group politics, and mass marketing. As they make the leap, vaulting optimism gives way to skepticism and the apotheosis of public opinion is muted, if not repudiated. Indeed, East European intellectuals find themselves fighting off a mood of bitter disillusionment as their political revolutions, along with their literary renaissance, are threatened by the allure of Western-style commercialism and by the withering attention of the electronic media.

Mass education and mass literacy, radio and television, modern advertising and electioneering: all have contributed to the fact that the modern public is a far cry from the eighteenth-century ideal. Despite the continuity of language, the opinion now measured incessantly in surveys and polls cannot be "public" in the eighteenth-century sense; as the invisible will has become the measureable aggregate, the concept has lost its original promise of moral invincibility. In a process that eighteenth-century rationalists would have regarded as self-contradictory, public opinion breaks down into a melee of *opinions,* and endless argument among claimants for the allegiance of the real public. One hopes for a clear numerical majority, not an authoritative consensus.

To judge by historical experience since the eighteenth century, all this does not necessarily spell doom for the Eastern European experiments. The problem may lie with a kind of purism in the original ideal—an aversion to the uncontrollable messiness of pluralistic conflict and mass participation. Those who still indulge in such purism may set themselves up for a plunge into disillusionment. Only those who can reconcile themselves to the fact that public opinion does not produce a pure consensus of reason will be able to navigate democratic politics successfully.

In eighteenth-century Europe, the onset of disillusionment was gradual, but it gained pace at the end of the century. "Friends of the Revolution," Garve wrote some time in the mid-1790s, "take refuge in public opinion as a *Qualitas occulta* that explains everything—or as a higher power that can excuse everything." Garve had in mind the orators and journalists who had justified mob violence and the Terror in revolutionary France. Others had already observed that the expanding market for print was a mixed blessing for *belles lettres*. If it created a reading public, it also threatened to reduce literature to one more trivial commodity and to leave authors at the mercy of fickle consumers in search of effortless entertainment.

In its eighteenth-century apotheosis, public opinion was the voice of an educated and propertied elite. Faced with the Revolution's surge of democratic politics, and with the egalitarian momentum of an increasingly commercialized print market, the elite began to justify certain kinds of exclusion within the promise of openness. The sexual division of labor might exclude women from active participation in the new public, but how justify the continued exclusion of the broad mass of men? How could a part—the educated and propertied part—claim to speak credibly for the whole? Why were some people more capable of disinterested judgment than others? There were many answers, all justifying an elite's claim to speak with an authoritative voice. Authority now lay in the broad vision afforded by property ownership and education; in the professional's expert judgment on issues the "lay" public could not judge; in the literary critic's mission to guard "standards" against the onslaught of trash.

Public opinion would remain a court of appeal, but the size and composition of the jury had become a contentious issue. Public opinion may still evoke an ideal of rational consensus, but it turns out that the ideal itself is not exempt from political conflict or indeed from the struggle for profit. The new Eastern European democracies are learning this lesson very fast, though they have reminded us that, at least for a moment, public opinion can be the voice of conscience.

3 | P. T. BARNUM AND THE AMERICAN MUSEUM

A. H. SAXON

Could a present-day Manhattanite somehow be transported back to the mid–nineteenth century, he would find little to surprise him in the New York City of that time. Although its teeming boardinghouses and tenements, hotels, pleasure haunts, and thriving businesses were still located mainly in the area from the Battery to just north of City Hall, the inexorable march "uptown" was well under way, with well-to-do citizens erecting their opulent mansions as far north as Union Square at 14th Street, while some visionaries were already predicting the day when every inch of the island would be built upon.

Fueled by ambitious natives pouring in from the countryside and by a never-ending stream of immigrants, the city's population, from 60,000 inhabitants at the turn of the century, had been more than doubling every 20 years and by 1850 stood at slightly over half a million. The "Empire City," as some insisted on calling her, already had the reputation of being a cosmopolis—of being, owing to the large number of foreigners in her midst, the least "American" of American cities.

Commerce was the great engine that drove the city. American entrepreneurship had at last come of age, and huge fortunes were being made overnight by former petty tradesmen, farmers, and ship captains. The manners of these parvenus or "shoddyites"—with their ludicrous aping of foreign customs, conspicuous consumption, and putting on of what they considered to be aristocratic airs—were amusingly satirized at New York's Park Theatre in Anna Cora Mowatt's *Fashion* of 1845.

Reprinted from the autumn 1989 issue of *The Wilson Quarterly*.

But those in more modest circumstances and the industrious poor who jammed into the city were no less engaged in running after riches. And behind the kaleidoscopic whirl of life in Gotham was a darker, less salubrious aspect: in the back slums of Broadway and the city's notorious "Five Points" district, crime, drunkenness, and prostitution flourished amidst appalling scenes of misery and squalor.

In the spring of 1841 Phineas Taylor Barnum, aged 30 and "about as poor as I should ever wish to be," as he later wrote in his autobiography, was himself an eager participant in this hurried scene.

If we are to believe every word of his autobiography, it was not his first scrape with poverty. Born in 1810 in the rural village of Bethel, Connecticut, Barnum later harped upon the "deprivations" of his youth, complaining that he never had any educational "advantages." In fact, he had been no worse off than most of his boyhood companions. At both the Bethel common school and the private academy in neighboring Danbury, he had received a thorough grounding in mathematics, composition, and the classics of English literature.

Barnum's father, Philo, a tailor, innkeeper, and livery-stable owner, died insolvent when his son was 16. But the custom of the "widow's dower" allowed Mrs. Irena Barnum and her five children to keep their house and even a modest amount of personal property. The oldest of her five children, the future showman, enjoyed the further "advantage" of being the pet of one of the village's wealthiest citizens, his maternal grandfather Phineas Taylor, after whom young "Taylor"—as he was usually called by his friends and family—was named.

From his family, and his grandfather in particular—or so he liked to think—Barnum inherited a lifelong love of practical jokes. Phineas Taylor would "go farther, wait longer, work harder and contrive deeper, to carry out a practical joke, than for anything else under heaven," Barnum wrote admiringly in his autobiography, whose original 1855 edition describes many such exploits in hilarious detail. Young "Taylor" was himself often the accomplice in, and sometimes the butt of, his grandfather's elaborate pranks; and to the end of his life he could never resist the opportunity to cause other people temporary embarrassment.

The prankster was never an idler, however. By the time he was in his teens, with the encouragement of his doting grandfather, Barnum was successfully engaged in various business enterprises. After serving as a clerk in a country store, he opened two such establishments of his own in Bethel. At 19, too, he married a "fair, rosy-cheeked, buxom-looking girl" named Charity Hallett, who had traveled up from the coastal town of Fairfield to work for a local tailor.

Business and marriage did not consume all of Barnum's energy. He took an early and keen interest in public affairs, and when letters he wrote attacking religious interference in politics were rejected by the editor of a Danbury newspaper, he established a weekly paper of his own—the first in the history of Bethel—which he defiantly named *The Herald of Freedom*. The fledgling editor's heated opinions and outspokenness landed him in court on several occasions. At the conclusion of one such trial for libel, brought on by his accusing a local dignitary of being a "canting hypocrite" and a "usurer," he was sentenced to 60 days in the Danbury jail.

Eventually, the attractions of tiny Bethel began to pall. So in the fall of 1834, without any firm idea of what he might do there, he moved to New York City. After several months of unemployment and some rather desultory attempts to re-establish himself as a businessman, he "fell" into the profession of showman when he began taking around the country the exhibition known as "'Joice Heth."

This extraordinary attraction was in fact a blind, decrepit, hymn-singing slave woman, whom Barnum advertised as being 161 years old and as having once been the "nurse" of the revered George Washington. When Joice died early in the following year (at which time an autopsy revealed she could not have been much above 80), he continued to tour with several other entertainers, including an Italian juggler whom Barnum rechristened "Signor Vivalla" and a young blackface dancer named "Master Diamond."

The showman later confessed that this nomadic period in his life had been fraught with dangers to his moral well-being. "When I consider the kinds of company into which . . . I was thrown, the associations with which I was connected, and the strong temptations to wrong-doing and bad habits which lay in my path," he wrote, "I am astonished as well as grateful that I was not utterly ruined."

Meanwhile, his long-suffering wife, Charity, who had remained behind in Bethel or New York while her husband was off on his tours, had given birth to the first two of their four daughters. The showman faced mounting pressure to settle down and establish himself in some "respectable" line of business. From time to time—nearly always disastrously—he tried his hand at some "mercantile" enterprise. But his great opportunity came toward the end of 1841, when he learned the collections at New York's soporific American Museum were up for sale.

Barnum later wrote that he repeatedly visited the museum as a "thoughtful looker-on" and that he soon became convinced that "only energy, tact, and liberality were needed, to give it life and to put it on a profitable footing." The trouble was, his ill-fated business speculations had nearly exhausted his capital. He therefore wrote to Francis Olmsted, a wealthy merchant who owned the building in which the museum was housed, and persuaded him to purchase the collections in his own name, allowing Barnum, while leasing the building, to pay for them in installments.

The nucleus of the museum's collections had been assembled toward the end of the previous century by the Tammany Society and was originally exhibited in

City Hall. Since 1795, however, the collections had been owned and managed by a succession of private individuals, the latest of whom, the taxidermist and natural-history enthusiast John Scudder, had died in 1821. Thanks to squabbling among his children and to other turns of fortune (including the financial panic of 1837), the asking price for the collections, which might have been $25,000 a decade earlier, was now only $15,000. Barnum managed to bargain that figure down to $12,000.

Proprietary museums have largely disappeared from the American scene, and few people today would look upon them as likely business opportunities. But in the mid–nineteenth century, before the great public museums and zoological gardens got under way, nearly every city of any size boasted at least one such establishment, and often these were the principal, most popular cultural institutions of their day.

The theater, still held in low regard by many respectable citizens, reached its nadir in 1849 with the bloody Astor Place Riot, the climax in the long rivalry between the brawny American actor Edwin Forrest and the English tragedian William Charles Macready. Opera and ballet, then barely under way in America, were tainted by their theatrical associations. Circuses, which sometimes performed in theaters or buildings of their own when not on the road, were fairly common by this time. But here, too, shady practices and loose behavior on the part of employees—not to mention the coarse jests and indelicate references that figured in many clowns' repertoires—frequently outraged the moral element in communities.

Menageries were more acceptable, since they were patently "educational" and their denizens were commonly referred to in scriptural terms ("the Great Behemoth of Holy Writ," etc.). Exotic animals, brought to these shores and sold by enterprising ship captains, had been exhibited in America since the colonial period. Taken about the countryside individually or in small groups, they were a profitable investment for those who bought them.

Pleasure gardens such as William Niblo's in lower Manhattan, to which the novelist Henry James recalled being taken as a boy, were obviously respectable. Here, on a fine summer's evening, a family party or group of friends might take refreshments served in one of the elegantly decorated boxes or "bowers" that surrounded the garden, stroll along its illuminated pathways, and enjoy the light entertainment presented in the adjacent "saloon" or garden itself.

Waxworks, too, were deemed innocuous family entertainment, provided they did not dwell too luridly on female anatomy or the horrors of the French Revolution. Music of the nonoperatic variety, performed in numerous "concert halls," was eminently respectable; so were "ethiopian" entertainments or minstrel shows, whose greatest period of popularity, however, was to come in the second half of the nineteenth century.

An appreciation for the fine arts was noticeably on the increase, although here, too, there were as yet no great public institutions to bring together such works. At a time when photography was in its infancy, Americans' curiosity about the Old World and their own nation's remote fastnesses was satisfied by the number of spectacular pictorial entertainments—panoramas, dioramas, etc.—whose huge paintings, often viewed under shifting lighting conditions, with three-dimensional objects in the foreground, special sound effects, and musical accompaniment, were exhibited in specially constructed buildings.

One might as well add that lovers of the arts also had at least one "adult" outlet around this time: tableaux vivants of the "model artists" variety, whose generous display of undraped female charms pointed the way to another cultural development. But striptease and the raucous "girly-show" phase of burlesque were still some years in the future, as was the cleaner, full-fledged vaudeville show.

Americans were hardly starved for amusement at mid-century, and when one adds to the above the numerous other entertainments then available to them— "legerdemain" or magic shows, puppets, balloon ascensions, annual expositions of arts and industries, county fairs, lectures and other visitations sponsored by local lyceum societies, itinerating freaks, and such prodigies as Joice Heth that Barnum and his fellow showmen took around the country—one sees to what extent the old Puritans' influence over such godless goings-on had by now declined.

But of all these entertainments, museums were undoubtedly the most inclusive and least objectionable, combining as they did, rather incongruously, elements of nearly all the above, while at the same time stressing their dedication to "rational" amusement.

Such had been the announced policy of America's first great museum, that of the painter, inventor, and naturalist Charles Willson Peale, whose Philadelphia establishment, from the 1780s on, featured wax figures and a notable collection of the founder's own paintings. It also offered lectures, scientific demonstrations, musical evenings, magic-lantern shows, and a scenic spectacle with changeable effects, which Peale eventually advertised as "moving pictures." As at the present-day Smithsonian Institution, almost everything having to do with man and nature was cheerfully accommodated, from a chip of the coronation chair in Westminster Abbey to the tattooed head of a New Zealand chieftain and a living cow with five legs and two tails.

Peale sometimes expressed impatience with sports of nature and weird acquisitions, but their inclusion in earlier "cabinets of curiosities" was a well-established practice by the time he founded his Philadelphia museum, and neither he nor later museum proprietors dared disappoint their patrons.

The American Museum continued the tradition of catering to such expectations—not without a frequently humorous note—and under Barnum's direction exhibited such quaint objects as the preserved hand and arm of the pirate Tom Trouble, a hat made out of broom splints by a lunatic, and (a traditional Connecticut specialty) a wooden nutmeg.

But the bulk of the museum's collections was decidedly of a more legitimate nature and possessed, as Barnum often boasted, considerable scientific and cultural value, even if scholarly visitors did complain about the inadequate labeling and lack of systematic display they sometimes found in their favorite areas. For the American Museum aspired to be—and probably was under Barnum's management—the largest and most comprehensive establishment of its kind in America.

Unfortunately, no complete catalogue of its eclectic holdings was ever compiled, and the various guidebooks that were published give but a faint indication of the extent of its contents. Still, some idea of the "million wonders" Barnum was himself trumpeting in 1864, when the museum was as its most congested, may be gleaned from a guidebook published around that time. There was, to begin with, the usual profusion of skeletons and stuffed animals. A collection of wax figures—some, like the one of Queen Victoria, notoriously bad—was on display, as were paintings, statues, and daguerreotypes of Barnum and his famous dwarf Tom Thumb. Elsewhere were Roman, Oriental, and American Indian artifacts; trick mirrors, optical instruments, and a large magnet; collections of insects and butterflies, minerals and crystals, shells and corals, and horns. A separate room was devoted to 194 "cosmoramas," in effect peepshows, through whose apertures visitors raptly gazed at famous scenes and buildings around the world.

All this was but the beginning, however. Continuing another tradition established by Peale, the American Museum had its menagerie of living animals. They were so numerous and at times so large, in fact, that one cannot help wondering how Barnum found space to fit them all in, let alone get them to the museum's upper stories, where most of them were kept. Besides the usual lions, tigers, bears, ostriches, and primates, the museum boasted the first hippopotamus seen in America, a rhinoceros, the delicate giraffe or "camelopard" as it was still sometimes called, and the entire "California Menagerie" of the legendary "Grizzly" Adams.

Entirely new at Barnum's establishment was the first public aquarium in America. The idea for this project had come to the showman while he was on a trip to England, where he had seen a similar display at London's Regent's Park zoo. Procuring glass tanks and two able assistants from the same institution, in 1857 he inaugurated an elegant exhibit of "Ocean and River Gardens" at the American Museum. By the early 1860s a large collection of native and exotic fishes was on display, as were sharks, porpoises, and "sea flowers" or anemones. To keep his "Aquarial Gardens" supplied, he regularly fitted out sailing expeditions to the Tropics that returned laden with angel, porcupine, and peacock fish, and a variety of other brilliantly colored specimens. (The young Albert S. Bickmore, who had studied with Harvard's famed Louis Agassiz and was later to found the American Museum of Natural History, was on board the vessel that visited Bermuda in 1862.)

Even more remarkable was the expedition Barnum himself made to the mouth of the St. Lawrence River in 1861 to supervise the capture of beluga whales. Transported to New York in a special railway car, the first two of these beautiful creatures were exhibited in a brick and cement tank in the museum's basement. When they died after a short time, Barnum promptly set about procuring additional specimens, which were now housed on the second floor in a plate-glass tank measuring 24 feet on each side. To supply them and his other exhibits with fresh salt water, pipes were laid from the museum to New York Bay, and a steam engine was set up at dockside to pump the water. The showman also exhibited his white whales in Boston, and when rumors began circulating that they were only porpoises, Professor Agassiz himself showed up to vouch for their authenticity.

Although Barnum sometimes spoke disparagingly about his knowledge of natural history and told his friends that he didn't know a clam from a codfish, he had the reputation of being a great zoologist among his contemporaries, many of whom addressed queries to him and sent him specimens to identify. Many of his animals, like his beluga whales and his genuine white elephant of later circus fame, were of the greatest rarity or the first of their kind to be exhibited in America. Others, like the four giraffes he bragged about in an 1873 letter to Spencer F. Baird, secretary of the Smithsonian Institution, were difficult to transport under the best of circumstances. When these animals died, they were quickly replaced and their hides and skeletons given to scientific institutions, which often entered into fierce competition for them.

For half a century Barnum was actively involved with and made important contributions to the study of natural history. Yet today, predictably, he is remembered almost exclusively for such patent frauds as his Little Woolly Horse and the notorious Fejee Mermaid—those "skyrockets" or "advertisements," as Barnum liked to explain, by which he attracted attention to the bona fide objects he had to offer. At times even he was genuinely puzzled and in danger of being taken advantage of.

In the 1880s, in the midst of a spate of sightings of sea serpents and lake monsters (including the perennial "Champ" of Lake Champlain fame), he issued a standing offer of $20,000 to anyone who could capture a specimen and deliver it to him "in a fit state for stuffing and mounting." There seemed to be no reasonable doubt of the creatures' existence, he stated in his announcement, so many "intelligent and respectable" people had reported seeing them. The reward went unclaimed, needless to say, although several such monsters were manufactured around this time. In the early 1880s, too, the showman entered into correspondence with one J. D. Willman of Vancouver, British Columbia, who had the notion he might succeed in capturing a living mammoth.

And indeed, why should there not have been great woolly mammoths shaking the earth of the Canadian wilderness? Had not Charles Willson Peale, who at the turn of the century excavated the first nearly complete skeleton of a "mammoth"—more accurately, mastodon—for years cherished the belief that this "Great Incognitum" still lived?

The idea that species might become extinct, that breaks could occur in the "Great Chain of Being" linking God to the lowliest of his creations, had only recently gained acceptance in the scientific community, and was still vigorously opposed by many outside it. For that matter, were not new species like *Gorilla gorilla,* whose existence had been reported but generally doubted until the explorer Paul du Chaillu showed up in London with his specimens in 1861, being discovered all the time?

Even more unsettling than the notion of species becoming extinct, to many of Barnum's contemporaries, was the idea that they might be subject to a process of gradual change. It was left to Alfred Wallace and Charles Darwin to formulate the theory of natural selection. But even before the publication of the latter's controversial *Origin of Species* in 1859, sufficient evidence had accumulated to convince many scientists that evolution occurred, although its mechanism was then but dimly perceived. The immense geologic record of the earth itself was at last being read, and soon the race would commence for fossil remains far more ancient and unsettling than Peale's mastodon.

To those with an interest in natural history—and this included nearly everyone in nineteenth-century Europe and America—it was an exciting, if confusing, age. Barnum, who supplied as best he could legitimate examples of the subject, was not above exploiting his patrons' ignorance and credulity from time to time. This he certainly did with the Fejee Mermaid and Little Woolly Horse, not to mention a tantalizing procession of unicorns, frogs with human hands, phoenixes, and similar curiosities manufactured for him by the ingenious Japanese, who even then seem to have had a good idea of what would appeal to the American market.

Equally challenging to spectators were his exhibits in the "missing-link" and "descent-of-man" categories. There may have been some excuse, in the 1840s, for touting "Mlle. Fanny," his celebrated orangutan, as "the connecting link between man and brute." But the succession of "What Is Its?" he exhibited from the same period onward were out-and-out frauds. The most famous of these was the cone-headed Negro William Henry Johnson, known to generations of Americans as "Zip," who continued at his strange vocation until his death in 1926, when he was variously reported as being anywhere from 63 to 84 years old. "Is it man? Is it monkey? Or is it both?" queries one bill dating from 1861, describing "Zip" or one of his predecessors.

In a pamphlet published the previous year, the speech of this curiosity's "keeper" is even given. He had been captured, according to this account, by a party of adventurers in quest of a gorilla and had only recently been taught to walk upon his feet. After pointing out a number of interesting physical traits—"the ears are set back about an inch too far for humanity," etc.—the speaker concluded with the announcement that he had been examined "by some of the most scientific men we have, and pronounced by them to be a connecting link between the wild African native and the brute creation."

It was no accident that the advent of this particular "What Is It?" coincided so closely with the publication of Darwin's *Origin of Species,* whose original English edition had sold out on the first day of issue the previous November. The diarist George Templeton Strong, who was then, like many of his contemporaries, immersed in reading and privately arguing with the work, stopped by the museum on two consecutive days in early March 1860 to view the "What Is It?" On his first visit he thought the keeper's story "probably bosh" and the "What Is It?" itself "clearly an idiotic negro dwarf." But its anatomical details, he conceded, were "fearfully simian, and he's a great fact for Darwin."

Aside from exhibits that can most charitably be termed "ethnographic," there was always a floating population of human abnormalities or freaks to be seen at the American Museum, generally on a platform in one of the saloons, but, in the case of more choice specimens like General Tom Thumb, sometimes on the stage of the Lecture Room. There was a formidable assortment of giants and giantesses (their heights nearly always exaggerated, of course), including Barnum's sensational "Nova Scotia Giantess," Anna Swan, who in time married the irascible Captain Martin Bates, another giant, and went off to an Ohio farm in the hope of settling down to a "normal" life.

At the opposite end of the spectrum were Isaac Sprague, the 50-pound "Living Skeleton," and the "Living Phantom," R. O. Wickware, "whose body is so thin that it is almost transparent, whose limbs, like walking canes, are only about an inch thick, and yet who enjoys a hearty meal, and can wrestle successfully with men of robust constitution and powerful physical development."

There was always a pleasing variety of little people—"dwarfs," as Barnum and his contemporaries usually referred to them, but which spectators today, since they were perfectly proportioned, would more likely term "midgets." And what more interesting entertainer could one wish for than the armless wonder S. K. G. Nellis, who played the accordion and the cello with his toes and could also expertly manage a bow and arrow, hitting a quarter held up by any visitor intrepid enough to hazard the experiment?

Equally interesting were those individuals possessing abnormal pigmentation or none at all. The albino family of Rudolph Lucasie—husband, wife, and son, whose marmoreal likenesses are immortalized in a Currier and Ives print—was the best-known example. At one time Barnum also featured two Negro girls, "Pure White, with White Wool and Pink Eyes," alongside their black mother and baby sister.

Freaks and ethnographic curiosities were by no means the only living hominids to be seen at the American Museum. The halls and saloons were populated by a variety of industrious individuals, for the most part concessionaires, who offered their wares and services at small additional charge. There were Bohemian glass-blowers and phrenologists like Professor Livingston, who was advertised to examine his customers and produce correct charts of them in less than ten minutes. During the first few years of Barnum's management visitors might purchase multiple silhouettes of themselves made by an individual using an outlining apparatus known as the physiognotrace; in later years daguerreotypists and photographers took over this function. Further entertainment might be had in a rifle and pistol gallery in the museum's basement, while those in need of nourishment could refresh themselves in an oyster saloon.

Finally, there was the Lecture Room. By Barnum's own admission a "narrow, ill-contrived and uncomfortable" place when he took over the museum, this feature had been common to all museums since the days of Peale. And originally such rooms had been just that: places in which lectures and scientific demonstrations were given. As time went on, however, their educational goals were subverted by less rigorous entertainment—magic-lantern shows, exhibitions of juggling, ventriloquism and legerdemain, dancing and musical numbers, comic skits, etc.—until their programs were barely distinguishable from those of variety halls.

From this, once their auditoriums and stage facilities had been suitably improved, it was only a short step to full-scale dramatic entertainments, rivaling or even excelling those of neighboring theaters—but always under their earlier designation of "lecture room" or "hall," thereby ensuring the continuing approbation of spectators who would never dare think of entering a "theatre" but who had no qualms whatever about taking themselves and their families to such entertainments as Barnum and his contemporary, Moses Kimball, proprietor of the Boston Museum, presented on their stages.

So much has been made in the past of this subterfuge, of the supposed hypocrisy of Barnum, Kimball, and their fellow museum proprietors, that one tends to overlook the genuine service they rendered to the American stage.

During the first half of the nineteenth century theaters were hardly the decorous places to which we are accustomed today. Spectators, particularly those in the upper galleries, were given to demonstrating their disapproval of actors and play-wrights in no uncertain terms; drunkenness was rife in the front of the house and, to a somewhat lesser extent, on the other side of the footlights as well; pros-titutes openly solicited in corridors and boxes. Unless he were hopelessly addicted to the drama or determined to see some great itinerating "star," a respectable person thought twice about going to the theater. He thought even harder before exposing his wife or sweetheart to these conditions. Children were almost never taken there.

But all this was gradually to change during the second half of the century, thanks largely to the determined efforts of Barnum and a handful of other man-agers. They made theater into something it had rarely been before: a place of family entertainment, where men and women, adults and children, could inter-mingle safe in the knowledge that no indelicacies would assault their senses either onstage or off. In addition to such sterling temperance and abolitionist dramas as *The Drunkard, Ten Nights in a Barroom,* and *Uncle Tom's Cabin* (the last in an adaptation even Mrs. Stowe had difficulty following), the Lecture Room regularly regaled its audiences with domestic and romantic melodramas and with plays based on biblical subjects.

From Barnum's acquisition of the American Museum at the end of 1841 until its destruction by fire $23^1/_2$ years later, nearly 38 million admission tickets were sold; close to a million additional tickets were dispensed at his second museum uptown during the two and a half years it was in existence. Many of these were bought by repeat customers, of course, but the record is nevertheless remarkable, especially when one considers that the total population of the United States in 1865 was only around 35 million. Indeed, calculations reveal that the first American Museum, during its years under Barnum's management, actually sold more tickets in proportion to the population than did Disneyland during its first $23^1/_2$ years in operation.

Nor did the American Museum ever cater to any particular "class" of specta-tor. Barnum once claimed, rather unconvincingly, that he had "often grieved that the taste of the million was not elevated." With no financial support for his museum other than what he took in at the door, he had been "obliged to pop-ularize it," and while he had indeed offered his visitors a "million" bona fide curiosities, "millions of persons were only induced to see them because, at the same time, they could see whales, giants, dwarfs, Albinoes, dog shows, et cetera." It was all an undigested hodgepodge, of course, and in later years the showman was sometimes apologetic about the museum's lack of system and some of the methods he had employed to lure its patrons.

Yet among these same customers, rubbing elbows with farmers fresh in from the countryside, tradesmen, apprentices and laborers, and "respectable" citizens with their families in tow, were famous scientists like Louis Agassiz and Joseph Henry of the Smithsonian Institution, authors like Walt Whitman and Henry David Thoreau, eminent statesmen, religious leaders, and ambassadors from abroad, and even, in 1860, the visiting Prince of Wales.

In an age when public-supported cultural institutions were still the exception rather than the general rule, Barnum's museum filled a definite need in American society. And, if it did not always strive to elevate their taste, at least it offered its visitors wholesome entertainment. From sunrise until 10 P.M., seven days a week, its untold wonders summoned the democratic multitude. It was one of the greatest, most universally popular institutions of its day. And all this—museum, menagerie, lecture room and freaks—for what was even then the bargain price of 25 cents.

Barnum's first American Museum burned to the ground on July 13, 1865. Unruffled, the showman immediately set to work to assemble a new collection and less than two months later opened his second American Museum farther up Broadway, between Spring and Prince Streets. When this second American Museum burned during the night of March 2–3, 1868, he decided to take his friend Horace Greeley's advice to "go a-fishing" and announced his "retirement" from museum management. But his interest in the business did not die. Besides offering advice and lending his support to newer institutions like the Smithsonian, the American Museum of Natural History, and eventually even the Smithsonian's National Zoo, he paid for and endowed the Barnum Museum of Natural History, which continues to this day as a center for the study of the biological sciences on the campus of Tufts University in Medford, Massachusetts.

As the century drew to its close, the old showman had sense enough to realize that proprietary museums of the type he had owned had nearly run their course. The great public institutions were at last coming into their own, and they were infinitely better organized, more specialized and "scientific," than his museums had ever been. If these successors were not half so entertaining—if they contained no fat ladies, "What Is Its?" or wooden nutmegs—why, such "curiosities" could still be accommodated in the museum or "sideshow" department of a traveling circus.

And so they were, beginning in 1871, when "P. T. Barnum's Museum, Menagerie, and Circus" (the ordering of the words was deliberate) first took to the road. The showman's connection with what came to be called "The Greatest Show on Earth" is a story in itself, and even there—despite his advanced age, the sniping of fierce rivals, and the perverse delight of latter-day critics in pointing out what he did *not* do in this field—his contributions were considerable.

As indeed they were in nearly every entertainment he touched. Aside from his acknowledged mastery of publicity, his almost intuitive grasp of human nature, and his skill in exploiting public opinion, Barnum, for over half a century, not only expanded but in large part defined the notion of popular entertainment in America. Like Walt Disney's in a later day, his view of such entertainments was that they should be eminently wholesome, family-oriented, "educational" and occasionally even didactic, but above all amusing. By the 1880s, when he had achieved almost mythic status, the showman's more notorious frauds and hoaxes had long been forgiven, and the "Prince of Humbugs" had been metamorphosed into "The Children's Friend" and "The World's Greatest Showman." In posters advertising his circus around this time, he was sometimes proclaimed "The Sun of the Amusement World." For one who let light into so many lives, that title will serve as well as any.

THE RISE OF AMERICAN ADVERTISING

T. J. JACKSON LEARS

In older downtowns across America, the casual observer may still happen upon spectral presences from the commercial past. Where there is available space on brick or stone, ancient advertising murals preside over parking lots, littered playgrounds, and construction projects. Often partly obscured by banks and fast-food franchises, some announce products: Uneeda Biscuit, Wilson's Whiskey; others are populated by fading fantastic characters: the Gold Dust Twins, the winsome White Rock Girl. Once part of the landscape of everyday life, these cultural graffiti somehow exert more fascination as they recede from view.

Those advertisements were part of a new visual environment that emerged around the turn of the century, as American corporations began to advertise "brand-name" products to a national market. Advertisers painted brick walls and billboards, caught the gaze of straphangers with subway-car cards, and bought acres of space in metropolitan newspapers and the new mass-circulation magazines. And they played a major part in the evolution of a new way of life, in which the acquisition of specific goods was somehow associated with psychic self-betterment, fulfillment, and happiness.

The earliest advertising agencies sprang up in the 1870s and 1880s. Two- or three-man operations, they were mostly clustered on Park Row in lower Manhattan, in stuffy backstairs rooms that smelled of printer's ink. As the business historian Daniel Pope observes, early advertising agents merely procured "a shadowy, uncertain commodity—advertising space"—from publishers and provided it to "businesses whose own products were often equally obscure"—magic elixirs, investment opportunities, or self-help schemes.

Reprinted from the winter 1983 issue of *The Wilson Quarterly*.

Like jobbers and merchants, advertising agents were middlemen, mistrusted by farmers, manufacturers, laborers, and anyone else who believed himself more engaged with the realities of production. Indeed, the agents' work was even less tangible than that of other middlemen: the only commodity they sold was that (sometimes dubious) service; they received commission from the publisher on the value of the space bought by the advertiser.

During the next 50 years, this method of compensation survived, but the agencies themselves were transformed. The more successful firms grew flush with money, moving from Park Row to more elegant midtown headquarters. Their clients were no longer marginal patent-medicine firms but established corporations selling brand-name products—Camel cigarettes, Dodge automobiles. As the agencies expanded, they became more bureaucratically organized and functionally specialized and provided a widening spectrum of services: advice on the choice of appropriate media, marketing information, and most important, design of the advertisements themselves.

THE RHETORIC OF SINCERITY

The question of designs, and of the strategies that lay behind them, was of particular concern to the first admen. Throughout the early days of the industry, agency spokesmen sought to establish their dignity as part of "the great distributing machinery brought into existence by the era of great combines." Yet they never fully banished the taint of hokum, the sense that their profession, like that of circus impresario P. T. Barnum, merely manufactured appearances to bemuse and bilk the public.

Fearing that they would be lumped with patent-medicine vendors or even with confidence men, members of the fledgling industry—most of whom were from the Midwest, many of them sons of Protestant ministers—resorted to the rhetoric of sincerity. It was a time-honored Protestant tradition. Throughout the nineteenth century, the sincere man had been the antidote to the confidence man—a reminder that morality could somehow be preserved amid the amoral ambiguities of the marketplace.

But achieving sincerity in one's copy was no easy matter. Sincerity required that the advertisement be seamless, that its artifice be concealed, that it seem straightforward and honest. For advertising men, as for other "impression managers," truth was insufficient and sometimes irrelevant. The important job was, in the words of the leading trade journal *Printers' Ink,* "making the Truth 'Sound True.' " Sincerity had become at once a moral stance and a tactic of persuasion.

Few advertising spokesmen were willing to acknowledge that ambiguity. As advertising images became more fantastic and surreal during the 1910s and

1920s, many admen clung to nineteenth-century notions of reality, truth, and meaning. Debate over strategies revealed a persistent conflict within the industry.

During the 1890s the trade press had generally been suspicious of the ad that was "too pretty." As one adman wrote in 1895, "It's the great public you are after and they don't give a continental whether you have been to college or not, what they want is facts; if they are reading your ad for amusement in all probability you don't want their trade." The no-frills, informative approach helped aspiring professionals to distance their methods from the sensational tactics of their patent-medicine predecessors.

At the same time admen realized that they faced a novel difficulty. As advertisements for brand-name commodities multiplied, the description of a product's qualities, such as one finds in a Sears catalogue, proved an inadequate strategy for selling.

AN "EPIDEMIC OF ORIGINALITY"

As early as 1903 a writer in *Judicious Advertising* complained that "there is so much that is exceedingly good, it is harder than ever to know how to devise creations that are 'different' enough to attract attention." By the early twentieth century, slogans, jingles, and trademarks were familiar sights in the advertising landscape—all designed to catch the eye of a busy distracted public. Illustrated advertising, containing virtually no information, aimed at "general publicity" for the product by associating it with attractive girls, healthy children, or prosperous family scenes.

Proponents of fact fought back, first by ridiculing the "epidemic of originality," then by invoking the formula that advertising was "salesmanship-in-print." That phrase was coined by the copywriter John E. Kennedy in 1904 and popularized by Albert Lasker and Claude Hopkins as "reason-why" copy.

Each piece of reason-why copy contained a vigorous sales argument, crammed with facts and pockmarked with dashes, italics, and exclamation points. For a time this approach threatened to sweep all before it. In December 1906 a prominent trade magazine contained an obituary for "advertising ideas," the puns and pretty girls that bore no relation to the product: they "passed with the notion that advertising is literature or art."

The obituary proved premature. Many advertising men continued to define their task not as "salesmanship-in-print" but as "the persuasive art." As Clowry Chapman, a legal consultant to ad agencies, argued in 1910, "mental images," not rational arguments, move the prospective buyer to buy.

According to this view, the advertiser's task was not merely to construct product-oriented arguments, but to turn the potential buyer's emotion into money. Fact men fumed. In 1906 one of them wrote an article bewailing the lack of information in American car ads. He noted that one maker claimed "his car is the Car of Destiny. What does that mean? Who could find any meaning in such a fact, even if it were true?"

Troubled by the absence of clear-cut meaning, opponents of "atmosphere" warned that it was time to talk sense to the American people. But automobile advertisers increasingly surrounded their product with emblems of style, status, and personal fulfillment. In 1910 the Chalmers Motor Company revived lagging sales by switching from reason-why to "word painting the auto's seductive joys." The strategy won praise in the trade press. By 1920 the factual auto advertisement had virtually disappeared.

One reason for the decline of factual auto ads was the increasing difficulty of distinguishing one brand of product from another. The problem was not confined to automobiles. Confronted by standardization born of technological advances, advertisers sought to make a particular beer seem "special" (1907) or to establish that "Bread Isn't Just Bread" (1930). Marketing journals urged manufacturers to devise new specialties, new ingredients, new features.

Colgate dental cream provided a model. In 1911 Palmolive Peet spent a huge sum of money on advertising to demonstrate that their toothpaste lay "flat" on the brush like a ribbon." The key, as one adman had observed in 1902, was to recognize "the importance of trifles." The search for trifles led to a proliferation of new, improved features, secret ingredients, and fantastic product claims. As product differentiation became more difficult, reason-why copy became less reasonable.

Ultimately, reason-why and atmosphere advertising converged. There had always been potential for irrationality in reason-why. It could include not only sober statements of a product's merits, but also strings of superlatives, inflated sales arguments, and an insistence that the product could transform the buyer's life. In 1925, when corset advertising rejected "the Bolshevik figure," promising an "ideal posture" that would "reflect good breeding and class distinction," advertising analysts found it possible to praise the copy because it appealed to intelligence rather than to emotion. "Romance and reason-why" could coexist in the same advertisement or in different campaigns for the same product.

"PUTTING YOURSELF IN THE CONSUMER'S PLACE"

But admen were wrestling with challenges even greater than the debate over romance and reason. The trade press, shifting its orientation from the product to its potential buyer, began to advise "Putting Yourself in the Consumer's Place," puzzling out his or her yearnings and anxieties.

The important change in trade press usage from "customers" to "consumers" that began around 1900 reflected a growing awareness that the audience for national advertisements was remote, impersonal, and difficult to visualize. Customers carried on face-to-face relations with local entrepreneurs; consumers were the target of standardized persuasion sponsored by corporations. The problem for advertisers was how to bring the target into sharper focus. Slowly admen inched toward the "science" of modern marketing. In the process, they increasingly viewed consumers as a manipulable, irrational mass.

Early speculation on consumers combined confident pronouncements about "human nature" with lists of consumer traits. The first composite portrait to emerge was that of a shrewd customer—subject to flattery but suspicious of bombast, capable of cupidity but essentially reasonable.

But as early as the turn of the century, the picture began to change. Some spokesmen, pointing to "the breathless rush and scramble" of twentieth-century life, noted that "men and women take their knowledge, like their lunches, on the run."

This perception called for either brevity or novelty to catch the busy eye. And for some admen, the power of silly or emotional copy stemmed from human nature itself. "You must take [people] as they are," wrote a *Printers' Ink* contributor in 1897, "grown-up children to a great extent . . . tired and bored by too much argument, by diagrams and prosaic common sense." From this perspective, the most effective advertising was aimed at consumers' irrational impulses.

In the emerging conventional wisdom, the typical consumer was especially susceptible to emotional appeals because he was bored much of the time. "His everyday life is pretty dull. Get up—eat—go to work—eat—go to bed," wrote freelance copywriter John Starr Hewitt in 1925. Yet Hewitt also believed that the typical American compensated "for the routine of today by the vision of what his life is to be tomorrow. It is the vision of getting ahead. Everything he buys comes as a partial fulfillment of that vision."

The notion of consumption as compensation was given a further turn by Paul Nystrom, professor of marketing at Columbia University. In *The Economics of Fashion* (1928), Nystrom noted the importance of boredom, "the desire for a change in personality," and among "not a few people in Western nations . . . something that may be called, for want of a better name, *a philosophy of futility.*" With the decline of religious faith, Nystrom believed, the "tendency to challenge the purpose of life itself" grew and made superficial consumer choices seem all the more important. This view of the consumer as anomic "mass man" strengthened advertisers' faith in the manipulability of the public.

There remained a rival faith in the consumer as rational individual, making knowledgeable choices. "In 1911 when the consumer buys," *Printers' Ink* asserted, "he does the choosing. He asserts his particular individuality."

Advertising made choice possible: "It has *educated* the consumer into being a connoisseur—which apt word means 'one who knows.'"

THE PSYCHOLOGICAL APPEAL

But the image of the consumer as connoisseur did not strictly conform to the rational economic man of liberal lore. The new model man exercised his sense of self not through labor or civic responsibility, but through consumer choices, often quite trivial ones.

Notions of "consumer individuality" ended up promoting the strategy of "personal appeal" rather than genuine respect for the diversity of the mass market. By seeming to single out the individual ("Imagine *your* picture here"), the personal appeal sought to create a sense of uniqueness in the consuming self, to make the buyer forget he was part of a mass market, to convince him that he was a conscious, choosing person.

Psychological theory underwrote that indirect approach and reinforced notions of consumer irrationality. Beginning in 1903, when Walter Dill Scott published *The Psychology of Advertising,* admen flocked to psychological lectures, hired psychological consultants, and wondered, "Can You Sell Goods to the Unconscious Mind?" The long flirtation between psychology and advertising was consummated in 1925, when John B. Watson dedicated *Behaviorism* to his employer, Stanley Resor of J. Walter Thompson. The vogue of psychology provoked grumblings among no-nonsense business types, but to many advertising men, it held the key to the mysterious mind of the consumer.

The most alluring use of psychology lay in the area of suggestion. Marketing professor Arthur Holmes summarized the conventional view of the process in 1925 when he wrote:

> People unacquainted with psychology assume that men have the power to say "Yes" or "No" to an advertisement. The assumption is only partly correct. A man has the power to decide in the first stage of the game, not in the last . . . if the printed word can seize his attention, hold him chained, drive from his mind all other thoughts except the one "Buy this!," standing at the head of an organized sentiment from which every opposing idea, perception, feeling, instinct, and disposition have been driven out or smothered to death, HE CANNOT SAY "NO!" His will is dead.

Few admen would have uncritically embraced Holmes's inflated view of the power of suggestion, and some, such as Claude Hopkins, lamented "the fearful cost of changing people's habits." But growing numbers of advertising men were confident they could do almost anything with a consumer through unconscious manipulation, and psychological theory bolstered their confidence.

"SCIENCE" OF MARKET RESEARCH

Besides psychology, the other major effort to understand consumer behavior was the infant "science" of market research. By the 1910s a number of advertisers were trying to base their strategies on information derived from questionnaires; by the 1920s at least a few were convinced that "the research basis of copy" had been established. The rise of market research offered new possibilities for admen such as J. George Frederick to assert their superiority over "the mere 'word-slingers.'"

By 1925, Frederick asserted, copy had become "the apex of a solid base of merchandising plan" that included data questions for advertisers as well as research into consumer types and preferences. The marketing approach was compatible with psychology. In the final stage of Frederick's merchandising plan, an analyst used proofs of varied copy to "conduct a carefully guarded test upon consumers (so planned that their unconscious judgment and not their conscious judgment would be obtained)."

The spread of marketing orientation, by revealing the diversity of the audience and its predilections, might have made more advertising men question their tactics. Every few years, a writer in the trade press remarked that most Americans did not employ maids, play golf, or wear evening clothes to dinner; perhaps the working-class majority could be represented in national advertisements. But these early calls for "market segmentation" were largely ignored, as advertisements continued to present a homogeneous portrait of the American people.

Justifying this homogeneity, advertising spokesmen revealed some fundamental assumptions about their craft. To critics who charged that "art directors snootify homely products," an agency art director replied that the homely scene had been "touched by the wizardry of the clever artist." He went on to argue that modish clothes and fine furnishings were "the kind our wives yearn for but seldom have enough pin money to buy." One industry magazine reasoned that this sort of "idealism" was "understood by consumers who do not take life too literally" as an inducement to strive for an ever higher standard of living. From this, it was only a short step to the admission that advertisements were primarily marketing fantastic visions rather than products.

Many advertising spokesmen had already taken that step. As early as 1912, a writer in *Judicious Advertising* had proposed that it was "possible through advertising to create mental attitudes toward anything and invest it with a value over and above its intrinsic worth." By the 1920s mention of a product's "intrinsic worth" had virtually disappeared, as advertising spokesmen argued that consumers could "buy" all sorts of ethereal qualities. James Wallen, who started his own agency after working with the flamboyant Elbert Hubbard, agreed that "you do not sell a man the tea, but the magic spell which is brewed nowhere else but in a teapot." What made an effective advertisement, in this view, was not the product but the symbolic context that surrounded it.

This was a long way from the older, business-oriented approach to advertising, but many admen embraced the newer perspective. One herald of the new strategy, James Collins, argued in 1901 that advertising had created an "economy of symbolism," in which symbols, not commodities, were exchanged. Within twenty years it was a common view that the product could be subordinated to its symbolic attributes. Face powder, for example, could be sold to both flappers and antiflappers—depending on whether the copy appealed to restless sexual energy or self-conscious sophistication.

The most commonly used symbolic attributes were meant to animate the inanimate commodity with "richer, fuller life." Like many of their contemporaries, advertising strategists were preoccupied by the pursuit of "life" amid a culture that seemed increasingly to deny it. Restless men, they moved from job to job, eager for variety and stimulation. In their preoccupation with escaping ossified forms and capturing movement in design, they resembled artists such as Georges Braque and Pablo Picasso. In their reverence for what one copywriter called "the divinity of common things," they resembled Ezra Pound and William Carlos Williams, who sought to reconnect words with things and rescue poetry from the vapors of Victorian abstraction.

THE MAGIC OF IMAGERY

But for admen, the problem of animating the inanimate was specifically commercial: how to make inert commodities resonant with vitality. The trick lay in the imagining.

One avenue to animation involved the imaginative use of language. In the early years, though most admen preached the gospel of simple and direct, there were many calls for "ginger" in copy; ad writers were advised to "pick out the vital words and form them into sentences that possess the breath of life."

By the 1920s a more overtly literary viewpoint emerged, as writers discussed ways of using the "magical powers" of words. One such writer, Richard Surrey, argued that literary metaphor soothed people by assimilating human travails to larger natural processes. Advertising metaphor moved in a different direction:

"Machine-made products, turned out by the millions, must be assimilated to the destiny of things not machinelike; must be translated . . . into human terms."

A number of rhetorical devices served that purpose, but perhaps the most striking was the "'I am' vogue," which lasted throughout the early 1920s, personifying commodities, ideas, and technical processes. Progress, electricity, and light joined adding machines, radios, and locomotives in adopting personae and speaking directly to the audience, often with what was thought to be biblical eloquence. ("Verily I shrink the world. . . . But never am I my own master," intoned one modest radio.)

In visual strategies the movement toward magic and fantasy was even more apparent, but it developed alongside a powerful countercurrent of realism. One approach incorporated the techniques of cartoonists and avant-garde artists; the other sought increasing proficiency in illustration and photography. In either case, the aim was to avoid the wooden and "unreal."

But real life remained an elusive quarry. Even photographs could be full of "'rubber-stamp' faces and expressions," the advertising art critic W. Livingston Larned complained in 1930. Unless the faces seemed to project spontaneous emotion, the "advertising language" remained unpersuasive.

"What do the faces in your advertising illustration *say?*" asked Larned. "Are they animate with action?" There were realistic ways to escape still life—placing a pat of melting butter on a stack of pancakes, for example—but ultimately the quest for "sparkle" led realists to the borders of fantasy.

While realism persisted, surreal images proliferated. In 1922 the same issue of *Printers' Ink* that contained a commercial art manager's plea for "Real People, Doing Real Things" also presented an ad for Poster Advertising, Inc., with an example of their work: a billboard showing the earth afloat in space, encircled by a gigantic Goodyear Tire, with the slogan "Goodyear means Good Wear." This technique, according to the ad, had "Strength Beauty Dignity."

Surreal attention-getting devices stretched back several decades, but by the 1920s, an infusion of "foreign art ideas" had generated a wider array of nonrepresentational modes. In 1925 the trade press noted that "Futuristic Monstrosities are all the Rage"—distorted figures, vaguely cubist designs in backgrounds and borders. Technical advances also accelerated the movement toward the bizarre. Airbrushing, double exposures, fadeaways, and various means of "doctoring" photographs could all help the advertiser "write a sales message across the human face"—as Pompeiian Massage Cream did when it showed a man's face in a hairnet with the caption "your face is a net . . . it traps the dirt." Like Barnum's hoaxes, these tactics called as much attention to the techniques of illusion as to the article for sale.

The more common means of visual animation were cartoons and allegorical figures. Since the turn of the century, advertisers had enlisted cartoon figures as trademarks—Sunny Jim for Force Food, the Campbell's Soup twins. But as cartoonists began to realize that anything could be animated—not merely human figures but trees, butter, buildings, or automobiles—advertisers embraced the more advanced forms of cartoon art.

By the 1920s trade journal writers were praising a host of animated characters: the oat who "experienced the thrill of a lifetime" when judged plump enough to be ground into three-minute Oat Flakes, the fairy characters who embodied the vitamins in Comet Rice.

Strategists seeking animation had one other option: to approach the ad as a drama in which the consumer could participate. "Even a casual examination of a few magazines proves that many of the national advertisers are borrowing dramatic appeal from the motion picture," a writer in *Judicious Advertising* noted in 1925. Static compositions could be vitalized by small details: an open box of bonbons in a living-room set piece advertising radios; a lighted candelabrum atop a piano in a candle ad. All sought to create the impression that the scene had just been vacated and was about to be occupied by the consumer. The advertising man thus became a stage manager, charged, as one copywriter put it, with "introducing the thing advertised in a natural, unaffected, casual manner, with no outward signs of the commercial."

By the late 1920s American advertising had acquired the characteristics it would retain for at least six decades—and perhaps will retain for as long as there is a competitive market economy. This "highly organized and professional system of magical inducements and satisfactions," as social critic Raymond Williams described it, has continued to have as its goal the selling of a panoply of goods among which there are frequently few salient differences. Working from the premise of the irrationality of the consumer, this vast fantasy machine employs every conceivable visual gimmick and rhetorical device to turn the public's attention from the product to its symbolic attributes.

In retrospect, perhaps the two most remarkable aspects of the advertising business are, first, how quickly after the emergence of mass media it assumed its shape, and, second, how durable that shape has proven to be. Its perdurability is all the more remarkable when one considers that advertising is the business of manufacturing evanescent appearances.

EXPANDED OPPORTUNITIES IN THE ELECTRONIC MEDIA

Not that things have remained unchanged on Madison Avenue since 1930. The rise of color magazines such as *Life, Look,* and *Vogue* allowed advertising artists and photographers to hone their skills, creating scenes of such voluptuousness and sensual ease that readers might *almost* overlook the item being sold.

And, of course, the electronic media—radio and particularly television—have greatly extended advertising's magisterial sway, further complicating and obscuring elusive "reality." Indeed, television seems almost tailor-made for the advertiser's art: its speed, its shallow but alluring slickness, and its combination of the visual and aural make it the perfect medium for serving up 30-second segments of idealized life.

Television also makes it possible for the advertiser to use the most powerful device of suggestion—repetition. Thanks to endless, hypnotic repetitions, even the most sophisticated consumers find themselves in the thrall of the jingle of the hour, whether they are reaching out, with the help of Ma Bell, to touch someone, or receiving, from a generous Gino's, the precious freedom of choice. Whether it convinces all of the people some of the time or just some of the people some of the time, TV advertising *does* sell goods.

Riding on an extensive media network, advertising began to move beyond the world of commerce and into such areas as government and politics, particularly during the 1960s. Today, of course, the packaging and selling of politicians has become so widespread and professionalized as to seem commonplace. It is now almost inconceivable for a candidate for high office to undertake a campaign without the help of media consultants, acting coaches, and the usual speech (and joke) writers. And, though it is perhaps too easy to say so, one wonders if the outcomes of elections in America will not soon be determined even more strongly by the candidate's image and appearance—his "fatherly reassuring aura" or his "youthful confidence"—than by his current policies or his political record.

Advertising, then, has conquered important new terrain since 1930 and has done so with new forms and appeals. But despite outward changes, it remains, at bottom, what it was sixty or more years ago: the business of manufacturing illusions.

To some degree, it remains so because the admen of today, like those of the past, have experienced the same confusions felt by other members of twentieth-century American society. These confusions stem from a contradiction between our democratic ideology, with its emphasis upon individual choice and freedom of expression, and an economic arrangement that encourages, and indeed depends upon, conformity and predictability among both producers (employers as well as employees) and consumers.

Ours is also a society that has traditionally valued spontaneity, risk, and adventure; largely for that reason we cherish the myth of the frontier, where those qualities, we believe, once flourished. Yet most Americans today inhabit an urban or suburban world that is overly regulated, hemmed in by routine, and presided over by scores of specialists and experts. "Adventure" itself has become a commodity, a packaged trip down the Colorado, an organized trek across the

Himalayas, a fortnight on a dude ranch. Room for real adventure is limited, if it exists at all.

Advertising men and women have not been immune to these and other contradictions. Many have been, after all, creative and original thinkers, some outstanding artists (René Magritte), photographers (Richard Avedon), and poets (James Dickey and Allen Ginsberg). Yet even the least talented advertising people have recognized that their skills were harnessed to large, impersonal organizations and that the end of their efforts was to convince millions of consumers that they would be happier, even better, human beings if they used Whiz instead of Duz. Given the conditions of their work and of ordinary life, it is not really surprising that generations of advertising men have aimed to transform a prosaic world of commodities into a magical place of escape, illusion, and fantasy—an ephemeral empire of images.

For at least a century, scholars of writing have tried to determine how the alphabet spread—whether it emerged from a single source or was independently invented in several places, or whether there is some other explanation for the development of the letters that form the words you are reading. Among the notable works in this tradition are archaeologist Ignace J. Gelb's *A Study of Writing* (University of Chicago Press, 1963), linguist David Diringer's *The Alphabet: A Key to the History of Mankind* (Hutchinson, 1948), and the quite readable *A History of Writing* (Scribner's, 1984) by the British Library's Albertine Gaur.

The question of the oral versus the written tradition looms large in study after study. Language scholar Walter J. Ong, in *Orality and Literacy: The Technologizing of the Word* (Metuchen, 1982), and the anthropologists in *Literacy in Traditional Societies* (Cambridge University Press, 1968), edited by Jack Goody, offer examples of the links between language, literacy, and logic. Goody and Ian Watt, for instance, write that the Eskimos of Alaska and the Tiv of Nigeria do not recognize any contradiction between what they say now and what they said 50 years ago "because they lack written records." Myth and history for the nonliterate "merge into one."

On the other hand, psychologist Jean Piaget, in *The Development of Thought* (Viking, 1977) and anthropologist Claude Lévi-Strauss, in *The Savage Mind* (University of Chicago Press, 1967), argue that there are few, if any, differences between the cognitive or intellectual abilities of literate and nonliterate peoples. Nonliterate villagers in Africa, North America, or Asia, Lévi-Strauss contends, have their own sophisticated systems of classification and logic that do not depend on writing. The Navaho of old, for example, could identify more than five hundred species of desert plants off the top of their heads—a feat that any literate person would be hard pressed to equal. "The use of more or less abstract terms," writes Lévi-Strauss, "is a function not of greater or lesser intellectual capacity, but of differences in interests . . . of particular social groups."

Psychologists Sylvia Scribner and Michael Cole make much the same argument in *The Psychology of Literacy* (Harvard University Press, 1981), a report of their seven-year study among the Vai of Liberia. The two researchers found that nonliterate or literate, the Vai performed equally well on most tests of cognitive ability. Only those educated in Western-style schools surpassed their fellows in what Scribner and Cole call "logical functions."

The notion that simply learning the ABCs is not enough would not have surprised the female abolitionists who sought to "teach and civilize" illiterate free men and women after the Civil War in the United States. Historian Robert C. Morris, in *Reading, 'Riting, and Reconstruction* (University of Chicago Press, 1982) describes what W. E. B. Du Bois called "the crusade for the New England schoolma'am." To the dismay of white Southerners, the Yankee teachers taught more than seven thousand young African Americans everything from reading to arithmetic. In the process these schoolma'ams were successful in attracting many of their students to the Republican party during the 1870s and 1880s, and helped found many of the South's black colleges and universities.

Surely one of the major changes in reading in the United States began in the years just before the Second World War and exploded after that conflict ended. Paperback books made reading easy and relatively inexpensive. Today we not only get instant paperbacks (often versions of popular movies and television shows), but also a vast array of fiction and nonfiction, from mysteries to romance novels, from serious biographies to memoirs of the infamous. To better understand this modern-day reading revolution, read yet another paperback: Kenneth C. Davis's *Two-Bit Culture* (Houghton Mifflin, 1984). Here one can learn the details about an industry that grew from Dr. Spock's phenomenal best-seller on baby care, issued as the baby boom commenced in 1945, to the variety of fodder about the O. J. Simpson trial that filled every Border's and Barnes & Noble.

One of the most significant selling tools of the paperback has been its creative covers. The image of Holden Caulfield and his red hat on the cover of J. D. Salinger's *Catcher in the Rye,* for example, inspired a generation of writers to try to pen the next great American novel. More about this key popular-culture phenomenon can be discovered in *Paperbacks, U.S.A.* (Blue Dolphin, 1981), by Piet Schreuders, who traces book designs from the initial Art Deco inspirations to the photorealism of the late twentieth century.

We may buy and read more books than at any point in history, yet many critics and scholars remain worried. In *Bonfire of the Humanities: Television, Subliteracy, and Long-Term Memory Loss* (Syracuse University Press, 1995) David

Marc comes off as "a man in heat," outraged and frightened that TV is killing the humanities in general, and reading in particular. In *Literacy in the Age of Television: The Myth of the TV Effect* (Ablex, 1995) Susan B. Neuman more objectively reviews the vast body of research about TV's presumed negative effects, and finds that while television has influenced everything, its effects on reading have not all been negative. Indeed, more books are published and purchased today than at any time in history.

Regardless of TV's effects, the book industry has become a billion-dollar media machine. To appreciate how it is organized, and how ruthless its leaders can be, read *Books: The Culture and Commerce of Publishing* (Basic Books, 1982) by Lewis A. Coser, Charles Kadushin, and Walter W. Powell. These three authors skillfully lead one through the history of the industry, the process of devising a title, and the maze of agents and reviewers. They agree that throughout the history of publishing one fact has not changed: great editors help. One who is properly celebrated is Bennett Cerf, and he tells his story in *At Random* (Random House, 1977), a lovingly written tome in which Cerf, ironically best known to the general public as a longtime panelist on TV's *What's My Line?*, tells how he acquired and edited the books of James Joyce, Sinclair Lewis, and Truman Capote.

Still, for an industry that generates billions of dollars in sales each year, economists all too rarely tackle the book trade. A rare insightful exception is Fritz Machlup's *The Production and Distribution of Knowledge in the United States* (Princeton University Press, 1962). At the center of the knowledge industry are the institutions of reviewing (newspapers and magazines), and selling (for example, the Book-of-the-Month Club). Joan Shelley Rubin's *The Making of Middle Brow Culture* (University of North Carolina Press, 1992) tackles both, as well as the surprising rise of the "Great Books" movement and the underappreciated influence of book reviewing on radio.

Americans still read, but on average we spend far more time in front of the TV set. And, tellingly, TV's programs get on the air, at least in the United States, because advertisers pay. "[But] to be for or against advertising these latter years of the 20th century is about like being for or against weather. Advertising is ubiquitous, incessant, and inescapable." So writes James Playstead Wood in *The Story of Advertising* (Ronald Press, 1958). Wood's book is among the best of the early descriptive histories of American advertising. From 1885 to 1905, according to Wood, advertising was brash, bold, vigorous, and fun. The industry tried to reform itself in the period from 1905 to 1914, toning down the more extravagant and misleading claims for products it was touting to the public. It lent itself to the federal government's propaganda efforts during the First World War, and then returned to excesses of reckless salesmanship during the 1920s.

Sobered in the depression years of the 1930s, the ad industry, writes Wood, redeemed itself again with its efforts to create public awareness and spirit during the Second World War. Frank W. Fox's *Madison Avenue Goes to War* (Brigham Young University Press, 1975) examines the precise role advertising played during both world wars.

It was during the interwar period that advertising took on new scope and maturity: the number of ads, the variety of products advertised, and the available media grew rapidly. This was the era of optimism and expansion, asserts Roland Marchand in his classic study, *Advertising and the American Dream: Making Way for Modernity, 1920–1940* (University of California Press, 1985). Marchand explains how advertisers learned to play off the public's anxieties and promise answers for all the ills of modern America. For Marchand the dream puffed by advertisers was a distorted image: "Ad creators tried to reflect public aspirations rather than contemporary circumstances, to mirror popular fantasies rather than social realities." After all, he writes, "the central purpose of an ad was not to reflect reality but to 'move merchandise.' "

The ad industry grew increasingly defensive between the wars, and many of the early books about advertising were personalized praise for a Madison Avenue that heralded the great new wares available to the average American. Pioneers like Claude C. Hopkins, once said to be the highest-paid ad creator in the world, extolled the advertising business in books like *Scientific Advertising* (1923) and *My Life in Advertising* (1927; both books reprinted by Crain Communications, 1966). Hopkins was the person who persuaded Quaker Oats to change the name "Wheat Berries" to "Puffed Wheat"; the cereal he advertised "shot from guns"; and it was Hopkins who "discovered" dental plaque to help justify hawking more and more toothpaste.

Stephen Fox takes a different tack in his *The Mirror Makers: A History of American Advertising and Its Creators* (Morrow, 1984). Writing about the relationship between advertising and American culture in the 1950s, Fox examines some of the leading personalities of the advertising business (J. Walter Thompson and Albert Lasker, among others) and argues that advertising had reached its peak of influence during the 1920s and thereafter declined in power and influence. "When restricted, more or less, to the truth," writes Fox, "advertising lost some of its powerful, frightening devices. Advertising became less deceptive, the public grew more sophisticated and skeptical. As advertising grew and prospered, it lost influence."

Many disagree. James B. Twitchell's *Adcult USA: The Triumph of Advertising in American Culture* (Columbia University Press, 1995) stresses that during the final years of the twentieth century the average adult was seeing and hearing some three thousand advertisements each day! Children, who watch an average of more than 28 hours of TV a week, will spend years in the glow of advertisements costing far more in toto than is spent on public schools in the United States. Can this be good? Is this a decline? Not according to Twitchell.

In today's TV age, with a return to hard-sell marketing practices, David Ogilvy, long an industry leader, could not be more happy: "The pendulum is swinging back our way—[our] way," he says. For more on this amazing transformation dip into *Ogilvy on Advertising* (Random House, 1985) and his *Confessions of an Advertising Man* (Atheneum, 1980). Indeed advertising practitioners have never been less shy when it comes to defending themselves and justifying what they do. Among the better examples of this genre is Bart Cummings's *The Benevolent Dictators: Interviews with Advertising Greats* (Crain Books, 1984). More objective is sociologist Leo Bogart's *Strategy in Advertising* (NTC Business Books, 1996).

The power of advertising has long been taken seriously by its critics. *Advertising and a Democratic Press,* by C. Edwin Baker (Princeton University Press, 1994), offers the concerns of a University of Pennsylvania law professor who is disturbed by the impact of advertising on news, where advertising "distorts and diminishes the mass media's contributions to a free and democratic society." Stuart W. Ewen pursues a Marxist approach in *Captains of Consciousness: Advertising and the Social Roots of the Consumer Culture* (McGraw-Hill, 1975), which views advertising as an arm of advanced capitalism bent on selling products and services to working-class folk, things they hardly need and can ill afford. Non-Marxist, but avowedly skeptical, are Michael Schudson's *Advertising, the Uneasy Persuasion: Its Dubious Impact on American Society* (Basic Books, 1984) and Jib Fowles's *Advertising and Popular Culture* (Sage, 1996). In particular, Schudson uses the phrase "Capitalist Realism" to describe advertising art and argues that, like the art of Soviet Socialist Realism, it portrays the ideals and aspirations of the system more than it reflects reality. Surprisingly this sociologist contradicts his fellow social scientists and argues that advertising has less impact than many lead us to believe. For every success story, there are many forgotten Edsels.

Although "new" is the most frequently used word in the advertising lexicon, the industry, in fact, has really not changed as much as it would like us to believe. Warren Dygert's *Radio as an Advertising Medium* (McGraw-Hill, 1939), which includes chapters on music in commercials, contests, and market testing, offers the prediction that "those who are nearest to television are optimistic about the place advertising is to play in this coming field." We need to remember that in 1939 the world was seeing TV for the first time, most notably at the World's Fair in New York. New or old, Judith Williamson's *Decoding Advertisements: Ideology and Meaning in Advertising* (Boyars, 1978) begins the tricky task of trying to figure out what all those ads really mean. This surely will be the thrust of scholarly analysis of advertising as we enter the twenty-first century.

But the printed word and visual persuasion hardly constitute the sole means of human expression. Sitcoms, pulp fiction, and country music must also be included in a seemingly endless list of media through which a cacophony of messages are spread to a mass audience, many who rarely ponder how frequently they are "targeted." Taken together in its broadest sense, these disparate forms of mass communication and entertainment produce a vibrant, restless, ever-changing "popular" culture.

To make sense of all the forms of American pop culture it is best to begin with Frenchman Roland Barthes's *Mythologies* (Hill and Wang, 1972). Barthes argues that popular culture hardly arises spontaneously from "the people." He sees it as imposed by entrepreneurs seeking to maximize profits, not public satisfaction. Columbia University sociologist Herbert Gans tried, in his *Popular Culture and High Culture: An Analysis and Evaluation of Taste* (Basic Books, 1977), to craft a set of popular culture hierarchies or "taste cultures." These Gans defines as encompassing both "values" and "cultural forms," everything from music, art, design, literature, news, "and the media in which they are expressed," to consumer goods "that express aesthetic values or functions, such as furnishings, clothes, appliances."

Maybe nothing illustrates the problems of analyzing pop culture more than the challenge of making sense of the vast and lasting appeal of *Reader's Digest*. Long the Rodney Dangerfield of journalism, beloved by untold millions but denied a scintilla of respect by the academy, the *Digest* has been consistent in its vision of a simpler, more innocent time. To understand how this powerhouse publication came to be (and to dominate), read John Heidenry's *Theirs Was the Kingdom: Lila and DeWitt Wallace and the Story of Reader's Digest* (Norton, 1993).

The seemingly mundane are also contemplated by pop culture more scholars. *The Man in the Bowler: His History and Iconography* by Fred Miller Robinson (University of North Carolina Press, 1993), for example, offers a fascinating case study of a hat, introduced in London in 1850, that eventually made its way to the heads of Charlie Chaplin and Laurel and Hardy. Indeed some of the greatest studies of popular culture come from a close examination of what are usually labeled "ephemera." No better case can be made than that of the ubiquitous fast-food emporia. *Roadside Empires: How Chains Franchised America* (Viking, 1985), by Stan Luxenberg, is a study of the economic organization and history of the movement to standardize the hamburger, the chicken wing, and other delights. Since the central symbol of the fast-food phenomenon is McDonald's, it is not surprising that we have both an authorized and unauthorized version of how founder Ray Kroc brought the burger to the byways of suburbia. Kroc's own *Grinding It Out* (Contemporary, 1977) is best summed up in his own words: "I have had the satisfaction of seeing McDonald's become an American institution.

Such a dream could only be realized in America." Max Boas and Steve Chain, the authors of *Big Mac* (Dutton, 1976), find the basis of Kroc's success in exploited labor, dull mass-production routines, and uniformity, all merged in an attempt not to sell superior food but to offer the consumer a vision of a "way of life," and in the process make its franchisees very rich.

The study of popular culture has attracted leftists critical of American society. Stuart and Elizabeth Ewen's *Channels of Desire* (McGraw-Hill, 1982) emphasizes the contradictions in the development of American popular culture over the past century. "On the one hand," they write, "people have experienced industrial hardship and alienation: urban loneliness, dehumanized work, loss of traditional culture and skills, erosion of family and community life. On the other hand, industrialism has broadened horizons, spread literacy, stepped up communications, and promised material abundance beyond the wildest dreams of previous epochs." *Roll Over Beethoven: The Return of Cultural Strife* by Stanley Aronowitz (University Press of New England, 1993) seeks to survey all the hot contemporary debates in which popular culture turns out to be a touchstone: multiculturism, political correctness, and high and low culture.

Popular culture is difficult to study because it seems to be everywhere. To make sense of this ubiquity historians have looked at a single genre across multiple media. No better set of studies can be found than those of the dominant form of a generation ago, the Western. Through the first half of the twentieth century tales of the Old West seemed everywhere, from the movies of Gene Autry to the music of Bob Wills and his Texas Playboys, from cowboy and cowgirl outfits to TV and radio serials. John G. Cawalti studies them all in *The Six-Gun Mystique* (Bowling Green University Popular Press, 1971) and *Adventure, Mystery, and Romance* (University of Chicago Press, 1976). Jane Tompkins's *West of Everything: The Inner Life of Westerns* (Oxford University Press, 1992) uses skills in reading texts and applying feminist criticism to locate surprising thematic unity in varied tales of the Old West, whether penned in the 1880s or filmed in the 1980s. More than any other medium the movies spread the Western across the world. An authoritative guide to the Western cinema can be found in *The BFI Companion to the Western* (Andre Deutsch, 1988), edited by Edward Buscombe. This beautiful and well-informed book comes from the British Film Institute, not some American academic factory.

Finally sports have been written about endlessly since they became mass entertainment with a dedicated newspaper section. Most sportswriters lack objectivity and their books simply prop up the genre's conventions and stereotypes rather than illuminate the functions of sports in society. A rare exception is *Ty Cobb* (Oxford University Press, 1984) by historian Charles C. Alexander. Cobb was surely the greatest baseball hitter in the first half-century of the professional game, but he also made it respectable, even valued, to play as a ruthless competitor, to do anything to win. Behind the scenes Cobb was as ruthless in his business dealings, in the process making himself the first millionaire athlete.

G. Edward White's *Creating a National Pastime* (Princeton University Press, 1996) surveys even more territory in the history of baseball. White tries to determine why baseball has enjoyed mythic status in American popular culture. He traces its appeal from the first World Series in 1903 to the relocation of the Boston Braves to Milwaukee a half-century later. In between, the more things changed about America, the more baseball tried to stay the same—by design. White argues that baseball was a Progressive Era game, an important part of the "City Beautiful" movement. The owners sought—successfully—to transform baseball from a rough, working-class sport to a game that symbolized small-town, pastoral times.

The complete history of popular culture remains to be written. For the moment one thus needs to admire historian Lawrence W. Levine's *Highbrow/Lowbrow: The Emergence of Cultural Hierarchy in America* (Harvard University Press, 1988) and Warren I. Susman's *Culture as History* (Pantheon, 1984). Both clearly situate popular culture, not at some scholarly extreme, but at its heart. We can only hope more such studies are researched, written, and published.

NEWS AND POLITICS

LEO BOGART

When World War II ended, eight daily newspapers in New York City reported the story, as did seven in Boston, four in Philadelphia, five in Chicago, four in San Francisco. Now, some five decades later, New York is down to three (the *Times, Post,* and *Daily News*), and Boston, Philadelphia, and Chicago have only two newspapers apiece. Major casualties have included the *Baltimore News American, Washington Star, Philadelphia Bulletin,* and *Cleveland Press.* In St. Petersburg, St. Paul, Louisville, New Haven, New Orleans, Des Moines, Portland, Tampa, Minneapolis—all one-ownership newspaper towns—publishers have discontinued their less successful papers, usually their afternoon papers. The troubles of other newspapers are still making news. In 1923 there were 503 cities with more than one separately owned daily newspaper; by the mid-1980s there were only 49. And in 20 of those cities, competing papers had joint business and printing arrangements.

After the evening *Minneapolis Star* (circulation 170,000) was discontinued in April 1981, its editor, Stephen Isaacs, responded to a query from *Editor & Publisher:*

> What do I see ahead? I talked to many publishers recently and was startled by the number who have in effect told me that the newspaper business is a dying industry. A dinosaur. Some will survive—the very big and the very small—but the in-betweens are going to face rough going in the electronic era. . . . Frankly, I was stunned by their comments.

Reprinted with revisions from the 1982 special issue of *The Wilson Quarterly.*

DEMOGRAPHIC SHIFTS AND THE DECLINE OF CITY PAPERS

The deaths of great metropolitan dailies are stunning events, and not only to publishers and editors. But do they mean that newspapers, as such, have outlived their function?

The fallen giants in the business have been stricken by the sickness of their home cities. In the twenty largest American cities, newspaper circulation dropped by 21 percent between 1970 and 1980, while population fell by 6 percent. This does not tell the whole story, because the big cities have changed character even more than they have lost people. Their white population fell by 20 percent, and the whites now include a higher proportion of Hispanics and the elderly poor.[1] In many blighted inner-city areas, crime, vandalism, and collection problems have wreaked havoc with both home deliveries and street sales.

Changers in the urban economy and social structure have also had disastrous effects on downtown retailers, who have been the mainstay of metropolitan newspaper advertising. Retail chains followed the middle class to the suburbs— and began to put advertising money into suburban papers, give-away "shoppers," and direct-mail advertising. Metropolitan evening papers had to print earlier (usually well before noon) just to permit delivery by truck through traffic jams to the sprawling suburbs. Because their circulation was more concentrated in the central cities, they were more vulnerable than their morning rivals to the pressures of urban change. The deaths of metropolitan newspapers help explain why total daily circulation has declined since World War II; the ratio of newspapers sold to U.S. households dropped from 128:100 in 1948 to 71:100 in 1987.

The reasons are many and complex. The price of a subscription has gone up, and some papers have stopped distribution in outlying areas because of the expense. Young people of the TV generation now read newspapers less often than their parents did. Changes in family life have altered the use of leisure. With more wives at work, both husbands and wives have less time to read when they get home.

INNOVATIONS IN FORM AND CONTENT

Still, the worst appears to be over. In spite of the losses in the big cities, overall newspaper circulation and readership stabilized during the mid-1980s, following eight years of steady decline. The real question is not whether newspapers will thrive in the twenty-first century, but rather *what kind* of newspapers they will be. The answer lies both in the economics of the press and in the perceptions of editors and publishers. Their perceptions have already led to rapid changes in newspaper style and character during the past two decades and to an extraordinary amount of editorial innovation.

One theory that quickly gained favor was that TV news was taking away readers—although no evidence directly supported this notion. To the contrary, newspapers have done better (in terms of the ratio of circulation to all households) in metropolitan areas where TV news ratings are high rather than low. Television news viewing went down, not up, in New York City when the *Times, Post,* and *Daily News* were on strike in 1978.

Moreover, many editors appear to have been convinced during the 1970s that more and bigger photographs, and more "features" and "personality journalism" were necessary counters to the visual and entertainment elements of TV in general. Indeed, the *Miami News* billed itself as the newspaper "for people who watch television."

There were other less obvious changes, particularly among dailies with less than 100,000 circulation. One was the emphasis on local, staff-written news—leaving more of the wider world to the TV network news, the *Wall Street Journal,* or *Time* and *Newsweek.* Thirty-five percent of *all* editors who were asked about editorial changes in 1977–9 reported a shift toward "localizing" the news. "What sells papers is the ability to identify with the news content," said Milton Merz, who in 1976 was circulation director of the Bergen County, (N.J.), *Record* (circulation 150,796). "And people identify with things that affect them directly. Once you get outside their town, their interest drops like a rock." Among big-city papers, in particular, zoned editions, aimed at specific regions within a metropolitan area, seemed a good response to competition for readers from the mushrooming smaller suburban dailies and weeklies.

Yet the belief that people are mainly interested in "chicken dinner" news runs counter to reality. First, Americans as a whole today are increasingly well educated, cosmopolitan, and mobile, with weak ties to their home communities. Second, as is well known, fewer of any big-city daily's readers now live or work in the city where the newspaper is published and where it deploys most of its reporters (only 32 percent of the *Chicago Tribune's* circulation, for example, is within the city limits); the suburban dispersion of homes and jobs in scores of distinct communities over hundreds of square miles means that any particular local event is likely to affect relatively few people. A high proportion of what editors think of as local items that appear in a big-city paper are actually "sublocal"; they deal with events—school board disputes, village politics, accidents—that matter little to most of the paper's readers.

What some editors forget is that TV network news, for all its "show business" flaws, has made national and foreign figures, from Reagan to Begin, vivid and familiar to average Americans, to a degree unimaginable twenty years ago. Of

What Adults Read and Watched in 1986
News and information sources and "serious" television programs

	Each Day		Each Week
63.0%	Any daily newspaper	24%	*TV Guide*
2.8	*USA Today*	22	*Reader's Digest*
2.4	*Wall Street Journal*	14	*Time*
1.7	*New York Times*	10	*Newsweek*
35.0%	Early evening local news	19%	*60 Minutes* (CBS)
29.0	Late local TV news	10	*20/20* (ABC)
27.0	Network evening news	9	*National Geographic Specials* (PBS)
9.0	Morning TV news	6	*Nature* (PBS)
2.0	*MacNeil/Lehrer Newshour*	6	*This Week with David Brinkley* (ABC)
		6	*CBS Sunday Morning*
		5	*Nova* (PBS)
		4	*Face the Nation* (CBS)
		3	*Masterpiece Theater* (PBS)
		3	*Meet the Press* (NBC)
		3	*Mystery!* (PBS)

Sources: Simmons Study of Media & Markets, 1986. For PBS the percentage is of homes, A. C. Nielsen; PBS figures do not include several repeats of programs outside of prime time each week.

course, as always, people want *both* kinds of news, not just one or the other. Still, national research shows that the average item of local news attracts slightly fewer people who say they are "interested" or "very interested" in it than does the average item of foreign or national news. The same study shows that the "memorability" of local events as "big news," "upsetting news," or "good news" is extremely low relative to the amount of space they occupy in newspapers or relative to more dramatic stories from the wider world.[2]

The *Chicago Tribune*'s publisher, Joseph Medill, was once asked the secret of his success. "Just publish the news," he said. Today, not every publisher would agree. The most notable change in newspaper content since 1970 has been a new stress on "soft" features, often concentrated in special sections aimed at "upscale" suburban consumers, especially women. Under such umbrellas as "Lifestyle," "Living," or "Style," editors and writers have sought to impart the latest in television, movies, celebrities, self-help, women's issues, fashions, food, parties, recreation, and manners. (Less regular coverage has been devoted to the old specialized side dishes of the traditional newspaper menu: stamp collecting, chess, gardening, and photography.) The new "sectional revolution" was led by the *Washington Post*, the *Los Angeles Times,* and the *Chicago Tribune*.

At the *New York Times,* "Weekend," started in 1976, was followed by "Living," "Home," "Sports Monday," and "Science Times." The strategy worked; the *Times's* circulation rose by 33,000 during the sixteen months after "Weekend's" birth. In 1977–9, almost half of all newspapers with circulations of over 100,000 added weekday "lifestyle" sections; many of the remainder already had them. Said Derek J. Daniels, a former Knight-Ridder executive:

> If [newspapermen] are to meet the new challenges, they must, above all, recognize that reading is work. . . . I believe that newspapers should devote more space to the things that are helpful, enjoyable, exciting, and fun as opposed to undue emphasis on "responsible information."

In some ways newspapers were coming to resemble consumer magazines. Editors had always used feature material as "good news" to lighten the "bad news" that dominates the headlines. But did readers really want newspapers to entertain them rather than to inform them? Not really. A majority (59 percent) of a national cross-section of people questioned in 1977 indicated they would prefer a newspaper devoted *completely* to news rather than one that just provided a news summary and consisted mostly of entertaining features.

This response should not be dismissed as merely the expression of a socially acceptable attitude. For what it really indicates is that people expect newspapers to do more than cater to their personal tastes. Americans recognize a newspaper's larger responsibility to society; and they want it to cover a multitude of subjects, including ones about which they themselves normally would not care to read.

People perceive that some newspaper articles are "interesting," but others are "important." Thus according to the 1977 study, half of those who found the average sports item "very interesting" also rated it as "not very important." When people's responses to specific newspaper items are surveyed, entertainment features—except for TV and radio program logs, advice columns, and travel articles—all score below average in interest. A typical entertainment feature is rated "very interesting" by only 20 percent of those surveyed, while a typical straight news story is rated "very interesting" by 31 percent.

Editors, then, in remaking their newspapers during the 1970s, may have under-estimated their readers. But newspapers in those years were not just changing—they, collectively, were growing. In smaller and middle-sized communities, daily newspapers, most of them without local daily competition, continued to enjoy high levels of readership and prosperity. And the reader got more for his or her money. For a typical (surviving) major metropolitan daily, the number of pages of editorial matter went from 19.8 in 1970 to 32.4 in 1986, keeping pace with an increased volume of advertising.

So, despite the alterations, cosmetic and substantive, newspapers were actually providing more "hard" news and more national and world news. But the proportions were different. There was more icing on the cake, and often the cake itself was a bit fluffier. The *character* of newspapers was changing.

Editorial ingenuity and experimentation did not save the *Chicago Daily News* or the *Cleveland Press*. An article in the *Minneapolis Star,* after announcement of that paper's impending demise, recalled the editors' rescue efforts:

> Suddenly, or so it seemed, the newspaper's most basic ingredients—City Council meetings, news conferences, speeches—were gone. In their place was an unpredictable front-page mixture of blazing illustrations, Hollywood features and all sorts of things that had once been tucked away inside the paper.

The *Star's* radical changes did not halt its decline in readership.

THE ECONOMICS OF ADVERTISING

Yet the disease that kills off competing newspapers is not lack of readers; it is lack of advertising, which accounts for three-fourths of a newspaper's income. This disease has struck down even highly respected newspapers with considerable numbers of high-income readers, from the *New York Herald Tribune* in 1966 to the *Washington Star* in 1981. From an advertising point of view, "duplication" is considered highly wasteful.

Once a newspaper, good or bad, falls into second place even by a small margin, it becomes a "loser" in the eyes of advertising agencies and big retail chains; more of their advertising goes to the winner, accelerating the decline of the loser.

Why has this winner-take-all doctrine taken hold on Madison Avenue—with all its pernicious side effects on local diversity of information and editorial opinion? Part of it stems from the desire of advertisers for an exact fit between the kinds of people who buy their products and the characteristics of the media audience. The computer has created an insatiable appetite for marketing data, and the result is that advertising is bought by the numbers, by formula.

This practice has been fostered by the overall trend toward concentration. An increasing percentage of all retail sales goes to chains that operate in a number of different areas, with most of the growth since 1960 in the suburbs. The top hundred national advertisers (for example, Procter & Gamble, General Foods, and Philip Morris) in 1987 accounted for 53 percent of all advertising outlays in all media, up from 35 percent in 1960; and in the same year the top ten advertising agency groups (led by the British-owned Saatchi and Saatchi) directed the spending of 43 percent of all advertising dollars, up from 17 percent in 1955.

What this means is that the decisions to allocate advertising dollars among newspapers (or among newspapers, magazines, TV, cable, and other media) are increasingly made by fewer people in fewer places. And the decisions are increasingly made on the basis of strictly quantitative data, covering everything from income to lifestyle and personality types ("psychographics").

The established doctrine in marketing on Madison Avenue and elsewhere says this: if 30 percent of the people in a given area buy 60 percent of the product, then you target 100 percent of the advertising dollars at this group. (And for practical purposes you forget the others.) The media attracting the highest percentage of this group get the advertising dollars. What this means is that in Philadelphia, the *Bulletin,* with over 400,000 circulation, strangled on a deficit of $21 million in a market where advertisers spent $1.8 billion on all media in 1981. In that same year, the *Press* had 43 percent of the daily circulation in Cleveland, but only 28 percent of the advertising.

Advertisers try to direct their messages only at the most likely customers, and media have responded by defining their audiences in terms of particular market "segments" in which advertisers might be interested. There are thousands of specialized magazines, from *House and Garden* to *The Runner.* Radio audiences have long been broken up into fractions identified with various tastes in music. As cable television spreads, the regular TV networks' share of "prime time" is waning. There are dozens of cable networks that advertisers can use to reach specific types of viewers. The newspaper will probably remain the only mass medium in a given community—each day supplying the body of information that provides a shared experience for people who share a geographic space.

To be sure, the death of a metropolitan newspaper is a dramatic story—big news. When a small-town weekly goes daily, that is not such big news. Yet since the end of World War II, newspaper births and deaths have approximately balanced each other out so that the total number of daily newspapers in 1987 (1,657) was only somewhat less than what it was on V-J Day (1,763). Twelve daily newspapers stopped publication in 1980 and 1981, but twenty-five new ones were started. Despite the 1981 death of the *Washington Star,* total newspaper circulation in the Washington metropolitan area as of March 31, 1982, was down by only 4 percent from what it had been a year earlier. The reason: Five suburban *Journal* newspapers were successfully converted from weekly to daily publication when the *Star* fell, and a new competitor, the *Washington Times,* emerged.

Despite the funerals of great newspapers, the newspaper industry is, in fact, not faring badly. Daily newspapers are published in 1,525 American towns, more than ever before. Newspapers have 26 percent of all advertising investments (television, local and national, now gets 22 percent; magazines get 5 percent; radio, 7 percent). In 1986 newspapers made capital investments of about $1.2 billion, much of it in new production technology. The latter has transformed newspaper production and greatly cut blue-collar labor costs. Publicly owned newspaper companies have enjoyed considerable prosperity—with a profit rate double the average for all corporations.[3]

INCREASING READERSHIP

Nearly nine out of ten Americans still look at a daily newspaper in the course of a week—108 million on an average weekday. Sunday sales are bigger than ever. The 1980s saw a 42 percent increase in the number of people from age 35 to 44, a prime age group for newspaper reading. With smaller families, the number of households will keep growing faster than the number of people, further improving opportunities for newspaper sales. Despite all the concern about the state of the public schools, the average level of education has been moving upward. Educators are beginning to respond to public concern about students' reading skills. Publishers (and school administrators) have belatedly begun encouraging the use of newspapers in the classroom. And the members of the TV generation are heavy consumers of paperback books and magazines.

What really makes newspapers indispensable is that they give voice and identity to the communities where they are published, and their disappearance somehow diminishes local civic spirit and morale.

It has been suggested recently that newspapers should simply turn themselves into an "upscale" product, aimed at just the top half or third of the social pyramid. This would be folly. There is enough advertising to sustain "elite" newspapers in New York, Los Angeles, and maybe a handful of other places, but certainly not in the average town. Newspapers are inescapably for everybody—and

What People Watched and Read in Peoria, 1987

Sources of daily news for people in Peoria, Illinois

Daily Audience For	Homes	Percentage
Local evening news	72,000	33
Network evening news	82,000	38
Late night news	85,000	40
Newspaper circulation	151,000	70
Peoria-Journal Star	91,000	
Bloomington Pantograph	37,000	
Pekin Times	16,000	
Canton Ledger	7,000	

Source: Arbitron, November 1987.

in an era of ever more specialized audiences and markets, that is a significant distinction. Newspapers have a powerful argument to make to the advertisers of mass merchandise, who need to cast their nets as widely as possible so as not to miss any prospective customers.

Still, the trend toward "target" marketing is irresistible, and newspapers are adapting to it. Many of them are able to provide advertisers with "pinpoint" coverage in specific areas and to extend their coverage with supplementary distribution of advertising through mail or home delivery to nonsubscribers. But to be able to do this selectively for the largest number and variety of advertisers, newspapers must remain a mass medium.

As it happens, that is also what newspapers must remain if they are to fulfill their principal function, which is not to serve as a vehicle for advertising or entertainment, but to communicate to America's citizens what is happening of importance in their communities, their nation, and the world—and so to sustain informed public opinion in a free society.

NOTES

1. To illustrate this point with an extreme instance, the Bronx lost 19 percent of its total population between 1960 and 1980. The black population rose from 11 percent to 32 percent of the total, and Hispanics now represent 34 percent. The *New York Times* lost 56 percent of its Bronx circulation in those years, the *Daily News,* 26 percent.

2. This and other findings cited in this article are from a national survey of 3,048 adults conducted for the Newspaper Readership Project in 1977 by Audits and Surveys, Inc. A more comprehensive description of the study can be found in my book, *Press and Public* (Lawrence Erlbaum Associates, 1981).

3. For example, the Knight-Ridder, Gannett, and Washington Post organizations showed net incomes in 1986 of $182.6 million, $540.75 million, and $204.1 million, respectively.

JAMES BOYLAN

The press, wrote A. J. Liebling, is "the weak slat under the bed of democracy." Journalists have always liked to think the contrary—that the press keeps the bed from collapsing. They thought so even more after Vietnam and Watergate: journalism, its champions then argued, deserves the privileges and immunities of a fourth branch of government; and its practitioners should enjoy the status, rewards, and invulnerability that go with being known as professionals.

Unfortunately for the press, its critics took such claims at face value. The press, they said, had become imperial, and journalists an arrogant "elite." Vice President Spiro T. Agnew put an official stamp on this interpretation back in 1969 when he denounced the power of the "eastern establishment press." Agnew soon left the scene, but he was succeeded by more sophisticated and tenacious critics. Their target was the same as Agnew's—the Big League press and not American journalism as a whole. The latter, in fact, is a potpourri of wire services and syndicates, newspapers ranging in size from big-city tabloids down to mom-and-pop weeklies, and hundreds of magazines and broadcasting outlets.

However, focusing generally on the *New York Times,* the *Washington Post, Time, Newsweek,* and TV networks, such critics as Stanley Rothman, Kevin Phillips, and Michael Novak developed a wide-ranging indictment of journalism's upper crust. These journalists, they charged:

- are better educated and better paid than most Americans, with ideas and values alien to those of "the real majority";
- are concentrated in a few national news organizations that exercise disproportionate power over the selection of the news that reaches the American public;

Reprinted from the 1982 special issue of *The Wilson Quarterly.*

- seek to enhance their own power by taking an aggressive, even destructive, stance toward other major American institutions such as government, the political parties, and business, while making themselves invulnerable to retaliation by wrapping themselves in an absolutist version of the First Amendment;
- have abandoned standards of fairness, accuracy, and neutrality in news to pursue larger audiences and greater power.

Beneath the political animus that fueled such critiques was a residue of harsh truth. But what was not necessarily true was the assumption made by critics that the current state of journalism departed radically from what came before it, that there had been a distinct break with the past.

As British historian Anthony Smith observed in *Goodbye Gutenberg*, "Each decade has left in American newspaper life some of the debris of the continuing intellectual battle over the social and moral role of journalism." For 150 years, journalists have sought success and power and respectability, usually in that order, and society has responded with unease and occasional hostility.

INNOVATION AND CONSOLIDATION FROM THE PENNY PRESS TO PROFESSIONALISM

The press, in fact, has gone through at least four cycles of innovation and consolidation. America's first popular newspapers were the penny press of the 1830s and 1840s, typified by James Gordon Bennett's *New York Herald.* The penny press created a first generation of journalists by putting printers in waistcoats and turning young college graduates of literary inclination and poor prospects into reporters. So threatening was Bennett's frank and sensational news coverage that New York's establishment, led by the musty, older commercial papers that Bennett was putting out of business, conducted a "moral war" to stop him. Bennett survived.

A second and far larger journalistic generation appeared during the 1880s and 1890s. By then, the city newspaper had grown into the first mass medium, thanks to the showmanship of such entrepreneurs as William Randolph Hearst and Joseph Pulitzer. In the shrill Hearst-Pulitzer competition during the Spanish-American War, the sales of an individual newspaper for the first time exceeded one million. Critics again fretted over the power of the press to push the nation into war, to debase society. Like Bennett, Hearst had a "moral war" declared against him, on grounds that his papers had incited President William McKinley's assassin. Like Bennett, Hearst survived.

Each journalistic generation set its own distinctive "style," but each progressed from rebellion to consolidation, from breaking old rules to laying down new ones. The penny press and its ragtag of "bohemians" angered and shocked the mandarins of the old commercial-political newspapers. Yet it was the old penny journalists who, during the 1870s, declared bohemianism dead and all journalists henceforth gentlemen of clean shirt and college education. Bohemianism reappeared with the "yellow" journalists of the 1890s. When that generation matured, it too set bohemianism aside: its spokesmen began to claim that journalism was as much a profession as law or medicine, and universities established journalism schools in a flawed effort to prove the point.[1]

UNIONIZING THE NEWSROOM

For forty years or more, newspapers rode high, but during the middle years of the twentieth century, they were no longer unchallenged. *Time* and other magazines, radio, and TV began to claim a share of the news audience. (Even so, most journalists continued to ply their trade at newspapers, and 75 percent still do.) The character of the popular press, meanwhile, began to turn from yellow to gray, as befitted an aging institution.

The next generation, the third, rebelled not by reverting to impetuous iconoclasm, but by trying to change the harsh economic rules of the game. The Great Depression had sent reporters' salaries plummeting; by 1933 many were out of work. New York columnist Heywood Broun, summoning reporters to set aside snobbery and join together, wrote that he could die happy if, when a general strike began, he saw Walter Lippmann "heave a brick through a *Tribune* window" at a scab trying to turn out a Lippmann column on the gold standard. Broun became president (1933–7) of the first national union for journalists, the American Newspaper Guild, and led it into reluctant affiliation with the U.S. labor movement.

Unionization's immediate effect was to take from management some of the power it had long enjoyed—the power to fix newsroom wages and to hire and fire as it pleased. In the long run, unionization made newspaper life more orderly and predictable and made it possible for reporters to think of a career. During the years after World War II, as newspaper staffs grew, the newsroom became bureaucratized, even tame. "Somehow," lamented David Boroff, author of a 1965 Ford Foundation study, "the glamor and magic of the craft have leaked out of it." As before, consolidation had followed rebellion.

In fact, the glamour and magic were by then already leaking back in as a fourth generation of journalists came of age. Like its predecessors, the new generation challenged the rules—not the economic rules, for the 1960s was an era of unprecedented affluence, but the largely unwritten rules concerning the *substance* of a journalist's task: the definition of "news," the authority of the employing institution, and the relation of journalism to the larger society. The groundwork for many of these challenges had already been laid. What the new generation did most successfully was to combine the individualism and flair of *The Front Page* (that is, of yellow journalism) with the ideology and seriousness of "professionalism."

The recipe had several ingredients. The first was an erosion of "publisher power." By the beginning of the 1960s, most newspapers had lived down their colorful past. Although occasionally caught up in the fevers of, say, a sensational murder trial or sex scandal, most newspapers no longer consistently sensationalized the news. Most major newspapers did not let advertisers regularly control news content. Most publishers had learned to control their hostility to labor and provide balanced coverage of strikes. And most newspapers at least claimed to offer balanced political coverage. The figures most prominently associated with the legendary abuses of the past were fading from the scene. Hearst died in 1951, the *Chicago Tribune*'s Colonel Robert R. McCormick in 1955.

Professionalism was the catchword reporters invoked to insulate themselves from their employers. Aspirants were not required, like doctors or lawyers, to master a certain body of knowledge. But by defining themselves as professionals, journalists could, like doctors or lawyers, claim special rights, notably a degree of individual autonomy in writing and reporting. By the 1960s reporters commonly agreed that attempts, by editors as well as publishers, to shape the news to make it fit predetermined "policy" were wrong. Theoretically, wrote journalist-sociologist Warren Breed in 1955, the only controls should be "the nature of the event and the reporter's effective ability to describe it." In the newsroom the actual result was a chronic, usually muted struggle between editors and reporters, between managerial direction and reportorial autonomy.

In addition to the self-image of professional autonomy, the younger journalists inherited from their elders a long-standing antipathy toward officialdom. Publishers during the 1930s had tried unsuccessfully to use the First Amendment to thwart New Deal legislation strengthening labor unions. In the years after World War II, the press's suspicions of government shifted to an editorial, and a more subtle, level. Newspapers during the 1950s mounted a "freedom-of-information" campaign, implicitly suggesting that undisclosed records and closed meetings were a cloak for official misdeeds. Reporters who had submitted to the manipulations of Franklin D. Roosevelt now objected to those of Eisenhower and Kennedy. The term "news management" was coined by James Reston of the *New York Times* during the mid-1950s.

Pulitzer Prizes, as always, went to exposers of instances of city hall corruption and Washington chicanery. But steady, continuous muckraking—unless embod ied in an institutional "crusade" in the Hearst or Pulitzer tradition—was not yet the fashion. The press had not yet undertaken in its investigations, as Lippmann in his 1922 classic *Public Opinion* had stated it should *not* undertake, "the burden of accomplishing whatever representative government, industrial organization, and diplomacy have failed to accomplish."

News standards were also changing during the late 1950s and early 1960s. Increasingly, the old "objective" format for news was viewed as inadequate to the complexities of contemporary subject matter and to the reporter's desire to demonstrate expertise. The satisfaction of going beyond the facts, once reserved largely for Washington columnists, now came to ordinary reporters, given a new license to "interpret" the news.

One final element helped pave the way for the fourth generation: enhanced pay and popular prestige. Even after the Newspaper Guild helped to stabilize wages and working conditions, newspapers were justly accused of underpaying their employees. Polls taken during the 1950s, moreover, ranked journalism low—near the bottom in fact—in occupational prestige. By 1962 or 1963, however, all of that had begun to change. The combined appeal of gradually rising pay and gradually rising status became attractive enough to draw college graduates from other fields.[2] Journalism school enrollments began to swell.

Newspapering became more secure. In 1965 Walter Lippmann pondered the overall metamorphosis of the American journalist since World War II: "The crude forms of corruption which belonged to the infancy of journalism tend to give way to the temptations of maturity and power. It is with these temptations that the modern journalist has to wrestle." It was these temptations that confronted reporters as the 1960s unfolded.

THE TEMPTATIONS OF POWER

Although it was not the first cold war press-government confrontation over "national security," Vietnam set a decade-long pattern of mutual antagonism that ultimately verged on mutual paranoia during the Nixon years. In reality, the *New York Times*'s David Halberstam and other early birds in Saigon were not, as later painted, antiwar activists in 1963. Rather they heard (from U.S. military field advisers), saw, and wrote, not inaccurately, that U.S. policy in Vietnam was *not working*, even as Washington claimed the opposite.

This conflict between press accounts and official assessments of Vietnam was not all-pervasive, or even constant. But it grew, fed by the inherent ambiguities and rhetorical contradictions of an increasing costly "no-win, no-sellout" war policy. Under Lyndon Johnson and Richard Nixon, the resulting "credibility gap" began to extend to other matters—to CIA and FBI activities, to diplomacy, and to government generally.

At the same time that he slowly committed America to Vietnam, Lyndon Johnson invited high expectations of government from newsmen and ordinary folk alike with his Great Society programs to "end poverty," to "end inequality," to "end hunger." Few reporters then questioned the need for bigger government (they were, at heart, reformers too). But black riots in Watts in 1965, in Detroit in 1967, and in Washington and a dozen other cities in 1968 seemed to show that government at home as in Vietnam was failing, even as universities seemed unable to cope with campus unrest, and churches and businesses and other institutions seemed unable or unwilling to respond to rising demands for, variously, more equity, more freedom, a cleaner environment, more truth in advertising, more "power." The 1968 Democratic convention, with its attendant Chicago "police riot" against antiwar demonstrators, seemed to show that the political party system could not or would not respond either. Activists on behalf of Hispanics, women, homosexuals, the handicapped, the aged, followed blacks in claiming their due rights, not just in Washington, but in cities all over America.

The younger reporters who tried to keep up with all this were prepared to challenge authority, but they operated within the establishment. Unlike their "underground" contemporaries, they chose to work inside existing and prospering institutions, which alone could offer them the full material, moral, and status rewards of journalism—"status" meaning, above all, status in the eyes of other journalists. The impression given by complaining editors later that they had been overrun by activists hostile to newspaper traditions is largely false.

The claim to professionalism had two striking implications—first, that the press as an institution ought to be a kind of free-floating body in society, encumbered by neither governmental nor social controls; second, that the individual journalist ought to be free of institutional restraint as well. In working terms, this meant that reporters could try to shake free of editors; in social terms, it meant generational conflict even more intense than usual.

For the press as a whole, professionalization meant living more by one's own rules, living, in the words of communications scholar James W. Carey, "in a morally less ambiguous universe than the rest of us." This was the universe inhabited by many young reporters as they covered the civil rights movement, urban decay, campus unrest, the peace movement, and the congressional debates over the Vietnam War. So many things were wrong. The issues seemed so clear. And so dramatic.

The older newspaper generation watched the new breed uneasily. One *Washington Post* veteran later remembered an "often mindless readiness to seek out conflict, to believe the worst of government or of authority in general, and on that basis to divide the actors in any issue into the 'good' and the 'bad.'" This readiness was heightened, perhaps, by the influence of television news and the "thematic" approach that flavored (and often flawed) its documentaries, such as *The Selling of the Pentagon,* broadcast in 1971.

The attitude was replicated in many newsrooms, big and small. The institutional structure of the press was seen as a barrier to truth. Journalism would be purer and better if it were controlled by the reporters themselves. In the wake of the controversial coverage of the 1968 Chicago riots, young reporters throughout the country established new "journalism reviews"—sometimes in-house newsletters, sometimes magazines meant for a larger circulation. These usually attacked the residual power of publishers, the authority of editors, or the insufficient zeal of reporters in discomfiting politicians, business, and the military. The *Chicago Journalism Review* made its debut in late 1968, *More* magazine in New York in 1971.

These reviews—neither of which is still published—were allied with a reform movement that advocated, at least implicitly, newsroom governance comparable to that of a Swiss canton; or comparable to that of, for example, France's *Le Monde,* where newshands elect their own *redacteur en chef.* "Reporter power" enjoyed a brief heyday, then expired. It never achieved formally in the area of newsroom control what the Newspaper Guild had wrought in terms of security. In part, this was because the battle had been won—newspaper editors had already become more "permissive," and objectivity, as a journalistic standard like the straightedge and compass of classical geometry, was widely accepted as, if not obsolete, then insufficient.

The antagonism between editors and reporters was minor compared with the continuing clash of press and government. Amid the strains of the Vietnam War and civil disorders at home, the Nixon administration in 1969, through Vice President Agnew and others, had launched a public counterattack on the "elitist" media and their "liberal" bias. Then, in 1971, came the first serious confrontation, over the "Pentagon Papers."

Hawk-turned-dove Daniel Ellsberg had tried for a year to make public the secret Pentagon study of the history of U.S. involvement in Vietnam. He had approached prominent antiwar politicians, among them Senators William Fulbright and George McGovern, but had not achieved his aim. Finally, Ellsberg called *New York Times* correspondent Neil Sheehan, a former Vietnam reporter who had recently begun writing in opposition to the war. Sheehan was interested in the study, and so was his newspaper. ("You have permission to proceed, young man," Washington bureau chief James Reston has been quoted as telling Sheehan.) In June 1971, the *Times* began publishing the Pentagon Papers.

At first, there was no great stir, except at the rival *Washington Post* where editor Benjamin Bradlee hastened to order a "catch-up." But when the Nixon administration decided to suppress further publication on national security grounds, the confrontation was joined. The *Times*'s and the *Post*'s subsequent victory in the Supreme Court became a landmark in journalistic history. But had the Big League press gone too far in substituting its judgment for Washington's? Had it arrogated to itself a power unsanctioned either by law or by the public it claimed to represent? The debate over such questions continues.

In *Without Fear or Favor* (1980), a history of the *New York Times* centering on the Pentagon Papers case, Harrison Salisbury claims that the *Times* (and, one would think, the rest of the national press) "has quite literally become that Fourth Estate, that fourth coequal branch of government of which men like Thomas Carlyle spoke." The implications of such a claim are immense. "Fourth-branch" rhetoric has been around a long time, of course. (Douglass Cater's *The Fourth Branch of Government* was published in 1959.) But when Salisbury and others take the fourth-branch metaphor as literal truth, they imply that the press, like Congress, for example, enjoys not only independence, but also constitutional privileges and immunities. Time and again, this case, widely accepted among newsmen, has been made before the Supreme Court, but so far, at least, a majority of the justices has refused to concur.

Salisbury puts forth another expansive claim in his book: that Watergate itself and hence the Watergate exposés (in which the *Post* took the lead) would not have happened except for the Pentagon Papers case (in which the *Times* took the lead). Given the security hysteria the Pentagon Papers case touched off in the Nixon White House, the proposition is supportable but unprovable, like much else about Watergate.

WATERGATE: A BREEDER OF MYTHS

Watergate was a breeder of myths. The chief myth is that Hardy boys Joe and Frank (i.e., *Post* reporters Bob Woodward and Carl Bernstein) solved the mystery and toppled a president. Actually, as political writer Edward Jay Epstein noted back in 1973, the government itself cracked the case in its early stages. "What the press did between the break-in in June (1972) and the trial in January," Epstein wrote, "was to leak the case developed by the federal and Florida prosecutors to the public." Congress and Judge John Sirica carried the burden thereafter.

But it was difficult for the mere facts of a complicated story to compete with a glamorized version as compelling presented in the popular 1974 movie *All the President's Men*. The "Woodstein" model was credited with filling the journalism schools (although, in fact, the influx of students had begun years earlier) and restoring to newspaper work much of its lost glamour.

Watergate also signaled the start of what has been seen as a period in which the press's confrontation with the federal government became excessive and unreasoning. Although some editors noted that the behavior of the government had been far from normal (necessitating, in their view, an abnormal response), others urged journalists to draw back. "The First Amendment is not just a hunting license," warned Associated Press general manager Wes Gallagher in 1975. "We must put before the public ways and means of strengthening the institutions that protect us all—not tear them down," he said.

Under considerable criticism for a variety of sins, the media undertook during the Watergate era to overlay a veneer of public interest on their operations. In 1973 a coalition of foundations and media created the National News Council, a media-dominated, unofficial "ombudsman-at-large" for the national press. At the same time, many publications named their own in-house ombudsmen to handle readers' complaints, explain journalism to the public, and monitor the newspapers' performances. Reporters and editors often greeted these newcomers coolly; their presence seemed not only to promise the embarrassment that accompanies public discussion of newsroom frailties, but to diminish professional autonomy. Newspapers also began running corrections regularly, sometimes in a reserved space, although victims of errors still complained that the corrections lacked substance and prominence.

The temper of journalism after Watergate, as these reforms suggest, was not that of Agamemnon after Troy. To all outward appearances, the press was still acquiring new influence. Investigative, even accusatory, journalism had become more rather than less popular. Yet journalists were uneasy. Chris Argyris, a Harvard management consultant who published in 1975 a thinly disguised study of the inner workings of the *New York Times,* observed (perhaps with some malice) that "the innards of the newspaper had many of the dynamics of the White House. I found the same kinds of interpersonal dynamics and internal politics; the same mistrust and win/lose competitiveness."

Although surveys showed that most journalists liked their work, despite its deadline pressures, many reporters seemed fueled by a sense of being under attack or of being in a race; indeed, the Knight-Ridder newspaper chain administered tests to job applicants to gauge just such desirable qualities. Was it surprising then that journalists, especially during the 1970s, tended to see government and politics in the same terms of aggression and competition?

POST-WATERGATE: DEFINING NEW LIMITS

For a decade the key issue remained control. "Young reporters have always wanted to change the world," wrote Charles B. Seib, then the *Washington Post's* ombudsman, in 1978. But, he went on, "in the old days, when a reporter let his opinion show he was quickly brought to heel by an editor" and eventually was turned into "what we called an objective reporter—meaning a reporter who stuck strictly to the raw, unvarnished facts. Nowadays editors are inclined to be more permissive." Seib said he was glad "the days of trying for blind objectivity are over," but he warned, "Too often the new permissiveness is carried too far."

That newspapers indeed at times carried the "new permissiveness" too far became very clear to all in the spring of 1981, when a story by a *Washington Post* reporter was awarded a Pulitzer Prize for feature writing. It turned out, however, that reporter Janet Cooke had simply made up "Jimmy's World," her tale of a (nonexistent) eight-year-old heroin addict. Despite certain clues, *Post* editors, including Bob Woodward of Watergate fame, had failed to discern the deception. Cooke resigned, and the *Post* returned her Pulitzer. The next day, the newspaper assured in an apologetic editorial that "more of the skepticism and heat that [we] traditionally bring to bear on the outside world will now be trained on our own interior workings. One of these episodes is one too many."

The uproar over the Cooke affair did not soon abate. Shortly afterward, a *Daily News* columnist in New York was fired when he could not back up some of his reporting from Northern Ireland. Reporters in Minnesota and Oregon were punished for inventing quotations. The Associated Press admitted that an account it had distributed about a California joy ride had been a "composite" story. In February 1982 the *New York Times* admitted on page one that an article written by a freelance writer about his trip to Cambodia, which appeared in December 1981 in the *New York Times Magazine,* had been a fabrication. The writer, in fact, had not left Spain.

As a result of the Janet Cooke affair and the ensuing "crime wave" of newly disclosed hoaxes, fakes, and frauds, editors vowed to reassert their authority over reporters. A survey of 312 editors conducted for the American Society of Newspaper Editors Ethics Committee found 30 percent of them had changed their policies because of the Cooke scandal. More than a third said they were keeping a closer eye on reporters and the accuracy of their stories. Fewer than 2 percent of the editors said they would allow reporters to keep identifications of sources from editors; 55 percent said identification had to be provided on request; and 41 percent said it must always be provided.

To outsiders, the press now seemed a little on the defensive. The first "hot" newspaper movie since *All the President's Men* appeared toward the end of 1981: *Absence of Malice*—whose script was written by former *Detroit Free Press* editor Kurt Luedtke—portrayed a venal press cloaking its mischief in the First Amendment.

As the pendulum swung back, journalists began asking tougher questions about their own performances. The *Wall Street Journal* in 1982 attacked other newspapers' coverage of El Salvador as cut from the same cloth as the journal-ism of John Reed in Russia, Herbert Matthews in Cuba, and David Halberstam in Vietnam. (Halberstam defended himself ably.) When the public appeared to support the Reagan administration's exclusion of the press from the Grenada invasion in 1983, there was a further wave of journalistic soul-searching.

Such intramural debates, however acrimonious, may be a healthy sign that a dilemma, underlined by publication of the classified Pentagon Papers, is at least being brought into the open. Journalists are committed to serving the truth, or at least the "facts." Yet they are unable to avoid wielding influence. Any big story may produce some damaging social or political effect. The public knows this instinctively, but journalists have usually said, "Damn the consequences!" Now, it seems, they are being put on notice that they can be called to account. As Wes Gallagher of the Associated Press warned after Watergate, "The press cannot remain free without the proper functioning of the government, the judicial branch and private institutions in a democracy. The press also is an institution. All rise and fall together."

Journalism's responses so far have been imperfect. One of the most publicized was that of the *New York Daily News*'s Michael J. O'Neill, in a May 1982 farewell address as president of the American Society of Newspaper Editors. He seemed to be accepting, almost point by point, the critique advanced since 1970 by neo-conservative intellectuals. Journalists, he said, should "make peace with govern-ment," should cure themselves of their "adversarial mindset."

Thus, the most recent generation of journalists, the one that grew up in the Vietnam and Watergate years, received the message that the heyday of autonomy had ended. The nostalgic in that now-aging generation may briefly have glimpsed new dreams of glory in the guerrilla war in Central America and the Iran-Contra scandals of 1986–7. But while the press has pitched in earnestly, neither in Central America nor in the Contra scandal have its exposures proved better than sporadic or marginal, or both. No new Halberstams or Woodsteins have emerged.

The sobering historical lesson is that journalists, however bright or idealistic, cannot pretend in the long run to live outside society and to live by their own rules. Society wants and needs their services, but at its own price. In the long run American society will determine what kind of journalism it wants; only to a far lesser degree will journalists determine what kind of society America will be.

NOTES

1. Ironically, the romance of bohemianism was even then being forever stamped on the psyche of journalists, most indelibly through *The Front Page* (1928) by Ben Hecht and Charles MacArthur. The playwrights conceded, however, that Hildy Johnson and his feckless colleagues were a vanishing breed—"the lusty, hoodlumesque, half-drunken caballero that was the newspaperman of our youth. Schools of journalism and the advertising business have nearly extirpated the species." Films about the news business (*Broadcast News*, 1987, and *Switching Channels*, 1988) are about TV journalists—suggesting that the "glamour" side of the media is television, not print.

2. Journalists' salaries vary considerably, even at the 139 Newspaper Guild–organized dailies. As of 1987, a reporter at the *New York Times* with two years' experience earned a minimum of $929.16 a week; at the *Chicago Sun Times,* after five years, $866.03; at the *Sacramento Bee,* after six years, $649; at the *Terre Haute* (Ind.) *Tribune,* after five years' experience, $400.88. The average top reporter minimum for all Guild papers in mid-1987: $590.26. At non-Guild papers (that is, at most papers), the pay is usually lower.

7

AMBIVALENT VICTORIAN: H. L. MENCKEN

T. J. JACKSON LEARS

One gray autumn day in the early 1950s, James T. Farrell stopped off in Baltimore, took a cab to H. L. Mencken's house on Hollins Street, and spent a depressing afternoon with the critic who had befriended him years before. Though Mencken seemed physically healthy, he had suffered a cerebral hemorrhage in 1948, and its effects were painfully apparent. His talk wandered; he could neither read nor write. While Mencken maintained a wry good humor, Farrell recalled a persistent refrain in their conversation: "I'm finished," Mencken repeatedly told the novelist. "I'm out of it." Mencken's predicament was a poignant coda to a vigorous career. The impresario of words, for whom language had been life, was surrounded by letters he could not read and books he could not understand.

There was a sense, though, in which Mencken had been "out of it" for many years before his stroke. During the earnestly nationalistic 1930s and 1940s, Mencken's levity seemed an echo of the frivolous Jazz Age. Even during the years of his greatest influence, the 1920s, his ideas betrayed a curiously anachronistic quality. Mencken assaulted Prohibitionists, Rotarians, and genteel custodians of culture, but the attack was launched with the well-worn weapons of positivist science and classical liberalism. He clung to the same late-Victorian brand of iconoclasm for fifty years, while American culture passed him by.

To understand what Mencken meant to people when he stood at the height of his power, let us follow a black teenager as he made his way to the public library in Memphis in 1926. As a black, Richard Wright was not allowed to check out books, but he was determined somehow to smuggle out one by

Reprinted from the spring 1989 issue of *The Wilson Quarterly.*

Mencken, for Mencken was the only white man more vilified in Southern newspaper editorials than any black ever was, and Wright wanted to find out why.

The book that Wright finally secured was full of the discoveries Mencken was then championing—T. S. Eliot, Dostoevsky, Gide—names that Wright had never heard of. Yet Mencken's book itself was the most liberating book Wright said he ever read. It filled him with a sense that there was another, a better world elsewhere.

Mencken intoxicated many others. His critique of middle-American smugness stirred writers as diverse as Ernest Hemingway and Walter Lippmann. In 1926, Lippmann called him "the most powerful influence on this whole generation of educated people." Sinclair Lewis said Mencken should be made "Pope of America" for spreading the gospel of sophistication. In *The Sun Also Rises,* Hemingway noted that "so many young men got their likes and dislikes from Mencken." To the young talents of this new generation, for whom American culture with its Prohibition and Babbitt-like boosterism was stiflingly provincial, Mencken's gibes at American complacency went down like invigorating tonic. They delighted in piss-and-vinegar attacks like this one: "The normal American of the 'pure-blooded' majority goes to rest every night with the uneasy feeling that there is a burglar under the bed, and he gets up every morning with a sickening fear that his underwear has been stolen."

Especially appealing was the way Mencken could offend both sides—say, Communists and 100 percent Americans—simultaneously. He argued that the Reds should be allowed to "spew out their garbage" on every street corner, because it wouldn't do any good: the American mind didn't work that way, Mencken said; it would choose a Ford over the Constitution every time.

The great irony of Mencken's career, however, is that although he attacked American complacency with an unprecedented fierceness, in many ways he was himself complacently at home in it. Mencken, in short, was a bundle of contradictions, an ambivalent Victorian in the modern world.

Mencken admitted he was born "a larva of the comfortable and complacent bourgeoisie" in Baltimore in 1880. His father, August Mencken, was a second-generation German who owned a cigar factory and a part interest in the Washington baseball club. Young Mencken grew up amid the amusements of the Baltimore Germans—a beery atmosphere, heavy with cigar smoke, and Biedermeier sentimentality. Not a bad atmosphere to grow up in, Mencken thought, as years later he recalled being "encapsulated in affection, and kept fat, saucy, and contented."

In Mencken's recollection, the Baltimore of the Eighties was a city of tidy rowhouse neighborhoods, pestilential plagues of mosquitoes, vile sewer stenches—and gastronomic delights, given its proximity to the truck-garden of Anne

Arundel County and "the immense protein factory of the Chesapeake Bay." After enormous midday meals, the male population transacted the rest of the day's business in bars, where no-account Virginia "colonels," down on their luck after "The War," hoisted bumpers of rye with the local business community; and August Mencken, with young Henry beside him, checked the blackboard for the ball scores. Out in the streets, black or Italian hucksters (always called "Ay-rabs" by the Baltimoreans) clattered carts along the cobblestones, hawking strawberries or oysters "with loud, raucous unintelligible cries, much worn down by phonetic decay." The city mixed Northern and Southern, provincial and cosmopolitan styles, and the mix marked Mencken's own cast of mind throughout his life.

After emerging from "the caves of learning" at Knapp's Institute and the Baltimore Polytechnic, young Mencken reluctantly entered the family business. His miserable career as a cigar salesman was cut mercifully short by his father's death in 1899. The day after the funeral, Mencken presented himself at the offices of the *Baltimore Herald,* a paper with less prestige but more dash than the rival *Sun* (even then a bastion of maiden-aunt respectability). Night after night, he kept coming back, until finally the editor sent him out to cover the theft of a horse and buggy. Mencken broke into print the next morning, and so began a decade's apprenticeship as a reporter.

The experience reinforced his preference for "life itself" over things academic. "At a time when the respectable bourgeois youngsters of my generation were college freshmen, oppressed by simian sophomores and affronted by balderdash daily and hourly by chalky pedagogues, I was at large in a wicked seaport of half a million people, with a front seat at every public show, as free of the night as of the day, and getting eyefuls and earfuls of instruction in a hundred giddy arcana, none of them taught in schools." Small wonder that Mencken, like so many other writers of his generation, disdained the anemic idealism of polite literature in the name of "real life."

Mencken rose rapidly. After six years of haunting police stations and waterfront dives, he was made managing editor—a reward for his hard work and talent. Mencken's lifelong belief in the mythology of self-made manhood was a projection of his own experience as a newsman in an individualistic era—a proud and manly age, he believed, when newsmen would no more think of calling themselves "wage slaves" and joining a union than they would imagine tying up a studhorse's mane in pink bowknots. Yet for Mencken there was a value in the newspaper experience that went beyond masculine posturing. On the docks and in the back streets, he had abundant opportunity to acquire a taste for "raw reality"—but he never followed Frank Norris and Theodore Dreiser into a self-parodic *nostalgie de la boue*. He developed a fascination with vernacular language:

the pungent Baltimorese of the local whites, the patois of the African Americans, the Polish or Yiddish or Italian variations of the more recent immigrants. The many voices of the city inspired the research that led to his monumental *The American Language;* they also enriched his own prose style.

In 1906 the *Baltimore Herald* collapsed, but Mencken stayed in Baltimore, as he would throughout his career. He joined the staff of the *Sun*—first as editor of the Sunday edition, later as editor of the *Evening Sun,* and in 1911 as author of a daily, signed editorial column he called the "Free Lance." The column gave Mencken a chance to air his idiosyncratic political views: a compound of ambivalent enthusiasm for the "progressive" civic reforms then raging through the city, tempered by a Nietzschean faith in the need for an iconoclastic elite. His contempt for Anti-Saloon Leaguers and other militant moralists provoked a vitriolic response from his readers, whose letters he printed alongside his columns. The role of pamphleteer/*provocateur* was one Mencken would relish all his life.

But it was in the realm of arts and letters that Mencken first began to acquire a national reputation during these years. In 1908, he began writing book reviews for the New York-based magazine *The Smart Set;* in 1914 he took over the editorship with George Jean Nathan. Like Van Wyck Brooks, Mencken assaulted "Puritanism as a Literary Force" and busily set about toppling such icons of gentility as William Allen White (*A Certain Rich Man*) and Marjorie Benton Cooke (*Bambi*). Thus began the epochal struggle, now enshrined in all literary histories: the Rebellion of the Angry Young Men against the Genteel Tradition. According to conventional wisdom, World War I broke the back of Old Gentility, after the Young Men had pummeled it into stupefaction. In actuality, the psychic foundations of respectable bourgeois culture had been crumbling for decades, as WASP elites succumbed to a sense of "overcivilized" languor toward the end of the nineteenth century. The harshest critics of the Genteel Tradition spoke from within that tradition, ranging in subtlety from Theodore Roosevelt to Henry Adams. The war merely made the weakness of the old ideals more obvious, less avoidable.

Nevertheless, there is no question that the ethnic tensions aroused by the war intensified the cultural conflicts. Mencken, Brooks, Randolph Bourne, and other dissenters mounted a major attack on the Genteel Tradition in the name of cosmopolitan ideals *versus* 100 percent Americanism. For Mencken the issue was more personal. He had never been a professional German in his youth. His father and grandfather were detached from their homeland and annoyed by self-conscious ethnic posturing. There was little or no German spoken in August Mencken's household. But as a young man Mencken found himself inexorably drawn to German culture. He cut his intellectual teeth on Nietzsche, and when he visited Germany in 1913, he found, he believed, a land of beauty, tradition, and order—a sharp contrast to the "muddled mass of individuals" on this side of the Atlantic. The outbreak of hostilities in 1914 confirmed Mencken's Germanophilia. He felt surrounded by Anglophile cant and paranoid suspicion of things German—as indeed he was, especially after 1917 when the United States entered the conflict. In Mencken's mind, the war merged the cause of civil liberties with the rights of the German-American minority. It intensified his sense of isolation, and his embittered rage at Anglo-Saxon hegemony in letters as in politics.

After the war, there were growing divisions in the tattered army of Angry Young Men. Bourne was dead; Brooks was shuffling from one sanatorium to another; Mencken was alive and kicking, but increasingly impatient with the aestheticism of *The Smart Set.* He wanted to shift his gaze from literature to society, and in 1924 he founded *The American Mercury* in order to set up shop as a social critic. For several years he won a national following by aiming accurate barbs at the pretensions and pomposities of a business civilization. But after 1927 circulation began to slip, and the Depression accelerated the decline, as Mencken remained stuck in his rigid iconoclast's pose. In 1933 he resigned from the *Mercury,* returned to the *Sun, The American Language,* and comparative obscurity. He had married Sara Haardt of Alabama in 1930, but she died five years later, leaving him utterly bereft. In 1939 he began to write his memoirs—it was as if he sensed he would be forever associated in the popular mind with a historical moment that had passed. Perhaps his obsolescence stemmed from his inability to adapt, chameleon-like, to changing cultural fashion. (One thinks of Van Wyck Brooks's reincarnation, in the 1930s, as a celebrant of mainstream American culture.) Throughout his career, Mencken's ideas remained remarkably consistent. In some ways that consistency was a weakness; in others it was his greatest strength.

From his freethinking father and grandfather, Mencken inherited the mental furniture of the "enlightened" nineteenth-century bourgeoisie. A positivist belief in progress through empirical science; a literalist disdain for fantasy, myth, and metaphysics; a fear of anarchists, socialists, and labor unions—August Mencken's prejudices shaped his son's outlook from an early age. As his biographer, Charles Fecher, has observed, even as a child Mencken was "repelled by the improbable fantasy" of Grimm's fairy tales. His discovery of Charles Darwin, Herbert Spencer, and Thomas Henry Huxley reinforced his distaste for religion and his reverence for "fact."

By the late nineteenth century, such attitudes were anything but rebellious. During Mencken's boyhood, Calvinism was dead, except in rural backwaters. The official creed was not "puritanism" but a liberalized, nondenominational

Christianity which was hardly at odds with Mencken's own positivism. But there were fissures in the liberal-positivist consensus. The 1890s were hardly an era of complacent mediocrity, as Mencken's memoirs suggest; they were marked by social, intellectual, and moral ferment. Nationwide labor unrest threatened the bourgeois social order. A rediscovery of the nonlogical and unreasonable elements in the psyche undercut the intellectual order. From Nietzsche to Henri Bergson, from William James to Freud, serious thinkers showed an unprecedented fascination with primal irrationality. And lesser men popularized that fascination on both sides of the Atlantic.

Despite his engagement with broad cultural issues, Mencken remained immune to much of the intellectual ferment surrounding him. He clung to the ponderous schemes of evolutionary progress mapped out by Huxley and Spencer. He dismissed James and Bergson, railed against "the Freudian rumble-bumble," and transformed Nietzsche from a Dionysian mystic into a Spencerian progressive in his youthful treatise *The Philosophy of Friedrich Nietzsche* (1908). Mencken and Nietzsche shared a common contempt for "the masses," but there was a profound philosophical gulf between the two men. Mencken's *Treatise on the Gods* (1930) was a restatement of nineteenth-century notions that religion was an immature stage in human development, gradually being outgrown as "the race" progressed; Nietzsche's life work was an effort to discredit positivism and restore an ecstatic dimension to religious life.

Mencken's literary tastes also revealed his inflexible literalism. Impatient with psychological subtleties, he dismissed "the flabby, kittenish realism of Howells," and declared Henry James to be "of less interest than Richard Harding Davis." He had a tin ear for poetry, which seemed to him "very deficient as an agent of progress." He admired Dreiser as "a really implacable reporter of facts"; he also praised Sherwood Anderson, Sinclair Lewis, and Joseph Conrad—novelists he could fit within his naturalistic frame of reference. But he rejected many twentieth-century writers in baffled irritation. He admitted that "the Thomas Mann stuff simply eludes me"; he believed that Hemingway wrote novels simply to prove he was a "naughty fellow" and that there was no more sense in Faulkner than in "the wop boob, Dante." During the 1920s, Mencken's *Smart Set* was the magazine where most major new talents (Fitzgerald, Edmund Wilson) first broke into print. But as he aged, the prophet of modernity, who had once championed Ezra Pound, became anesthetized to much of serious modern literature.

Mencken's political thinking remained less philistine. His classical liberalism never wavered; he remained devoted to free speech during periods when more "pragmatic" liberals abandoned it. He defended novelists against censors, publishers against smuthounds, socialists and anarchists (whose views he abhorred) against superpatriots. In 1925, Mencken focused attention on Carlo Tresca, the proprietor of a small, radical anti-Fascist paper in New York, whose views offended Mussolini's ambassador to the United States. Under pressure from the ambassador, the United States government shut down the paper and offered Tresca the non-choice of being deported to Italy or going to jail. Tresca shrewdly chose the latter option. In the *Sun*, Mencken fumed: "What becomes of the old idea that the United States is a free country, that it is a refuge for the oppressed of other lands? . . ."

In the *Mercury*, he published articles by Emma Goldman, an anarchist writer who had been deported during the Red Scare of 1919; he urged the Justice Department to return the papers it had seized from her office and the Bureau of Immigration to allow her to return to America to visit her relatives. While his own thinking was shaped by German ethnocentrism, he nevertheless rose above the racial mythologies of his time. He publicly denounced lynching in a town where race-baiting was a way of life, and the last thing he ever wrote was a stinging assault in the *Sun* on segregation in Baltimore parks. His libertarian principles led him to perceive national prohibition as an emblem of the moral hysteria pervading small-town America in the 1920s. One can only imagine how he would skewer the "Just Say No" panicmongers of the 1980s.

It is tempting to see Mencken as the last liberal, the last genuine devotee of individual freedom who refused to make that "pragmatic" genuflection to bureaucratic authority—who refused to elevate technique over ultimate principle. He never twisted his libertarianism to sanction corporate or military power, as today's pseudo-libertarians have so often done. And, though his critiques of the New Deal became formulaic, Mencken had spotted weaknesses in pragmatic liberal thought long before the accession of Roosevelt. Mencken remained committed to a classical republican vision of politics—the eighteenth-century vision of Jefferson, Madison, and Adams.

To be sure, Mencken does not always deserve to be grouped in such august company. Though he trained a sharp eye on the meanspirited moralism of prohibitionists and 100 percent Americans, Mencken displayed a meanspiritedness of his own. His was the narrow smugness of the urban bourgeois, addicted to his creature comforts and convinced that he has earned them through his superior ability. With the significant exception of his concern for civil liberties, Mencken's "Jeffersonianism" could be heard in any barbershop full of Right-thinking Citizens. His father had divided all mankind into "those who paid their bills and those who didn't," and Mencken shared the old man's tightfisted morality. The New Deal, Mencken charged, was a "political racket" based on the proposition that "Whatever A earns really belongs to B. A is any honest or industrious man or woman; B is any drone or jackass." Mencken's obsession with the tyranny of the "inferior man" blinded him to mass suffering. "Even in a great depression few if any starve," he wrote. He was as much a defender of Victorian complacency as a rebel against it.

Despite his concern for culture, Mencken never considered its relationship to social and economic circumstances. True to the classical republican tradition, he tended to trace the shortcomings of American political life to the ignorance or venality of individual politicians. He seemed unable to conceive of power relations in systemic or structural terms, and so he missed the significance of the organizational revolution that was insulating the political process from popular control during the early twentieth century. He all but ignored the steady concentration of power in bureaucratic and economic elites, and attributed the vapidity of American culture to an (undemonstrated) excess of democracy. An even more serious problem was the tendency of Mencken's cultural criticism to slip into self-indulgence and superficiality: He often remained preoccupied with surfaces. He arraigned fundamentalists because they were ridiculous and businessmen because they were boring. In one sense his legitimate heir is that contemporary merchant of *chic,* Tom Wolfe.

But there was more than Wolfe's snobbery in H. L. Mencken. His talents were various; in many ways they resembled Mark Twain's. Both men were artists of language rather than ideas; both reached wide middle-class audiences through outrageous humor and vigorous colloquial style. (Mencken said that Warren Harding's prose reminded him "of stale bean soup, of college yells, of dogs barking idiotically through endless nights." It was a characteristic simile.) Without that style, neither man's reputation would have survived a generation. Both men sustained ambivalent relationships with majority culture: they mocked it, exploited it, made literary capital out of it, but they never dismissed it. To do so would have been to reject their own birthright as American provincials. Restive and rebellious as they were, they nonetheless remained committed to most values of the respectable bourgeoisie (including its sentimental ideal of domestic life).

Yet Mencken sought to be more than a National Funny Man. He used humor for serious purposes. Mencken's writing at its best was like that of Alexis de Tocqueville and other critics of American society: He lamented the homogenizing effects of democratic culture on public discourse, and he sought to promote a genuine "battle of ideas" for its own sake. He kept alive a tradition of personal journalism during decades when newspapers and magazines were passing increasingly under corporate control. His voice rose above the rumble of "responsible opinion," and for a time his disdain for official pieties leavened the intellectual life of the nation.

Unlike many of us, Mencken was ultimately forced to test the courage of his intellectual convictions. As he grew older, more concerned about his health and prone to thoughts of death, Mencken increasingly followed his materialist premises to their logical conclusion.

For him, as for his late-Victorian predecessors, the only alternative to religious or secular humanism was a mechanistic materialism that was nearly as arrogant in its human-centeredness, in its assumption that human science had already cracked the code of the cosmos. He was willing, Mencken said, "to stand up single-handed against the eternal and intolerable mysteries." The assertion sounds sophomorically Faustian, until one recalls the pain of his later life. When he married Sara Haardt, he knew she was dying of tuberculosis; when her death finally came it was still hard to accept. "What a cruel and idiotic world we live in!" he cried in a letter to *Atlantic* editor Ellery Sedgwick.

Mencken's own stroke was the final demonstration of that cruelty and idiocy. It was one of the "harsh and meaningless fiats of destiny" he found in Conrad's stories, a destiny undreamt of in positivist optimism. Mencken the maestro of language was destined to end his days groping for words and forgetting the names of his closest friends. ("How are my friends?" was one of his refrains to Farrell.) He was sad, his voice was thick, sometimes the right word would not come; yet he still could sometimes summon his playful old persona. "When I see God," he would tell visitors, "I'm going to speak sharply to him." Nothing in his life became him like the close of it. We may permit ourselves to imagine that the old man on Hollins Street was not merely an anachronism, that he was "out of it" in a more honorable sense as well, providing a kind of stoical witness against the self-congratulatory certainties of America's national creed.

8

POLITICS TRANSFORMED

ROBERT J. DONOVAN AND RAY SCHERER

As a young reporter for the *Richmond Times-Dispatch,* Charles McDowell was one of the first inside witnesses to television's impact on politics. By sheer chance he observed at the Republican National Convention in Chicago in 1952 how people's reaction to what they saw on television influenced political decisions—a phenomenon that would profoundly change the workings of the political system.

The Republican convention in 1952 was the first at which television news had the technical resources and the large audience to enable it to exert significant political impact. In 1940, NBC had broadcast scenes of the Republican convention in Philadelphia to a few stations. That year the network also made newsreels of the Democratic convention in Chicago and sent them to New York for broadcast the next day on a small scale. Although the Democratic and Republican conventions of 1948 in Philadelphia were fully covered by television, few people around the country had sets, and the networks' reach from Philadelphia was limited mainly to the East.

McDowell was in Chicago in 1952 as a member of his newspaper's convention bureau covering the fight between General Dwight D. Eisenhower and Senator Robert A. Taft of Ohio for the Republican nomination. Although it seemed unlikely that the Republicans would reject a war hero of Eisenhower's stature, the Taft forces nominally controlled the party machinery. Before the convention Taft had more delegates committed to him, on paper at least, than did Eisenhower. Sentimentally, most delegates probably preferred Taft, "Mr. Republican," as he was called. A critical issue at the convention was whether pro-Eisenhower or pro-Taft delegations from Texas, Louisiana, and Georgia should

Reprinted from the spring 1992 issue of *The Wilson Quarterly.*

be seated. In these three states pro-Eisenhower delegates had been chosen by precinct conventions. The respective Republican state committees, however, had brushed these actions aside, alleging that Democrats were allowed to vote. The committees selected alternative slates of delegates favorable to the Ohioan and demanded that they be seated at the convention. The whole nominating process thereupon descended into a labyrinth of charges, countercharges, negotiations, and proposed compromises.

Much in need of a decisive issue, the Eisenhower camp seized the moral high ground in the delegate dispute. Shrewdly, Eisenhower's people used television to tell the whole nation that the general was the victim of those who would spurn fair play. On the eve of the convention Eisenhower said that the dispute over southern delegates was "a straight-out issue of right and wrong." He accused the Taft campaign of "chicanery."

According to Edward R. Murrow, one of the CBS staff covering the proceedings, the Taft people wanted to keep the whole convention off television. This would have included a hearing in which the credentials committee was taking up the question of the disputed delegates. In a news broadcast from Chicago, Murrow reported that Eisenhower's staff sided with broadcasters in favor of having television cameras at the credentials committee hearing, and in the end, despite the resistance of the Taft forces, Eisenhower's staff succeeded.

When the hearing opened in the Gold Room of the Congress Hotel, McDowell came to listen. Well known in later years as a stalwart on the PBS television program *Washington Week in Review*, he was then a junior member of the *Times-Dispatch* convention staff. Lacking the proper credential for this particular event, he slipped unnoticed into a kitchen just off the main room in the hope of being able to hear what went on. Soon strategists for the Taft side ducked into the kitchen to assess the progress of the hearing. If the politicians noticed McDowell, they evidently assumed he was one of the hotel employees and made no effort to keep their voices low. McDowell's listening post proved to be a good one. He learned, as he later wrote, that "the Taft managers were talking about conceding the Louisiana delegates to Eisenhower." From what the Taft managers were saying, McDowell also learned that the television coverage of the hearing was affecting viewers' opinions of the two candidates.

"What was happening," McDowell explained, "was that people back home, following the debate on television, were telephoning and telegraphing their delegates to say that Taft's case was coming through as weak. Republicans of consequence were saying that a steamroller approach would look bad on television and hurt Taft more than yielding the delegates."

The credentials committee awarded the Louisiana delegates to Eisenhower. Taft's position crumbled. Eisenhower was nominated on the first ballot.

Television contributed to the outcome. Over a period of days, it had conveyed the impression that the conqueror of Normandy was getting a raw deal from the Republican Old Guard.

Beginning in 1952, television caused structural as well as superficial changes in American politics. That year, delegates of both parties were warned that the probing television lenses could capture every movement they made in their chairs. They were admonished to be careful about what they said to one another lest lip readers pick up the conversation from the television screen. Women delegates were cautioned against affronting blue-collar viewers by wearing showy jewelry. Another change was so startling that CBS put out a news release on it: the bald, gruff Sam Rayburn, chairman of the 1952 Democratic convention in Chicago, had agreed to wear makeup from gavel to gavel.

Memories of the 1948 convention had convinced broadcasters to change convention coverage. The traditional style—with the endless nominating speeches, the proliferation of seconding speeches, and hours of parades and whoopee in the aisles—was boring for television viewers. At the disorderly Democratic convention in 1948, the nominee, Harry S. Truman, did not begin his acceptance speech until 2:00 A.M. In 1952, when events on the rostrum grew dull, the networks diverted their cameras to cover interviews or meetings in downtown hotels. For the first time, television producers, not party officials, decided what aspect of the convention would be shown throughout the nation at any given time. Advances in electronics enabled NBC anchors to converse with their reporters and cameramen, who were roving the aisles with hand-held portable cameras, then called "creepie-peepies." This gave coverage a new range and mobility. Any delegate or other politician trying to strike a deal on the convention floor was fair game for an interview. The television audience was provided a broader look at how the politics of conventions worked. The unfavorable side was that in future years roving reporters and camera crews began to clog the aisles in their search for pundits, charlatans, and celebrities of all kinds, as well as delegates. Unfortunately, this generated competition among the networks for often meaningless, not to say misleading, scoops on the floor, sometimes blurring the true picture of the convention proceedings.

When the Democratic convention opened in Chicago in 1952, the party cooperated with the networks. The Democrats limited nominating speeches to 15 minutes and individual seconding speeches to 5 minutes. Floor demonstrations were limited to 20 minutes for each candidate placed in nomination. At the start, five candidates were in the running for the party's nomination. Almost before the rap of the opening gavel had faded away, however, the field narrowed. It was customary for the governor of the state to give an opening speech on the first day, and the governor of Illinois was then Adlai Stevenson. Truman had once favored Stevenson for the nomination, but the president later backed away. The governor had not tossed his hat into the ring, and he had no pledged delegates. His welcoming speech, however, was so exciting, so filled with music and good sense, that the convention was over almost before it began. The delegates were thrilled. Television viewers around the country sent telegrams. Truman again threw his support to Stevenson.

Before the week was out Stevenson was on his way to a hopeless campaign. The Democrats had been in power for 20 years. The Korean War had shredded Truman's popularity. The electorate was hungry for change, and the voices of the people said, unmistakably, "I like Ike." Stevenson never succeeded in recapturing the magic of the welcoming speech, and it was the Eisenhower campaign that grasped the new techniques of the television age. Indeed, in their desperation for a winning issue, the Democrats charged that Madison Avenue had taken over Eisenhower. Stevenson said, "I don't think the American people want politics and the presidency to become the plaything of the high-pressure men. . . . [T]his isn't Ivory Soap versus Palmolive." Stevenson stood aloof. One of his leading advisers, George Ball, lamented that Stevenson "obstinately refused to learn the skills of the effective television performer."

Eisenhower, however, did learn them. In fact, his campaign used the first spot television commercials in the history of presidential politics. When Eisenhower was president of Columbia University after the war, he became friends with Bruce Barton and Ben Duffy. During the 1952 campaign, Eisenhower trusted Duffy, president of the large advertising agency Batten, Barton, Durstine, and Osborn, and followed his advice and that of professional Republican politicians. They told Eisenhower that the formal set speech of earlier campaigns could not convey the warmth of his public personality. Of course, some such speeches would have to be made, but the new emphasis should be on informal television productions in which the candidate appeared to be talking to Americans individually. Where a set speech was necessary, it should be part of a large drama, a rally staged for paid political television and glittering with all the hoopla of a Hollywood premiere.

In city after city the Eisenhower campaign rolled into auditoriums bathed in spotlights. Arms overhead in his famous V-for-victory sign, he stepped out of the wings as a band was blaring. Mrs. Eisenhower beamed from a box, the crowd roared, and the television cameras caught it all.

Television speeches were held to 20 minutes, with frequent pauses for applause. On the road Eisenhower cut a handsome figure in a double-breasted camel-hair coat and brown fedora. At airport rallies or on the rear platform of a campaign train, he would often pull an egg from his pocket and ask the crowd, "Do you know how many taxes there are on one single egg?" If no one answered, he would reel off a list of levies that would make any good Republican shudder.

The men behind Eisenhower's television commercials were Rosser Reeves, Jr., of Ted Bates and Company advertising, and Michael Levin, a former Bates associate. In the early days of television, Bates had pioneered the clustering of spot advertisements before and after entertainment programs. Reeves was confident that television could market a politician as well as it marketed toothpaste. When he started to work on the campaign, Reeves first watched an Eisenhower political speech in Philadelphia on television. Reeves counted 32 separate points Eisenhower made and then dispatched a research team the next morning to ask people at random what Eisenhower had said. None of those questioned could say. Reeves then read all of Eisenhower's speeches and extracted a dozen important issues, but found them too diverse for sharp focus. From George Gallup he learned that the issues that most bothered Americans were the Korean War, corruption in Washington, and rising taxes and inflation. Thereupon, Reeves drafted 22 scripts and, in mid-September, joined Eisenhower in a Manhattan studio to have him read them from cue cards. What Eisenhower was reading were ostensibly his own answers to questions that had been written by Reeves. Reeves later insisted the answers were framed in words from various Eisenhower speeches. But who would ask the questions? They would be asked by randomly chosen citizens, reading in front of a camera from the same cue cards. The respective questions and the respective answers would be spliced together. The questioners would never see Eisenhower. On the television screen, however, it would appear that they were face to face. "To think that an old soldier should come to this," Eisenhower commented in the studio as his brother, Milton S. Eisenhower, cleared the scripts.

Executives of NBC and CBS at first hesitated to run such simplistic material, arguing that the commercials were not up to the standards of a presidential campaign. Under pressure from Batten, Barton, Durstine, and Osborn, however, they yielded. Beginning in mid-October, 28 of the commercials were broadcast in 40 states. Commercials faking conversations between a candidate and citizens would be unacceptable today. Yet compared with the ugly commercials of later campaigns, the Eisenhower spots were mild fare. Overall, the campaign was a moderate one. Eisenhower never attacked Adlai Stevenson or Harry Truman. He surely did not need to rely on theatrics to defeat the Democrats in 1952. Unquestionably, the stagings and the commercials enlivened his campaign. More than that, they were harbingers of a style of politics that Eisenhower could not have foreseen and would not have liked.

The year 1952 was also pivotal in another way. Television networks for the first time covered state primaries. The coverage attracted national audiences. In January 1952, President Truman, a product of an era of political bosses and machines, had told a news conference, "All these primaries are just eyewash when the conventions meet." But he was wrong. The victory of the Eisenhower forces over Taft in New Hampshire, the first primary of the year, provided strong impetus for the general's drive at the Chicago convention. In the years that followed, primaries and caucuses multiplied as a result of democratizing reforms and the decline of party organizations. And to an extent Truman would not have believed, television coverage turned the primaries into crucial stepping-stones for candidates.

Instead of being eyewash, primaries determined the outcome of the nominating process. Once decisive, national conventions were reduced to gaudy gatherings that ratified decisions already made. When the selection of delegates to the conventions was largely in the hands of state party bosses, television had little to cover. But in 1952 the presidential aspirants began to campaign openly for delegates, and television moved in and covered the events for the public to see.

As primaries increased in number, the costs of running for office soared. With incalculable effect on the health of the political system, television advertising required candidates to raise vastly more money than ever before. In 1948, Truman's supporters had to pass the hat to collect enough cash to move his campaign train out of the station in Oklahoma City. By 1990 the amount of money spent just on political advertising was $227.9 million. "In Washington today," Richard L. Berke wrote in the *New York Times* in 1989, "raising money takes nearly as much time as legislative work."

After 1952 the next stage in the magnification of television's role in elective politics came with the televised debates between John F. Kennedy and Richard M. Nixon in 1960. The networks that year were striving to improve their image and reassure viewers of their dedication to the public interest. Television had just sloshed through an embarrassing ordeal resulting from the fixing of weekly quiz programs. Cheating on two highly popular shows—*Twenty-One* and *The $64,000 Question*—genuinely shocked the American public. Network executives, eager to demonstrate their civic-mindedness, conceived of the idea of televised debates between the Democratic and Republican nominees. In addition to huge audiences, the debates promised another benefit to the networks: a change in the Communications Act of 1934. Section 315 of that act had long rankled broadcasting executives. It required that candidates for the same office be given equal treatment on the air. Long-shot presidential contenders from every party, not just the Democratic and Republican nominees, would have to be included, making the debates, in the networks' eyes, an impractical multilateral affair.

The networks invited Kennedy and Nixon to debate, subject to congressional action on the Communications Act. Kennedy immediately accepted. The debates would give him a great deal of national exposure, which he then lacked and might not readily get otherwise. Although he had less to gain and more to lose, Nixon, proud of his debating skills, agreed to face Kennedy, and Congress suspended Section 315.

Four debates were held at staggered intervals during the campaign. They covered different issues. "Since there was no precedent for this kind of televised debate," Nixon later wrote of the 1960 encounters, "we could only guess which program would have the larger audience. Foreign affairs was my strong suit, and I wanted the larger audience for that debate. I thought more people would watch the first one, and that interest would diminish as the novelty of the confrontation wore off." He was right. Nixon, however, heeded his advisers, all of whom were convinced that the last program, nearest election day, would attract the biggest audience. Domestic issues were the focus of the first debate, which was held at the CBS studio in Chicago on September 26.

Both candidates arrived in Chicago the day before. Kennedy was much the more rested of the two. Ill luck had befallen Nixon at the start of his campaign. In Greensboro, North Carolina, on August 17, he had bumped his knee getting into a car. An infection that set in forced him to stay in the Walter Reed Army Medical Center in Washington from August 29 to September 9. He lost eight pounds—and looked it. As soon as he was discharged, he began campaigning furiously to make up for lost time and caught a cold.

Nixon did not arrive in Chicago on September 25 until 10:30 P.M., and even at that hour he visited some street rallies that kept him up until well after midnight. On the morning of the 26th he had to address a meeting of the United Brotherhood of Carpenters and Joiners of America. Meanwhile Kennedy rose early and spent four hours with members of his staff preparing for the debate. After lunch he, too, made a brief speech to the same union and then took a nap, while Nixon spent practically the entire afternoon reading in preparation for the debate. Nixon later wrote, "The tension continued to rise all afternoon. My entire staff obviously felt it just as I did. As we rode to the television studio, conversation was at a minimum as I continued to study my notes up to the last minute." When he got out of the car at the studio he painfully bumped his sore knee again. On greeting Kennedy inside, he was impressed by how fit the senator looked. "We could see that Nixon was nervous," Kennedy aide Lawrence O'Brien recalled. "He tried to be hearty, but it didn't come off."

CBS's Don Hewitt was the program's director. Ted Rogers was present, as Nixon's adviser, as was Kennedy's adviser, Bill Wilson. The vice president's pallor disturbed both Hewitt and Rogers. Aware that Nixon's skin needed makeup under bright studio lights, Rogers had requested that the vice president's makeup artist be brought to Chicago, but the campaign staff declined. Hewitt asked Nixon if he would like to be made up. "No," Nixon replied. Kennedy, well suntanned, did not need makeup. And, according to Hewitt, Nixon did not want to run the risk of having it reported that he was made up (an unmanly advantage) and Kennedy was not. In the end Nixon did use "Lazy Shave," a powder meant to cover his five o'clock shadow, but Hewitt did not think it was satisfactory.

Nixon used poor judgment in wearing a gray suit against the gray backdrop. He did not stand out on television screens nearly as sharply as Kennedy, who was handsomely dressed in a dark suit, blue shirt, and dark tie. Kennedy's manner throughout the debate was serious. By contrast, Nixon smiled often and somewhat nervously. Perhaps because of his sore knee, he sat awkwardly when he was not speaking. His tendency to perspire under studio lights quickly became noticeable, and it caused a quarrel in the control booth during the debate. Rogers was shocked when, without warning, Hewitt called for a reaction shot that caught Nixon apparently off guard. The shot showed Nixon wiping his brow and upper lip. Furiously, Rogers maintained that reaction shots had been disallowed by the rules and that Nixon had been brought into the picture unfairly in an undignified pose.

Many people who tuned in to the first debate on radio rather than on television thought that Nixon had the better of it. He was careful about making effective debating points. But, as Theodore H. White, the shrewd chronicler of presidential elections in the 1960s and 1970s, observed, Nixon "was debating with Mr. Kennedy as if a board of judges were scoring points; he rebutted and refuted, as he went. . . . Nixon was addressing himself to Kennedy—but Kennedy was addressing himself to the audience that was the nation."

In retrospect, Nixon characterized the first debate as a setback for him. He was in much better health for the last three and at the very least held his own. But those debates did not engage the public to the degree the first one had. Even the first debate failed to cause anything like a decisive swing in either direction in the Gallup poll. Kennedy retained the slight lead he had held through September. Nixon's sense of a setback contrasted with renewed optimism around Kennedy. His staff was ecstatic because when Kennedy resumed campaigning after Chicago, he suddenly seemed to attract more excited crowds, as though people were flocking toward a winner. Certainly, the concerns of Eisenhower and other Republicans had been realized: Kennedy, the younger and supposedly less experienced candidate, had looked more presidential on television than Nixon.

Because no overriding issues defined the 1960 campaign, the importance of the Nixon-Kennedy debates lay largely in the images projected on television. Whether these images determined the election outcome is hard to say. The margin of Kennedy's victory—112,881 votes—was so narrow that it is impossible to single out as decisive any one factor, even one as important as the debates.

Nixon learned his lesson, though. His campaign against Hubert Humphrey in 1968 marked a radical turn toward reliance on television. From his disastrous debate with Kennedy in 1960, Nixon concluded, "I had concentrated too much on substance and not enough on appearance. I should have remembered that 'a picture is worth a thousand words.'"

Surrounded by advertising men, consultants, lawyers, and speechwriters, Nixon centered his campaign in 1968 not just on television but on controlled, manipulated television. In this way his election strategy foreshadowed those of Ronald Reagan and George Bush. Nixon's daily appearances were carefully staged to project a certain image of himself and his programs. Vestiges of old-style campaigning, still pursued by Hubert Humphrey, were largely swept aside by Nixon. Only four years earlier Lyndon Johnson and Barry Goldwater had stumped the country tirelessly. As far as Nixon was concerned, that kind of campaigning was as far gone as the torchlight parades for William McKinley in 1896.

Nixon's campaign staff read excerpts from Marshall McLuhan's book *Understanding Media* (1964). "The success of any TV performer," one of the excerpts said, "depends on his achieving a low-pressure style of presentation." Lowering the intensity of Nixon's earlier political behavior was a crucial part of the strategy for Nixon in the 1968 campaign. Reliance on controlled appearances on television facilitated this. He would not debate Humphrey. He avoided reporters. A memorandum to Nixon on November 16, 1967, by Leonard Garment, one of the bright and reputable persons on his staff, said that Nixon must try to get "above the battle, moving *away* from politics and *toward* statesmanship." To this end Garment advocated "a fundamentally philosophical orientation, consistently executed, rather than a program-oriented, issues-oriented, or down-in-the-streets campaign."

The availability and lure of television completely transformed Nixon's customary manner of running for office. This strategy was followed even more rigidly four years later in his re-election campaign. Likening Nixon to "a touring emperor" rather than a candidate for president, the *Washington Post*'s David Broder declared that the "Nixon entourage seems to be systematically stifling the kind of dialogue that has in the past been thought to be the heart of a presidential campaign." The age of the "handled" candidate had fully arrived.

The arts of handling were not lost on the Democrats. Well before the presidential election of 1976, Jimmy Carter received a memorandum from his assistant Hamilton Jordan. Recently retired as governor of Georgia, Carter was thinking about running for president. Jordan gave him this advice: "We would do well to understand the very special and powerful role the press plays in interpreting the primary results for the rest of the nation. What is actually accomplished in the New Hampshire primary is less important than how the press interprets it for the rest of the nation."

If recognition of that kind was important to Dwight Eisenhower and John Kennedy, both nationally known figures when they ran for president, it was surely essential to Carter, unknown to most of the country in the mid-1970s. Grasping this reality, he made a shrewd decision to focus first on the Iowa Democratic caucuses of 1976, which would precede the New Hampshire primary. It was a testing ground that had been largely ignored by presidential aspirants in previous years.

Carter began cultivating Iowa Democrats in 1975. His strategy clicked. On October 27, the Iowa Democrats held a Jefferson-Jackson Day fundraising dinner at Iowa State University in Ames, at which a straw vote was to be taken. Jimmy Carter and his wife, Rosalynn, were on hand. Carter's staff, especially pleased that R. W. Apple, Jr., of the *New York Times* was covering the affair, did their best to pack the place with Carter supporters. When Carter won a definite victory—23 percent of the 1,094 respondents, the largest individual share— Apple filed a story about the Georgian's "dramatic progress." Carter, he reported, "appears to have taken a surprising but solid lead" in the race for Iowa delegates.

On January 19, 1976, the day of the caucuses, Carter flew not to Iowa but to New York City, where he talked about his victory on the late-night television specials and the next morning's network news shows. At one point Roger Mudd said on CBS, "No amount of badmouthing by others can lessen the importance of Jimmy Carter's finish. He was a clear winner in this psychologically important test." This was exactly what Hamilton Jordan had had in mind. Carter went on to win the New Hampshire, Florida, and Ohio primaries and was nominated at the Democratic National Convention in New York in July.

Seldom had there been a better time for a Democrat to run. In the previous four years, Vice President Spiro Agnew had resigned in disgrace, Nixon had resigned to avoid impeachment, and Watergate had horrified the country. In 1976 the Republican nominee was Gerald Ford, who had succeeded Agnew as vice president and then Nixon as president. As chief executive he had soothed the nation's shock over Nixon and Agnew. Yet he had damaged himself with a sudden, surprising, and ill-prepared announcement that he had granted Nixon a presidential pardon. On top of that, in a televised campaign debate with Carter, Ford blundered by asserting "There is no Soviet domination of Eastern Europe." Run and run again on the networks, in the familiar way television magnifies an incident, it caused people to say, in effect, what Ford himself was to say 13 years later: "I blew it." Carter won the election.

Ford was an exception among Republicans. Beginning with Eisenhower in 1952, the Republicans—Nixon (except in 1960), Ronald Reagan, and George Bush—have gotten the better of their opposition on television. These Republican candidates were not necessarily better or more honest than their Democratic opponents, but their appeal to television audiences was somehow more compelling. In experts such as Michael Deaver, Roger Ailes, and Lee

Atwater, the Republicans enlisted more skillful tacticians than the Democrats employed. Certainly, the Republican edge was clear in the 1984 campaign between Reagan and former vice president Walter Mondale. In his book on the campaign, journalist Martin Schram wrote that President Reagan had "skillfully mastered the ability to step through the television tubes and join Americans in their living rooms." Schram called Reagan and Deaver "pols who understand TV better than TV people themselves."

Indeed, by 1984 television news executives were striving to keep their news programs from being manipulated by political image-makers. In a picture medium, however, this was not always easy to do. "If Ronald Reagan makes a speech in front of the Statue of Liberty, and the speech has news in it," Joseph Angotti, then an NBC political director, said, "there is no way we can show Reagan without showing the statue behind him."

On July 4, 1984, the best shot Walter Mondale could offer television evening news was of himself at home in Minnesota, talking with Mayor Henry Cisneros of San Antonio, a potential vice-presidential nominee. Reagan, aboard Air Force One, was on his way to the annual Daytona 500 stock car race and a picnic with 1,200 of the fans. As the plane, equipped with television cameras inside the cabin to catch the president, swooped down, he picked up a radio-telephone, sang out the traditional "Gentlemen, start your engines," and then sent the cars thundering down the track. Furthermore, after he arrived at the stands, packed with 80,000 spectators, he sat in for a while as guest commentator on the racing circuit radio network. It was all lively fare on the network evening news.

By October 7, 1984, the date of the first televised debate in Louisville between the candidates, Mondale was trailing so badly in the polls that practically his only hope lay in this confrontation with Reagan. So much aware of it was Mondale that he practiced in the dining room of his house in Washington, which, for the purpose, had been converted into a mock television studio with two podiums. Under bright lights members of his staff fired questions at him before a camera. His answers were played back until he had memorized them. Then, to almost universal surprise, he went to Louisville and so unmistakably carried the day that the polls indicated an incipient turnabout in the campaign. It was not the dining room rehearsals that changed things. Rather, for the first time the Gipper, at the age of 73, blew it on television. He hardly seemed the telegenic master campaigner who had ousted the incumbent Carter four years earlier. He was worn out. He was confused. He was not himself. "Reagan is really old," Mondale told an aide after the debate. "I don't know if he could have gone another 15 minutes."

What had been seen on television suddenly changed the overriding issue of the presidential campaign. Two days later a headline in the *Wall Street Journal* read, "New Question in Race: Is Oldest U.S. President Now Showing His Age? Reagan Debate Performance Invites Open Speculation on His Ability to Serve."

Other newspapers and the networks took up the question. Some television news programs spliced scenes from the debate with shots of the president dozing during an audience with Pope John Paul II.

By the time of the second debate on October 22 in Kansas City, the drama centered on Reagan's appearance and the state of his alertness. Beforehand, his technicians went to the studio and changed lighting angles and candlepower to give him more of a glow. When the two contenders appeared, the president was poised and wide awake. He seemed more rested than before. His self-confidence was palpable. "They pumped him up with sausage and he looked okay," Mondale recalled long afterward. Reagan knew what pitch was coming. His eye was on the center-field stands when, sure enough, a reporter on the panel reminded him of the youthful John Kennedy's ordeal over the Cuban missile crisis and asked Reagan if he himself was "too old to handle a nuclear crisis." Crack went the bat: "I am not," the president replied, "going to exploit, for political purposes, my opponent's youth and inexperience." The whole country watched the ball sail over the fence. "When I walked out of there," Mondale said, "I knew it was all over."

The 1988 campaign was the culmination, in many ways the nadir, of practices, strategies, manipulations, and distortions that had been multiplying in elections almost since the advent of television news. Television spots, or commercials, were more numerous and, on the whole, more unpleasant than in any previous campaign. Discussion of issues was more than ever reduced to sound bites measured in seconds. Mostly, the blame for the tone fell not on the loser, Governor Michael S. Dukakis, but on the winner, George Bush, whose campaign nevertheless was the more effective.

Bush advocated, among other measures, a day-care program for children. He promised a vigorous attack on the drug scourge. But after he was inaugurated on January 20, 1989, it was evident that the more conspicuous issues with which he had saturated the campaign—which candidate liked the flag better, which disliked murders more—had little to do with governing the country.

The previous June, Michael Dukakis, the Democratic frontrunner, had swept four states, including California and New Jersey, on the last primary day. A *Wall Street Journal*–NBC News survey taken June 9–12 showed Dukakis leading Bush for the presidency, 49 to 34. A Gallup poll of June 10–12 indicated that Dukakis enjoyed a lead of 52 to 38. Then the lead sagged. Dukakis did not do much to sustain it. Bush managed to make more news. Dukakis was nominated in Atlanta in mid-July by a well-unified party. As best he could, he finessed the ambition of Jesse Jackson and, hoping the choice would help him in the South, selected

Senator Lloyd Bentsen of Texas as the vice-presidential nominee. As a climax, Dukakis delivered a good acceptance speech.

For the Democrats it was an uphill struggle after Atlanta. Probably the elements made it a Republican year, willy-nilly. Bush was riding a tide of peace, prosperity, conservatism, and enduring resentment in some regions of the country against the civil rights reforms of past Democratic administrations. A sharp Republican team knew the rough way to play, and the Democrats did not know how to fight back. Republican veterans created television commercials and photo opportunities on emotional subjects such as blue-collar crime, prisons, patriotism, and the welfare state. Although Dukakis considered himself a moderate, the Republicans effectively branded him a 1960s-style liberal and, *ipso facto,* soft on crime, committed to heavy civilian public spending, and niggardly on defense appropriations. For all the vulnerabilities of the Reagan administration, Dukakis failed to frame a winning issue.

The Bush team had no such trouble. Well before the conventions, Lee Atwater asked Jim Pinkerton, the chief researcher, to make a list of issues that might help bring Dukakis down. Pinkerton returned with a three-by-five card on which he had noted Dukakis's positions on taxes and national defense, his veto of a Massachusetts bill requiring the Pledge of Allegiance in the classroom, the state of pollution in Boston Harbor, and Dukakis's opposition to the death penalty. The list also contained something Pinkerton had discovered in the text of a debate among Democratic contenders before the April presidential primaries in New York. Senator Albert Gore, Jr., of Tennessee had questioned Dukakis about a Massachusetts prisoner-furlough program. Pinkerton went on to discover that an imprisoned murderer named William (Willie) Horton, Jr., an African American, had received a weekend pass and then raped a woman. After this atrocity Governor Dukakis had the procedure changed to bar furloughs for convicted murderers. Nevertheless, the Bush campaign seized on this tragedy as a way to accuse Dukakis of being soft on crime.

To make, in effect, a market test of issues, Bush consultants had two so-called focus groups of voters organized in Paramus, New Jersey. The participants chosen were Democrats who had voted for Reagan in 1984 but who, four years later, intended to vote for Dukakis. Out of sight behind two-way mirrors, the Bush experts watched with increasing jubilation the reactions of these voters as moderators in each group introduced them to the issues on Pinkerton's card. According to later reports, 40 percent of one group and 60 percent of the other said they would switch to Bush. "I realized right there," Atwater was reported to have said, "that we had the wherewithal to win . . . and that the sky was the limit on Dukakis's negatives."

A conference was held the following weekend at the Bush home in Kennebunkport. According to a report in *Time,* Bush was hesitant about a negative campaign of attacks on Dukakis, but then yielded. Most states had a prisoner-furlough program. The one in Massachusetts had been enacted under former governor Frank Sargent. The fact that Sargent was a Republican did not bother Roger Ailes, who proceeded with work on a commercial showing prisoners exiting jail through a revolving gate. A voice said, "[Dukakis's] revolving-door prison policy gave weekend furloughs to first-degree murderers not eligible for parole. While out, many committed other crimes like kidnapping and rape and many are still at large. Now Michael Dukakis says he wants to do for America what he has done for Massachusetts. Americans can't afford that risk." This first commercial did not use a photograph of Horton.

It was a second prison-furlough commercial, sponsored by the National Security Political Action Committee, that used a photograph of a glowering Horton. "Bush and Dukakis on crime," an announcer said. Then a photograph of Bush and the comment, "Bush supports the death penalty." Next a photograph of Dukakis and the observation, "Dukakis not only opposes the death penalty, he allows first-degree murderers to have weekend passes from prison." Finally, a mug shot of Horton. The ad appeared throughout the country on cable television for 28 days. The *New York Times* assigned three reporters to get the story of its production. According to the investigation, the National Security Political Action Committee claimed the quiet support of the Bush staff. Lloyd Bentsen was among the first to label the commercial racist. The Bush people earnestly retorted that Horton was not chosen because of his color. Yet, as a symbol of white fear of African American criminals, his menacing visage could scarcely have been improved upon. At an early point Pinkerton told Atwater, "The more people who know who Willie Horton is, the better off we'll be."

In the history of the republic, political campaigns have at times been so full of strife, libel, nastiness, and brawling that the Willie Horton ad does not stand alone on the horizon by any means. The resonance and impact of political attack, however, have been magnified beyond measure by the technology that brought the menacing image of Horton into millions of American homes simultaneously. Reaction to people and events can be massive and immediate nowadays. In their book on the 1988 campaign, Peter Goldman and Tom Mathews likened television "in the hands of the new managers" to what napalm might have been in General Sherman's hands. "You could scorch a lot more earth with a lot less wasted time and effort."

After Bush's victory at the polls, NBC called in its campaign reporters and producers for a critical reassessment of the problems of covering the campaign for television. The names of the participants were not disclosed, but here is what one Washington-based reporter said: "The great ugly secret of campaigns is this: Not much happens. The candidates give the same speech over and over again to different audiences. Because we won't report the same speeches over and over again, we are left to do the photo-ops and the inner workings of the campaign." Another reporter complained about the problems of logistics. "[Airplane] coverage involves so much shlepping around from baggage call to staged events and then a frantic race to the television feed-point [that] there is little time and less energy for the kind of research and reporting that shapes a thoughtful report, and that's when it's very easy to accept balloons and sound-bite candy."

The tendency toward an ever more pivotal role for television in presidential campaigns reached new and troubling heights in 1988. The candidates' so-called media managers had become masters of getting their messages across in television commercials and in events staged for television. For the television industry this produced the deep dilemma of how to use the pictures without becoming entrapped in stagecraft. Television techniques all but displaced old-time political campaigning as the focus of coverage. Reporters began to sound like drama critics.

The waves of changes that began with the televising of the national conventions in 1948 had, by 1988, transformed the mode, mechanics, and theater of elective politics. To be sure, television has not eliminated ethnic, religious, and racial preferences among voters, or the ancient division between Left and Right, or people's tendency to vote their pocketbooks. The effect of television is secondary to what ABC's Jeff Greenfield has called "the shaping influences of American political life . . . embodied in political realities." Politicians, more than political scientists and journalists, have exalted the importance of television. They have done so not only in words but in actions. For more than 40 years they have not been able to stay away from television. It is the thing that matters most to them. By listening to their own words it is possible to judge where the dividing line lay between what politics was before 1948, when television news was born, and what politics has been since. The day after his dramatic victory over Dewey in 1948, Truman articulated the essence of the "old politics" when he said, "Labor did it." A mere 12 years later, after defeating Nixon in 1960, Kennedy's comment went to the heart of the "new politics": "It was TV more than anything else," he said, "that turned the tide."

9 HOW TO READ THE CAMPAIGN

MICHAEL CORNFIELD

An autumn 1991 episode of America's most consistently intelligent and fiercely realistic prime-time television series opened with Homer Simpson watching the news. "And, to conclude this Halloween newscast on a sca-a-ry note," said the anchorman, "remember, the presidential primaries are only a few months away. Heh-heh-heh."

There is no escaping now. From mid-January 1992, the *Washington Post* and *New York Times* allocated at least one full inside page to the presidential campaign every day. CNN aired at a minimum a half-hour program every weekday. The newsmagazines and the other broadcast networks devoted similar space and time to the campaign. "Coverage" seems too mild a word to describe the reports, round tables, polls, predictions, analyses, profiles, rumors, shoptalk, advertisements, call-in shows, and comedy routines geared to the presidential campaigns. We now have super-coverage, a Niagara of coverage—or, in the vernacular of television, "our continuing coverage."

Increasingly, such coverage continues by covering itself. Expressions of concern about the power of the media to distort campaign results and to sour the electorate on national politics have become part of the usual campaign clamor. (Such media self-criticism reached a crescendo, for example, during the controversy over candidate Bill Clinton's alleged adultery.) In the universities and think tanks, critical reports proliferated; Harvard University alone published three by the end of 1991. Many reform proposals have merit, but their oft-repeated condemnations of the "vicious cycle" of trivialized discourse, as it is frequently called, only serve the literary function of absolving all parties of guilt. To gather journalists, politicians, and

Reprinted from the spring 1992 issue of *The Wilson Quarterly*.

scholars around a conference table and emerge with lists of recommendations on improving the process is also to give the screw another downward turn.

The "vicious cycle" also refers to a second problem: the irresistibility of the version of events that media coverage generates. The source of this irresistibility has less to do with the conduct and motives of individual politicians and journalists than with the dynamics of the whole subculture to which they (and thousands in the audience) belong.

Members of this subculture—the self-proclaimed "junkies" of presidential politics—share a language, perspective, and set of priorities. They are the audience for the daily *Presidential Campaign Hotline,* a kind of campaign tip sheet that is sent by fax or computer to subscribers. It is a safe bet that many *Hotline* clients grew up reading the books of Theodore H. White, beginning with *The Making of the President, 1960.* White's great discovery was that the news swapped among campaign insiders could be consolidated into the classic story form of a melodramatic contest. Journalists have long since learned how to weave the foreground events of a campaign (speeches, debates, elections) together with the daily mass of background talk and memoranda to generate White-like narratives on a daily basis. This form of storytelling, however, is a source of the irresistibility that afflicts campaign journalism.

What is it that cannot be resisted? Call it "Topic A." At any moment during the campaign, one topic dominates the subculture buzz: the David Duke phenomenon, Mario Cuomo's indecision, the president's bout of stomach flu in Japan, the Clintons' marriage, Patrick Buchanan's surprise showing in the primaries. Topic A is often symbolized by a segment of videotape on which a "defining moment" has been recorded. Whenever the topic comes up thereafter, images and dialogue from the videotape will spring to mind.

Ah, but what meanings will be associated with the defining moment? For the few days a story topic is Topic A, elite members of the subculture rush to shape its most widely accepted connotation. To many people inside the subculture, the identity of the next president seems to hinge on the battles for authority that each Topic A sets off and that each defining moment seems to resolve. There lies the devil's lure. Most journalists do not want to be manipulated; most politicians want to (and do) stake out serious positions on issues; and most academics want to compose scholarly accounts of the election. But each party to the vicious cycle gets yanked along the wayward story line that the string of Topic As constructs. Wherever coverage continues, there all eyes and ears are drawn.

The "vicious cycle" and "defining moment" are recent examples of storytelling conventions that have emerged from this subcultural vortex—alas, with consequences that are not always helpful to the public's understanding. Such conventions enable junkies to quickly encode the latest Topic A into a readable account of presidential campaigns.

Sometimes reliance on these conventions—and I shall examine four of them: the "road," "momentum," the "professionals," and "tests of character"—makes for apt descriptions of what is going on in presidential campaigns. Too often, however, an almost unconscious reliance on these stock formulas causes the subculture to miss the real story. And what we get instead, as *The Simpsons* joke suggests, too often resembles a shaggy dog story.

"THE ROAD"

TV reporters who cover the day-to-day workings of government can do stand-ups in front of the Capitol or the State Department, but those who cover campaigns have a problem: their story may take them to many places and settings. To make sense of all this, they collectively draw a chronological line through all of the moves of the top candidates and call it the "road to the White House." This enables them to tell a story of a journey with a clear destination.

On the campaign road the race is run, the motorcade passes through, the bandwagon rolls, and the press bus follows. This is where losers come back after a period in the wilderness (Nixon '68), and unknowns come from out of nowhere (Carter '76). Democratic candidates travel the road low to high, carrying the historically marginal groups they personify (e.g., Irish Catholics, Southerners, women, Greek immigrants) into the capital city of national respectability. Republicans head down to Washington alone, reluctantly, on leave from the private sector, to right a capital sunk in corruption and mismanagement. The road warriors of both parties are outsiders with new ideas who lead grass-roots movements against entrenched interest groups. It is a simple matter to drop each of this year's contenders into one of these categories; indeed, many have tried to shape their image to fill a particular role.

Journalists hope for a close race to sustain audience interest, and their reports can subtly influence perceptions. In 1979 political scientist C. Anthony Broh noted several ways that reporters stoke the feeling of suspense. They highlight "quotes" from representatives of undecided segments of the populace, adjust the length of the time period in which "recent" results are displayed (to emphasize the narrowing gap between candidates), and provide technical information about the range of error in opinion polls to intimate the unpredictability of the impending election.

Long before it became a journalistic convention, "the road" for Americans was a mythic place where individuals escaped conformity, oppression, and deprivation, where the romance or friendship of a lifetime might be forged, and where pilgrims searched for a higher ground. But the reality of contemporary politics makes it difficult to maintain such a convention. Campaign information from one stop on the road is instantaneously dispatched through an electronic grid to every other potential stop. Primaries and caucuses that occur simultaneously in states—notably "Super Tuesday"—also fracture the sense of a journey. And the political nominating convention, that crucial way station on roads past, now seems as superfluous an institution as the Electoral College. The outcome has already been networked.

In order to reconstruct the road, the campaign story has been stretched back to the weeks and months prior to the first official events, the Iowa caucus and the New Hampshire primary. This change, in conjunction with the rise of primaries as the preferred method of delegate selection (from 17 Democratic and 16 Republican primaries in 1968 to 37 and 39, respectively, in 1992), has led to a "front-loading" of the campaign process.

Front-loading has stirred concern that the news media (and the citizens of Iowa and New Hampshire) exercise undue influence over the nomination process and the election. (To Broh's list of suspense-building techniques, for example, may now be added the quite familiar phenomenon of journalistic swarming around an early front-runner to expose his debilities and perhaps bring about a fall.) Thanks to the long buildup, Chapter One—or even the Preface—of the official Campaign Story sometimes delivers the climax.

More generally, front-loading has detracted from the campaign's inherent interest and truncated political debate. The greater story potential of the early stages of the race helps explain why William C. Adams of George Washington University found that Iowa and New Hampshire provided the setting for 32 percent of the coverage that ABC, CBS, NBC, and the *New York Times* devoted to the first six months of the 1984 presidential campaign. In another study, Syracuse University's Thomas Patterson found that voter interest peaked early in 1976 despite dramatic developments during the conventions and fall debates: the hard-fought contest for the GOP nomination and the close race between Gerald Ford and Jimmy Carter. There is no reason to doubt that these findings have been duplicated in the years since.

The Democratic party had attempted to avoid an early wrap-up of its 1992 nomination. It mandated proportional, congressional district-by-district selection of delegates rather than winner-take-all primaries and increasing the percentage of appointed "superdelegates," who would presumably not commit to a candidate until late in the primary season. Even if this stratagem delayed the emergence of a victor, even if the convention proved exciting (to say nothing of what happened in the GOP race), much of the story of the campaign would be resolved too soon. This is because, apart from the potential for a quick resolution of the main conflict, the first sections of the road have most of the fascinating bumps and turns. Early in the campaign the candidates are new faces, with untold biographies and undiscovered characteristics. Interest-group and voter allegiances are up for grabs. The possibility of victories by ideologically "pure" candidates is greater. There are more shifts in candidates' positions. And there is a real score to update each week (the delegate count), not just media-made opinion poll standings.

In the general election, a tight race is one of the few major story attractions campaign coverage can offer. But the excitement is muted by the fact that the two major party nominees seem by then to be few voters' first choice—a sentiment that spreads whenever "also-rans" or "never-rans" (such as Mario Cuomo) make great speeches at the conventions. And since media scrutiny of the finalists has been going on for months, there is little left to learn about them except how they interact in each other's presence. That inflates the significance of the presidential debates.

The problems with the "road" convention, then, are that it goes "downhill" too early and that it has few stopping places that seem to matter any longer. This makes for misshapen stories. Not least, it often leads to citizen disaffection.

THE FAIRY DUST OF "MOMENTUM"

In campaign coverage, interpretation ("This is what I think just happened"), explanation ("This is why"), and speculation ("This is what I think will happen next") usually blur together into road-race commentary. "Momentum" has become the byword of choice for the commentators. It can be divined from poll results, debate performances, crowd size, Federal Election Commission reports on fundraising, and virtually any news event that catches a commentator's eye (including, of course, the incidents that touch off and define a Topic A). But the beauty of the concept of "momentum" is that it need not be tied to anything whatsoever. Momentum may be conferred upon a candidate on a hunch—and simply saying that a candidate has momentum sometimes is enough to make it so.

Since 1976, when Jimmy Carter benefited from the momentum of the Iowa caucus results and the exclamations of commentators over his victory, candidates and their teams have been poised to interpret, in the most self-serving way, the momentum-ability of upcoming campaign occurrences. The politicians' entry into this expectations game provides commentators with yet another category of interpretable events: "momentum" may be awarded to a candidate on the basis of his persuasive publicity. In the world of narrative, every announced shift of momentum whets reader interest whether it correctly foreshadows the action or not. Thus there is a perennial incentive to say the magic word.

Even when "momentum" accurately refers to a campaign that is gathering (or losing) strength, it is a poor explanatory term. It leaves out too many crucial determinants of electoral results. Off-road events—diplomatic breakthroughs, economic upswings, and other "surprises"—may have more impact. Some of these off-road events do get reported in other sections of the newscast or paper, but even the sharpest observers tend to slight electoral forces that change too slowly to qualify as news under any category, such as the simple partisan predisposition to vote as one has in the past. And while Theodore H. White thought enough of demographic changes to devote a chapter or two of his campaign chronicles to the latest findings of the U.S. Census Bureau, few of his literary progeny maintain that tradition.

THOSE CUNNING "PROFESSIONALS"

The constant invocation of the momentum cliché makes voting appear more volatile and random than most retrospective studies reveal it to be. This, in turn, enhances the mystique surrounding campaign consultants. Continuing coverage endows those who advise winners with shamanistic, momentum-creating powers.

Many stories improve with bad guys on the scene. Campaign stories have few prospects for the role. That leaves campaign advisers, especially paid consultants. These "professionals" are portrayed as shadowy figures, often evil geniuses, who rely on their expertise in campaign law, finance, organizing, and communications technology to make money off the democratic process. Some professionals have become celebrity Svengalis (Roger Ailes, Pat Caddell), lending their candidates credible deniability for dirty politics. In 1988, James Baker and John Sasso appeared on a *Time* cover proclaiming the election a "Battle of the Handlers." The star of 1992 was James Carville, Bill Clinton's adviser. No doubt some consultants resent the stereotyping. Others relish it, on the assumption that, for client-building purposes, negative publicity is better than no publicity at all.

Campaign professionals, like the "pols" and "bosses" of yesteryear, are conventionally portrayed as meeting in secret. Huddled behind one-way mirrors and airplane curtains, they map out how they can run interference between the press and their candidate, control the flow of information, and thereby hoodwink the electorate. In a front-page Sunday story after the 1988 election, for example, David Hoffman and Ann Devroy of the *Washington Post* attributed George Bush's victory to "an immensely complex, largely hidden machine" maintained by an army of supporters. The lead sentence implied that electoral triumphs are properly won through "a crusade of ideas." but the only idea advanced by the Bush campaign was "to leave nothing to chance":

Almost everything that could be controlled, influenced, or bargained in favor of Bush was attempted. For example, when he was being photographed outside his home in Kennebunkport, Maine, for the covers of news magazines just before the Republican convention, his aides insisted that photographers aim their lenses above the horizon, and not capture the craggy rocks of the shoreline. Rocks, the photographers were told, would be "elitist." Nearly all the photographers obeyed the rule—no rocks.

In this passage the identities of the consultants were obscured by the passive voice and collective nouns. Vagueness fosters the illusion that professionals have more power than they do. It also cloaks the reality that the consultants are often the primary sources for the very articles that castigate them. Hoffman and Devroy convincingly described the hiddenness and thoroughness of the Bush campaign's stagecraft. But how crucial was it to his election?

The professionals' techniques also come in for narrative mystification and criticism. The black magic roster is now familiar: Spin control. Focus groups. Photo opportunities. Sound bites. Attack ads. Exit polls. Tracking polls. PACs. Such innovations *are* news. Like most instruments, they have been used to confuse, distort, and lie. Even when used honestly, they can make citizens (and candidates) feel like meat. But the usual condemnation of professionalized politics rests on several fallacies. First, campaign stories sometimes imply that if the consultants who vend their mastery of these techniques were replaced by party officials, or regulated by nonpartisan boards, the techniques would be used strictly for good. Second, news stories imply that if the techniques disappeared altogether, candidates and constituents would engage in Platonic dialogues. A third notion, echoing the sentiment distilled into fiction by Edwin O'Connor in his novel *The Last Hurrah* (1956), holds up the previous era of campaigning as a more humane brand of trickery. A fourth fallacy confuses pithiness and effectiveness with evasiveness—as if "Read my lips: No new taxes" belongs in the gutter with the Willie Horton television spot. Finally, many of the same "sinister" techniques the professionals are said to foist upon press and public—such as the sound bite and the focus group—are used by the news media as a matter of course in their own productions.

TESTS OF "LEADERSHIP"

The media employ many gauges of campaign strength: endorsements, facility with travel logistics, matching funds won, cleverness at "spin control," poll numbers. Of these, the indicator with the greatest narrative appeal is the performance of the candidate in a well-publicized—and often well-advertised—

stressful situation: the character test. Those who pass such tests are often said to have demonstrated "leadership."

The rise of the character test is in part a response to the role of consultants, the idea being that character cannot be contrived. The character test also has narrative advantages. Literary theorists teach that the ideal road hero (Ulysses) is a goal-directed person who nevertheless remains open to change and growth. But presidential character testing makes good political as well as literary sense. After all, character does matter. And while party leaders once monopolized the power to screen presidential aspirants, today, the press presides.

At any time in the process, of course, a campaign crisis may pose a character test. Before and during the primaries, however, the conventional test is for candidate "weight," or simple viability as a campaigner on a national level. At the conventions, the criteria shift to how well the nominee controls the show and to the quality of his vice-presidential selection. In the general campaign, stamina moves to the story fore (the road is now the long and winding road), along with broadening of appeal (including the ability to attract the best people from the campaigns of vanquished primary opponents) and a comparative advantage over the other nominee. Whenever feasible, the press fits character-testing information into the sequence found in a thousand American success stories: "early failure," "learning the lesson," "gathering resolve," "better preparation," and "eventual triumph." In *Newsweek*'s special edition on the 1988 campaign, both Michael Dukakis and George Bush gritted their teeth and grew tougher in order to defeat Richard Gephardt and Robert Dole, respectively. Then Dukakis turned moody (as he had in the past, always a bad sign) and lost his 17-point lead over Bush.

Televised presidential debates loom large as character tests because they are the only occasions on which candidates do battle directly. The "big game" treatment given to the fall debates has overwhelmed some nominees. One can understand why Jimmy Carter and Gerald Ford did not move a millimeter for 27 minutes when the power went out in one of their 1976 debates. By contrast, a seasoned Ronald Reagan used the test of his second debate with Walter Mondale in 1984 to recover from his poor performance in the first.

Until 1972, most tests of character hinged on political skills, that is, on the candidate's ability to form and maintain a majority coalition. But the Eagleton affair of that year marks the point when the private side of (vice-) presidential character became legitimate story material. Since then, it has increasingly seemed that testing for how well the candidate keeps together his stable of supporting groups matters less than how well he or she keeps the self together against the onslaught of press exposés and national chatter. Bill Clinton won almost as many plaudits for keeping a smile on his face during his early travails as he did for keeping voters on his side.

The cruelty such personal tests can entail, especially toward a candidate's family, has produced a backlash against the media, which it has acknowledged through self-coverage and, at times, a moderation of tone. But campaign narrators have shown no signs of pulling away from developments of this ilk. Who can resist a scandal? (Scandals, it should be pointed out, sometimes allow the nation to work out important conflicts over values, such as the fundamentalist and feminist challenges to the Establishment code of conduct.) Excess and tawdriness are not the worst consequences of such "feeding frenzies." The larger civic defect lies in the failure of the media to get beyond Topic A.

There is nothing wrong with the basic news conception of the presidential campaign as a nationwide search for leadership. While it cuts corners somewhat to explain campaign events through stories in which the winning team prevails because leadership suddenly emerged in an incident along a road, attracting followers and creating momentum for the next incident, such tales do serve as adequate summaries of and introductions to political history. The big problem is that continuing coverage induces queasiness. Too much of it no longer rests on a foundation of observational reporting. It now takes skilled effort for a reader or viewer to find authentic political journalism about a campaign. Many are employed by the news media to monitor the campaign, but few record what they see and hear of it.

On October 16, 1988, the *New York Times* carried a piece by Andrew Rosenthal entitled "After Third TV Debate, Networks' Policy Shifts." This article announced the television networks' decision to declare George Bush the winner in his third debate with Michael Dukakis, even though they had not picked a winner in the previous two. Rosenthal quoted network personalities who, along with one professor, commented on their own previously televised commentary. He also brought in the results of an ABC poll conducted instantly after the debate. There was not a single reference to anything said in, or about, the debate itself.

This is a shame, and members of the subculture do not even fully understand why. A campaign event may constitute a defining moment. It may involve an eventual winner. But it is, regardless, a living instance of the precious American commitment to democratic governance. The presidential campaign consists, at bottom, of forums in which powerful people must ask for things from less powerful people. When such solicitations occur (and when they do not), that is campaign news. Unfortunately, the political subculture's preoccupations have drawn journalists away from the literal commemoration of such campaign discussions. The emphasis is on sampling the legitimate crosstalk as quickly as possible so that it can be converted into fodder for "Crosstalk" and other insider forums.

Reformers' various efforts to promote campaign discourse have been largely self-defeating. After 1988 the *Washington Post's* David Broder and others called

for more newspaper analyses of campaign ads. This has been widely imple-
mented. Yet these "truth squad" boxes are twice removed from political reality.
Journalists wind up analyzing the campaigns by watching television. ABC's
"Town Meeting" shows, perhaps the best of several pseudo-discourse formats
intended to raise the level of debate, tend to sink into speechmaking because of
a surfeit of name-brand guests on stage with Ted Koppel. To the degree that covering talk among the people has become fashionable, the people have been squir-
reled away in focus groups or reached through pollsters' phone banks and asked
to talk about, not with, the politicians.

The irony of American campaign coverage today is that the solution to the
problem is so simple. Campaign journalism ought to describe what politicians
and people say to each other, and how they look as they talk. (Reporters should
also chronicle discussions between voters and the candidates' surrogates—it
would have been useful, for example, to have more records of John Sununu's
appearances in New Hampshire on behalf of George Bush in 1988.) Perhaps
coverage of such encounters seems superfluous to the media. Candidates already
make efforts to speak to the people clearly, directly, and as often as possible. But
covering these exchanges is also difficult. While less translation is necessary,
much campaign conversation needs to be edited out, and the remaining dialogue
often requires expository context. Exposition, in turn, often necessitates investigation. (Reporters who accept the duty to check the veracity of candidate claims
can never get enough praise.) In short, good campaign journalism may be as simple to describe as it is hard to produce.

Talking with citizens is the best kind of campaign activity that journalists can
encourage candidates to do. For no one talks *with* a president. The campaign is
the last best chance to talk with the individuals who become president.
Americans do not need to elect a great president every time out; they have
learned to cope with mediocrity. But year in and year out they need to sense that
they can tell the two apart. The narrative conventions of campaign journalism
have dulled this sense.

FURTHER READING
NEWS AND POLITICS

"News and truth are not the same things, and must be clearly distinguished." So, in 1922, wrote Walter Lippmann in *Public Opinion* (4th ed., Macmillan, 1965). "The press is no substitute for [other] institutions. . . . Men cannot do the work of the world by this light alone. They cannot govern society by episodes, incidents, and eruptions." Such lofty talk was long in coming to American journalism. Only a half-century after the founding of the United States did the newspaper come into its own. Jacksonian democracy, with its egalitarian politics and free-market philosophy, not only encouraged entrepreneurs to start newspapers, but also helped create the middle-class audience with the necessary time and money.

Pioneering newspapers, such as the *New York Sun,* covered not just commerce and politics, but the "activities of an increasingly varied, urban, and middle-class society," writes Michael Schudson in *Discovering the News: A Social History of American Newspapers* (Basic Books, 1978). Still, in 1830, Schudson estimates, the combined circulation of all daily newspapers in the United States was but 78,000. Within ten years, however, the total had shot up to about 300,000. *The Sun Shines for All: Journalism and Ideology in the Life of Charles A. Dana* by Janet E. Steele (Syracuse University Press, 1993) offers the complete history of the *Sun,* a great innovator in the nineteenth century, and a great failure in the twentieth.

In the years after the Civil War a muckraking, manic depressive Hungarian immigrant named Joseph Pulitzer further expanded the newspaper audience. Biographer W. A. Swanberg, in *Pulitzer* (Scribner's, 1967), tells how he wedded reform to sensationalism and developed the newspaper crusade as a way of hooking America's giant new working-class immigrant population on the daily newspaper habit.

Pulitzer was topped by William Randolph Hearst. Expelled from Harvard in his junior year, Hearst went to work at Pulitzer's *New York World,* and that experience for a rich boy looking for direction served as an apprenticeship to "yellow journalism." In 1885 Hearst took over the *San Francisco Examiner,* bought by his father with the riches from the Comstock Lode. Swanberg writes in *Citizen Hearst* (2d ed., Bantam, 1963) that, like Pulitzer, the flamboyant outsider Hearst was excruciatingly shy in person but explosive in print. Hearst took a lower road to journalistic success, following a "crime and underwear" recipe. He sent his reporters to hunt grizzly bears, or to fall overboard from ferry boats, or to escort Sarah Bernhardt to a San Francisco opium den.

By 1923, two young men fresh out of Yale, Henry R. Luce and Britton Hadden, decided that daily news was so abundant in urban America that busy people needed it organized, condensed, and (because the dry facts did not suffice) interpreted. Thus was born a new genre of journalism, the newsmagazine. With Hadden and Luce's *Time* came a style notable for its Homeric epithets ("bumper-jawed," "long-whiskered") and odd linguistic shrinkages ("in time's nick"). Former *Time* editor Robert Elson tells the story in the company-sponsored *Time, Inc.: The Intimate History of a Publishing Enterprise, 1923–1941* (Atheneum, 1968). Outsiders have a less sanguine view of the publishing giant. W. A. Swanberg's *Luce and His Empire* (Scribner's, 1972) shows how Luce used his considerable power to advance a cold war agenda. The publisher had moved far beyond useful summaries of the news in trying to fashion the "correct" foreign policy for the United States.

Luce died in 1967, but his successors continued into television, giving Home Box Office to the world in the 1970s. They were not so successful, however, in tying a magazine to their new world of cable TV, as recounted in *The Fanciest Dive: What Happened When the Media Empire of TIME/LIFE Leaped without Looking into the Age of High-Tech* (New American Library, 1986) by Christopher M. Byron. How could a corporation with the tradition of Time, Inc., have lost hundreds of millions of dollars starting a *TV Guide* rival? Byron offers a sad tale of a journalistic institution gone sour.

That Luce's empire would be swallowed into a Hollywood studio would have been unthinkable in his lifetime, but in 1990 the Warner Bros. Hollywood colossus took over Time, Inc.—despite the Time-centric title of the new company— and created the most diversified, largest media company in the world. *Time* magazine became a bit player, as Richard M. Clurman laments in his *To the End of Time: The Seduction and Conquest of a Media Empire* (Simon & Schuster, 1992). Clurman, long a *Time* staffer, has become a very, very bitter person.

Others besides Luce and company began to learn how to use the media for their own purposes by the mid–twentieth century. Harried reporters, trying to fill a daily "news hole," were susceptible to calculated manipulation, systematic leaks, and controlled press conferences. No sadder case can be found than the rise of Senator Joseph McCarthy (R-Wisc.), as chronicled by Edwin R. Bayley in his *Joe McCarthy and the Press* (University of Wisconsin Press, 1981). Leaking to newspapers made McCarthy somewhat of a national hero in the early 1950s, but, Bayley argues, it was McCarthy's inability to use the new medium of television that did him in. In 1954 the televised Army-McCarthy hearings (on the ABC and DuMont networks) brought the ugliness of the senator's attacks directly into America's living rooms, and led to McCarthy's censure by his Senate colleagues.

The study of the press means to most people the study of great men and women, yet such a narrow focus on personality has limits. Too often the exploits and flamboyance of the mogul inspires only book-length biographies; some controversial figures, such as Rupert Murdoch, are treated over and over again. Thomas Kiernan's *Citizen Murdoch* (Dodd, Mead, 1986) best tells the tale of Murdoch's remarkable life; William Shawcross's *Murdoch* (Simon & Schuster, 1992) is more typical, fawning, and admiring.

No newspaper mogul has attracted more attention, in no small measure due to the rarity of female owners, than Katharine Graham of the *Washington Post.* The official version of the growth of the U.S. capital's leading newspaper during the latter half of the twentieth century is Chalmers R. Roberts's *The Washington Post: The First Hundred Years* (Houghton Mifflin, 1977). Roberts argues that the *Post* rose to dominance because of its reporting about presidents and Washington power, cresting with the 1970s Watergate scandal. Katharine Graham has her detractors, too, who claim that the reputation of the *Post* is undeserved and overblown. Deborah Davis's *Katharine the Great* (Sheridan Square, 1991) is unrelentingly negative, while Carol Felsenthal's *Power, Privilege and the Post: The Katharine Graham Story* (Putnam, 1993) brings the story up-to-date as Katharine Graham begins to turn her creation over to son Donald.

Newspapers, properly managed, have made their owners very rich. Richard H. Meeker's *Newspaperman: S. I. Newhouse and the Business of News* (Ticknor & Fields, 1983) offers a rare look inside one of the largest but least-known newspaper chains. The founder of this press empire, S. I. Newhouse (1895–1979), successfully sought to preserve his privacy by not listing on the New York Stock Exchange. Meeker, skillfully using the tools of an investigative journalist, tells us much about how Newhouse, and later his two sons, bought and sold media properties and in the process penetrated the daily lives of millions of Americans. The Newhouses care little about the big issues of the day, but seek monopolies of their local markets and so become leading agents for local advertising. Father and sons spent more time on newspaper distribution than on developing an enterprise skilled at exposing a Watergate, "travelgate," or Iran-Contra scandal, however.

But the story of newspapers in America ranges far beyond vivid tales of ruthless entrepreneurs. What is the current state of the newspaper business? *Press and Public: Who Reads What, When, Where, and Why in American Newspapers,* by Leo Bogart (Lawrence Erlbaum Associates, 1990), covers the array of influences that define today's newspaper business. Ellis Cose's *The Press* (Morrow, 1989) seeks to answer the same question by profiling five corporations that account for a quarter of the 60 million newspapers sold each day: the New York Times Company, the Washington Post Corporation, Gannett, Times-Mirror, and Knight-Ridder. This is a book for the uninitiated, though, because unfortunately it contains little new information. Indeed, those who have read Harrison Salisbury's *Without Fear or Favor* (Times Books, 1980), Robert Woodward and Carl Bernstein's *All the President's Men* (Simon & Schuster, 1974), Gay Talese's *The Kingdom and the Power* (World, 1969), and David Halberstam's *The Powers That Be* (Knopf, 1979) will recognize many of the anecdotes that bulk up *The Press.*

Then there are the workers who report and edit the news. David H. Weaver and G. Cleveland Wilhoit's *The American Journalist: A Portrait of U.S. News People and Their Work* (Indiana University Press, 1986) provides a snapshot of these skilled laborers, their education and training, their working conditions, their values and ethics. Weaver and Wilhoit find that, contrary to the prevailing popular view of journalists as elites, the average news reporter or editor is a typical well-educated, middle-of-the-road professional. The history of the profession of the reporter and editor is just beginning to be researched and written. For a series of pioneering essays dip into *News Workers: Toward a History of the Rank and File,* edited by Hanno Hart and Bonnie Brennen (University of Minnesota Press, 1995). Focusing on the period 1850–1930, the contributors tell how unions and training began to define the reporter as a kind of modern-day service worker.

Newspapers began to change in the late twentieth century, faced with a serious new competitor in television, and targeting a transforming society (for example, most customers living in far-flung suburbs). One notable victim has been the afternoon daily newspaper, a rarity as the twentieth century ends. In *Death in the Afternoon* (Andrews, Mcneel & Parker, 1984), Peter Benjaminson describes the demise of such venerable dailies as the *Washington Star,* the *Cleveland Press,* and the *Philadelphia Bulletin,* and concludes that only under very special circumstances (a rare blue-collar town) can an afternoon daily survive the instantaneous access of television and the long commute to and from the suburbs.

The most controversial new newspaper of recent times has been Gannett's *USA Today.* Its creator and first publisher, Al Neuharth, tells his version of its founding in *Confessions of an S.O.B.* (Doubleday, 1989). A self-described conniver and backstabber, Neuharth was one of the most successful executives in the modern newspaper business. Neuharth's rise from impoverished South Dakota farm boy is nothing short of extraordinary. Richard McCord's *The Chain Gang* (University of Missouri Press, 1996) ruthlessly attacks Gannett because its corporate culture treats newspapers as "units" and seeks to squeeze every penny from its monopolies.

Fewer and fewer editorial decisions are made in hometown newsrooms. Increasingly, newspapers depend on copy from outside wire services. Too little has been written about these stalwarts, but three books are extremely helpful. Jonathan Fenby's *International News Services* (Schocken, 1986) lays out the workings of such key wire services as Reuters and the Associated Press. Fenby, a former correspondent for Reuters, provides an exhaustive account of not only how they operate on a daily basis, but also assesses their considerable impact in the creation of a modern newspaper. The history of wire services has its Boswell in Richard A. Schwarzlose. His exhaustive *The Nation's Newsbrokers* (Northwestern University Press, 1989) examines the creation of the wire services; a second volume, subtitled *The Rush to Institution: From 1865 to 1920* (Northwestern University Press, 1990), brings the story into the twentieth century.

Make no mistake: today's newspapers, however comprehensive and balanced, have their detractors. William A. Rusher's *The Coming Battle for the Media: Curbing the Power of the Media Elite* (Morrow, 1988) surveys the news business from a conservative perspective, arguing that the liberals who run the editorial offices around the nation are injecting bias into the news. Surely it is no surprise to learn that many reporters tend to be liberal in their outlooks, but liberal views do not necessarily lead to bias. Rusher does not admit that news reporters should challenge the status quo because it is their job to be skeptical.

More and more scholars are studying the social influence and importance of newspapers in America's history. Louis Liebovich in *The Press and the Origins of the Cold War, 1944–1947* (Greenwood, 1988) focuses on four major news organizations—the *New York Herald Tribune,* the *Chicago Tribune,* the *San Francisco Chronicle,* and *Time* magazine—and describes how they dealt, fairly unsuccessfully, with the major foreign policy issues of the post–World War II era. Covering a slightly earlier period, Betty Houchin Winfield's *FDR and the News Media* (University of Illinois Press, 1990) examines how President Franklin Roosevelt managed relationships with newspapers, magazines, and radio with considerable skill.

Indeed the press coverage of presidents and their decisions has long been a scholarly staple. The last major military conflict involving the United States, as of this writing, was Desert Storm, the war against Iraq in 1991. Within a couple of years a bookshelf of analysis of the coverage by the major media had appeared. Douglas Kellner's critical *The Persian Gulf TV War* (Westview, 1992) and Bradley S. Greenberg and Walter Gantz's *Desert Storm and Mass Media* (Hampton Press, 1993) rank as readable early entries. Wars do not provide the only subjects for case studies. Lee Wilkins, in *Shared Vulnerability: The Media and American Perceptions of the Bhopal Disaster* (Greenwood, 1987), chronicles the media's coverage of the 1984 chemical spill in India. David E. Morrison and Howard Tumber, in *Journalists at War: The Dynamics of News Reporting During the Falklands Conflict* (Sage, 1988), offer an in-depth look at the 1982 confrontation between Argentina and Britain over the Falkland Islands (or Malvinas). Thomas Fensch's *Associated Press Coverage of a Major Disaster: The Crash of Delta Flight 1141* (Lawrence Erlbaum Associates, 1990) is a detailed study of the crash at the Dallas–Fort Worth airport in August 1988. These content analyses seek to understand how journalists might improve their coverage of such conflicts in the future.

The social science that matters the most to the media, at least to practitioners, is economics. With news media profits reaching into the millions, applied analysis tries to lay out the best ways to manage the business of news. Jim Willis, in *Surviving in the Newspaper Business: Newspaper Management in Turbulent Times* (Praeger, 1988), provides a concise overview of who does what in today's newsrooms. *Press Concentration and Monopoly: New Perspectives on Newspaper Ownership and Operation* (Ablex, 1988), edited by Robert C. Picard, is a first-rate study of the contemporary economics of the newspaper business but offers no definitive conclusions. Its strength lies in its vast fund of useful information about the degree of modern media consolidation.

Social science can also remind us of important lessons. For example, Carolyn Martindale's *The White Press and Black America* (Greenwood, 1986) presents a comprehensive study of press coverage of black Americans between 1950 and 1980. This carefully researched analysis of past deficiencies pushes the press and the public alike to be always on guard. Too often press coverage is so blinded by the ethos of the day that we all lose sight of obvious improvements that are needed. *The Black Press, U.S.A.* by Roland E. Wolseley (Iowa State University Press, 1990) is an update of a fine 1971 study and, sadly, is still the only available one-volume study of this important subject.

There is no end of books about the way journalists shape the political process. In *Behind the Front Page: A Candid Look at How News Is Made* (Simon & Schuster, 1987) David S. Broder, the highly respected political reporter of the *Washington Post*, analyzes how political events are processed and reported, based on his considerable experience. Broder is more optimistic than most: examples of poor reporting fill many bookshelves. Lewis W. Wolfson's *The Untapped Power of the Press: Explaining Government to the People* (Greenwood, 1985) presents offensive examples of poor reporting from Washington, D.C., but all could be found in almost any state capital. Mark Hertsgaard's *On Bended Knee: The Press and the Reagan Presidency* (Farrar, Straus & Giroux, 1988) argues that the public-relations teams of President Reagan "reduced the press . . . to virtual accessories to the White House propaganda apparatus." His harsh critique may be overdrawn, but Hertsgaard's evidence is disturbing.

Because more and more news comes from the capital of the United States, the observations of longtime Washington media watcher Stephen Hess are especially useful. In *Washington Reporters* (Brookings Institution Press, 1981), Hess examines the select few who actually cover the federal government. In a subsequent work, *The Government/Press Connection* (Brookings Institution Press, 1984), Hess switches his attention to that small army of government information officers who struggle—usually unsuccessfully—to control the way news is played in the media. His major point is this: there is little that can be kept secret in Washington once someone determines that it is newsworthy. Hess takes on these same issues, for different institutions, in *The Ultimate Insiders: U.S. Senators in the National Media* (Brookings Institution Press, 1986) and *Live from Capitol Hill! Studies of Congress and the Media* (Brookings Institution Press, 1991).

Critics cite all this evidence, and more, to buttress their point that poor news coverage has negative consequences for American democracy. *Going Negative: How Political Advertisements Shrink and Polarize the Electorate* by Stephen Ansolabehere and Shanto Iyengar (Free Press, 1995), the result of six years of investigation by two veteran political scientists, concludes that the conventional wisdom—that it is easier to drive people away from the polls than to convince them to vote for a specific candidate—is indeed true. The media are often the tools used to force eligible voters not to participate.

It was Edith Efron's *The News Twisters* (Nash, 1971) that first focused serious attention on TV's inadequate coverage of presidential candidates and campaigns. Efron argued that all three networks—then ABC, NBC, and CBS—were "strongly biased in favor of the Democratic-liberal-left axis of opinion," and during the 1968 campaign portrayed Hubert Humphrey as a "quasi saint" and Richard M. Nixon as "corruption incarnate." This point has stuck despite careful scholarly rebuttal. For example, after the Nixon-McGovern campaign of 1972, more than a dozen studies of TV's coverage concluded that neither side was favored.

Still, even by then analysis of campaigns had become a scholarly cottage industry. One Republican in Tennessee, upset at the three networks' coverage of the 1968 GOP convention, induced Vanderbilt University to begin regularly taping the network evening news. As a result, researchers now have at their disposal tapes and an index—all now described on a World Wide Web site—to analyze coverage of that aspect of TV news. Studies generated from the Vanderbilt data vary widely in their conclusions, of course. For example, S. Robert Lichter, Daniel Amundson, and Richard Noyes's *The Video Campaign: Network Coverage of the 1988 Primaries* (American Enterprise Institute, 1988) finds fault. *The Media in the 1984 and 1988 Presidential Campaigns* (Greenwood, 1991), edited by Guido H. Stempel III and John W. Windhauser, does not blame TV in general but loathes the development of the sound bite. These nine-second chunks lead the authors to conclude, "Our results leave no doubt that the coverage of issues was minimal. Two-thirds of the stories in newspapers and newsmagazines and on television newscasts dealt with politics and government, candidate strength, and poll results. We believe the lack of coverage of the economy, education, and science largely reflects what candidates did with these issues. They didn't get coverage because the candidates did not address them in significant fashion."

By 1990 the scholars had made their point and the media began to react. By the 1992 campaign season newspapers and CNN regularly were providing reports assessing candidates' claims in their slick TV spots. Still, campaign rhetoric has never been complex or clear; the decline in voter turnout in presidential elections in the United States began a century ago, long before the invention of television. The "debasement" of presidential campaigning, notes historian Gil Troy in *See How They Ran: The Changing Role of the Presidential Candidate* (Free Press, 1992), is an old story. During the nineteenth century, the nation's republican tradition made it seem undignified for presidential candidates to speak on their own behalf. But gradually the democratic demand for "the personal touch" drew candidates to campaign, first from their back porches and later on the hustings. Increasingly, voters were interested not only in the characters and ideas of the candidates but in their personalities and the details of their personal lives. Refreshingly, in *The Reasoning Voter: Communication and Persuasion in Presidential Campaigns* (University of Chicago Press, 1991), political scientist Samuel Popkin argues that Americans are not bamboozled by today's media barrage: "voters know how to read the media."

One solution to his mess is public or civic journalism. This movement of the 1990s builds on a simple idea: newspaper readers are citizens and they should be informed about the issues that impact their lives. The ideas, beliefs, and assumptions of the public journalism movement are well detailed in *Doing Public Journalism* (Guilford, 1995), by Arthur Charity, in which the author builds on case studies of nine newspapers that exemplify the best type of journalism for democracy.

In the end Herbert Gans's *Deciding What's News* (Vintage, 1980) reminds all who study this classic tome that news is about "the economic, political, social, and cultural hierarchies we call nation and society." They are more important than coverage of campaigns or wars. For the most part Gans says we regularly view news reports about those at or near the top of the hierarchies and about those, particularly at the bottom, who threaten them. The bulk of the audience for all forms of news reports on the top and bottom is America's vast middle class. The news business is not something to be taken lightly, but stands at the core of the functioning of modern society.

MOVIES AND MUSIC

DOUGLAS GOMERY

Stars lunch poolside, amid palm trees and exotic bird-of-paradise flowers. It's a typical afternoon: in yellow-and-white-striped cabanas one well-known executive "green lights" a film; an equally famous director reads scripts while sunning himself on one of the two hundred chaise longues. Gossip hounds from around the world, invariably led by *Entertainment Tonight*'s Mary Hart, sniff out hints of the latest breakups and alliances.

Some luxury resort? No, just another day at the Beverly Hills Hotel pool, long the watering spot where movie stars and Hollywood moguls make deals. The hotel management even furnishes poolside secretarial service.

A mile or so down Sunset Boulevard sits the campus of the University of California, Los Angeles (UCLA). Across town is the University of Southern California (USC). Their film schools emerged during the 1970s as the launching pads for success, and thus a seat at the Beverly Hills Hotel pool. Enroll in a script-writing workshop, whisper those in the know, and before long one of the alumni of those two well-placed institutions, perhaps George Lucas (B.A., USC, 1966) or Francis Coppola (M.A., UCLA, 1968), will discover you.

Unfortunately, neither the "by-the-pool" nor at "at-school" method has ever guaranteed a successful career in the American film industry. In 1921 Carl Sandburg, later a Pulitzer Prize–winning biographer of Abraham Lincoln, but then a struggling movie reviewer, correctly recognized Hollywood for what it was and still is: "The production of motion pictures is first of all an industry and only secondly an art."

This is a revised and updated version of "Hollywood's Business," which appeared in *The Wilson Quarterly* in the summer 1986 issue.

Sandburg surely would have agreed that the best way to make it to the top of Hollywood in the 1990s, to have the power to make poolside decisions or hire (and fire) the latest UCLA or USC prospect, would be to follow a much clearer path: go to law or business school, land a job with one of the conglomerates that dominate the movie business, and slowly work your way up.

Successful Hollywood executives preside over an industry whose public profile far exceeds its economic heft. The annual net *profits* of General Motors are regularly greater than the entire domestic box-office revenue of all of America's movie theaters. Including Hollywood's actors, film editors, and the innumerable "assistants to the assistants," as well as the hundreds of ticket takers and projectionists around the country, movie industry workers hardly equal the number of America's PhDs and MDs. So why all the fuss?

Hollywood's aura comes from the high-stakes, high-profile character of the movie business. The difference between expensive flops, such as 1997's *Speed 2: Cruise Control,* and smash hits, such as the same year's *My Best Friend's Wedding,* can mean—in the long run—an extra billion dollars added to (or subtracted from) a company's balance sheet. Blockbusters, from *Jaws* (1975) to *Out of Africa* (1985) to *Jurassic Park* (1993), have left their mark on fashion, fads, behavior, and even public debate. But above all, through one film Hollywood can capture the popular imagination, projecting hopes and fears, fantasies and dreams onto a screen for all to see and share.

Despite some considerable changes in the way Hollywood does business, an industry "insider" from the 1930s would still recognize the names of today's dominant companies: Warner Bros., Disney, Universal Studios, Paramount Pictures. What has changed in recent years has been Hollywood's expanding participation in nearly all phases of mass media production, distribution, and presentation—from movies to television to music to book publishing. All of those famous-name motion picture production companies are now parts of very large, very active corporations. And although many fans may look back to the 1930s and 1940s as the "Golden Age" of the movie business, in fact the closing decades of the twentieth century stand as the era when Hollywood—as a diversified subset of six mighty corporations—achieved its greatest power and profitability.

HOLLYWOOD'S BIG SIX

Six multinational companies formed more than a half-century ago still have hegemony over the creation and distribution of movies throughout the world. Studio executives can make or break the careers of the Demi Moores, Harrison Fords, Francis Coppolas, Jessica Langes, and Eddie Murphys. They can also decide whether to distribute the films of James Cameron, Ridley Scott, or any of Hollywood's legion of aspiring producers, directors, and writers. Without a studio distribution contract, filmmakers and stars find it nearly impossible to raise the $40 million required for the average Hollywood production budget, even if they spend a lifetime by the Beverly Hills Hotel pool. (Distribution and advertising costs add at least another 50 percent to the average feature film's costs.)

The continuing need to borrow millions and regularly produce box-office hits guarantees that Hollywood studios are not (nor ever will be) run by "wild and crazy guys." Executives have worked their way up the chain of command because they know how to play it safe, how—when all others things are equal—to "green light" another *Batman* sequel rather than some quirky, independent, but risky project, however meaningful the latter might be as a statement about the fate of humankind. Orson Welles, the brilliant director of what may still be the best film ever made in Hollywood, *Citizen Kane* (1941), never directed another major release after *Touch of Evil* (1957) because the studio chiefs viewed him, as his biographer Joseph McBride put it, as a "wastrel, a rebel, a continuing challenge to the Hollywood system."

The Hollywood majors are a rugged corporate lot, having survived repeated challenges over the past 50 years: the breakup of their theater chains, the rise of network television, the advent of cable and "pay" television, the home-video revolution, and, most recently, the advent of satellite TV and its two hundred channels. They show no signs of weakening. If anything they are getting stronger. The Hollywood studios may not be America's biggest companies, but they surely are among the most adaptable and agile of business enterprises.

Today, individual entrepreneurs control three of the six majors—Twentieth Century Fox, Viacom's Paramount Pictures, and Seagram's Universal Studios. There are no powerful people in today's Hollywood than Rupert Murdoch, Sumner Redstone, and Samuel Bronfman, Jr. The reach of these modern movie moguls vastly exceeds anything ever dreamed of by Louis B. Mayer, Darryl F. Zanuck, or Harry Cohn during Hollywood's Golden Age, because they not only own but also operate on a day-to-day basis major Hollywood enterprises.

The Australian-born, Oxford-educated Murdoch, for example, skillfully fashioned a vertically integrated movie-television company when he bought Hollywood's Twentieth Century Fox in 1985 and combined it with his chain of six big-city independent television stations to launch the Fox television network. This means that a Fox-made film such as *Predator* (1987) or *Volcano* (1997) can (and will) be shown not only in theaters around the world, but also by Fox television a year or two later. No monies stray far from Murdoch's bulging coffers.

Sumner Redstone is hardly as famous (or infamous) as Murdoch, but he is just as powerful. His Viacom conglomerate owns Paramount Pictures and the UPN television network. Feature films flow from Paramount's Melrose Avenue studio, from the regular stream of *Star Trek* sequels to 1997's *Breakdown* and *'Til There Was You*. Viacom comprises not only television and film units, but also the largest book publisher in the world, Simon & Schuster. Viacom's cable channels include MTV, Nickelodeon, and Showtime; it also owns a chain of movie theaters and the national Blockbuster video store chain. It is hard to be a consumer of mass media in America and not regularly hand over a dollar or two to at least one of Viacom's billion-dollar divisions.

In 1996 millionaire Samuel Bronfman, Jr., heir to the Seagram's liquor fortune, sought to match the power of Murdoch and Redstone by acquiring for more than $5 billion the fabled Universal Studios. Throughout the 1960s and '70s, there was no greater force in Hollywood than Universal, but when Lew Wasserman looked to retire the company went on the auction block. In 1990 the Japanese electronics giant Matsushita (whose best-known trade name is Panasonic) acquired Universal and tried to merge manufacturing and filmmaking. The effort failed, and the company was glad to sell to Bronfman. As the century ends, Bronfman will seek to take Universal to the heights of *E.T.,* which when it was released in 1981 ranked as the greatest blockbuster in movie history.

Murdoch, Redstone, and Bronfman are proud, rich, and exceptions. Most of the rest of Hollywood is a series of faceless multinational media conglomerates, parts of the largest media corporations in the world. Columbia Pictures is a division of Tokyo-based electronics giant Sony, Warner Bros. is part of Time Warner, and the Disney studio is part of a corporate colossus known throughout the world. Depending on your measure either Time Warner or Disney ranks as the largest media company operating today.

As the 1990s commenced, Sony paid more than $4 billion for Columbia Pictures Entertainment. Through that purchase Sony acquired not only a productive movie and television studio, but also an extensive library of nearly 3,000 movies and 23,000 television episodes. Since its acquisition, however, Sony has been unable to turn this Hollywood studio colossus into a money-making operation; Sony's music label has earned far greater profits. Sony may have turned the corner in 1997—with hits like *Air Force One, Men in Black,* and *My Best Friend's Wedding*—which may stand as the year the company reasserted itself as a major force in Hollywood.

Warner Bros. was a struggling studio in 1969 when outsider Kinney National Services, Inc. (which dealt in parking lots, construction, car rental, and funeral homes), bought it up. Three years later the renewed colossus Warner Communications was born and over the years its founder, Steven J. Ross, expanded it to include significant positions in popular music, book publishing, and cable television. Ross added Time, Inc., in a controversial merger, and upon his unexpected death in 1992 Time Warner controlled the number-one music distributor, the second-largest operator of cable systems in the United States, and the most profitable pay-cable network (HBO), and enjoyed a worldwide presence with cable's Comedy Central and magazines such as *Sports Illustrated.* His successors added Turner Broadcasting and with it CNN, TNT, and a host of other television properties. At the core, however, stands the Warner Bros. studio, with not only a seemingly endless stream of top-grossing films, most notably its *Batman* series, but also TV hits from *Murphy Brown* to *Night Court* to *Dallas.*

Disney challenges Time Warner for the mantle of the world's largest media corporation. Led by Michael Eisner, Disney has taken bold steps to become a full-service media conglomeration. Its heralded 1995 takeover of Capital Cities/ABC climaxed a decade of expansion. In the mid-1980s the formerly clean-cut Disney began making R-rated films for adults through its new subsidiaries Touchstone and Hollywood Pictures as well as its acquiring distributor Miramax. The company also opened new theme parks in Japan and France. The Disney cable channel consistently made money, targeting its youthful audiences and their parents. Disney has gained high ratings with TV's *Home Improvement* and *Ellen.* But best known to the moviegoing public have been the string of Disney animated features, from *The Lion King* to *Hercules.*

In Hollywood parlance these six corporations—Twentieth Century Fox, Viacom's Paramount, Seagram's Universal, Sony's Columbia, Warner, and Disney—are known as the majors. Year in, year out they control almost 80 percent of the movie business in the United States and approximately half the market in Sweden, West Germany, and several other nations in Western Europe, not to mention Asia. Every few years a couple of bold pretenders (Orion Pictures and New World Entertainment in the 1980s) emerge to challenge the majors, and soar into the headlines on the basis of one or two modest hits. But no challenger has survived over the long haul. In contemporary Hollywood, there are dozens of independent producers, but virtually all of them pay one of the six big studios to distribute their films.

FILM DISTRIBUTION AND PRESENTATION: THE SECRETS OF THEIR SUCCESS

The continuing power of the Hollywood majors derives, as it has since the 1920s, from their exclusive ability to distribute their blockbuster films. At considerable expense, they maintain offices across North America (and up to 50 more overseas), where their representatives are in constant contact with the heads of the dominant theater chains, TV networks, and video rental and sales stores.

The studios "hit parade" record at the box office is what impels theater owners, TV station proprietors, and owners of video outlets—all conservative business-people aspiring to maintain double-digit profits from their investments—to consistently rent or buy their movies.

Year in and year out, the Hollywood majors control markets from Sweden to Australia, from West Germany to nearly all the nations of Africa. Hollywood derives roughly one-third to two-fifths of its total box-office revenues from overseas; only in the rare nation does Hollywood not capture more than half the business. Hollywood's regular production of hit films provides a strong incentive for foreigners to consistently deal with the six majors rather than take a flyer with an independent.

The majors and the leading chains of movie theaters around the world engage in a never-ending tug of war. The studios' revenues comes from a percentage of the take at the box office. This percentage is negotiable. To enlarge "profit centers" in which the studios cannot share, theater owners, particularly in the United States and Western Europe, allocate considerable time, space, and effort to hawking popcorn, soft drinks, and candy. One reason: three cents worth of popcorn can be sold for one dollar. A well-run concession stand generates at least one dollar of sales and as much as 75 cents of profit for each and every ticket buyer who enters the theater, and when totaled across the United States adds half a billion dollars more to the coffers of theater owners.

In 1945, during the high tide of moviegoing in America, the majors owned most of the nation's best movie theaters. Their downtown "picture palaces"—the Paramount in New York, the Fox in St. Louis, the Warner in Washington, D.C.—were the showcases for movie entertainment as well as hubs of community nightlife. In their heyday of the 1920s and 1930s, these marble citadels of fantasy and opulence offered the average American some of the best-loved, most exuberantly romantic architecture ever seen in the United States. In the 1920s Marcus Loew, founder of MGM, proclaimed, "We sell tickets to theaters, not movies."

From these Xanadus, with their baroque architectural splendor and acres of seats, came the bulk of any film's revenues, even though smaller neighborhood houses, with less than five hundred seats, outnumbered dream palaces by ten to one. In the mid-1940s, America's movie houses, large and small, sold some 90 million tickets per week.

That all began to change in 1948, when the U.S. Supreme Court forced the majors to sell their theater holdings. They gradually divested themselves during the 1950s—just in the nick of time, as it turned out. As middle-class Americans migrated to the suburbs, downtown movie theaters decayed, shuttered, and over the four decades since have been torn down or converted into centers for the performing arts.

Today 25 regionally based companies control the film exhibition business, led by American Multi-Cinema (AMC) and United Artists Communications, each with more than one thousand screens. (The total number of screens in the United States now tops 25,000.) Many of these new film exhibition giants got their start as operators of drive-ins, the "passion pits" of the 1950s. They prospered not only because they offered a trysting place for older adolescents but because they offered a cheap night out for young parents—put the kids in the backseat, no babysitter needed.

Opening a drive-in required only a fence, some speakers for the cars, and an enormous screen. Best of all, the drive-ins could be built on cheap land at the edge of town. With the migration of the middle class from cities to suburbs during the 1950s, Hollywood's best customers literally moved out to the drive-in, away from the traditional downtown picture palace.

As the suburbs matured and land became more expensive, "hardtop" cinemas enjoyed a comeback, usually in the form of mini-cinemas with a few hundred seats squeezed into a series of plain boxes adjoining or integrated into a shopping center. Gradually, during the 1970s and 1980s, evolved the multiplex, with 10 to 20 screens in one complex. The economics, as *Fortune* magazine noted in 1986, is simple: "A theater with four screens [then the national average] is four times more likely than a one-screen house to book a hit picture." An unexpected blockbuster can be shifted to the largest auditorium in the complex, a dud to a smaller one.

During the mid-1980s the major Hollywood studios went on a buying spree, acquiring theaters before the deregulation-minded Ronald Reagan left the White House. In 1986 the Department of Justice quietly agreed not to press the long-time restrictions against theater purchase by Hollywood embedded in antitrust decrees signed 40 years before. Paramount kicked things off by buying the Trans Lux circuit and the Los Angeles–based Mann theaters. But the bombshell hit when in January 1986 MCA, parent company of giant Universal Studios, acquired a major interest in the second-largest circuit of theaters in North America, Cineplex Odeon. Once again Hollywood's majors were top powers in the theater end of the business.

Indeed despite ever-rising ticket prices, the merger of Universal and Cineplex Odeon has meant generally good news for patrons. Cineplex began to bring back the luxury, diversity, and technical superiority of the movie theater. Seats in Cineplex Odeon theaters are wide and comfortable; the butter on the popcorn is "real"; the sound and image achieve a standard many had long forgotten. In Canada, where it began, Cineplex has long had a policy of commissioning original art works for its theater lobbies as well as offering elaborate drink and dessert menus rather than just the usual popcorn, candy, and soft drinks. Film critics give the company four stars. Jay Scott of the *Toronto Globe and Mail* extolled, "Toronto has a film culture because of Garth Drabinsky['s Cineplex]. For movies he's been wonderful."

The 1980s world of multiplexes, plain and fancy, instituted a new pattern for releasing feature films. Before TV, the studios turned out a new feature each week and opened it at a downtown picture palace. Film fans knew the film would return a month later for a run at a larger neighborhood cinema, then appear on successively lower rungs of the distribution ladder. At each step down, the price of admission dropped.

THE AUDIENCE

The multiplex world focuses on one season of the year: summertime. Regularly the "majors" withhold their hoped-for blockbusters until just before Memorial Day and then launch them in waves throughout June, July, and August, ending on Labor Day weekend. According to *Variety,* the industry's trade newspaper, the summer movie season accounts for more than 40 percent of the domestic box-office take. The Christmas and Easter school vacation periods add another 20 percent. The major studies—and their "independent" divisions, such as Disney's Miramax—save their more risky projects for the fall and spring.

Viewing patterns have also changed. After 1948, television siphoned off part of the film audience, and moviegoers who once went to the movies no matter what became far more selective. "Filmgoing used to be part of the social fabric," Art Murphy, longtime writer at *Variety,* has observed. "Now it's an impulse purchase." After dropping from a peak of 4.5 billion tickets sold per year during the late 1940s, annual admissions in the U.S. leveled off at about 1 billion per year during the 1960s and have remained steady at that number for three decades. The total of monies taken in goes up every year as multiplexes regularly raise their ticket prices—in the $9 range in New York City in 1997.

At the same time, the composition of the moviegoing audience has changed. The new schedule targets today's biggest ticket buyers: teenagers on school vacations. According to the *International Motion Picture Almanac* young people ages 12 to 19 make up 40 percent of the typical movie theater audience. Moreover, as reported by the Opinion Research Corporation for the Motion Picture Association of America, teenagers go out to the movies almost three times as often as their parents.

Where have all the older folks gone? Literally nowhere. Most are staying home, parked in front of their television sets. (Sometimes they cue up for a theatrical feature such as *Driving Miss Daisy* or *The English Patient.*) The "tube" not only offers up soap operas, situation comedies, action-adventure shows, and news, but a surprising number of Hollywood productions. A quick survey of *TV Guide* reveals that about a quarter of the average television broadcast day is devoted to rerunning Hollywood feature films, principally on independent stations. Add cable television's film-heavy menu and the movie time available on television vastly increases.

And there is always a visit to the local video store, where an average Blockbuster retail outlet in a big city will have more than ten thousand titles available. (It only sometimes seems that they are all the *same* title—one you have seen before.) And the largest cities in the United States are sprinkled with specialized video stores, from French-only shops to the predictable X-rated sleaze merchant.

CAUSES AND CONSEQUENCES OF HOLLYWOOD POWER

The six Hollywood majors possess a host of advantages that enable them to maintain their considerable economic power and keep out the competition. One of the most important, cross-subsidization, enables a Hollywood media conglomerate with interests in a number of markets to take profits from a thriving area to prop up another, less financially successful area. Single-line corporations do not have this luxury, and so aspiring Hollywood operations invariably fail. Another, reciprocity, enables Hollywood media conglomerates to choose to whom they will sell and then only deal with those companies that cooperate with other units of the media conglomerate. For example, Viacom's Paramount Pictures might refuse to sell movies to Time Warner's HBO unless Time Warner's cable franchises book Paramount's cable Sci-Fi Channel.

In the end this leads media conglomerates that own the Hollywood studios to integrate vertically by taking over the means of production, distribution, and presentation to the public, the latter in a wider and wider variety of forms. Consider—in the most telling example of the late twentieth century—that all six of the majors "instantly" became the defining producers and distributors in home video even though others came to home video first. Now the Big Six dominate home video almost exclusively.

Indeed, as the twentieth century is ending, the Hollywood majors have for a generation been building up more and more vertical power by spending millions to acquire interests in movie theaters, cable television operations, over-the-air television stations, and even networks. All felt that controlling the markets "downstream" (i.e., distribution and exhibition) was vital for the long-term survival and prosperity of any Hollywood-based operation, whether downstream meant a movie theater, a television station, or a rented videotape. Two economic motivations led the CEOs of the major Hollywood companies to spend millions to secure vertical control.

First, vertical integration enables a company to take full advantage of reductions in costs associated with having to "sell" only to another part of the same company. Time Warner can take a Warner movie and book it into a Warner-owned theater, present it on HBO, show it to the millions of households that subscribe to a Time Warner cable system, and then tender sales through Warner's video arm. This can be coordinated without a fleet of salespeople to drum up business.

More important, however, is the issue of market control. A vertically integrated company need not worry about being shut out of one of those key ancillary markets. Indeed, one of the majors would rather work with a known "rival" than see a new competitor arise. So, despite all their alleged struggle in the merger talks of 1989, Paramount and Time Warner continued to jointly own and operate vast theater circuits that gave both a strong, dependable position in key cities (principally Los Angeles), guaranteeing that their movies would receive the best possible opening in their jointly owned chain. Indeed today's "theatrical window," despite all the talk of the impact of cable television and home video, remains the most important venue to create the blockbusters that can be exploited in other media.

For Hollywood studios the process of creating profits only begins in theaters. "Downstream" profits, in what euphemistically are still called "ancillary" markets ("pay" cable, home video, foreign distribution, and over-the-air television), far overwhelm the monies that flow into ticket booths. The movie house has been reduced to a "voting booth" where fans can elect a hit and then the studios can reap the dollars (and pounds and lira and yen, etc.) from their newest blockbuster. A theatrical blockbuster virtually guarantees millions in additional revenue from the home-video and pay-television arenas. That is why Hollywood works so hard to craft a hit in the theaters, for once a commodity is proven there, the rest of the way is usually smooth sailing.

Even as recently as 20 years ago, movie theaters supplied more than three-fourths of the revenue for an average Hollywood feature film. Today, theaters provide less than one-fourth because of the extraordinary cable TV and home-video markets. In 1980, the Hollywood majors collected about $20 million from worldwide sales of videocassettes. By 1997 the figure was well in excess of $16 billion. In 1980 an average feature film expected to take in precious little from home video; today that "ancillary" revenue contribution usually is the leading contributor to the revenue stream.

Home video leads the parade of revenue sources, but hardly stands alone in Hollywood's pantheon of ancillary markets. HBO and its cousins continue to rake in millions in the "mature" pay-cable market, both for feature films and made-for-cable-TV movies. The final runs for feature films and Hollywood-made TV shows come with presentation on basic cable and reruns by an over-the-air television channel. It usually takes a couple of years for important feature films to make their way to independent television (less for box-office failures), but once released into syndication, the feature films are repeated to faithful audiences on independent TV stations or cable channels like American Movie Classics. (Reruns of hit TV series work the same way, and make up with old films the libraries that Wall Street values in the billions of dollars when studios are sold.)

A BRIGHT FUTURE

Since the mid-1950s, television has played an indispensable role in Hollywood money making. By the end of that decade, all the major studios had plunged into the production of TV series. In the mid-1980s Universal's television division, the studio's principal profit center, boasted such hits as *Miami Vice* and *Murder, She Wrote*. During the late 1950s the presentation of old Hollywood favorites first whetted the public's appetite. Now we expect "Night at the Movies" every evening of the week, usually in the form of a studio made-for-TV film.

It is fashionable to dismiss TV movies as low-budget dramas inspired by the "disease of the week," but truth is, the public will flock to a miniseries like *Hollywood Wives* or *The Thorn Birds*. Since their turnaround time (from production to presentation) is so short, made-for-TV films can deal with topical issues, and even in some cases provoke discussion of important ideas, as with *The Day After* and *The Burning Bed*.

All of these changes, from cable to pay television, from the multiplex to the VCR, add up to one clear trend: more and more people are going to be watching more and more movies. And to filmdom's "majors," that is nothing but good news, for they will still be financing, producing, and distributing most of what people watch.

In Hollywood, the past exists only on film and in memory, and many of the film colony's older folk wax nostalgic about the Golden Age. The parties seemed grander, the celebrities more glamorous, the studios more efficient. But if we keep our eyes on the facts, the historical evidence reminds us how little the business of Hollywood has changed during the past 60 years. Hollywood's majors remain steadfastly in charge.

And they will continue to. Nothing looms on the horizon that might change that vise-like grip. Indeed, the takeovers of Columbia by Sony, MCA by Seagram, and Paramount by Viacom only point out that it is far easier to buy into the Hollywood oligopoly than to form a new company.

Many who find fault with Hollywood's excess power look to the coming of some new technology to alter Hollywood's long-held economic power. One new technology that many argue will make us stay home and never venture out to the movies again is high-definition television (HDTV)—provided in a digital form. Presumably its superior, wide-screen, cleaner video image will finally allow new entrants into the elite Hollywood oligopoly.

This is wishful thinking. HDTV, however digital, offers no real substitute for a feature film shown on a movie screen. The quality of the motion picture image, for example, has not "stood still." Chemical celluloid images provide more information per square inch than the best HDTV can offer. More important, during the 1980s we learned that image quality does not matter so much. If it did, why did the technically superior Beta format for home video fail so badly in market competition with the inferior images of VHS? Fans seek out their favorites for many reasons, not simply to experience the most technologically advanced image reproduction.

Nothing looms on the horizon that will threaten the oligopolistic power of the major studios. The Hollywood majors will continue to enjoy the fruits of their formidable economic power. Their influence will keep spreading throughout the world, more powerfully than any other mass medium. The Hollywood oligopoly has learned to thrive in the age of advanced technologies, based on skilled use of media economics.

THE MOVIES AND TV: A REVISIONIST HISTORY

DOUGLAS GOMERY

There are two images from my youth that I shall never be able to shake. There was that clear Saturday afternoon in October when I rode my bicycle downtown to see a show at the Rialto, only to look up at the marquee and see the chilling announcement, "20 lanes of bowling." No movie I have ever seen has jolted me more.

The thousands of hours I spent in the wondrous Rialto Theatre of Allentown, Pennsylvania, formed the core of my adolescent education. I learned "lessons" in proper teen rebellion from the experts: James Dean, Sal Mineo, and Natalie Wood in *Rebel Without a Cause* (1955). From the master, Alfred Hitchcock, I learned the true nature of panic in *Rear Window* (1954). How could my beloved baroque movie palace become just another bowling barn, of which Allentown already had more than a dozen?

The second jolt came a few years later, in the summer of 1960, when I spied spread across a page of *Life* a photograph of a crumbled Roxy Theatre, with silent film star Gloria Swanson standing amid the ruins. My mother had taken me to that mecca of movie palaces as a special treat during infrequent trips to New York City. Now even that five-thousand-seat, gilded, festooned "wonder theater" at the corner of 51st Street and Sixth Avenue had been torn down. None of it seemed to make sense. Or did it?

Even in isolated Allentown I could stare across the living room and guess the answer. During the 1950s television hit the United States with a force unmatched by any other technical innovation of this century. When my family

Reprinted with revisions from "Who Killed Hollywood?" which appeared in the summer 1991 issue of *The Wilson Quarterly*.

moved to Allentown in 1950, few of my friends had a set. I would race over to Dave Gearhart's house to watch; his father was a doctor and rich enough to pay the $500 a new set cost—about $2,000 in today's inflated dollars. A decade later, when my teachers forced me to watch the Nixon-Kennedy presidential debates (the very year that the Roxy was torn down), everybody had a TV set.

If the death of the glamorous Hollywood these palaces represented is viewed as a kind of film noir murder mystery, the identity of the killer seems all to obvious. Scholars have tended to agree: TV killed Hollywood. After all, the "murder" happened right before their eyes, as it did before mine. And TV already had a criminal record, having helped undermine the habit of reading and the academic vigor of America's children. In his encyclopedic *Movies and Society* (1970), I. C. Jarvie of Canada's York University writes, "Until the advent of television in the late forties Hollywood was peerless. Then television began to eat into film audiences, cinemas began to close in America, and the production figures fell seriously." This is one of the great dividing lines in film history. Before TV we had Hollywood's Golden Age; after TV, a Tarnished Age.

Moviegoing in America reached a statistical peak in 1946: attendance at America's 20,000 movie houses roughly equaled the total national population, 79.4 million. Seventeen years later, attendance had been cut in half, and then cut in half again—all while the population was growing to historical highs.

Going to the picture show ceased to be a regular habit. Cinema buffs attended only recommended films, after pondering a number of serious reviews. Otherwise, it took a blockbuster on the order of a *Godfather* (1972) or *M*A*S*H* (1970) to lure the average couch potato to a theater. In its heyday Hollywood released nearly 500 features annually, plus 1,000 short subjects and newsreels. As the 1960s turned into the 1970s, the American movie industry was lucky to turn out two hundred features in a year. The average studio went from producing a new feature each week to one each month by 1970. The age of Hollywood movie factories masterminded by legendary moguls like Nicholas M. Schenck gave way to an era of blockbusters "packaged" by fast-talking agents. A part of American mass culture has been lost forever.

The movies as kitsch had been transformed into cinema as art. Directors became "filmmakers," with framed graduate degrees in film from places like UCLA and NYU hanging on their office walls. It became possible to major in film studies at Harvard and the University of Michigan. The *New York Times* treated film as a meaningful form of art. And commentators seeking to gauge the national mood could be counted on to take some bearings from the relative popularity of Rambo and Jane Fonda.

Could all of this change have been caused by the coming of television? Could the Rialto and the Roxy have disappeared for some other reason?

Apart from simple observation, the "blame TV" argument rests on a straightforward principle of microeconomics known as the substitution effect. If we use a good or service for a certain purpose and a cheaper substitute comes along, we ought to abandon the former and adopt the latter. No one ever considered the flickering black-and-white images on television a perfect substitute for a movie show, but even as a child I could appreciate that no one charged you admission to see *The Many Loves of Dobie Gillis* or *The Untouchables*.

But in applying any theory—economic or not—one must square the logic with the facts. And the basic figures for movie attendance do not square with the "blame TV" explanation. Simply put, attendance at America's movie houses began to drop in 1946 and slid most steeply in the late 1940s, long before most American families even had a set. Indeed, before 1950 only a tiny minority of U.S. citizens had even laid eyes on a television. By 1950, there were still only one million TV sets in use in the country, most of them in the Northeast. New Yorkers and Chicagoans had TV, but to their cousins in Wichita and Green Bay it was as exotic as a skyscraper or subway.

The technology was ready, but because of a four-year freeze on the licensing of new stations that the Federal Communications Commission imposed while it pondered the best way to divide the TV spectrum, most communities in the heartland of the nation did not have TV stations until 1954. It was not until that year and the next that large numbers of TV sets began appearing in America's living rooms. But these very TV-less folks had quit going out to the movies years earlier.

Perhaps they switched to something else, something that historians and others have since, unaccountably, failed to recognize. If, during the late 1940s, growing numbers of families in the suburbs abandoned the movies, they should have begun to look for something in the way of cheap, mass entertainment that would be available at home while caring for young children. Like radio.

In fact, there was a brief surge in the radio business in the years immediately after World War II. Radio advertising and profits increased, cresting in 1952. For stockholders, at least, the late 1940s were radio's true Golden Age. CBS and NBC made millions programming to new suburbanites. Probably the best manifestation of that forgotten prosperity was the famous talent raids conducted by CBS in 1948 and 1949. CBS founder William Paley was making so much money in radio that he could bid millions to lure away *Jack Benny* and *Amos 'n' Andy* from NBC. Paley's rival at NBC, David Sarnoff, believed that TV was right around the corner, so he let Paley steal his best radio talent. Upstart CBS made a killing, and with its big earnings from radio was able to catch up to NBC. When TV did emerge in the mid-1950s CBS was ahead, and it would continue to win TV's prime-time ratings race for an entire generation.

So Hollywood lost out to radio, not television. And the best way to understand what happened to Hollywood, it turns out, is not in terms of the mesmerizing effects of that brilliant new technology in a box but in terms of a far more elemental restructuring of American life that occurred during the late 1940s and early 1950s.

During World War II, most Americans had earned more than they had since the heady days of the Roaring Twenties. But there was precious little to buy. Auto factories were turning out tanks, not Fords, and lumber was used to build barracks, not houses. At the urging of film stars and other famous Americans, people put their money in savings bonds. As soon as the war was over, refrigerators and autos began to appear—and then rapidly disappear—in record numbers as Americans cashed in their bonds for all the things that promised to make life fun again.

This spending spree focused on home buying. Americans accelerated a trek which they had begun at the turn of the century, the movement to single-family dwellings in the suburbs. To appreciate the scope of this internal migration one should compare it to the transatlantic pilgrimage from Europe around the turn of the century. In 1907, when that migration was at its peak, more than one million Europeans landed in the United States. This also was precisely the yearly magnitude of the great suburban migration of the late 1940s. Underwritten by Veterans Administration mortgages, home ownership in the United States increased by nearly 50 percent between 1945 and 1950. Ten years later, for the first time in history, more Americans owned houses than rented.

Coupled with this massive move to the suburbs was another historically important change. Two-child households, so common since the turn of the century, gave way to the large families of the baby boom.

This overpowering demand for suburban life is, I think, the only plausible explanation for the abandonment of the moviegoing habit. Virtually overnight, the core of the movie audience vanished. After the war, Americans married at younger and younger ages; the average age of first wedlock fell from 24 to 19. There were few singles left to go on dates to the movies, and young couples were in no position to go: they were having more children, and having them sooner, than their elders had. In the Great Depression (and today) young couples got themselves "established" before they thought of starting a family. But in 1950 a typical 18-year-old bride and her 20-year-old husband were having their first child before either could vote. The new domesticity left little time or money to catch a show.

In a stunning reversal of another long-term demographic trend, well-off and well-educated Americans had more children than any other portion of the population. Lawyers, doctors, and executives contributed proportionally more to the baby boom than did factory and farm workers. And who since the age of the nickelodeon had been Hollywood's best customers? As Robert Sklar writes in *Movie-Made America* (1975), "The more education a person had, the more often he or she went to the movies; people at higher income levels attended movies more frequently than people in lower brackets."

Cutting out the weekly picture show made sense when one had to worry about inflated mortgage payments. The move to the suburbs also made it vastly more difficult simply to get to a show. The matrix of movie houses that had served Hollywood so well prior to 1945 was centered at the heart of the American city. Downtown movie palaces had run the best Hollywood could offer. My beloved Rialto and Roxy were located in central shopping districts, positioned for easy access by streetcar. After its premiere run downtown, a Hollywood feature of the 1930s snaked its way through a network of neighborhood theaters. For a year (or more), it would appear as part of the packages at the network of more than ten thousand neighborhood theaters that served up double features, Saturday afternoon matinees of "B" serials and Westerns, and newsreels and cartoons for the whole family. People generally walked to their local Paradise and Uptown, often without bothering to check what was playing beforehand.

The postwar suburbs were built miles from downtown; no one could (or wanted to) walk back to the old neighborhood Bijou. No streetcars ran from Levittown, New York, or Greendale, Wisconsin, to the old downtown. Walking was passé; suburbanites piled the family into the new Olds '88 or Hudson Hornet and rode in style. Besides, everyone knew there was no parking downtown. Gone were the days of simply grabbing a coat on the spur of the moment and heading for the neighborhood Egyptian or Rialto.

Of course, the Hollywood movie moguls did not simply sit still and watch the suburbs steal away their customers. At first they reined in costs. Any Hollywood studio employee who was not actually working on a feature was fired; an entire special effects unit might be wiped out and only a single guard left at the studio gate. Even stars were let go. Suddenly by 1952 Hollywood seemed like a ghost town.

The new studio bosses also cut the number of films released. Increasingly, each motion picture had to be a potential blockbuster, able to stand on its own as a media event. Studio units making "B" movies, never-ending serials, animated cartoons, and newsreels—all regular movie-palace fare during the 1930s and 1940s (and now seen in perpetual rerun on cable television's TNT and American Movie Classics)—saw their production slowed from weekly editions to special attractions and finally to nothing. All disappeared from the American movie industry by the mid-1960s. Hollywood, which had released a new feature every day of the year, was reduced to producing and releasing but a handful of new feature films each month.

Studio bosses returned to their bag of tricks for strategies they had scoffed at less than a decade before. In the late 1940s, Hollywood began for the first time to regularly offer feature films that catered to an audience serious about its cinema. If young men and women were staying home to raise families, perhaps the "older" folks—for Hollywood, people aged 30 and above—might venture to the movie house to see film art. So Andy Hardy and Roy Rogers gave way to *Gentleman's Agreement* (1947), an Academy Award–winning tale in which Gregory Peck discovers anti-Semitism; *The Snake Pit* (1948), a tale of mental illness starring Olivia de Havilland; and *Pinky* (1949), a pioneer drama about a black woman passing for white. Oscar honored the adult film when *On the Waterfront* (1954), a grim, realistic tale of union corruption on the New York docks, won eight statues. Films such as *Marty* (1955), with Ernest Borgnine's portrayal of a lonely, alienated man, and *Judgment at Nuremberg* (1961), a complex examination of the guilt and shame associated with World War II, became intellectual reference points for a generation.

Before the late 1940s, studio executives shunned serious movies that dealt with complex subjects. Jack L. Warner is reputed to have told one producer, "If I want to send a message, I'll use Western Union."

Many a theater owner, seeing increasing red ink and wanting to rescue his investment, began to program "art" films, which were flowing into the United States from abroad. By the mid-1950s, even Allentown had its Nineteenth Street art theater. Roberto Rossellini's *Open City* (1946) and Vittorio De Sica's *Shoeshine* (1946), masterful, grim, Italian neorealism at its best, proclaimed the coming of film as art. For a time, Hollywood even tried to capture the mood and tone of the best of the European filmmakers by making a number of features abroad.

Serious films showed that they could make money; Brigitte Bardot's . . . *And God Created Woman* (1957) kept many a neighborhood theater in business. Moreover, it set new standards for portraying sexuality on the American movie screen. (Today it can be shown on cable television's Arts & Entertainment channel without provoking any comment or objection.) It became possible for Hollywood to deal frankly with sexual mores and with relationships that were not innocent and pure and which did not always come to a happy ending. Among the best-known products of the new Hollywood were *Peyton Place* (1957), *Butterfield 8* (1960), and *Lolita* (1962).

But Hollywood executives generally remained far more comfortable with variations on the "sell the sizzle not the steak" formula. Beginning with Cinerama in 1952, they rolled out new technology after new technology to wow the public. As promised, film fans of all ages were thrilled by the famous roller-coaster ride in the original Cinerama. For a time during the last months of 1953, "3-D" added another dimension to films, from George Sidney's *Kiss Me Kate* (1953) to Alfred Hitchcock's *Dial M for Murder* (1954). But the required cardboard glasses and frequently out-of-focus images doomed 3-D.

CinemaScope and VistaVision offered clear images of a size and range unmatched in movie history—not to mention by those little boxes in American living rooms that Hollywood was blaming for its troubles. Roman gladiators appeared ten feet tall in Twentieth Century Fox's CinemaScope *The Robe* (1953). John Wayne was never more towering than when he roamed Monument Valley in John Ford's *The Searchers* (1956), shot in VistaVision.

With this surge of wide-screen systems came stereo sound. Music and dialogue were now expected to wash over the spectator from all sides. Movie theaters were remodeled and refitted and new, larger screens were installed, but few new theaters were built. The core problem, the suburban audience, was never addressed.

Moreover, buying a new screen and installing stereo sound meant less money for other amenities. Splendid service with an usher in every aisle gave way to a single teenager taking tickets. What space remained in lobbies was transformed into cafeterias, filled with the smell of popcorn, stray candy wrappers, and trash cans overflowing with cups and wrappers. Luxurious carpets and ornate chandeliers faded into frayed floor coverings and dingy lighting.

There were a few changes for the better. After 1960 all major Hollywood films glowed in reds, yellows, and blues that made their predecessors seem grimy and dark. Producers selected from a multitude of color processes, from the highbrow Technicolor to the lesser lights of Cinecolor and Pathe Color. In films such as Douglas Sirk's *Written on the Wind* (1956) and Vincente Minnelli's *Gigi* (1958) filmmakers stunned spectators of the day with vivid colors. Soon after, movies in color became the industry standard, and have remained so to this day.

By the late 1960s, the movie industry had found itself. The fad of multiple "Scopes" and added "Dimensions" ended; features were shot in Eastman Color with Panavision cameras in some wide-screen ratio larger than the four-by-three images that set the industry standard before 1952, yet smaller than CinemaScope. No one could mistake these theatrical films for television images.

Hollywood slowly came to recognize that it must take its new films to the suburbs. First came the drive-in. Across the country, shrewd entrepreneurs began clearing cornfields, putting up massive screens, and installing speakers in semi-circular rows. Admission was just a dollar a carload. While mom and dad enjoyed the show, the kids could sleep in the backseat—or at least pretend to. In 1946, there were fewer than 100 drive-ins; 10 years later there were more than 3,000 and they were still spreading. Families from the suburbs flocked to the new auto theaters, and by 1960 one of every four exhibition dollars was coming from these "ozoners" (to use industry lingo).

But even the drive-in's ardent proponents agreed that viewing a CinemaScope film from the backseat through a dirty windshield could not provide the basis for a new mass-entertainment industry. The ultimate theatrical solution was, like one of those grand old Hollywood extravaganzas, many years in the making: the suburban shopping-center movie complex. The movie industry followed the department store as it searched out its lost customers. As late as 1967, one still had to go downtown to see a first-run movie. By the early 1970s, the anonymous multiplexes, located near highway crossroads, were becoming the new locus for moviegoing. Today, the movie theater is just one more outlet next to Sears and Waldenbooks.

But the multiplexes did bring back the theatrical movie audience. Theatrical revenues picked up and surged into the billions of dollars per year. The young baby boomers, though weaned on TV, became a faithful teenage movie audience. The movie season came to consist of summer and the Christmas and Easter holiday seasons, when these young people were not in school. This new moviegoing audience made the blockbusters *Jaws* (1975), *Star Wars* (1977), and *E. T.* (1981) possible. The overwhelming success of these films confirmed the new dominance of the suburban multiplex theaters—and also meant the end of my beloved Rialto and Roxy.

Simple explanations developed while events are unfolding seldom turn out to be as neat and clean as we would like. Blaming TV for Hollywood's fate is like saying the butler did it. The argument was developed in the 1950s and has stuck. But just because one thing seems to happen at the same time as another (the fall of movie attendance and the rise of TV viewing) does not mean that one caused the other. We ought to keep our historical thinking clear and systematic, even when something as fun as the movies is involved.

There is another lesson. We ought to stop blaming television for everything. It was not so long ago, in fact, that movies were seen as the source of all evil in American society. One influential academic study of the movies' baneful influence was titled *Our Movie-Made Children* (1933). By 1960 television had replaced the movies as the cause of all that was bad in society. Although no scientist has ever proved a direct connection between the ills of society and watching too much TV (or too many movies), it is easy to find fault with the Boob Tube. TV is just too seductive, too much fun. Not being able to shake the puritanical spirit of our forebears, we can't resist fingering it for everything from declining SAT scores to an increasing crime rate.

TV and movies certainly influence our lives, but so do our changing lifestyles affect the development of these mass media. The movie audience after World War II was "lost" not because of anything the movies or television did, but because those institutions, like all others in American society and culture, were transformed by a wholesale, radical break in social and economic history. No aspect of life in the United States escaped the forces of suburbanization and the baby boom. Universities were turned from institutions for the wealthy few into instruments for mass education of an advanced society. Cities declined. Could we have imagined the enormous popularity of rhythm and blues repackaged for teen suburban audiences before the arrival of the Beatles? All of this—and more—happened because of the vast changes in American lifestyle after World War II.

But not all has been lost. The audience for movies has never been larger. True, few of today's viewers are trekking to the neighborhood movie house, but millions stare at the unspooling of Hollywood's past glories and the continual rerunning of contemporary blockbusters—on television. And with a VCR anyone can become the "house manager" of his or her own home theater. It is a wonder that any contemporary movie buff ever ventures outside. Hollywood has benefited and has never been more healthy. The Japanese paid $4 billion for Columbia Pictures in 1989 and twice that for Universal Studios because they knew there was only one Hollywood. Even with their billions they could not fabricate their own Tinseltown in Tokyo. Not accidentally, movies are one of the nation's most popular exports. Movie stars advise members of Congress and often become the centers of presidential campaigns. One of them even became president.

So TV did not kill Hollywood. In the great Hollywood whodunit there is, after all, not even a corpse. The film industry never died. Only where we enjoy its latest products has changed, forever.

FRANK D. MCCONNELL

At one point in Graham Greene's *The Confidential Agent,* the hero—a hunted spy—hides out in a movie theater. A nondescript Hollywood romance is on the screen, but the hero discovers in it a significance deeper than any intended by its makers: "It was as if some code of faith or morality had been lost for centuries, and the world was trying to reconstruct it from the unreliable evidence of folk memories and subconscious desires."

A splendid film critic in his own right, Greene realized that the movie comes closer than any other product of our culture to the happy status of the novel in Victorian England. It is at once attuned to individual human concerns and sensitive to the daydreams of the masses. And, a rarity in this century of lugubriously self-conscious art, the movies are genuinely fun.

That is why they have taken so long to be accepted as a legitimate object of study in the university. American academics, good Calvinists all, have operated for years on the assumption that "Kulchur" (as poet Ezra Pound contemptuously called it) should hurt, at least a little; that there must be a gulf between asthetics and entertainment. This attitude was concisely captured by the turn-of-the-century wit who said of Wagnerian music, "It's better than it sounds." By contrast, our best "serious" novelists and poets have understood that we live in a creative and often profoundly humanizing popular culture—and that much of this culture is stored on celluloid.

THE MYTHOLOGY OF FILM

American literature of the twentieth century is filled with writers who built their vision of America upon a vision of Hollywood: F. Scott Fitzgerald in *The Last*

Reprinted from the summer 1978 issue of *The Wilson Quarterly.*

Tycoon, Norman Mailer in *The Deer Park,* and Saul Bellow in *Humboldt's Gift.* Others, like Brock Brower in *The Late Great Creature,* and especially Thomas Pynchon in his towering novel *Gravity's Rainbow,* have begun using not simply the fact but also the basic themes and myths of popular film genres in their work. To understand *Gravity's Rainbow,* for example, it is not sufficient to have a background in modern fiction and physics. One must also understand that this awesome tale, which seeks refuge in fantasy from the terrors of the modern city, swings unfailingly and recognizably between the extremes of *King Kong* and *The Wizard of Oz.*

The popular film, of course, is not of value simply because it prepares us to read Brower, Pynchon, and the rest. The serious celluloid fairy-tale genres—science fiction, melodrama, the Western—are much like officially sanctioned myths; their formulas are predictable. At the same time, these formulas undergo subtle shifts with time. To understand these shifts is, in its way, to excavate that mental city we all inhabit privately—and in common.

As Norman Mailer wrote in his 1961 open letter to President John Kennedy on the Bay of Pigs invasion, "I can't believe the enormity of your mistake: You invade a country without understanding its music." Substitute "movies" for "music" and one comes close to stating the necessity of understanding film. In movies that catch the popular imagination, we see ourselves as in a funhouse mirror: distorted, yes, but distorted in a way that reveals more than photographic accuracy ever could. For it reveals who—and where—we really are, what we want and want to believe.

ROCKY: A WESTERN FOR THE EIGHTIES

It is widely believed, for example, that our post-Vietnam, post-Watergate mood is one of moderate self-congratulation. But what is the real shape of this mood? How do we, in our film daydreams, project the new confidence in ourselves we think we have earned? Sylvester Stallone's *Rocky* is a film of obsessively unbounded optimism. It insists so strenuously that everything will be all right that we are forced to ask, What is it that we were afraid would go wrong?

The continually implied and finally averted possibility of disaster in *Rocky* is the failure of community. Rocky Balboa is a never-was, a club fighter in the Italian neighborhood of Philadelphia who supplements his scanty fight earnings by breaking bones for the local loan shark, a nobody whose great romance is with the clerk in the neighborhood pet store, a drab girl named Adrian.

In a bizarre public-relations gimmick, Rocky is selected to fight heavyweight champion Apollo Creed on New Year's Day. The whole community falls in behind him, helps him train, gives him money, lets him pound away on beef carcasses. The night before the fight, Rocky tells Adrian he wants, if not to win, at least to go the full fifteen rounds. "If I can do that, I'll know I wasn't just another bum from the neighborhood." He lasts the fifteen rounds, losing to Creed only by a split decision. At that moment, bruised, bloodied, exhausted, he is able to tell Adrian, for the first time, "I love you."

Sentimental, of course, but intelligently so. We can trust it because it is so aware of its own sentimentality. Rocky begins as a lonely man trying to be a lonely hero. He discovers that he becomes a hero when he stops being alone. The film is a celebration of the single man who redeems the honor of his town.

It is, in other words, a Western. For in the Western—despite the bitter inversion of such films as *High Noon* (where the town abandons the hero) or *The Magnificent Seven* (in which the Seven are driven from the town they save)—our hopes for the tiny communities of the film West are always, implicitly, our hopes for the larger community in which we all live. Main Street is always Main Street, and *Rocky,* complete with final showdown, simply translates the myths into elementary terms. It tells us that little people can survive, but only if they are faithful to each other.

STAR WARS: THE POSSIBILITY OF HEROISM

George Lucas's *Star Wars* makes the assertion in a different key. Far from simply a science-fiction adventure, this highly self-conscious film is a virtual history of past motifs, situations, and even characteristic bits of dialogue from old Westerns, swashbucklers, war movies, and of course, science-fiction movies. Ontogeny recapitulates phylogeny, at least on the celluloid level.

This does not mean that *Star Wars* is "camp"—to use that shibboleth of critics who are excited by popular works they don't understand. Like *Rocky, Star Wars* is an experiment to see if the myths of popular culture have any life left in them. That these myths are still alive is reflected by nothing so much as the movie's phenomenal success—in cold cash ($500 million), the most successful film in history. And for all its self-consciousness and formula predictability, it is a serious film about the possibility of heroism, not within a community but within our own imagination: can we still believe in ourselves as heroes?

A hero, after all, is a corny thing to be; a century of psychoanalysis, sociology, and political science has taught us that. But *Star Wars,* great popular myth that it is, reminds us that the corniness of heroism, like that of love or honor, does not render it less important. The real "force" behind the famous *Star Wars* blessing— "May the Force be with you"—is that of fairy tales and their power to humanize even after we no longer believe in their literal reality.

CLOSE ENCOUNTERS: EVERYMAN AND A VISION OF TRANSCENDENCE

If *Star Wars* attempts to revivify some of the oldest conventions in the movies, Steven Spielberg's *Close Encounters of the Third Kind* does something more subtle, risky, and important. A resolutely popular myth, it is also an uncanny critique of the relationship between popular mythology and our nostalgia for the sublime—for a desire to believe, as the film's advertising copy announced, that We Are Not Alone. Roy Neary, the Indiana electrical worker who sees a UFO and is thereafter compelled to visit the site where the alien visitors will show themselves, is a modern Everyman who in his boredom and confusion has become obsessed by a vision of transcendence—a terrible thing to experience, as St. Paul told us long before director Spielberg got around to it.

But Neary is an Everyman whose vision is itself shaped by the pop mythologies of transcendence that surround us. When we first see him, he is watching television: watching Cecil B. De Mille's *The Ten Commandments,* that earlier translation of miracle into special effects, of transcendence into kitsch. Later, his daughter watches a Bugs Bunny cartoon about invaders from Mars. And in the climactic sequence, when the UFOs land and speak to us, they speak through a lovely, funny jazz fugue, transforming the giant mother ship into a cosmic synthesizer playing the Muzak of the spheres.

The point is not that *Close Encounters* is a pop gospel of transfiguration. It is something better, an examination of our lives as already transcending their own limitations, if only we can understand our own daydreams. We are not alone because we speak to one another—and nowhere at a deeper level than through the mythology of film.

To say this much implies that the hieroglyphics of popular myths are at once naive and highly sophisticated about their own naiveté. For they rediscover the dignity of clichés and tell us again and again what we can never hear too often: we are most human not in despair or self-loathing but in shared laughter and delight—when, indeed, we are having fun.

A FOOTNOTE TO HISTORY: MGM MEETS THE ATOMIC BOMB

NATHAN REINGOLD

In February 1947, barely eighteen months after an American-made atomic bomb known as Little Boy leveled the Japanese city of Hiroshima, Metro-Goldwyn-Mayer (MGM) released to the world what would today be called a "docudrama" about the making and deployment of that bomb. It was the first such movie of the atomic age, the first full-length feature film describing what *Life* magazine called the "biggest event since the birth of Christ."

In theaters across the United States, before millions of moviegoers, the MGM lion growled his customary two growls. Below his mane appeared the company's celebrated motto: *Ars Gratia Artis,* "Art for art's sake." Then came what purported to be a newsreel, showing canisters of film—supposedly, copies of the film that the audience was about to see—being buried in a grove of California redwoods. "A message to future generations!" the voice-over proclaimed. "Come what may, our civilization will have left an enduring record behind it. Ours will be no lost race."

Thus began *The Beginning or the End,* Hollywood's ambitious and ultimately ill-starred portrayal of the World War II Manhattan Project and the people behind it.

No one man or woman was responsible for the way this motion picture turned out (badly). Then as now, docudrama filmmaking in Hollywood involved a triad of conflicting interests: the commercial hopes of the producers, the perceived demands of a mass audience for entertainment, and the personal qualms of the participants in the events described in the film. Taken together, these proved to be a recipe for a fiasco, in terms of both historical veracity and box-office receipts.

Reprinted from the autumn 1984 issue of *The Wilson Quarterly.*

Happily, we can reconstruct what happened, thanks to a legal requirement that no longer exists. In order to depict living, well-known public figures, MGM had to secure their permission in writing. These individuals, in turn, often demanded the right to review the script. The result is a vast harvest of correspondence scattered among MGM files, the National Archives, the Library of Congress, and various universities. The letters, along with the film, supply a bizarre footnote to the dawn of the atomic age.[1]

The idea for *The Beginning or the End* grew out of contacts between MGM producer Sam Marx and members of the so-called atomic scientists' movement, a group of young, liberal, rather antimilitary Manhattan Project alumni who hoped to educate the lay public about the nature of atomic weapons and their disturbing implications for both domestic and foreign policy. (The movement soon developed into the Federation of American Scientists.) Edward R. Tompkins of the Clinton Laboratories, now the Oak Ridge National Laboratory, in Tennessee, seems to have been the first to suggest the idea of a movie—in a letter to a former high-school student of his, actress Donna Reed, who brought the concept to MGM's attention. MGM eventually paid Tompkins a modest honorarium of $100.

Sam Marx was as much in awe of the new atomic weapons technology as the scientists were of Hollywood; initially, at least, Marx approached the subject of the bomb with unusual care. During the autumn of 1945, in preparation for his film, the producer visited the Clinton Laboratories and on the same swing east visited President Harry S. Truman in Washington. MGM officials later assured the president that "a great service to civilization" might be done if "the right kind of film could be made."

MIXING FACT WITH FICTION

High-minded though its intentions were, MGM faced a forbidding challenge: how to present complex, often cerebral, feats of science and engineering in a way that American audiences would sit through, without fidgeting, for 120 minutes. Then as now, the solution, inevitably, was to veer, often sharply, from factual accuracy in the interest of entertainment.

Screenwriters Robert Considine and Frank Wead, abetted by Marx and by director Norman Taurog, added several fictional characters and the mandatory "love interest" to the story. To build tension, they depicted the Manhattan Project as a race pitting America against both the Germans and the Japanese, who were said to be nearing completion of their own atomic bombs. (In reality, there had been little concern about Japan.) The filmmakers invented numerous other aspects of both nuclear technology and the development of the Manhattan Project.

The members of the atomic scientists' movement, active in shaping the script during its early stages—they naively hoped to determine its point of view and, through a substantial contribution from MGM, to swell their organization's meager coffers—withdrew their cooperation when they saw what Hollywood was doing to the story. In the opinion of Sam Marx, who did not want his film to be "a big, long speech for world government," this was just as well.

The scientist-activists withdrew with the expectation that the senior scientists and military men in the Manhattan Project, people such as J. Robert Oppenheimer, General Leslie R. Groves, Vannevar Bush, and James B. Conant, would likewise withhold their endorsements. In this they proved to be, for the most part, wrong.

Why? One reason was that some of the key military participants in the Manhattan Project had already accepted fees from MGM—$10,000 in the case of General Groves—in return for their permission to be depicted on film. For their part, many of the important scientists (none of whom accepted money) seem to have assumed that helping the filmmakers was a professional obligation. Moreover, only by cooperating could the Manhattan Project's "big shots" exercise any control over the film's content. MGM's need to get waivers gave all of them a certain leverage that the younger, unknown scientists did not possess.

To be sure, the senior Manhattan Project personnel protested the direction in which the movie appeared to be heading when, in the spring of 1946, the first screenplay was sent to most of them for approval. MGM, in response, agreed to make some small changes. Some of the scientists protested once more after viewing the first completed film version in autumn of the same year. Once again MGM made some changes. But when it came to what the studio insisted was a matter of both artistic principle and commercial necessity, MGM stood its ground.

In the words of an MGM memo passed on to Albert Einstein by studio head Louis B. Mayer in 1946, "It must be realized that dramatic truth is just as compelling a requirement on us as veritable truth is on a scientist." The studio reminded General Groves, who headed the Manhattan Project in its later stages, that MGM was not an endowed institution "like Harvard" but a commercial enterprise. The requirements of "dramatic truth" helped shape the film into a familiar narrative form with stock characters and stock situations.

In the original screenplay, the movie begins with J. Robert Oppenheimer (who would be played by Hume Cronyn) recounting the flight of physicist Lise Meitner from Berlin when Nazis overrun her laboratory in 1938. She takes refuge with Nobel laureate Niels Bohr in Denmark. Soon, word of the pair's work in nuclear fission reaches America; Albert Einstein, at the behest of a fictional physicist named Matt Cochran (played by Tom Drake), writes his historic 1939 letter to Franklin D. Roosevelt suggesting the theoretical possibility of constructing an atomic bomb. An Office of Scientific Research and Development (OSRD) is set up, leading to physicist Enrico Fermi's first controlled chain reaction at the University of Chicago's Stagg Field in 1941. ("Dr. Fermi, scientifically detached from the world, enters," reads the screenplay.)

Among the scientists at Stagg Field, the fictional Cochran is the most vocal in airing doubts about going forward with the atomic bomb. His concerns are typically dismissed out of hand. ("Get it done before the Germans and the Japs, then worry about the bomb," he is told.) After the successful experiment at Chicago's Metallurgical Laboratory, a small group of scientists is shown resigning from the bomb project; both correspondence and the script make it clear that these men were intended to be perceived as Quakers. The walkout, which never occurred, gives the Enrico Fermi character an opportunity to say, "Sometimes, it takes greater principles to stay than to go." In general, *The Beginning or the End* slides over issues of morality that some atomic scientists at Stagg Field, hardly pacifists, debated intensely among themselves.

Skipping over much important scientific work of the period, the screenplay shifts to the domain of the Manhattan Engineer District, which superseded the OSRD. General Groves (played by Brian Donlevy) is shown exhorting industry to support the weapons effort. We see the DuPont representative grandly waive all potential patent rights, an easy position for DuPont to take fictionally since the real Leslie Groves and Vannevar Bush would never have let atomic weapons technology fall into private hands. The movie screen bustles with a panorama of factories, railway yards, and busy assembly lines.

The action moves to Los Alamos, where rather little is shown, given the requirements of military security. (Until 1958, the town of Los Alamos was off-limits to the general public.) Then comes the first test explosion. For the movie, the A-bomb blast at Alamogordo, New Mexico, would be impressively re-created in the MGM studios in Culver City, California. Right after the test, a turtle is seen walking across Ground Zero, a symbolic affirmation that, yes, life can survive a nuclear blast.

Declaring in the original script that "I think more of our American boys than I do of all our enemies," President Truman decides to drop the bomb on Hiroshima. Matt Cochran and his equally fictional friend Jeff Nixon (played by Robert Walker), an Army colonel on General Groves's staff, travel to Tinian, a small Pacific island, to prepare the first of two atomic bombs for use against Japan. In an impossible accident, Matt suffers a fatal radiation injury while setting up the bomb one evening all by himself.

Then, the *Enola Gay* takes off on its historic mission, braving heavy flak over Hiroshima. (In reality, the B-29 encountered no hostile fire.) Little Boy devastates the city in a spectacular film sequence that demonstrates Hollywood's skill at special effects. (The special effects won the movie an Oscar.)

Matt dies, though not before writing the obligatory final letter, resolving his own doubts about the bomb. The screenplay (like the movie) ends with Matt's pregnant widow, along with Jeff Nixon and Jeff's girlfriend, standing before the Lincoln Memorial in Washington and talking inspirationally about how the world will be better for the young scientist's sacrifice.

This, in outline, was the screenplay that those Manhattan Project alumni depicted in *The Beginning or the End* were asked to review and approve during the spring of 1946.

ELIMINATING "UNREASONABLE DISTORTION"

The senior participants in the Manhattan Project did not like what they read and said so in no uncertain terms. The first hurdle for MGM was physicist J. Robert Oppenheimer, who had served as director of the atomic laboratory at Los Alamos. Oppenheimer's chief complaint was artistic; the characters appeared "stilted, lifeless, and without purpose or insight." Producer Sam Marx wrote back, agreeing to fix certain minor factual details and to spruce up the personalities. In particular, Marx said, "the character of J. Robert Oppenheimer must be an extremely pleasant one with a love of mankind, humility, and a fair knack of cooking." Marx added that the film would make it plain that Oppenheimer, not Groves, was in command at the Alamogordo test.

Somewhat mollified, Oppenheimer signed a release in May 1946. He would be depicted in the movie as an earnest scoutmaster who accidentally had a doctorate in theoretical physics from Gottingen. Queried later by an incredulous member of the atomic scientists' movement, physicist James J. Nickson, Oppenheimer replied that while the screenplay was not "beautiful, wise, or deep . . . it did not lie in my power to make it so."

Although Oppenheimer withdrew from further involvement in *The Beginning or the End* after May 1946, both General Groves and Vannevar Bush corresponded with MGM throughout the year. Groves was determined that the movie not violate national security (a sensitive issue in the immediate postwar era) or discredit anyone involved in the Manhattan Project. He sought assiduously, though with limited success, to correct inaccuracies.

Among other things, Groves was disturbed by the way he was shown barking orders at industrialists; relations with business, he insisted, had always been polite and respectful. The general was outraged by his fictional subordinate, Jeff Nixon, the long-haired (for an officer) womanizer and wise guy. Such a man, Groves argued, would not have been tolerated in the Corps of Engineers and would never have been asked to join his personal staff. As to his own film image, the rumpled, pudgy Groves raised no objection to being portrayed by the handsome Brian Donlevy.

In the end, the general won some small concessions, notably the elimination of a highly imaginative scene in which Groves tells Roosevelt and Secretary of War Henry L. Stimson that if the United States did not use the atomic bomb at once against Japan, Japan would greet a U.S. invasion of the home islands with nuclear weapons of its own. Essentially, though, Groves went along with MGM's plans. He was no doubt relieved by the report of an aide who attended a sneak preview of the final film version in 1947. The aide concluded that the public impact of the movie would be minimal because the film would be a box-office flop.

Vannevar Bush, formerly director of the Office of Scientific Research and Development, had better luck than Groves with the creative folks at Culver City. Bush had held the crucial discussion with FDR about launching the Manhattan Project, but in the screenplay, MGM gave the credit to another man, the National Bureau of Standards' Lyman J. Briggs. Bush objected and the moviemakers rewrote the script accordingly.

Bush did not like the rewrite either. In the new version, Bush was shown with Roosevelt (and with FDR's Scotch terrier, Fala, who leaves the room when Bush announces that he has a top-secret matter to discuss); he was portrayed as uncertain over whether an atomic bomb could be built "in time" or would even be small enough to fit inside an airplane. On the contrary, Bush insisted, he had had no doubts on either score.

Sam Marx agreed to soften but not eliminate this angle. It was Hollywood fiction that had been deliberately introduced to heighten dramatic tension—to suggest the possibility that the Axis powers might get the bomb first.

Bush also disliked being shown leaving the White House disgruntled at not getting an immediate go-ahead from the president. The scene implied, he believed, that American scientists were "arrogant enough to feel [they] should either make the decision [themselves] or force the Commander-in-Chief into making it then and there." Again, MGM gave way. The released film shows a rather prosaic parting of Bush and Roosevelt, followed by the president placing a transatlantic call to Winston Churchill to give him the details.

On the eve of the film's release in 1947, Bush could write to financier Bernard Baruch that, insofar as his own role was concerned, "history was not unreasonably distorted" by *The Beginning or the End.*

Harvard president James B. Conant, a key administrator in the A-bomb effort, proved even more persnickety than Bush. Conant was hardly publicity shy. Indeed, he and Bush willingly played themselves in a 1946 March of Time documentary, *Atomic Power,* which showed the pair stretched out on the desert (actually, a sand-strewn garage floor in Boston) awaiting the first nuclear blast at Alamogordo. *The Beginning or the End* was another matter. Conant agreed to being shown at Alamogordo but not to having any words put in his mouth.

The foreign-born scientists depicted in the movie gave Sam Marx his biggest headaches. Having been told by members of the atomic scientists' movement that *The Beginning or the End* would reflect the Pentagon's viewpoint, Albert Einstein twice refused his consent to be portrayed, reluctantly giving in only at the urging of colleague Leo Szilard. Appalled by inaccuracies and outright fabrications, Lise Meitner and Niels Bohr spurned all of MGM's entreaties and had to be written out of the movie altogether.

From MGM's standpoint, the most serious refusal was that of Bohr. The early scenes of the screenplay featured him in Europe. To highlight the race against the Nazis, much was made of smuggling the physicist out of Copenhagen and then bringing him to the United States. That Bohr was essential to the A-bomb project was more than strongly implied—though in fact he was not a member of the Manhattan Project. For dramatic effect he was placed at the Alamogordo test site; but in fact he had not been there.

To make up for the absence of Bohr and Meitner, MGM in December 1946 hastily began cutting the movie and reshooting scenes, a process that continued into January.

The intransigence of Bohr, Meitner, and others cost *The Beginning or the End* one of its more vivid fictional interludes. In the original script, Niels Bohr shocks Oppenheimer when he brings the news that the Germans are sending atomic experts and know-how to Japan. Later, the screenplay has a U-boat leaving Hitler's doomed Reich with a fictional German physicist aboard named Schmidt—identified as a former worker in Lise Meitner's Berlin laboratory. The submarine surfaces in Tokyo Bay, and the Japanese promptly rush Schmidt off to a modern laboratory they have built for him—in the city of Hiroshima.

Columnist Walter Lippmann was responsible for another excision. After previewing the original version of the movie in the fall of 1946, Lippmann complained that Truman's order to drop the bomb was depicted as a snap decision. This, he wrote, was an "outright fabrication and reduces the role of the President to extreme triviality in a great matter." Lippmann also objected to the movie Truman's seeming unconcern for the loss of Japanese lives. The entire scene was reshot.[2]

Neither Herr Doktor Schmidt nor a shoot-from-the-hip Truman appeared in the final film version, but many of MGM's other revisions of the record made it through. Before a first atomic bomb is tested at Alamogordo, for example, Oppenheimer and General Groves's deputy, Brigadier General Thomas F. Farrell, discuss the frightening possibility that the nuclear chain reaction would go around the world, converting the planet into one big fireball. In the movie, Oppenheimer rates the possibility at less than one in a million. Asked after the test if he really had been worried, the Oppenheimer character says, "In my head, no, in my heart, yes."

In fact, the Manhattan Project physicists had no such worries; the possibility was raised only *after* the bombings of Hiroshima and Nagasaki, by people with little expertise in nuclear fission.

A BOX OFFICE "BOMB"

Until the world premiere of *The Beginning or the End* in Washington, at least some MGM officials were certain they had a hit on their hands. Carter T. Barron, MGM's man in Washington, cabled to Culver City on January 7, 1947:

> Seldom have we experienced more enthusiasm for the dramatic entertainment of a film than that demonstrated by small preview groups comprised of immediate friends, staff members, and associates of persons impersonated or otherwise associated with the project. It appears to be a daringly strong audience picture.

Then came the reviews. *Time*'s critic wrote that "the picture seldom rises above cheery imbecility" and scolded Hollywood for "treating cinemagoers as if they were spoiled or not-quite-bright children." (Few reviewers, however, questioned the factual accuracy of the movie.) At least 75 films in 1947 grossed more at the box office than what MGM billed as "the story of the most HUSH-HUSH secret of all time."

The reaction of groups of scientists invited to special screenings was typically one of disappointed silence punctuated by outbursts of raucous laughter. Sam Marx had once allowed that he was interested "not in how a scientist would talk but how the public thought he would talk." Hollywood's notion of how science was done—amid batteries of blinking lights and a cacophony of electronic noises—proved irresistibly comic to real scientists.

Ironically, had the reactions of Bohr and others not forced so much cutting and reshooting of scenes, MGM might have produced a box-office hit. At a sneak preview in October 1946, the first, uncut version of the film won an overwhelmingly enthusiastic response from the audience. Imagine the impact on popular memories of World War II if tens of millions of American moviegoers had watched the fictional Herr Doktor Schmidt disembarking from his U-boat in Tokyo Bay, with a blueprint for an A-bomb in his briefcase!

Did *The Beginning or the End* really matter? Not in any way that is easy to describe. Although its distortions went largely unremarked, they also went largely unseen. The making of *The Beginning or the End* is chiefly of value as a parable of sorts. And it may serve as a timely reminder that, as the years go by, Hollywood fictions sometimes take on lives of their own. "Engrossing account of atomic bomb development, depicting both human and spectacular aspects"— that is how *The Beginning or the End* is described in Leonard Maltin's *TV Movies* (1983–4 edition). The film gets three stars, no less.

NOTES

1. For related reading, see also Alice K. Smith's A Peril and a Hope (1965) and Michael J. Yavenditti's "Atomic Scientists and Hollywood: The Beginning or the End?" in Film and History (December 1978, vol. 8, no. 4).

2. Because Truman's visage did not actually appear—the camera shot over an actor's shoulder—MGM did not need a signed waiver from the president. Truman read the screenplay of the first film version and, judging from private letters, disliked the same sequence that Lippmann criticized, and for the very same reasons. However, wishing to avoid charges of censorship, he refused to intervene.

14 HOLLOW ROCK AND THE LOST BLUES CONNECTION

MARTHA BAYLES

People used to tap their feet and smile when they listened to American popular music. Now they sit open-mouthed and stare: at "speed metal" rockers with roadkill hair who, despite a certain virtuosity on guitar, treat music as a form of warfare; at "grunge" bands in thrift-shop flannels who throw tantrums and smash their instruments; at "gangsta" rappers in baggy gear who posture as rapists, pushers, prostitutes, murderers, or terrorists. Tune into MTV and you will occasionally come across something wonderful. But more likely the sonic abuse and verbal-visual ugliness will appall and repel you.

Appall and repel, that is, if you belong to one of two groups of listeners: either to those who have always disliked popular music and regard what they see on MTV as the inevitable outcome of commercialization, or to those who once liked popular music but cannot stomach the current fare. For the latter, among whom I count myself, the main problem is finding a way to articulate objections without echoing earlier gripes about music we relish, whether jazz, swing, blues, rhythm and blues, or rock 'n' roll. "Turn that racket down," we yell, realizing we sound just like our parents.

So we chalk the problem up to age, telling ourselves that people prefer the music of their youth, and that's all there is to it. But this explanation conjures up a most unlikely prospect: today's teenagers 60 years from now attending Saturday-night dances in their retirement communities, their eyes misting over to the sounds of Megadeth, Sonic Youth, and Niggaz With Attitude. Such a future seems unlikely for the obvious but underappreciated reason that much of today's popular music evokes only the more intense, unsettling emotions of

Reprinted from the summer 1993 issue of *The Wilson Quarterly*.

youth: anxiety, lust, anger, aggression. In the narrow gauge of its effects, such music could not be more different from the best of American popular music, which balances such unsettling emotions with tenderness, grace, and wit. Indeed, the great vigor of our music has always been its ability to blend opposites.

What happened to this vigor? The answer, or at least part of it, is found in the undisputed heart of American popular music, the blues. The story of our music's decline, as I shall show, is strongly bound up with the history of what happened to the blues starting in the mid-1960s: how it got bludgeoned into "rock," "hard rock," "heavy metal," and even more grotesque offshoots—developments that you need not be a philistine, prude, or old fogy to deplore.

Defining the blues is itself a vexed question, given the historic conundrum of race and sex that has long distorted white reactions to African American music in general and to the blues in particular. The task is further complicated by the fact that generations of folklorists have evaluated different blues forms in ideological, as opposed to musical, terms. Many of these earnest souls have engaged in a prolonged but fruitless debate over whether certain changes in blues practice (lyric content, instrumentation, electric amplification) have destroyed blues artistry and reduced the blues to commercialized entertainment. The debate is fruitless because it ignores the fact that the blues has always been commercialized entertainment.

While scholars disagree over many particulars of blues history, most agree in tracing the music to two sources: to African American religion and ritual, including spirituals, ring shouts, field hollers, work chants, sermons, and toasts; and to early forms of American popular culture, including plantation music, minstrel "coon songs," and popular ballads performed by itinerant street singers for the loose change of passersby.

From its beginning, then, the blues was both noncommercial and commercial. The form as we know it—one performer, usually male, singing and playing a guitar—dates back to the years immediately after the Civil War, when emancipation sent former slave musicians on the road to earn a living. This image of the solo, itinerant bluesman appeals to aficionados steeped in the romantic ideal of the lonely artist pitted against a hostile society. But for two reasons, the blues rarely fits the ideal. First, the blues has always been played by groups as well as by individuals. And second, it has never ceased to sell itself. For over a century, the blues performer's motto has been not "art for art's sake" but "make way for the paying customers." The latter have included everyone from travelers waiting at a railroad depot to sharecroppers crowded onto segregated benches for a country "medicine show," from families gathered for a barbecue on a Mississippi cotton plantation to low-life rowdies raising hell in a Memphis juke joint, from city dwellers strolling in a public park to transplanted southern factory workers in a hole-in-the-wall Chicago club.

In recent years, the blues performer most frequently forced into the art-for-art's-sake mold has been the renowned Mississippi Delta bluesman Robert Johnson (1911–38). Because Johnson was a lone wolf who wrote many of his own lyrics, some of them strikingly original, reissues of his 1930s recordings have been greeted with glowing tributes, many of which depict him as the true romantic hero who lived only for the purity of his art. The deflating truth, however, is that Johnson spent most of his career working as a human jukebox. Journalist Peter Guralnick cites one of Johnson's contemporaries, who recalled that the bluesman "was as likely to perform 'Tumbling Tumbleweeds' or the latest Bing Crosby hit as one of his own compositions. 'You didn't play what *you* liked, you played what the people liked. That's what you had to do.' " Had Johnson lived past 1938, he might have been one of the first Delta bluesmen to perform on radio. The price of appearing on tiny KFFA in Helena, Arkansas, was singing jingles for the King Biscuit Flour Company and allowing your face to adorn a cornmeal label. But Johnson would have paid it, just as his stepson and protégé, Robert "Junior" Lockwood, did.

To stress this commercial aspect is not to disparage blues artistry. It is only to point out that the leading practitioners of African-American music have never drawn a sharp, uncrossable line between commerce and art. The great figures of blues and jazz have understood all too well that commercial priorities often conflict with artistic ones, and that those who profit from the music are rarely those who create it. But they have nonetheless striven to make commerce and art dovetail. As Duke Ellington remarked about his famous predecessor, "I loved and respected Louis Armstrong. He was born poor, died rich, and never hurt anyone on the way."

Unlike folklore purists, musicians have always defined the blues as a structure, as a way of playing and singing, and (equally important) as a ritualized way of coping with the harshness of life. As crystallized in the early twentieth century, the traditional blues is a 3-line, 12-bar stanza with lyrics following a variety of rhyme schemes, usually *a a b.* Typically in the key of E or A, the blues stanza starts with four bars on the tonic, with the fourth shifting to the dominant 7th; then it proceeds to two bars on the subdominant, two more on the tonic, two on the dominant 7th, and two final bars back on the tonic. Not all blues have this structure; far from it. The oldest known blues are almost free-form, and many "classic" blues, such as those recorded in the 1920s by Bessie Smith, Mamie Smith, and other female performers, have the familiar structure of the 32-bar popular song.

But blues artistry consists of more than strumming a simple sequence of chords and singing the somewhat constrained melodies that arise from them. First and foremost, the blues is polyrhythmic, meaning it possesses that elusive but essential quality known as "swing." At some point, every critic tries to explain Ellington's famous title "It Don't Mean a Thing If It Ain't Got That Swing." The task is not easy, but the French musicologist André Hodeir comes close when he explains that swing depends on five things: "infrastructure" (meaning a regular structural beat, often implied rather than played), "super-structure" (meaning the numerous other pulses surrounding the structural beat, usually given equal, if not greater, accentuation), "getting the notes and accents in the right place," "relaxation," and "vital drive." As Hodeir admits, "The first three are technical in nature and can be understood rationally; the last two are psycho-physical, and must be grasped intuitively."

Blues artists further define their music in terms of distinctive vocal and instru-mental techniques, such as "moaning" and "string bending," which produce a rich variety of timbres and microtonal shadings. Like polyrhythm, these tech-niques are indisputably the heritage of Africa. As a slave musician remarked to a white visitor in the 1830s, "Notes is good enough for you people, but us likes a mixtery." The same "mixtery" is found in all forms of African-American music. In blues, as well as in jazz and gospel, the best performers range across the whole spectrum, from tones pure enough to pass muster in a European concert hall to "impure" textures evocative of every imaginable emotional state.

Emotion brings us to the spirit of the blues, a subject frequently misunder-stood, even by its admirers. The music gets its name from the Elizabethan phrase "the blue devils," meaning a fit of bad temper or melancholy. But bad temper and melancholy are merely the starting point of the blues, not its destination. Of course, some people view the blues as depressing, as would befit "the devil's music." This view prevails in the gospel field, where many agree with Mahalia Jackson that "blues are the songs of despair, gospel songs are songs of hope." It is more sympathetically expressed by blues historian Paul Oliver: "The blues is primarily the song of those who turned their backs on religion." But both eval-uations miss the point. If the blues teaches us anything, it is that despair is not the only alternative to faith. For all the emotionalism found in blues perfor-mance, the music's basic philosophy is stoic.

To put the matter another way, "having the blues" is not the same thing as "playing the blues." The former refers to a negative state of mind, such as lone-liness or grief, anger or fear, disappointment or jealousy; the latter, to the art of leavening, tempering, or (possibly) transforming such a state. Because it does not expect to achieve heavenly bliss, the blues aims lower than gospel, at what can be achieved in this world—usually enough irony or humor to give a modicum of freedom in even the grimmest circumstances. Novelist and jazz critic Albert Murray explains:

The church is not concerned with the affirmation of life as such. . . . The church is committed to the eternal salvation of the soul after death. . . . But the Saturday Night Function [the blues performance] is a ritual of purification and affirmation nonetheless. Not all ceremonial occasions are solemn. Nor are defiance and contestation less fundamental to human well-being than are worship and propitiation. Indeed they seem to be precisely what such indispensably human attributes as courage, dignity, honor, nobility and heroism are all about. . . . The most immediate problem of the blues-bedeviled person concerns his ability to cope with even the commonplace. What is at stake is a sense of well-being that is at least strong enough to enable him to meet the basic requirements of the workaday world.

Robert Johnson's blues never suggest any hope that coping with trouble in this world will lead to rewards in the next. One of his best-known lyrics goes, "You may bury my body down by the highway side/So my old evil spirit can catch a Greyhound bus and ride" ("Me and the Devil Blues"). Yet Johnson makes it just as clear that if despair is allowed to rule in small things, it will rule in large: "If you cry about a nickel/You'll die 'bout a dime" ("Last Fair Deal Gone Down"). Like gospel, the blues involves both performer and audience in a communal, ritualized re-enactment of extreme emotional states. The purpose of the blues ritual is, like that of gospel, to *return* from those states—to *survive* trouble, not succumb to it. The difference is that, unlike the preacher, the bluesman tempers every extreme. His stoic stance toward life eschews pain, but his focus on bitter realities also distrusts joy.

Historically, the topics addressed by the blues make for a very long list. Here are just a few, taken from Paul Oliver's landmark study of traditional blues lyrics, *Blues Fell This Morning:* employment and the lack thereof; the need to migrate, usually by railroad, and the personal costs of doing so; color prejudice among blacks as well as whites; standards of beauty and dress; flirtation, romance, courtship, and marriage; fidelity and infidelity; sex in all its permutations, including sexual boasting and insult; folk beliefs, magic, and "hoodoo"; gambling; carnivals, juke joints, and vaudeville; liquor, Prohibition, and drugs; conditions in various regions and cities; prostitution and vice; weapons and fighting; gangsters and crime; the Ku Klux Klan; prison and convict labor; the abuses of the criminal justice system; prison escape and family breakup; capital punishment; the Mississippi River; floods, tornadoes, dust storms, and hurricanes; housing, insurance policies, and fires; military service, wars, and veterans; diet, working conditions, injury, and disease; death, funerals, and cemeteries; heaven and hell; bereavement and hero worship.

Because the blues has long been embraced as an authentic "folk art" by the political Left, its stoicism tends to get overlooked. Old leftists, from Anatoli

Lunacharsky (Stalin's commissar of public enlightenment) to the poet-activist Amiri Baraka, have interpreted the blues as a form of coded political protest, thereby foisting upon the music a programmatic optimism about human affairs that is simply not present. And new leftists, from rock critic Greil Marcus to black nationalist Ron Karenga, have dismissed the blues as passive acceptance of injustice, thereby missing the hard gleam of resistance at its core.

When the rural southern blues moved to the urban North in the 1940s, both its sound and its lyric content changed. In Chicago, practitioners of Johnson's Mississippi Delta style such as Muddy Waters (McKinley Morganfield) and Howlin' Wolf (Chester Burnett) began using electric amplifiers to make themselves heard over the conversational din of clubs and saloons. At the same time, one theme came to dominate the lyrics: relations between the sexes. There were commercial reasons for this change. As sociologist Charles Keil explains, "Radio stations and other commercial interests have been most energetic in reshaping blues styles." But Keil also sees other factors at work, including the fact that "male roles in the [northern] Negro community are confused, anxiety-laden, and in need of redefinition." In other words, sex became the focus of the urban blues not just because sex sells but also because sex is freighted with meanings about the stability, and instability, of life in the urban North.

Yet too often these larger social and psychological concerns are lost on listeners who are put off by the blues' sexual frankness. Oliver puts it well: "As with all other subjects the blues, when dealing with matters of love and sex, is forthright and uncompromising." Oliver suggests that "polite society" takes "offence" at salty blues language. And so, in its way, does the Old Left. Ever since Maxim Gorky's 1928 essay "On the Music of the Gross," socialists of all stripes have considered the element of eroticism in African-American music proof of "decadent commercialism." To such listeners, there is nothing but a crude leer in the famous Johnson lyric "You can squeeze my lemon 'til the juice run down my leg."

But they, too, miss the point. Like all blues lyrics, "squeeze my lemon" has to be interpreted in context. The line appears in Johnson's "Traveling Riverside Blues," a song of wry complaint. The singer has a woman in every Mississippi port, but the one in Friar's Point, he laments, has "got a mortgage on my body, now, a lien on my soul." "Squeeze my lemon" expresses lust, of course, but in a deliberately banal way suggestive of what casual sex has become for this heartsick traveling man. The next (and last) line is crucial: "But I'm goin' back to Friar's Point, if I be rockin' to my head."

Unfortunately, this larger context is also neglected by a goodly portion of the 1960s generation, many of whom embraced the counterculture's project of total sexual liberation. Such listeners, who tend to be heavily represented in the ranks of rock critics, seize upon such lyrics as proof that the essence of the blues—the real *truth* of the form—is prurience. And it is this primitivist celebration of prurience, not the puritanical head-wagging of matrons and Marxists, that has fostered the systematic debasement of the blues in rock.[1] This primitivism is in turn related to some of the oldest misunderstandings that complicate relations between black and white Americans.

The phrase "blood knot" comes from the South African playwright Athol Fugard, but it is an apt metaphor for the complex racial-sexual dynamic that has for more than three centuries shaped American culture. To describe this dynamic properly, one must go back to the beginning—to the original clash of worldviews between black Africans and white Europeans in the New World.

Historian Eugene Genovese suggests that throughout the Americas the puritanical outlook of Anglo-Saxon slaveowners made them more restrained than their Spanish and Portuguese counterparts when it came to the sexual exploitation of slave women. But restraint had a cost, especially in cases where such exploitation might have led to sympathy. Interracial love was thwarted in the English colonies, Genovese argues, not only by the injustice of slavery but also by the white culture's powerful association of sex with sin:

> Miscegenation poisoned southern race relations much less through those acts of violence which lower-class women—and their men—have always had to suffer in hierarchical social systems, than through the psychological devastation it wrought. . . . What the white men might have viewed, even if perversely, as joyous and lusty, they generally had to view as a self-degradation.

As for the enslaved Africans, most historians agree that the coherence of their original religions was shattered by slavery. But as Albert J. Raboteau notes, it is significant that most North American slaves were not converted to Christianity until the Great Awakening of the 1740s: "In the face of this religious indifference," he writes, "some forms of African religious behavior seem to have continued." Genovese concurs, adding that even after conversion, most slaves had difficulty assimilating the puritanical view of sex.

This difficulty did not stem from the Africans' savage, concupiscent nature, as was commonly believed by white Americans in the eighteenth century. Instead, it derived from the fact that the religions of Africa (like most pre-Christian religions, including those of Europe) placed sex and fertility at the center of the cosmos. However shocking to seventeenth- and eighteenth-century European explorers, the graphic artifacts, dances, and rituals of West Africa symbolized a life force neither wholly material nor wholly spiritual. A recent interfaith study of Christian marriage in Africa captures this delicately balanced view:

In the African world view sex was not biological only; it was also sacred. It was to be "used" with care; it was mysterious and like all mysterious things it belonged to the gods. The pleasure of sex was, of course, legitimate, but its outcome, whenever possible, was to be children. Childbearing was a religious and social duty. It follows, therefore, that in almost all parts and cultures of Africa, rape, homosexuality, bestiality—all sexual acts which did not fulfill both of these conditions—were condemned and severely punished. They could bring nothing but disaster not only to the people concerned but to the whole community.

According to Genovese, this African worldview persisted among the slaves, who saw sexual misconduct as "primary a moral offense to the community rather than to God," and who rejected "the denigration of sex as sinful, dirty or anything other than delightfully human and pleasurable." The slaves were no puritans, but neither did they condone sexual excess. Premarital intercourse was tolerated, even encouraged, and there was no stigma attached to its issue. But tolerance did not extend to marital infidelity, by husband or wife; the cure for a bad marriage was dissolution, initiated by either partner. Genovese reports that many slaveowners were well aware of this sexual code among blacks. The more intelligent whites even acknowledged it—some with a trace of self-deprecating humor. Mary B. Chestnut, wife of a prominent Virginia planter and politician, wrote in her diary that "Negro women are married, and after marriage behave as well as other people."

Not only did the slaves have their own sexual code. They also held definite opinions about the somewhat different code of whites. Above all, they bitterly condemned white male adventurism among their own women, and many black men were willing even to die in defense of black women. In addition, the slaves took a dim view of certain aspects of the white sexual code, notably its insistence upon the permanence of marriage and its preoccupation with female purity. The slaves were starkly aware of the gap between word and deed in white sexual morality. The majority of North American slaves lived too intimately with whites to believe that the latter always abided by the stern morality they professed. Blacks understood all too well that most whites had two moral standards: a rigid one for themselves, which they frequently fell short of, and a lax one for their slaves, with whom they frequently did their falling short.

The blood knot acquired another twist after the Civil War, when, as Genovese explains, white attitudes shifted from guilt about sex between white men and black women to terror of sex between black men and white women:

The titillating and violence-provoking theory of the superpotency of that black superpenis, while whispered about for several centuries, did not become an obsession until after emancipation, when it served the purposes of racial segregationists.

Sociologist Calvin C. Hernton describes the ensuing dynamic: the ambivalence warping the white man's perennial exploitation of the black woman, the isolation of the white woman atop a pedestal of sexless virtue, the forbidden-fruit syndrome distorting all contact between the mythically potent black man and the mythically pure white woman, the resentments and hypocrisies afflicting relations between the sexes within each group, and, finally, the foul mist of irrational violence enveloping the whole.

Especially astute is Hernton's account of how blacks themselves have strengthened the blood knot. He cites the old southern tale about a group of white men walking through a cornfield, discovering a black couple making love, and joking, "That is another good reason for being a nigger!" Toni Morrison embroiders on this tale in her first novel, *The Bluest Eye,* where instead of merely joking, the white men gather around the couple (who are very young) and goad the boy to "get on wid it." Naturally, the boy is too terrified to do anything of the kind. But to keep his tormentors at bay, he fakes it. The effect, of course, is to humiliate him before his girl and add another trauma to his life. Yet Hernton's point is that white voyeurism has caused many black people to believe in their own fakery—or, worse, to put on a genuine performance when the white folks jeer, "Make it good, nigger."

The sad truth is that sexual prowess is one of the few traits for which blacks have received tribute from whites—albeit one of spiteful envy. For a people as systematically vilified as black Americans have been, any advantage over the vilifier is bound to exert a certain attraction. Combine that with a clear-eyed view of white sexual hypocrisy, and it seems inevitable that a certain segment of the black community would come to believe that black sexual "immorality" was superior to white "morality." Hence the strain in African-American folklore that regards any restraint as a sham and any license as honest, natural, and authentic. From this strain comes the folk hero Stagolee (the original "bad nigger"), whose sexual swagger is all too frequently imitated by men (and some women) lacking any other source of pride.

Does this mean that every black performer who pleases a white audience is the same as the boy in the cornfield? Even posing the question is an insult. Yet it needs to be posed, because the blood knot has a way of entangling everyone, white and black, who studies the interaction of black performers and white audiences. Consider this passage from James Lincoln Collier's biography of Louis Armstrong:

> Precisely why white Americans have been drawn to black entertainment is not easy to explain, but two factors are evident. First, the black subculture as it existed in the slave cabins and then in big-city ghettos has always seemed exotic to whites. . . . Second, blacks were also seen as more erotic than whites. They were not expected to abide by the sexual proscriptions of white society.

Why should Collier, a white admirer of jazz, find it "not easy to explain" the appeal of black entertainment? No doubt this disclaimer arises from the context, a discussion of the voyeuristic undercurrent of white interest in African-American music. Naturally, Collier wishes to distance himself from that undercurrent, with its unflattering image of the white jazz fan as a cold, uptight puritan secretly thrilled by the warm, relaxed sensuality of black performers.

Unfortunately, this undercurrent is real. To be sure, innumerable whites have straightforwardly embraced African-American music as an antidote to excessive inhibition—not just in relation to sex but also to emotion, bodily movement, even religious enthusiasm. To appreciate the complex beauties of the music in this way, however, one must sense the difference between the erotic, which preserves the connections between sex and the rest of life, and the obscene, which severs them. African-American music is sometimes erotic, but it is never obscene, because there is always a larger whole—whether spiritual ecstasy, physical exuberance, or emotional catharsis—to which its erotic qualities are joined.

During the 1950s, a great many whites embraced rock 'n' roll precisely because of its erotic component. The rock 'n' roll craze began in the South, when young whites began tuning in to black-oriented radio stations to hear the various 1940s hybrids of blues, swing, and gospel known as "rhythm and blues." Chuck Berry, Elvis Presley, and others added country music to the mix. The rhythm and blues influence remained strong through the mid-1960s, where it can be discerned in Motown, southern soul, and the early music of the Beatles.

Of course, rock 'n' roll elicited many of the same critical reactions that the blues did. To contemporary pundits, many of them influenced by the heavy-handed Freudianism of the day, rock 'n' roll was nothing but decadent trash mass-marketed to teens. To Jack Gould of the *New York Times,* for example, Presley had "no discernible singing ability," and his stardom rested wholly on "an accented movement of the body that heretofore has been primarily identified with the repertoire of the blonde bombshells of the burlesque runway."

Predictably, this prudish response was followed by a primitivist one. Like the prude, the primitivist focused exclusively on the sexual component of African-American music. But while the prude would censure, the primitivist would celebrate. Rock critic Greil Marcus, for instance, praised Presley's music purely in terms of sexual liberation, portraying this complex, troubled figure as the first open advocate of a centuries-long "secret revolt against the Puritans."

Reading Marcus, you would never know that most rock 'n' roll lyrics were as sugary as they were salty. Nor would you know that rock 'n' roll was, first and foremost, a *dance* craze. The fans who screamed and fainted for Berry and Presley were feeling their libidinous oats, to be sure. But that is not all they were feeling. The famous rock 'n' roll deejay Alan Freed once remarked that "rock 'n' roll was merely swing with a modern name." And he was right. By the 1950s, Americans had been driven from the dance floors—first by modern jazz ("bebop"), with its exploration of rhythms too subtle for human feet, and then by postwar "pop," with its preference for midtempo ballads.

Given this dearth of danceable music, it is hardly surprising that young people would seek out whatever dance music was available. Rock 'n' roll was different from swing because it was played by smaller groups in a bluesier, rhythmically heavier style. But it was similar in ranging from the sublime to the ridiculous. Bad rock 'n' roll, like bad swing, reduces the basic elements of a steady beat and repeated melodic "riffs" to a formula. Good rock 'n' roll, like good swing, enlivens these elements with rhythmic counterpoint, rich instrumental color, and adventurous solos.

Blues playing and blues feeling persisted right through the rock 'n' roll era. Some critics, patrons, and fans celebrated rock 'n' roll in primitivist terms, but not the musicians themselves. It was not until the mid-1960s, when primitivism became the province of musicians (and would-be musicians), that the loss of vigor really began.

The change took place in Britain, largely because the British admired African-American music but found it difficult to accept its commercial dimension. The Beatles' appealing early style drew upon such authentic sources as Chuck Berry and Buddy Holly, gospel quartets, and rhythm and blues. But because the Beatles did not stress the blues, purist British fans scorned their sound as commercialized "pop." This scorn was reinforced by class bias: the Beatles were working-class pubgoers from Liverpool, while most blues fans were middle-class clubgoers from suburban London. In their anxiety to avoid the taint of commerce, the latter gravitated toward a form of African-American music that had never really "crossed over" to whites: the Chicago blues.

In fact, the Chicago blues had never been all that popular with blacks. It sold well among the uprooted Mississippians of the Windy City, but most black listeners preferred other styles, such as the spare Texas blues of Sam "Lightnin' " Hopkins, the sprightly boogie-woogie of Jimmy Reed, or the lyrically swinging Memphis sound of T-Bone Walker, B. B. King, and Little Johnnie Taylor. Most of these strains negotiated the musical spectrum from sweet to salty, smooth to rough, pure to gritty, soft to loud, and slow to fast. Chicago blues, by contrast, emphasized the qualities at the cruder end of the spectrum—almost to a fault. Or so thought its leading exponent, Muddy Waters, who grew tired of the Chicago approach in the early 1960s and returned to a broader, mellower style closer to that of his native Delta.

Yet while Muddy Waters was broadening the Chicago blues, his British admirers were narrowing it to the point of caricature. The change shows up most starkly in the human voice. Most rock pundits dutifully report that Mick Jagger of the Rolling Stones learned to sing from the blues masters. Yet, as Rolling Stones biographer Philip Norman admits, the only black singer Jagger ever came close to imitating was Chuck Berry: "Berry's voice, light and sharp and strangely white-sounding, had a pitch not dissimilar to [Jagger's] own. Singing along to 'Sweet Little Sixteen' or 'Reelin' and Rockin',' he suddenly felt like something more than a mumbling impersonator." And Jagger surpassed most of his contemporaries, whose range is aptly summarized by critic Charles S. Murray: "British blues bands ran the emotional gamut from A (I'm feeling sorry for myself) through B (I'm well'ard, me) to C (I'm not tough really but I'm going to pretend that I am) to D (I'm pissed off)." Or, as Muddy Waters himself said of the "white kids" who had taken up the blues, "They play so much, run a ring around you playin' guitar, but they cannot vocal like the black man."

Back in America, blues vocalism fared no better. Janis Joplin, the 1960s rock heroine crowned "the greatest white, female blues singer of all time," claimed to have learned her art from Bessie Smith. But vocally Joplin could not have named a less appropriate model. Smith, whose range barely exceeded one octave, was a stunning practitioner of blues "mixtery," shading every note and beat with elaborate nuance. Joplin had a strong, three-octave voice, but rather than develop its potential, she began her career imitating Smith—only without nuance, in a painfully high register. Yet even this effort sounds better than Joplin in her heyday, when she cauterized her vocal equipment with a style consisting almost entirely of screaming. Reviewing a double bill featuring B. B. King and Joplin in 1969, music critic Henry Pleasants compared King's "consummate musicianship" with Joplin's reliance upon "a sound that little boys of four or five produce when trying to determine just what degree of aural torture will finally drive Mommy or Daddy into giving them a smack in the teeth."

The debasement of vocal artistry was intimately related to a debasement of instrumental artistry. Urban blues bands typically included several instruments—two or three guitars, acoustic bass, drums, harmonica, and piano—all involved in a constantly shifting interplay. Early rock bands, by contrast, stripped down to lead guitar, bass guitar, and drums. To be sure, the Beatles used the same stripped-down lineup, and a few early rock groups, notably the Rolling Stones, often included other instruments. But the rock bands that considered themselves "progressive" used the "power trio" lineup. Unfortunately, their notion of power was one that sacrificed musical interplay to self-indulgent soloing—what Charles S. Murray calls "the fetishization of lead guitar playing as an athletic event."

"Guitar heroes" such as Jeff Beck of the Yardbirds and Pete Townshend of the Who also manipulated the enormous amplification systems developed for stadium concerts in the late 1960s. In such systems, the electromagnetic pickups on instruments (especially guitars) receive two different kinds of signals: those manually produced by the musician and those produced when the pickups recycle the sound issuing from the huge loudspeakers. The result, familiar to anyone who has ever hooked up an amplifier, is "feedback," a sustained, distorted tone shrieking with high harmonic overtones.

The only person to turn feedback and other electronic effects, such as reverb, into blues was the black American guitarist, Jimi Hendrix. As white Chicago bluesman Mike Bloomfield explains, Hendrix used "an immense vocabulary of controlled sounds, not just hoping to get those sounds, but actually controlling them as soon as he produc[ed] them. I have never heard such controlled frenzy." As Townshend admits, "Jimi took some of our stuff, but he was doing a whole different thing with it. He took what I was doing and turned it into music."

Hendrix's closest rival was Eric Clapton, who, together with Jack Bruce (bass) and Ginger Baker (drums), started the archetypal power trio, Cream, in 1966. Blues devotees though its members were, Cream excelled at sheer virtuosity and volume—"a wall of noise," writes one critic, "that was physically palpable, and . . . almost literally bowled audiences over." But volume was not the only reason Clapton did not achieve Hendrix's "controlled frenzy." As one Hendrix biographer recalls, Clapton was also deficient in rhythm:

> Clapton could never seem to understand what Hendrix was getting at when he stressed rhythm accompaniment. Hendrix felt that Clapton was too intellectual about it, . . . insisting the guitar was now an instrument of the virtuoso, just like in classical music. Jimi tried to get across the message that the funk, the feel, and the boogie of the blues came from a subtle rhythmic combination . . . where the guitar put the electric fire crackling over the bass and drums, creating the dynamic that made folks want to dance and shout and get it all out.

Clapton himself agrees. Commenting on his early days, he admits he "forgot" about "time—when you hit the note and when you stop. How you place it exactly."

The glory days of guitar heroism were brief. Hendrix succumbed to drugs in 1970, leaving his "gauntlet," in Charles S. Murray's phrase, "still lying where he left it." And Cream broke up in 1969, despite its commercial success (its first three albums sold 15 million copies in the United States). To his disappointed fans, Clapton explained that Cream had taken "hard rock" as far as it could go. And he meant it. For all his diverse musical activity since then, Clapton has never returned to the sound that culminated in Cream. I say "culminated" because, although various offshoots of hard rock dominated the 1970s, they did so without progressing musically. To be sure, hard rock has produced a line of guitar virtuosos: from Beck and Townshend to Jimmy Page and Eddie Van Halen, to Steve Vai and Vernon Reid. But for all their virtuosity, the only musical values displayed by these idols are speed, dexterity, and athleticism. Guitar heroes scorn the high-tech music now made by computer, but their own playing sounds almost as mechanical.

Early rock also bludgeoned the spirit of the blues in two crucial areas: in its treatment of the erotic and in the relationship between performer and audience. In the first, the Rolling Stones led the way, understanding all too well that many rock fans were transfixed by the myth of black "hyperpotency." A few black performers were already trading on that myth in the mid-1960s, but the Rolling Stones had the advantage, and convenience, of not actually being black. They could cater to white primitivism without worrying about white self-consciousness. And it worked. One British reviewer exclaimed, "Never before has there been a sound to rival this—Except, perhaps, in the jungles of darkest Africa!" Another critic extolled Jagger as England's best "imitation black blues" singer—not just because he exuded "more aggression, more obvious sexuality," but also because he had "big flappy lips." Yet another admirer called guitarist Keith Richards "the world's only bluegum white man, as poisonous as a rattlesnake," and extolled the Rolling Stones for "inciting the crowd to orgasm."

Hendrix catered to the same fantasies, but for him primitivism was both a ploy and a trap. As Clapton explains,

> The English people have a very big thing about a spade. They really love that magic thing, the sexual thing. . . . And Jimi came over and exploited that to the limit. . . . He'd do a lot of things, like fool around with his tongue or play his guitar behind his back and run it up and down his crotch. And he'd look out at the audience, and if they were digging it, he wouldn't like the audience. He'd keep doing it, putting them on, playing less music.

The Rolling Stones also led the way in transforming the relationship between performer and audience. Unlike the Beatles' manager, Brian Epstein, who got his start selling records in music-obsessed Liverpool, the Stones' manager, Andrew Loog Oldham, entered the record business from the tangential fields of fashion and public relations. Thus, Oldham's ideas about performance came less from African-American music than from the visual arts—particularly from the stale avant-garde attitudes that he (along with many other early rock figures, including three members of the Stones) picked up in art college. For Oldham, it was only logical to market the Rolling Stones as the "artistic" alternative to the "commercial" Beatles. Here is the strategy, laid out in the group's first "official biography," published in 1964:

Many top pop groups achieve their fame and stardom and then go out, quite deliberately, to encourage adults and parents to like them. This doesn't appeal to the forthright Stones. They will not make any conscious effort to be liked by anybody at all—not even their present fans if it also meant changing their own way of life.

To prove themselves true artists, the Rolling Stones cultivated a posture of contempt for the audience: Instead of smiling at the camera, they scowled; instead of signing autographs, they spat; instead of ending a show at the London Palladium by greeting the fans, they turned and stalked off.

The irony, of course, is that this posture departed not only from the Beatles but also from the blues. Granted, the crowd-pleasing manner that is part of every bluesman's stock in trade takes a different form when removed from its original all-black setting. But it always reflects a basically positive disposition toward whatever audience happens to be out there. Even the notoriously moody Howlin' Wolf never failed to behave courteously when performing for his newly acquired white fans. Like most African-American musicians, he lived by the adage "The people can make you, and the same people can break you."

It was not long before rock's "artistic" posture became the whole show, with music taking second place to the spectacle of the superstar slowly destroying himself in an increasingly trite orgy of rampant promiscuity, alcoholism, and drug abuse. Hendrix's life—and music—sank into chaos while his fans cheered. Joplin dropped all pretense of blues artistry in favor of what *Rolling Stone* writer David Dalton calls "a myth of freedom and a disdain for boundaries." The "deadpan formality" of the blues may have been good enough for black folks, Dalton writes, but protean beings like Joplin needed to "experience not just the blues but the original impulse that created it: the violence, eroticism, craziness, and sputtering of rage." And the singer agreed:

> Young white kids have taken the groove and the soul from black people and added intensity. Black music is understated. I like to fill it full of feeling—to grab somebody by the collar and say "Can't you understand me?" . . . I was brought up in a white middle-class family—I could have anything, but you need something in your gut, man.

Unfortunately, all Joplin had in her gut at the time of her death in 1970 was hard liquor, hard drugs, and hard feelings toward the world for not loving her enough. And all she left behind was the widespread impression that singing the blues is the same as throwing a public tantrum.

By the end of the 1960s, a great many people, musicians as well as businessmen, were taking careful note of hard rock's commercial success and proceeding to turn the form into fool's gold. Celebrated guitar solos became codified so that less-gifted players could repeat them fast and loud; hard rock's heavy beat became fixed in a deadly pounding that fits the worst stereotypes of both foes and friends. Focusing on this monotonous pounding, political philosopher Allan Bloom observed that "rock has the beat of sexual intercourse." Steve Tyler of the hard-rock band Aerosmith makes a similar observation, though with pride rather than disdain: "It's rhythm and blues, it's twos and fours, it's fucking." No one seems to notice that this "dinosaur beat" is a travesty of the rich, tireless, complicated rhythms of the blues.

By the early 1970s, dozens of groups, from Steppenwolf and Grand Funk in America to Led Zeppelin and Black Sabbath in Britain, had adopted the formula. A few, such as Vanilla Fudge, Iron Butterfly, and Deep Purple, added arty organ noodling. But as the 1970s became the 1980s a seemingly endless parade of groups—Aerosmith, Judas Priest, Def Leppard, Iron Maiden, Twisted Sister, Poison, Motley Crüe, Guns N' Roses—prospered with a no-frills style described by the critic Jon Pareles as "stylized and formulaic, a succession of reverberating guitar chords, macho boasts, speed-demon solos and fusillades of drums." To the first MTV generation, this stuff is "rock 'n' roll," even though it sounds nothing like the music of the 1950s. But sound is no longer the point. To these fans, "rock 'n' roll" isn't music; it's *attitude*.

And where did this attitude come from? Not, it turns out, from African-American music. Instead, it grew out of the decadent, pseudoliterary sensibilities of Steppenwolf and certain other rock groups of the late 1960s and early 1970s. The music of these groups acquired the name "heavy metal," a phrase borrowed from William S. Burroughs's fictional celebrations of sadomasochism, drug addiction, and ritual murder—subjects that have over the years come to dominate rock lyrics. The champions of heavy metal may claim that there is no significant aesthetic or moral difference between Presley singing "That's All Right Mama" and a group like Slayer regaling 12-year-olds with simulations of human sacrifice, blood communion, mutilation, and necrophilia. But they are wrong.

To begin with eroticism, heavy metal's main accomplishment has been to polarize the sexes. Instead of the heartsore male-female dialogue found in the blues, heavy metal substitutes a male monologue. Musically and emotionally, it succumbs to an adolescent preoccupation with "hardness"—meaning not "hard singing" in the blues or gospel sense but the compulsion to prove one's masculinity by avoiding sounds and feelings that might be construed as "soft." The change is aptly summarized in Charles S. Murray's comparison of Muddy Waters's and Led Zeppelin's treatments of the same song:

> The former is a seduction, . . . warm and solicitous: [Muddy Waters] suggests that the woman to whom he is singing is both sexually inexperienced and starved of affection,

and volunteers to remedy both conditions. . . . Led Zeppelin, by contrast, come on like thermonuclear gang rape. . . . The woman is strictly an abstract, faceless presence; she is an essential part of the intercourse kit, but not as an individual. "Love," in this context, is a euphemism for something measurable with a ruler.

And that was back in 1970. By the 1980s, heavy metal had quit bothering with euphemisms—or with intercourse, for that matter. Good old promiscuity went the way of the dodo bird, as "speed metal" and "death metal" groups beefed up their acts with bloody sadism. The mid-1980s were the heyday of rock videos depicting female victims chained, caged, beaten, and bound with barbed wire, all to whet the appetites of 12- and 13-year-olds for onstage performances such as the famous one in which the group W.A.S.P. sang their hit song, "Fuck Like a Beast," while pretending to batter a woman's skull and rape her with a chain saw.

Offstage, performers regaled fan magazines with tales of strange sex acts with groupies involving wine and beer bottles. Metal stars bragged about having intercourse during performances, recording sessions, or video tapings. Heterosexual dancing disappeared, and metal concerts became all-male workouts consisting of "head-banging" (snapping the head up and down to the beat), "slam-dancing" (violently jostling one another), and "moshing" (pushing and shoving in the "pit" below the stage).

Then there was the semiofficial religion of heavy metal: Satanism and the occult. Every rock fan knows about Altamont, the 1969 rock concert during which a spectator was brutally murdered by members of the Hell's Angels motorcycle gang, hired to provide "security." Altamont is commonly viewed as the last gasp of the 1960s, the turning point after which the counterculture slipped from "peace and love" into a darker, more pessimistic phase. This view is accurate enough; Altamont certainly took the investment bloom off massive outdoor rock festivals. But the change did not happen in a day. The Rolling Stones had already darkened rock's mood with songs like "Sympathy for the Devil"—which in fact they had performed at Altamont just before the murder occurred.

A mere flirtation for the Rolling Stones, Satanism became a passion with Led Zeppelin's lead guitarist, Jimmy Page. So fond did Page grow of Aleister Crowley, Britain's most famous modern Satanist, that he purchased a former Crowley estate, the reputedly haunted Boleskine House on Scotland's Loch Ness. Next in line was Black Sabbath, a British group derided by critics for their "anguished screeching about war pigs, rat salads, iron men and similar gloomy topics set to an endlessly repeated two-chord riff," but capable of filling football stadiums with crowds eager to see lead singer Ozzy Osbourne do something vile—as when, later in his career, he bit off the head of a bat.

As every rock fan knows, Old Nick is also present in the blues—witness the many legends about blues performers (Robert Johnson, for one) gaining their talent through Faustian pacts. But the very extremes to which heavy metal carries Satanism suggests a radical break. For the fact is that African-American culture takes a very different attitude toward the devil than did a turn-of-the-century English decadent such as Crowley, who courted the London press with self-advertised sex orgies, drug marathons, and black masses. Reflecting its folk origins, the blues depicts Satan as a conjurer or trickster—wicked but also vain, mercurial, and susceptible to human wiles. Historian Lawrence Levine reminds us that, during slavery, "songs of the Devil pictured a harsh but almost semicomic figure (often, one suspects, a surrogate for the white man), over whom [the blacks] triumphed with reassuring regularity." Hence the strain of wry humor toward the devil and his works that pervades the blues, including Johnson's.

The other part of heavy metal's semiofficial religion is pre-Christian mythology, especially Celtic and Norse. When first touted by Led Zeppelin, this interest fostered a moody, quiet phase in hard rock's otherwise deafening sound. But overall, the main impact has not been musical. Led Zeppelin reverted to its "wall of noise," and its half-digested mythology set what biographer Stephen Davis calls "the tone of overwrought Dark Ages fantasy . . . that would be the standard psychic backdrop for all the heavy metal bands to come."

It is difficult, now that heavy metal is the theme music of Europe's neo-Nazi youth movement, to ignore the chillingly fascist flavor of this blood-and-soil backdrop. Equally troubling is metal's long-standing posture as an aggressively "white" music, in hostile opposition to whatever "black" music it happens to be competing with. To be sure, heavy metal started out paying homage to the blues. But in a way, that was exactly the problem. Nothing breeds resentment like homage. Rolling Stones biographer Stanley Booth remarked to Mick Jagger in the late 1960s that "we all want to be black, what we think black is." Jagger replied, with characteristic coolness, "*I* don't. I'm not black and I'm proud of it."

This reply speaks volumes about the transition from early rock to heavy metal. Jagger himself was never smitten with "blackness" so much as skilled at manipulating others who were. But those others were legion, and by the end of the 1960s it is likely that they were tired of the whole musical, folkloric, and (especially) sexual mystique of "what we think black is." What a relief, then, to recast primitivism as an affair of wild white savages lurching through the primeval mists of Europe!

Unlike heavy metal and its grotesque progeny, the blues comes by its supernaturalism naturally. Songs like Robert Johnson's "Hell Hound on My Trail" and "Me and the Devil Blues" emerged from a living tradition; they were not dug out of a source book for the self-conscious purpose of shocking the public, as when Motley Crüe adopted the Satanic pentagram in the hope that, as one band member allowed, "it would be able to get a rise out of normal citizens." Nor does the supernaturalism in the blues lead to a cult of obscenity and brutality, as in heavy metal and such unspeakable offshoots as "death metal," "grindcore," and (arguably) "gangsta" rap.

To some apologists, this cult of obscenity and brutality is justifiable as ritual, if not as art. To sociologist Deena Weinstein, heavy-metal concerts offer nothing less than "epiphany"—Dionysian ecstasy, brilliant theatrics, organizational genius, and idealized community, all in a perfect balance. Rock critics agree. To Mikal Gilmore of *Rolling Stone,* heavy metal is "a vital and reliable rite of passage." To Jon Pareles of the *New York Times,* "heavy metal concerts are theatrical events, community rituals." Of like mind, unsurprisingly, is heavy-metal producer Tom Werman, who reminds us that young people "need to be angry, they need to have music they can clench their fists by, to pump themselves up by. They're not always happy. They're confused and alienated. . . . They need an outlet."

Given my own account of the blues as a ritualized way of coping with harsh realities, I have a certain sympathy for this line of argument. But only up to a point. Werman says that heavy metal helps young people "feel angry." Yet he also implies that they are already angry, that society has made them angry. Does heavy metal offer a release for anger that is already there? Or does it whip up even more anger? Does whipping up more anger offer greater release? And what happens afterward? Does the head-banger go home after the concert with his troubled emotions under control, having experienced what Albert Murray calls "a ritual of purification and affirmation"?

Somehow I doubt it. As Albert Murray explains, the blues ritual is intended to help people "meet the basic requirements of the workaday world." The same cannot be said of heavy metal. To the contrary, the young people most deeply involved with metal, such as the dropouts, runaways, and "throwaways" who congregated in places like Hollywood Boulevard in Los Angeles during the 1980s, seem incapable of coping with anything. As a number of observers have noted, these young people display a bizarre combination of vaulting ambition and drooping despair, based on the conviction that the only alternative to stardom is death in the gutter. Nor do the stars provide guidance. They are just as nihilistic as their followers. But instead of being punished for self-destructive behavior, they are rewarded.

At some point, even apologists for metal quit praising its cathartic powers and say that most head-bangers grow out of their obsession anyway. This is the apologists' final argument, and it may very well be true. But it fails to explain how those same young people are supposed to make up for the months and years they wasted in the grip of something so ugly and useless.

I have no doubt that the youthful (and no-so-youthful) champions of rock and metal will ignore the substance of these arguments and dismiss them as the complaint of an aging flower child longing for the music of her youth. My reply is simple: the blues is not the music of my youth. It was not created by my generation or by any single age cohort. Quite the opposite: it is an American perennial, whose flowering and withering does not fit easily into the tidy decades so beloved of some pundits, critics, and historians. That is why serious attention to the blues is not a sign of regression but rather of renewal—that is, of hope for an imminent improvement in the quality of the music we hear. At the moment, such signs are appearing all over.

Take jazz, long considered defunct but recently revitalized by the so-called "neoclassical" movement, which seeks to identify with both the greater jazz past and the greater jazz audience. The name topping the charts is Wynton Marsalis, the New Orleans trumpeter who dazzles listeners with his facility in both the European classics and bebop. But there are many other names, and, as Marsalis would be the first to point out, neoclassicism is nothing new. Indeed, his heroes are those figures who over the past 40 years have exerted a steady counterpressure against such tendencies as free jazz and rock fusion. When Charlie Parker died in 1955, many of his fellow beboppers decided that the best way to move jazz forward was to reach back—into the blues. Thelonious Monk, Charles Mingus, John Coltrane, and Sonny Rollins did just that, and they were only following in the footsteps of Ellington.

Or take country music, currently the best-selling form of popular music behind the amorphous category "rock." In the mid-1960s, when rock first appeared on the scene, its fans considered country music a lily-white bastion, altogether hostile to the blues. And, indeed, country was dominated by the unbluesy "Nashville Sound," aptly summarized by Robert K. Oermann: "The procedure was to smooth over the roughness of the country style of a singer with violin sections, soft background voices, sophisticated arrangements, and studio technology. A typical Nashville Sound record features a high jangling guitar strum, country instruments overlaid with a soaring violin section, vocal background 'oooohs' . . . and a slight echo effect on the lead singer's voice."

Yet this image of country music blots out the memory of those legendary performers, from Jimmie Rodgers to Bob Wills to Bill Monroe, who learned their craft partly from bluesmen. It also obscures the importance of honky-tonk, the Texas strain of country heavily influenced by rhythm and blues during the 1940s. During the 1950s, the most respected names in country—Ernest Tubb, Lefty Frizzell, Hank Williams, George Jones—retained those rhythm and blues influences, even when besieged by violins. And by 1959, honky-tonk was poised to make a comeback, as the commercial success of Buck Owens's swinging, bluesy sound enabled him to build a recording empire in Bakersfield, California, and foster the 1960s careers of such honky-tonk stalwarts as Merle Haggard.

The abiding weaknesses of country music are two: love of sentimental cliché, rooted in its turn-of-the-century link with Tin Pan Alley, and an aversion to the rhythmic counterpoint of African-American music. The blues influence provides a welcome tonic for both ills, as proven most forcefully by "outlaw" country musician Willie Nelson. A successful songwriter who left Nashville for his native Texas in 1971, Nelson is an iron-willed character who proceeded to use country as a base from which to explore everything from jazz to gospel, blues to boogie-woogie, spirituals to swing. If the term "outlaw" means musical freedom, then Nelson is responsible for the happy fact that country music today contains more outlaws than law-abiders.

As for the lily-whiteness of country, I cannot assert that any part of the record industry, including the Nashville establishment, operates without white racism. But there is more than one kind of racism in popular music. After all, what is more degrading to blacks: country music's apparent exclusiveness or metal's (and "gangsta" rap's) increasingly sick primitivism? Moreover, it is not evident that the country audience rejects black performers out of hand. Beginning in 1965, black country star Charley Pride sold more records than anyone on the RCA label except Elvis Presley. It is also true that, despite the fondness for country music expressed by such legendary black artists as Ray Charles and Charlie Parker, the genre's pale complexion is partly the artifact of black attitudes. In 1992, rising black country singer Cleve Francis made an astute observation: "Maybe Nashville did discriminate against black singers, but in the black community, nobody encouraged you to sing country music—it's a two-way street."

Of course, both Pride and Francis avoid injecting blues into their country music. In this one respect, at least, country audiences resemble rock audiences: they are more tolerant of musical freedom in white performers than in black. But here again, the charge of racism is too easy because the best country musicians use their eminence to reaffirm their blues roots. And these reaffirmations—whether Nelson doing a TV special with Ray Charles or Randy Travis recording a duet with B. B. King—contain none of the leering condescension found in many rock tributes. It may seem odd to discuss country music in the same breath as neoclassical jazz, since their aims and accomplishments are so different. But they belong to the same family, and in their own ways they both provided a safe haven for the blues when the blues was under attack.

Finally, there are the musicians I call root doctors, those members of the 1960s generation who fell in love with the blues and, despite many changes, have remained stubbornly loyal ever since. Now in their forties or older, these people are as seasoned, in their way, as the blues performers they first admired. Their careers have been swamped, sometimes capsized, by the upheavals of their times. But the familiarity in the 1990s of names like Mike Bloomfield, Ry Cooder, John Mayall, Bonnie Raitt, Mac "Dr. John" Rebenneck, and Jimmie Vaughan suggests that maybe these people have been doing something right all along. The salient fact about these root doctors is that, unlike such 1960s rock icons as Mick Jagger, they are not perceived as "old." They are not getting any younger, to be sure. But their music is not "old," at least not in the sense of being stale, repetitious, or anachronistic. Instead, it occupies a special niche only slightly below that of the masters. Most listeners, young and old, understand that these root doctors have paid their dues.

Back in the 1960s, Muddy Waters tactfully passed judgment on his young British acolytes:

> I think they're great people, but they're not blues players. Really, what separates them from people like Wolf and myself, we're doing the stuff like we did way years ago down in Mississippi. These kids are just getting up, getting stuff and going with it, you know, so we're expressing our lives, the hard times and the different things we been through. It's not real. They don't feel it. I don't think you can feel the blues until you've been through some hard times.

Note well that Muddy Waters does not find the source of blues feeling in skin color, geography, social class, or relationship to the means of production. Rather, he sees it as the product of long, hard experience with life as well as with music. Yet once achieved, blues feeling has the power to transcend race, sex, generation, and most other human divisions. That is the source of its vigor, and that is why, if the blues does not return to our music, our music will remain in trouble.

NOTE

1. By "rock" I mean the white-dominated styles of music discussed herein, from the Rolling Stones to such contemporary forms as "speed metal" and "grunge." I do *not* mean the diverse strains of African American music lumped together as "rock 'n' roll" in the 1950s and early 1960s, and I do *not* mean the various black-dominated styles, from Motown and soul to funk and non-"gangsta" rap, now misleadingly classified as "pop."

15   THIS SURPRISING BUSINESS OF COUNTRY MUSIC

DOUGLAS GOMERY

Country music has become big business. Its stars make millions of dollars and appear in every form of mass media. Country music now ranks as the most-played musical form on U.S. radio. The Nashville Network and Country Music Television rate among cable TV's most-watched channels; total sales of country music on audiocassettes and compact discs are measured in the billions of dollars.

Like all media, the country music system is driven by its stars. Midway through the 1990s, if one totaled up music sales in the United States, the Beatles topped the list at $71 million, but "country hunk" Garth Brooks ranked second at $60 million. And Brooks was still in the middle of a remarkable rise to fame. The Beatles took three decades to establish their record; Brooks took but seven years, and in the process easily eclipsed such pop icons as Elvis ($50 million) and Michael Jackson ($48 million). No one has come close to Brooks's rate: selling an average of $8 million per annum. Pop stars Whitney Houston and Billy Joel settle for selling $3 million per year.

GARTH BROOKS AND THE "SUDDEN" POPULARITY OF COUNTRY MUSIC

The truth be told, country music has always sold well. It just hasn't gotten the attention that pop has because *Billboard* charts long undercounted its tallies. Garth Brooks soared to the top so quickly because a new computerized counting system directly and correctly measured his fans' devotion.

Prior to 1991, record charts were tallied by surveying music-store salespeople. Record companies understood, and paid off store employees with free albums, concert tickets, and even luxury vacations. Rock sales were overcounted, while country acts of the 1980s, not the favorites of young, male store employees in general, lagged.

In 1991 SoundScan began compiling *Billboard* charts using a "point-of-sale" computer system that tallied actual cash register receipts by picking up data from that ubiquitous bar code found on every cassette and compact disc. This unfiltered information was then sent directly to a Hartsdale, New York, central computer. Consequently the very first SoundScan survey, published in the May 25, 1991, *Billboard,* contained, "overnight," fifteen more country albums than had shown up the week before. Soon thereafter Brooks's *Ropin' the Wind* became the first country album ever to enter *Billboard*'s pop chart at number one.

TV proved the key. Musically Brooks claims that his brand of three-minute ballads deals with mundane reality: "The six o'clock [TV] news put to music." Before Brooks, country music recording was promoted simply and plainly through sounds on the radio; fans expected their favorites to sound like the record or compact disc. The ability to manipulate sound in the studio created a perfect *audio* performance. To promote their work Brooks and company skillfully employ music videos to create an image of Brooks's sound. Today Brooks's careful stage manipulation of space, time, costumes, and props creates far greater expectations; videos maintain that image through calculated editing and careful manipulation of mise-en-scène. They represent the perfect whole performance—the star, the band, the song, and the atmosphere.

The largest of the mass media in the United States—television—has embraced the Brooks performance. In the 1990s television's schedules became dotted with country music award shows that could feature a portion of the Brooks act. In the mid-1990s there were so many "specials" on the CBS television network that industry insiders joked that the network should be relabeled the Country Broadcasting System. In early 1997 few observers were surprised when CBS anted up $1.5 billion to purchase cable TV's Nashville Network and Country Music Television.

Suddenly Garth Brooks was topping sales charts not just in the United States, but around the world. He skillfully built on his music videos and television appearances, and only then went on the road to meet and entertain his new fans. He mounted a three-year world tour entitled "Fresh Horses," where he sought to top his previous world tour, which had climaxed with him singing "Ain't Going Down ('Til the Sun Comes Up)" by literally soaring 150 feet in the air above the stage (with the help of wires). With his computerized lighting system, he set off on a three-year odyssey, first entertaining audiences in North America, then scheduling concerts in Europe, Australia, and Asia.

Brooks's lure around the world is astonishing. From 1991, when he hit megastar status, to 1994, Brooks played some 211 shows around the world, grossing well in excess of $50 million. The stories of sellouts became legendary. In January 1994, for example, when tickets finally went on sale in Dublin, Ireland, so many fans called in that they overloaded the Dublin telephone system and blocked all incoming and outgoing calls across the nation in the process. In Japan Brooks's ballad "What She's Doing Now" because the theme song for the TV drama *Oka No Ue No Hi-mawari* (The sunflower on the hill). Fans in Barcelona and Madrid stunned Brooks and company by singing along to all the hits—in English, with an appropriate Oklahoma accent.

Because of Brooks and those who aspire to surpass him, by the middle of the 1990s, country music sales had quadrupled from a decade earlier. The star system—innovated by the movies some 75 years earlier—had worked again. And it spread Brooks and country music far beyond a simple niche market. Indeed at one point in the mid-1990s the best-selling country music album could not be found on *Billboard*'s charts because *The Garth Brooks Collection* was available only at McDonald's fast-food restaurants. In its first three weeks *The Garth Brooks Collection* sold more than 3 million compact discs as part of a month-long McDonald's promotion. My guess is that about the time the calendar turns to 2000 Brooks will be feted as the top seller of music in history.

DEFINING COUNTRY MUSIC

Until the 1950s it was called "hillbilly music," the plaintive and toe-tapping tunes of poor white Southerners. Twin fiddles, steel guitars, and distinctive Southern accents provided the sounds for dancing; close harmony singing flowed from front porches and churches alike.

Then the media intruded. The homespun Carter family trio became favorites through their pioneering phonograph recordings. Radio's *Grand Ole Opry* and *The National Barn Dance* turned amateur musicians into seasoned professionals by beaming their pickin' and singin' into homes all across the nation on Saturday nights. Early stars such as Jimmie Rodgers, Roy Acuff, and a host of others from the South took guitars, dobros, banjos, fiddles, harmonicas, and other cheap portable instruments, and borrowed from Tin Pan Alley, vaudeville, the blues, and even jazz to craft a sound that continually changed as new musicians innovated.

Gene Autry added the Western myth to the lyrical mix; Bill Monroe created the drive of all-acoustic bluegrass; rock forced country to smooth out its sound, add a beat, and sing it in a way urban Americans, used to Tin Pan Alley, would embrace. This was the "Nashville Sound" of Patsy Cline, Loretta Lynn, and Tammy Wynette, and it forever transformed country into a commercial popular music industrial segment and stamped its ballads and dance music into the national consciousness.

The 1960s Nashville Sound, with its ever-so-smooth harmonies and gut-wrenching love songs, thrust country music into America's musical mainstream. Nashville became the center of the production of this style and forced challengers to the margins. But since the 1960s, Nashville has not remained a simple-to-define musical monolith, but a musical center that through a series of constant transformations has ever broadened its appeal. Crooners such as Jim Reeves worked the pop music fields that Bing Crosby proved could make one not only a singing sensation, but also a movie star and a multimillionaire. Dolly Parton took Nashville to the limits of its country origins by exaggerating the myth so much no one could tell if she was putting her audiences on or not. Willie Nelson warbled his way into the Carter White House.

Today country is so broad that Nashville embraces Danny Davis and his brass, renegade Oklahoman Merle Haggard, and Texas child prodigy LeAnn Rimes, who if listened to closely sounds like a combination of Judy Garland and Kay Starr, not country predecessors Patsy Cline and Brenda Lee. Country represents a truly classical American popular musical hybrid, one that has taken a remarkable journey from homespun tunes sung in the hills and hollows of Virginia, Kentucky, and Tennessee to fans who filled New York's Central Park in August 1997 by the hundreds of thousands to cheer, sing along with, and idolize Garth Brooks.

The media may have fueled this musical diaspora and crossbreeding, but certain characteristics were always present. Country music is a commercial industry that did not begin until the 1920s, when phonograph records were sold in a national market and regional radio "barn dances" (today represented by WSM's *Grand Ole Opry*) drew new fans. In the 1950s television added more enthusiasts; a decade later the fragmenting specialization of FM radio made the current hits of the latest Willie Nelson, Dolly Parton, Tammy Wynette, and Johnny Cash available on more stations than any other playlist. During recent decades the audiocassette and compact disc enabled the devoted to take their country favorites wherever they would like to listen: in the car commuting to work, at home doing chores, or just sitting back and thinking about a simpler, easier world, one not yet suburbanized.

As a musical form country may have started on front porches in the Appalachian Mountains and the South with families singing hymns and folk tunes, but since its commercialization in the 1920s new genres such as Texas honky-tonk and Western swing, the Cajun and Bakersfield sounds, bluegrass, rockabilly, and the Nashville Sound have pushed the parameters of what is possible and what is accepted.

Still, at its core, country, however much its liberal aficionados sometimes protest, is white people's music, which at its best captures the strains of working-class life through telling lyrics, but often simply falls back to the verbal clichés that have driven pop music for a hundred years. Maybe the mythos of the lone romantic cowboy has best defined the pull of the lyrics and the music— at least since the days of Gene Autry in the 1930s.

And country, like its cousin rock 'n' roll ever changing, is the music of the American South. As geographer George O. Carney aptly noted, "Country music's audience is national, but it has been and continues to be performed, composed, and produced by individuals born in the so-called 'fertile crescent' of country music, an area running from the mountains of West Virginia to the prairies of east Texas." Only its fans are from around the world.

PAST AND PRESENT

The Nashville Sound is best represented today by the singing of Patsy Cline. Her life was cut short more than three decades ago, but today Patsy Cline sells more than half a million "units" (audiocassettes and compact discs) each year. In her thirty-one-year life she traveled outside the continental United States once for a brief stop in Hawaii, and for a couple of brief tours through Canada. Yet each Labor Day weekend fans from as far away as Russia, Australia, and Wales journey to her hometown of Winchester, Virginia, to pay their respects and see where she lived. Her life has been made into a movie; impersonators can be found on stage and in cabarets all across the world.

But none of this extraordinary fan embracing would be possible without the most corporate of commercial power. A Patsy Cline could have come to be only because of the distributional power of an oligopoly of multinational music companies. Her label might read "Decca," but the monies spent on Patsy Cline's "Greatest Hits" collection—which has sold more than 8 million copies as a record, an eight-track tape, a cassette, and a compact disc—have flowed directly into the coffers of MCA, as powerful a media conglomerate as has ever been formed. MCA and its five multinational rivals take full advantage of the modern-day fact that music, more than any other mass medium, crosses international boundaries and finds fans in every corner of the world, and thus has produced sales abroad that rival those of American movies and television.

How this international industry works is quite simple. Six multinational corporations dominate the music business; each exercises enough power to keep the newest Garth Brooks compact disc in stores just up the aisle from the albums of Patsy Cline, in shops from Tokyo to Tallahassee, from Poland to the Philippines.

With country music as top seller, it is surprising that only one of the "Big Six" music companies—Warner—is based in the United States. This music division of the world's largest media company, Time Warner, is based in New York City, with offices in Nashville and Los Angeles. While pop star Madonna has brought the company fame and fortune, Warner's current country stars, including Paul Brandt and Shelby Lynne, add mightily to Warner's bottom line. So do sales of the greatest hits of Dwight Yoakam and Emmylou Harris.

The other major record companies, which make so much money from music that originated in the American South, are based in Europe, Asia, and Canada. The Bertelsmann Music Group, for example, headquartered in Germany, still makes millions each year from the country boy who became rock's first great star—Elvis Presley. Other past favorites who still sell steadily include Jim Reeves, Connie Smith, and the Sons of the Pioneers. Current BMG heartthrobs include Travis Tritt, Randy Travis, Clint Black, and Alabama.

EMI, headquartered in London, still makes money from the Beatles, but earns far more from Capitol Records' biggest star, Garth Brooks. Yet it steadily earns from its country backlist, as a new generation discovers catalogue albums from the likes of Wanda Jackson and Tanya Tucker. Across the North Sea the Netherlands-based Polygram company, part of the Philips Electronics N.V. conglomerate, includes in its diverse list of present and past country stars the Statler Brothers, Hank Williams, Terri Clark, Kathy Mattea, and the Kentucky Headhunters. Sony Music of Japan owns the former CBS records, and today sells albums from Asleep at the Wheel, Ricky Skaggs, Willie Nelson, Ray Price, and Mary Chapin Carpenter. Finally, MCA, headquartered in Montreal, Canada, as a division of the vast Seagram's liquor empire, has long had the greatest sales from the deepest list of country stars, including Vince Gill, Trisha Yearwood, Brenda Lee, Kitty Wells, Webb Pierce, Patsy Cline, and Reba McEntire.

Each of the Big Six measures sales in the billions of dollars, year after year. Their power comes not only from having signed all the top stars, but also from relentless control and protection of their unique capability to distribute globally. Only the Big Six can promise an aspiring star that his or her music will get into customer hands in every nation on the planet. Independents, on the other hand, need to work through an expensive patchwork of agents, an awkward and logistical nightmare that leaves many markets unserved. Only the Big Six can showcase and maximize sales for decades, enabling new fans to discover a long-dead Patsy Cline.

COUNTRY MUSIC IS EVERYWHERE

Because of the Big Six, one cannot escape the presence and lure of country music wherever one might travel. The music of white, poor, hill folks, living outside the mainstream of America, far from the cities that fostered jazz, rhythm and blues, rock, and rap, has seen their music achieve middle-class appreciation and acceptance. In 1996 neopopulist presidential aspirant Patrick J. Buchanan, when interviewed, bragged that his favorite song was Patsy Cline's "I Fall to Pieces." H. Ross Perot, candidate of the people four years earlier, employed another Cline hit, "Crazy," as his official theme song.

In recent national surveys taken by the U.S. Census Bureau and the National Opinion Research Center, 50 percent of Americans stated that they liked country music, more than liked easy listening (49 percent) or rock (44 percent). Given that respondents needed to be at least eighteen years old, the figure for rock is admittedly understated, but even a reasonable adjustment upward would rank country and rock as the most popular music forms of the 1990s.

The surveys reveal that in the 1990s, as the baby boomers aged, they took their earnings and bought more and more country music. The average age of a country fan has remained in the mid-40s over the years, and in the 1990s there are more persons over 40 than ever before.

Expectations thus have risen. An early 1980s hit country album, by Willie Nelson or Dolly Parton, for example, was considered successful when it sold one million units. By 1997 the 18- to 34-year-old U.S. population segment and those households with incomes in excess of $60,000 a year were buying Garth Brooks albums in record numbers—to the tune of $2 billion per year. Country ranks as the fastest-growing segment of the music audience.

This rise to middle-class acceptability and respectability began in the 1970s, as radio formats moved from rock to country, as cheap audiocassettes brought easy-to-sing-along music into the cars of frustrated commuters, and as TV made Johnny Cash and Dolly Parton hosts of their own prime-time shows. The line between mainstream pop music and country had begun to blur as Cash, Parton, and a host of others began to exploit all the media available to expand their appeal and replace pop music as the favorite of the middle class. A notable achievement in this quest came in 1974, when Nashville's Country Music Association named Australian pop superstar Olivia Newton-John its "Entertainer of the Year."

Suddenly, going to Nashville replaced "Goin' Hollywood." A business formerly measured in millions of dollars came into a billion-dollar boom. Prime-time television appearances replaced tours of one-nighters in high-school gyms. Stage shows matched the techno-extravaganza of rock tours. As late as the 1980s country superstar Reba McEntire simply figured it was enough to stand center stage and croon her latest hits to adoring fans. By the 1990s her tour featured multiple costume changes and background videos with animation projections on a 25-by-60-foot screen; it requires eight Peterbilt trucks to transport Reba's production from coliseum to coliseum.

Music videos, too long associated simply with MTV, fueled this transformation during the late 1980s. Cable TV's Country Music Television (CMT) premieres the latest country songs, reaching a younger and more middle-class audience. Hillbilly was definitely out and almost forgotten; suburban-grown "hat acts" ranked among the biggest attractions in the music world.

Radio spread Elvis in suburbia in the 1950s; CMT did the same for Billy Ray Cyrus in the 1990s. His "Achy Breaky Heart" became an overnight hit, even though it received little play on radio and he had never toured. His song zoomed to number one in two weeks based on his sex appeal in the music video. He knew it. Just before being mobbed at a gathering of fans in mid-1992, the newly minted "hunk-of-the-year" threw his arms around Tracy Storey, the programming manager of Country Music Television. "Thank you," Cyrus gushed, "CMT has changed my life." He should have been happy; his compact disc broke the Beatles' record as the fastest-rising album debut in history.

The promotion of country music through radio and television has long been key to its ever-increasing popularity. If it were not so, a "Patsy Cline" would never have been discovered, and would simply not be known today. Born Virginia Patterson Hensley in the Shenandoah Valley of Virginia in 1932, she grew up in rural America and because of radio became a "hillbilly music" fan. Her radio favorites: *The Old Dominion Barn Dance* from Richmond, Virginia, and the *Grand Ole Opry* from Nashville, Tennessee.

As with most country music stars, poverty drove her. Singing in fraternal halls and in honky-tonk dives around Virginia, West Virginia, and Maryland paid poorly and was leading nowhere until in 1956 she found television. Thereafter, in fits and starts, her career took off. First it was a local TV show in Washington, D.C., alongside Jimmy Dean and Roy Clark. Then it was national network TV. On January 21, 1957, she appeared on and won first prize in CBS prime time's "Talent Scouts" as a gushing Arthur Godfrey introduced her to the nation. Her winning song, "Walkin' after Midnight," became her signature tune.

Her records were played on radio because her producer—Owen Bradley, a former big-band leader—gradually pushed her into a more pop sound, with violins backing up her velvet voice instead of steel guitars. Her biographical movie, *Sweet Dreams,* is named after a song that is as silky smooth as any of a Frank Sinatra or Jo Stafford. This Nashville Sound drew millions of new fans outside the South, yet her appeal to her basic country constituency never dissolved. In 1961, Patsy Cline finally cashed in on this radio play, and "I Fall To Pieces" and "Crazy" became national country and pop music chart hits. During the next 18 months Patsy Cline appeared everywhere. She sang frequently on television, from New York to Philadelphia to Nashville to Los Angeles. She played Las Vegas and vocalized in Carnegie Hall. Then the private plane she was flying home in crashed in a violent storm, and a great new star was lost.

But not completely. Her recordings (about 110 with new ones still being found and reissued) have kept her alive and popular with new generations. The media help, since all variety of musical artists—from the avant-garde k. d. lang (who named her band "The Reclines") to Madonna—publicly claim her as inspiration, and act on their admiration. Emmylou Harris and Reba McEntire have recorded "Sweet Dreams" as their homage to Patsy Cline.

Thus while she has been buried just outside Winchester for well into three decades, Patsy Cline's legion of fans has never been larger. Indeed people who claim they "can't stand" country music like Patsy Cline. Her magic speaks across decades through her constantly reissued songs on compact disc, a variety of radio appearances also on compact disc, and two home videos showcasing her TV appearances, and video testimonies by admirers. She is a constant media presence, and thus her career continues.

DIFFICULT CONTRADICTIONS AND OTHER VEXING QUESTIONS

Country music is truly a big business. And that business has come about because the mass media first spread it across the country, and then around the world. Its appeal is vast, and usually predictable. But what does all this mean? What is at the bottom of this fascinating popular-culture phenomenon? These questions cannot be answered simply, but in seeking their solution we do move to the heart of the key problem of the mass media: understanding its influence and power.

Country music began as the homemade sounds of a particular people and place: white, working-class Southerners, torn between the temptations of the city (all those honky-tonks) and the familiar feeling of rural farm life. But the South is no longer rural; it has become suburban, with attractive, well-stocked mega-malls replacing any vestige of the country store. Yet this has not caused country musicians to celebrate. They seem more likely to express and lament a sense of loss, a feeling of hopelessness and powerlessness, stranded in the present seemingly headed nowhere.

Fighting back, some offer a nostalgic, glowing, sentimental view of the past, one that could offer an escape from the troubles of the present. Inspired by a renewed sense of Christian faith, a Ricky Skaggs seems to rejoice in the face of the temptations of the suburbanized world. Yet if a certain brand of nostalgia is country's weakness, it is also its strength. Respect for the past offers a defense against simply being swallowed up in a new suburban world. By reviving and reveling in legendary singers and songwriters, country music has developed and held on to a lineage of sittin' on the front porch and makin' music with friends and neighbors.

Thus the bulk of the U.S. population, living in the suburbs, has taken to Garth Brooks and his songs alongside the six o'clock news. Here is no poor mountain boy, born on a tenant farm, unfamiliar with city ways. Like his fans Brooks graduated from college (Oklahoma State University with a degree in advertising), prefers the golf course to the pool hall, is proud of his IRA accounts, and visits prisons only to entertain, not serve hard time. Brooks and his rivals put Mercedes-Benzes and Volvos in their videos, not pickups and hot rods. When pressed they will admit they prefer white wine to bottled beer.

Country has taken up the mantle that Tin Pan Alley long possessed, servicing white America. Charley Pride, an African American, may demonstrate some cross-racial appeal, but scan the data: country is middle-class, white, and suburban. Survey after survey indicates that the typical fan is a white (94 percent compared to the national 78 percent) Sunbelt resident. Truth be told, country music does not seek to cross ethnic and racial lines, settling to appeal across all income levels of whites. Still surprises pop up that undercut the stereotype and give pause to simply categorizing country as white men playing for white suburbanites.

Scan the aging white fans in Branson, a tiny town nestled in the foothills of the Ozarks in the far southwestern corner of Missouri, 250 miles from the closest major airport, and properly expect that Branson's two dozen modern stages would offer yesterday's country stars, from Roy Clark to Loretta Lynn. Yet Branson's top attraction cracks the mold: Shoji Tabuchi, a native of Japan who as a violin student in the mid-1960s fell in love with the sound of the fiddle when he attended a Roy Acuff concert, and whose displays of fiddlin' close his shows now to standing ovations. Tabuchi formed his own band in Japan and then with his earnings journeyed to the United States to create The Osaka Oakies. Fans praise his "authentic sound," glittering costumes, and lavish stage productions, and as if on cue rush the stage at the close of his performance armed with flashing cameras and autograph books.

Breaking the stereotype even more is Jim Reeves, a white man from rural Texas who died in 1964 and yet today is a top-selling artist in Nigeria and Kenya. Like Patsy Cline, who died about 17 months earlier, Reeves lives on through an endless series of "Greatest Hits" collections. With a smooth baritone, he is best remembered in the United States for his hit "Four Walls," "a touch of velvet," a mellow and caressing sound that somehow accomplishes a cross-cultural miracle, pleasing the aspiring white middle-class faithful back in Texas while also winning a legion of black fans in Africa.

In the early 1960s Reeves actually toured in Africa, reaching South Africa three times, with one side trip to Rhodesia. But showing up is not the same as conquering and achieving long-run popularity. Superstars James Brown and Stevie Wonder drew only shrugs in Nigeria, while Reeves continues to sell and inspire. The Zanzibar Cowboys is no 1970s U.S. punk rock band, but a 1990s black band whose name honors its island homeland. In performance after performance, the Cowboys play homage to Reeves, dressing in homemade Western-movie costumes and singing Reeves's greatest hits to appreciative audiences. Africans so love Reeves's music they have given it a special name—sentimental music.

Despite this thickening complexity and many contradictions, country music is rejected as serious stuff worth study within the academic world. Not only does it have no place in the standard university curriculum, its harmonics are considered overtly simplistic, its lyrics too often maudlin. While it is surely the case that using the analytical terms employed to make sense of Bach and Mozart do not help understand the power and appeal of Patsy Cline or Hank Williams, that does not mean they are not worthy of study. Country music, like much of popular culture, needs to be completely rethought starting with Roland Barthes's dictum, "the text's unity lies not in its origin but in its destination."

Country music seems simple in both form and structure, yet it is so powerful and broad in its appeal that the task of analysis is just beginning. We need to abandon the criterion of European stylistics as the sole judge of great music, and look to intensity and unity as important terms of praise and evaluation. Country music at its best should been seen, heard, and appreciated like Hollywood cinema, a vast and powerful machine producing classical texts that sometimes are as complex and unified as any artistic work.

A BRIGHT FUTURE

If its appeal and categorization remain vexing, its continual popularity has not. Country's greatest stars continue to expand their lure in strange and unexpected ways and places. In June 1997, *Always . . . Patsy Cline* opened off-Broadway and fans found their way to Union Square to prove Patsy Cline's enduring appeal by packing the Village Arts theater to see and hear actresses try to capture a country legend.

Indeed, here we have a theatrical phenomenon. Some production of *Always . . . Patsy Cline* has been running somewhere in the United States through the mid-1990s, whether in Chicago, or San Francisco, or Denver. Through the flimsy narrative of a rise to fame and early death, crowds rediscover an image most barely know from a Hollywood movie and principally through a limited body of recordings.

But there is no mistaking the lure and power. One theatrical producer recalled, "I had no idea how broad Patsy's appeal was. It isn't just with older people who remembered her, either. She's loved by college kids, blue collar, white collar. She's sort of a female Elvis." The statistics back him up, and simply make the case that much more vexing. One Cline impersonator, Jessica Welch, as of 1997 had played Cline on stage more than 300 times in some 26 different locales. Fans seemed unable to get enough. Thirty years after it was recorded Cline's "Crazy" ranked as the most-played song on American jukeboxes.

In 1996, the hottest new country star, LeAnn Rimes, soared to the top of the charts, replacing Garth Brooks, by selling herself as "the second coming of Patsy Cline." The teenaged Rimes's 1996 album *Blue* sold more than three million copies in a year; the title track was no 1990s tune but a song written nearly two generations earlier for Cline herself. Rimes told interviewers, "Patsy Cline was one of the first country artists I listened to. I love her music, especially 'Crazy.' She's been a big influence on me." This from a singer born in 1982, a full generation after Cline died.

Here the past meets the present, and seems to assure a bright future for country music. Fueled by the mass media, country music has taken its place as part of world culture. Its appeal and impact have been exploited by the Big Six. Here we can praise the exchange of musical styles, while understanding that the vast global power of the Big Six has helped this American music flow around the world (good) while limiting the reverse flow of indigenous musics from elsewhere into the United States (bad).

The media have efficiently machined the production and distribution of country music, and should continue to do so. New media—from digital television to five hundred satellite-delivered channels of entertainment and news—will work with the Nashville machine to further sales. The journey of country music from the hollows of the American South to virtually every city and hamlet around the world will continue unabated as country music continues through what is best labeled its "Golden Age."

FURTHER READING
MOVIES AND MUSIC

William Randolph Hearst once observed, "The coming of the motion picture was as important as that of the printing press." For once the quixotic press lord was right.

The movies first appeared in the United States in 1895. By 1926 enough time had passed so a writer could offer up a historical analysis, and that year Simon & Schuster issued Terry Ramsaye's monumental survey (868 pages) of the American cinema, *A Million and One Nights*. "For the first time in the history of the world . . . an art has sprouted, grown up, and blossomed in so brief a time that one person might stand by and see it happen." Ramsaye crafted four types of portraits: pioneering inventors (Edison was his favorite), astute businessmen (here it was Adolph Zukor, founder of Paramount Pictures), glamorous stars (such as Charlie Chaplin and Mary Pickford), and a few great directors (of whom D. W. Griffith was the most important).

Since Ramsaye, thousands of writers have added volumes to these four categories, principally biography after biography of stars, important and obscure. A loyal book-buying public never seems to tire of confessions and exposés. Some authors, such as Richard Schickel in his *D. W. Griffith: An American Life* (Simon & Schuster, 1984), have tried to expand and reshape Ramsaye's categories. But, ironically, at the end of his exhaustive tome Schickel returns to an almost "Ramsayesque" conclusion: we can best understand the history of the first two decades of American cinema through the career of this single filmmaker. For a more balanced view of Griffith's contributions it is best to read Thomas Gunning's *D. W. Griffith and the Origins of the American Narrative Film* (University of Illinois Press, 1991), which carefully situates Griffith's accomplishments within the rise of the Hollywood studio system.

When I'm Bad I'm Better: Mae West, Sex, and American Entertainment by Marybeth Hamilton (HarperCollins, 1995) offers a rare non-Ramsayesque biography of a star, absent the usual fawning praise. Instead Hamilton traces the rise of the fabled movie queen of the 1930s from her working-class background, and argues that West's youthful experiences in New York City provided the material that she carefully re-enacted with an in-your-face, working-class sexuality. Moviegoers loved West's ironic self-parody and Hamilton uses careful analysis of this irony to shed light on how much America has changed since the Great Depression.

Recent scholarship has tried to move away from the "great man" or "great woman" approach to examine the creation and maintenance of the central institution of the movies, Hollywood. First of all a business, Hollywood must be studied as an industry, one in quest of ever-greater profits. In 1931, former film industry executive Benjamin B. Hampton surveyed the peaks and valleys of the first 35 years of business growth in his still-influential tome *History of the American Film Industry* (reprint, Dover, 1970). Hampton was the first to warn us to not be dazzled by "Lotus Land" and to remember that the monies enter the motion picture industry through box offices in thousands of theaters. Ben M. Hall, in his beautifully illustrated *The Best Remaining Seats* (Bramhall House, 1961), tells the story of those movie palaces, and through photograph after photograph lovingly embraces these fabled cathedrals of pleasure. Hall reprints one telling *New Yorker* cartoon in which a mother is seen dragging her gaping child through the rotunda of the now defunct Roxy Theatre as the child inquires, "Mama—does God live here?" Today the centerpiece of the moviegoing experience is found at a "multiplex" cinema in a suburban shopping center. How the exhibition side of the American film industry has moved from Ben Hall's mythic movie palaces to the cineplexes of the 1990s is the subject of Douglas Gomery's *Shared Pleasures: A History of Movie Presentation in the United States* (University of Wisconsin Press, 1992).

Early Hollywood defined a style and practice of narrative filmmaking that is by and large still with us today. David Bordwell, Janet Staiger, and Kristin Thompson in *The Classical Hollywood Cinema* (Columbia University Press, 1985) show how the story-driven conventions of film style (editing, camerawork, sound, acting, and decor) were established by 1920. A decade later, with the coming of sound, Hollywood's rules for proper filmmaking had become "naturalized" throughout the world. At the center of these stories, for the moviegoing public, were its larger-than-life stars. Richard deCordova's *Picture Personalities: The Emergence of the Star System in America* (University of Illinois Press, 1990) carefully traces the emergence of the star system within the discourse of the new American film industry. What deCordova calls the "conventions of stardom" were transformed into myth as Hollywood's features moved into movie palaces, abetted by publicity centered on puff profiles in fan magazines such as *Photoplay.*

William Randolph Hearst was not the sole American to recognize the power of the Hollywood cinema. Garth Jowett in his *Film: The Democratic Art* (Little, Brown, 1976) notes that "the first official court case involving a movie was *People v. Doris* in 1897." Both Jowett and Robert Sklar in his *Movie-Made America* (2d ed., Random House, 1995) examine in some detail how the Establishment has tried unsuccessfully to control the movies. Censorship did not begin with the now-familiar alphabetic ratings code of "G" through "NC-17," but became the rallying cry of reformers before the first decade of the twentieth century had ended.

Politics and cinema have long been intertwined, and Gary Crowdus and a score of contributors try to sort out the significant issues in *A Political Companion to American Film* (Lakeview Press, 1994). One of the key concerns that politicians long have touted has been cinema's extraordinary power over youth. These claims have long been exaggerated. In *Children and the Movies* (Cambridge University Press, 1996), authors Garth S. Jowett, Ian C. Jarvie, and Kathryn H. Fuller lay out the origins of scientific inquiries into movies' effects on children, and note that despite well-funded studies no one has yet figured out the effects.

We do know that by 1934 a rigid economic hierarchy of eight corporations controlled the movie industry, and to ward off possible governmental censorship they instituted self-censorship (the Hays Code), prohibiting certain forms of unacceptable behavior on screen. *The Dame in the Kimono: Hollywood, Censorship, and the Production Code* (Grove, Weidenfeld, 1990), by Leonard J. Leff and Jerold L. Simmons, offers a first-rate examination of the workings of the Hays Code. Through a detailed study of the records of the Production Code Administration, the authors provide an in-depth history of how Hollywood's leaders tried to have it both ways, celebrating the titillation in films such as *I'm No Angel, A Streetcar Named Desire,* and *The Outlaw,* while convincing the public they had film's effects under control.

The Hays Code was no government institution, but the work of eight collusive studios. As Douglas Gomery demonstrates in *The Hollywood Studio System* (St. Martin's, 1986), eight companies defined the conditions of classical film production, worldwide distribution, and ownership and operation of first-run picture palaces in the largest cities in the United States, Canada, and even in a handful of the capitals of Europe. We all know these companies by their symbols: Paramount's mountain, MGM's "Leo the Lion," the Columbia lady, and so on. These three companies plus United Artists, Universal, Warner Bros., RKO, and Twentieth Century Fox formed corporate Hollywood.

In this industrial system cinema artists had to struggle to express their own personal visions of the world. Those with certain skills survived, even thrived. Consider the case of the noted costume designer (and rare woman with power) Edith Head in her autobiography *Edith Head's Hollywood* (Dutton, 1983). Is *The Birds* (1963) a Hitchcock film or an Edith Head film? Should its composer and sound coordinator, Bernard Hermann, share in the credit? Scholars and fans alike still argue over these issues.

Whomever deserves the proper acclaim as the true author of the film, Hollywood as institution has relied on selling its features to the public based on certain categories or genres: yesterday's Westerns and gangster films, today's science-fiction and horror blockbusters. All these genres—and more—are truly significant American cultural innovations. Some of the most interesting writing on cinema has focused on the musical. Jane Feuer in *The Hollywood Musical* (Indiana University Press, 1982) and Rick Altman in *Genre: The Musical* (Routledge & Kegan Paul, 1981) skillfully dissect what seem to be the most obvious of cinema, particularly those made in the 1930s and 1940s, and conclude that the best of these works of music and dance were defined by a self-reflexivity and self-consciousness that any modern artist should admire.

The Philosophy of Horror or Paradoxes of the Heart (Routledge, 1990) by Noel Carroll systematically takes on the horror film, from *Frankenstein* to *The Exorcist.* An academically trained philosopher, Carroll carefully examines why this genre has become so persuasive, why audience members are so attracted at the same time they are so repelled, and why fans are frightened by what they "obviously" know does not exist. *The Philosophy of Horror* represents that rare book that takes something so familiar and analyzes it in a new and fresh way.

In the 1950s, as the great Hollywood studio system began to reinvent itself, pundits began to see more cinema from Europe and, within a decade, declared movies to be a serious art form. During the 1960s universities from Harvard on down began to offer film courses. Academics divide the study of the cinema into three parts: theory, criticism, and history. Three books artfully summarize the tools scholars have developed within this tripartite arena: J. Dudley Andrew's *The Major Film Theories* (Oxford University Press, 1976), David Bordwell and Kristin Thompson's *Film Art: An Introduction* (McGraw-Hill, frequent new editions), and Robert C. Allen and Douglas Gomery's *Film History: Theory and Practice* (McGraw-Hill, 1985).

The world of film theory is by far the most dense and impenetrable of these three. David Bordwell's *Making Meaning: Inference and Rhetoric in the Interpretation of Film* (Harvard University Press, 1989) offers an important, clearly written, and logically argued study about how we discover meaning in the movies. Bordwell systematically maps different strategies for making meaning out of films, illustrating his points with a vast array of examples. He examines how critical institutions constrain and contain the very practices they promote, and how the interpretation of cinema has become the central theoretical preoccupation of film studies as an academic discipline. David Bordwell and Noel Carroll, in their edited volume *Post-Theory: Reconstructing Film Studies* (University of Wisconsin Press, 1996), take up Bordwell's call for a new film theory, and their two dozen contributors advocate a renewed pluralism, a more open debate.

Because scholars have embraced film does not mean that in recent years Hollywood has altered its fundamental practices. It hasn't. We surely have new *auteurs,* best known to the filmgoing public through the work of Steven Spielberg and George Lucas. But as Michael Pye and Lynda Myles in their *The Movie Brats* (Holt, Rinehart and Winston, 1979) make quite clear, the true power rests elsewhere—with the major corporations that distribute the work of these filmmakers around the world. Today's Hollywood, if anything, is even more single-minded in its quest for maximizing profits. In contrast, aspiring filmmakers have become idealized in their desire to make a statement. David Lees and Stan Berkowitz, in *The Movie Business* (Vintage, 1981), write, "The uniformed [aspiring *auteurs*] show up at Hollywood and Vine and see nothing but tacky tourist traps and hookers of both sexes breathing in a lot of brown smog." A generation later official Hollywood has chased away the hookers, but the myth of making a significant statement in film remains strong among the youth seeking a way to comment upon the ills of society.

The contemporary film industry seems less and less separate from its visual cousin television. Hollywood used to have press agents, skilled at placing items in the gossip columns; today publications specialists release slickly packaged video clips to *Entertainment Tonight.* However, regularly (about every five years) a scandal brews and offers a peek at Hollywood's seamy underbelly. Investigative reports lay bare just how cutthroat the film business can be. Consider "one of the most remarkable boardroom dramas in history" in David McClintick's bestseller *Indecent Exposure* (Morrow, 1982), the most thoroughly reported of all Tinseltown's exposés.

Producers handle the money in making movies and thus often are at the center of Hollywood's frequent scandals. In the normal routine they organize the production, arrange for financing, and make sure copies get to theaters and video stories—all important tasks. They contract talent (stars and directors) through agents who peddle their clients' services for a 15 percent cut. We have no history of producers or talent agencies, but do have one fine case study, Frank Rose's *The Agency* (HarperBusiness, 1995), which tells of the rise to power and current methods of the William Morris Agency.

The mighty studio bosses hire and fire producers, directors, and stars. No individuals have more power and influence within the Hollywood system. Occasionally the studio boss and the corporate CEO work as almost a single unit. This was surely the case of one of the longest-running tandems: Warner's CEO (during the 1970s and 1980s) Steven J. Ross and his studio boss Robert Daly. Sadly Ross died before he could experience the spoils of victory through Warner's 1990 takeover of Time, Inc., the largest deal in Hollywood history. This mega-merger is well documented in Connie Bruck's *Master of the Game: Steve Ross and the Creation of Time Warner* (Simon & Schuster, 1994). Yet Hollywood is not always a story of industry success. Peter Bart's *Fade Out: The Calamitous Final Days of MGM* (Morrow, 1990) analyzes two decades of MGM ownership, when the grand studio was used as a Wall Street poker chip, nearly ending Leo the Lion's symbolic roar.

Finally, as befits a new scholarly field, cinema studies has begun to generate useful reference tomes. Only one is truly essential. To learn the cast and credits of nearly every Hollywood sound film dip into Leonard Maltin's *TV Movies* (issued yearly by Signet). Maltin and a half-dozen helpers offer reliable evaluations of the films and, even in the age of the World Wide Web, provide the easiest way to check a movie's stars and director.

Like Hollywood, the popular music industry has had a fascinating and complex history, and today it occupies an important place in modern culture. One of the key threads in popular music in the United States has been its African-American influence. West African ideas of pitch and rhythm involuntarily entered the New World, encountered both repression and appreciation from white society, and over the centuries emerged transformed as a family of musical forms—blues, jazz, and rock. All three—and their vast array of variants—prove capable of expressing the essence of modern life with great force and appeal.

But this historical tale of African American influence has been so interwoven with America's long-running, ever-festering problem of racism that authors who have tried to wrap its history into a neat linear package disagree at best, and frequently vehemently denounce each other. Is it a history of exploitation—of black creators ripped off by white imitators and their corporate sponsors—or of artistic triumph, as African American musicians permanently reshaped mainstream culture despite persistent warnings by conservative white cultural arbiters? These are the major arguments in a vast and growing literature.

Simply describing the music or its history can mean trying to have it both ways. In *The Music of Black Americans: A History* (Norton, 1971) Eileen Southern, a former professor of music and Afro-American studies at Harvard, shows little interest in questions of artistic ownership, probably because she is too busy documenting an immense and varied musical tradition. She meticulously traces lines of descent from West African singing to slave hollers, and then on to ragtime, jazz, and rock 'n' roll, in the process assembling a staggering catalogue of movements and ideas.

It is a straight line for Southern, but not for others. For jazz critic Albert Murray, author of *Stomping the Blues* (McGraw-Hill, 1976), the blues is a distinctly American creation, "a synthesis of African and European elements, the product of an Afro-American sensibility in an American mainland situation." European and African cultures met elsewhere in the world, Murray notes, and produced "calypso, rhumba, the tango, the conga, the mambo, and so on, but not the blues." Murray's arguments echo those expressed by French musician and critic André Hodeir in *Jazz: Its Evolution and Essence* (Grove Press, 1953). Writing from the perspective of a practicing musician who loves both jazz and European classical music and can discuss both with passion and precision, Hodeir defines jazz as the product of the blues and military marches, fostered in the melting pot of late-nineteenth-century New Orleans.

But not all scholars argue that there was a significant interaction between white and black cultures. Historian Lawrence Levine and musician Ortiz M. Walton would disagree—with different emphasis. In *Black Culture and Black Consciousness* (Oxford University Press, 1977) Levine admits black and white Americans living around the turn of the twentieth century sang many of the same songs, but he describes the blues themselves as thoroughly African, showing white cultural influence mainly through the emphasis on the solo performer—a rarity in African music. Walton, in *Music: Black, White, and Blue* (Morrow, 1972), goes one step further, insisting that the blues and jazz have been tempered by "the American experience" but draw little from white culture. Walton sees the relationship between black musicians and the mainstream as a steady pattern of exploitation and artistic theft. It is surely hard to deny his contention that the music industry has long preferred to promote fresh white faces, no matter who played the music first.

Hymns have played an important role in changing pop music as well. A living example can be found in gospel music, in both its black and its white exponents. The gospel form actually has a short history, going only as far back as Chicagoan Thomas A. Dorsey, as shown in Michael W. Harris's well-researched *The Rise of Gospel Blues* (Oxford University Press, 1992). In 1928 Dorsey began to write religious songs in blues arrangements. Ministers mocked them; transplanted Southerners loved them. In time, through such compositions as "There Will Be Peace in the Valley" and such disciples as Mahalia Jackson, Dorsey's "new old-time" music took on an altogether new meaning, reinventing and revitalizing traditional music, for both blacks and whites.

It may be more surprising that any chronicler of African-American music could go on paper supporting the record industry, but sociologist Charles Keil manages it. In *Urban Blues* (University of Chicago Press, 1996), Keil states that for all their faults, the record companies have introduced mainstream (i.e., white) America to a vital piece of black culture, and have given a select few blues artists an audience beyond the dreams of not a few music makers. "Is the opportunity to tell your story to hundreds of thousands of people an exploitation?" he asks. Considering the impoverished, nomadic lives of such blues greats as Robert Johnson, whose life was detailed by Peter Guralnick in *Searching for Robert Johnson* (Obelisk, 1989), Keil's answer that "many blues artists would pay for the privilege" sounds like the truth. Charles Wolfe and Kip Lornell have penned the biography of one of the most important figures of popular music in *The Life and Legend of Leadbelly* (HarperCollins, 1992). Huddie Ledbetter's "Irene, Good Night" was a big hit in the 1950s; his blues inspired a generation of folk singers and pop artists.

Questions of exploitation have dogged rock 'n' roll to a far greater extent than blues or jazz, in part because of the belief that rock is merely black music played by whites. But in *The Sound of the City: The Rise of Rock and Roll* (rev. ed., Pantheon, 1984) writer and independent record executive Charles Gillett argues that while rock may have begun life as repacked rhythm and blues (with Elvis as the innovator), rock is hardly unified. By 1960 it was, to the lament of many purists, blending country, swing, and a myriad of other musical forms to create something truly new. An important companion to *The Sound of the City* is Peter Guralnick's *Last Train to Memphis: The Rise of Elvis Presley* (Little, Brown, 1994) which offers, to date, the definitive story of the creation of one of the most important musical icons of the twentieth century.

If rock 'n' roll's rise seems a simple climax of important social and artistic forces, its continual transformation from the "Golden Age" of the late 1950s is not clear at all. There exist too many fragmenting figures and forces. For example, David Henderson's *'Scuse Me while I Kiss the Sky: The Life of Jimi Hendrix* (Bantam, 1981) examines the role race played in making Hendrix, an innovative black guitarist, into a mainstream pop icon. Tellingly Hendrix's management premiered him to a white audience in England, where locals were in love with African-American blues. His managers then brought Hendrix to the middle-class white teens of the United States. Rather than view Hendrix as an isolated figure, a lone black musician surrounded by whites imitating blacks, Henderson sees him as part of a larger music, as "essentially" a bluesman, sold and made rich by white audiences. Henderson describes the affinity Hendrix felt for such diverse but closely related artists as jazzman Roland Kirk and soul-funk groups War and Sly and the Family Stone. To Henderson, Jimi Hendrix was one black artistic hero out of many, able to win acceptance through the sheer strength of his powerful music.

Today pop music offers an eclecticism that few can make sense of, but some scholars are beginning to try. David Brackett's *Interpreting Popular Music* (Cambridge University Press, 1995) argues, through close analysis of the songs of Billie Holiday, Bing Crosby, Hank Williams, and James Brown, that a plurality of methods is necessary to fully appreciate and understand popular music. He asks scholars to break down the rigidity of current scholarly boundaries and cross disciplines. Simon Firth has collected five fascinating essays in his *Facing the Music* (Pantheon, 1988), dealing with such important subjects as Top-40 radio and its impact, the rise of MTV, and the power of marketing popular music as a commodity. His contributors explain what your favorite pop song is doing in a wine-cooler advertisement, and how black music and white music cross over to "new" audiences.

Cathy Schwichtenberg's edited volume *The Madonna Connection: Representational Politics, Subcultural Identities, and Cultural Theory* (Westview, 1992) uses postmodern theories to engage a truly postmodern figure. All her thirteen contributors acknowledge Madonna's cultural significance; all differ on Madonna's impact. Is she liberating, challenging the dominant culture and powers that be? Or is she just about the best mass-marketer since P. T. Barnum?

One rich vein of musical scholarship in recent decades has been opened as scholars have rediscovered country music. The most influential survey is Bill C. Malone's *Country Music U.S.A.* (rev. ed., University of Texas Press, 1985). From Jimmy Rogers to Jerry Jeff Walker, from Kitty Wells to Patsy Cline, country music emerged from the songs of the working-class whites of the South, the plain folk who later migrated to work in Detroit, Los Angeles, and Memphis (the case for Elvis's family). At their best country ballads offer painful expressions of the loneliness, frustration and alienation of rural white folk trying to fit into urban America. *All That Glitters: Country Music in America* (Bowling Green University Popular Press, 1993), edited by George H. Lewis, also examines country music's roots, its local and regional influences, its honky-tonk subcultures, its Nashville respectability, its possible futures. No bigger star ever appeared in country music's short history than Hank Williams in the decade after the Second World War. He died young, but his songs and singing live on, and their inspiration and origins are well analyzed in *Hank Williams: The Biography* by Colin Escott (Little, Brown, 1994).

Country "singin' and pickin' " started with families trapped in the hollows of the Smoky and Blue Ridge Mountains. A few, like the Carter family, became world famous. Others, like the Stonemans, became regional favorites. Lucky for us Ivan M. Tribe has researched and written *The Stonemans: An Appalachian*

Family and the Music That Shaped their Lives (University of Illinois Press, 1993). Here is a slice of Americana, some seventy years of a family trek from the mountains of Virginia to the slums of Washington, D.C., to the glitter of Nashville. The Stoneman family was named "musical group of the year" in 1967 by the Country Music Association; one year later their leader and founder, Ernest V. "Pop" Stoneman, was dead and family members scattered to pursue their own careers. Luckily the Stonemans left their singin' and pickin' on record.

Nashville has only relatively recently become the center of country music recording. Through the first half of the twentieth century, there were many regional centers. Wayne W. David chronicles the rise and fall of one in *Pickin' on Peachtree: A History of Country Music in Atlanta, Georgia* (University of Illinois Press, 1990). Technology killed these regional centers once live radio shows gave way to syndicated and network TV programming. Yet playing all over the nation never stopped. One can see this in the continuing craze for bluegrass music, with its acoustic instruments and absent drums and electric guitars. Neil V. Rosenberg's *Bluegrass: A History* (University of Illinois Press, 1993) explains that bluegrass, while "old-time" in spirit, was not introduced into the country music vernacular until after World War II by Bill Monroe, Lester Flatt, and Earl Scruggs. That Elvis, Buddy Holly, Patsy Cline, and Hank Williams studied their styles and sang their songs only attests to the vitality and positive influence of this musical form.

TELEVISION AND NEW TECHNOLOGIES

DOUGLAS GOMERY

It was a defining moment in American history, albeit one run over and over, like an episode of *Star Trek*. Into the tidy living room of a young family's suburban home, usually just days before Christmas, came the electronic marvel. The old mahogany radio set, already seeming a bit antique, was shoved into a corner, and two hefty deliverymen struggled to position the bulky new console across from the couch, between the easy chairs. Everyone gathered around as the first test pattern came on. Then the fun began—perhaps with giggling children on *Howdy Doody* or the Top-40 beat of *Dick Clark's American Bandstand* or the stars on *Ed Sullivan's Toast of the Town* or the magnificent coronation of Queen Elizabeth II. Thus was a new age born.

Pictures flowing through the air. That miracle had been much sought after and anticipated since movies and radio transformed American popular culture during the first quarter of the twentieth century. And like those two earlier marvels of mass communication, and with many times more power, television has so refashioned and reshaped our lives that it is hard to imagine what life was like before it.

During the Great Depression and World War II, families gathered in crowded city apartments or in the parlors of distant farms to listen to the radio. But TV was instantly and unalterably linked with mid-century America's rising suburban ideal. Indeed, certain TV offerings, such as *Ozzie and Harriet,* became synonymous with the ideal. Along with closely cropped lawns, two cars in the driveway, and a single earner so well paid that no one else needed to work, TV became a symbol of the "good life" in modern America.

Reprinted from the autumn 1993 issue of *The Wilson Quarterly*.

The TV boom was delayed first by the war and then for several years after 1948 by what might be called "technical difficulties." By 1948, the number of stations in the United States had reached 48, the cities served 23, and sales of TV sets had passed sales of radios. Coaxial cables also made possible fledgling networks, relaying live shows (there was no tape then) from the East to the Midwest. But as more and more stations went on the air it became clear that the Federal Communications Commission (FCC) had not allowed enough geographic separation between stations to prevent serious interference. The agency froze TV-station allotments and redrew the maps. It was only on April 14, 1952—with the FCC's Sixth Report and Order—that TV as we know it first began to flow to all sections of the United States.

So rapid and complete was TV's friendly takeover of the American imagination that when Lucille Ball gave birth to her second child the "same" night in January 1953 that her Lucy Ricardo character on *I Love Lucy* gave birth to "Little Ricky," it caused a national sensation, including an article in *Life* and a cover story in *TV Guide,* itself newly born.

Ubiquity may be the medium's leading characteristic. In 1950 far less than 10 percent of Americans owned sets. Those were folks lucky enough to have the $500 that a black-and-white receiver cost at a time when $3,000 was considered a good yearly salary and $5,000 would buy a splendid Cape Cod in Levittown. But TV's allure was powerful. By 1955 about two-thirds of the nation's households had a set; by the end of the 1950s there was hardly a home in the nation without one. By 1961, when Newton Minow, the newly appointed chairman of the FCC, proclaimed television a "vast wasteland," there were more homes in the United States with TV than with indoor plumbing. In less than a generation, the TV set had gone from being an expensive, somewhat experimental gadget to a home appliance considered more indispensable than the toaster or washing machine. With the possible exception of the videocassette recorder (VCR) in the 1980s, no other electronic gadget has been adapted so widely and with such alacrity.

Today, 99 percent of all households possess at least one TV, and most have two or more. There are nearly 200 million sets in use. More American homes have TVs than have telephones. (One study of the tiny minority of people who spurn TV found that the archetypal naysayer is a university professor of literature, wedded professionally to the printed word.) We take them to the beach, plug them into our automobiles, and even strap them on our wrists when we go jogging. Now a company called Virtual Vision promises to make TV even more omnipresent. Its $900 wraparound TV eyeglasses can be worn anywhere; they project an image that appears to float about ten feet in front of the wearer.

In the space of only a few decades, watching TV seems to have become one of life's essential activities—along with eating, sleeping, and working. TV has become the Great American Companion. Two-thirds of Americans regularly watch television while eating dinner. The A. C. Nielsen Company, which monitors sets in a carefully selected nationwide sample of four thousand households, regularly reports that the TV is on about seven and a half hours a day—virtually all of the time remaining if one subtracts eight hours for sleep and eight hours for work. Collectively, the nation tunes in to a staggering 250 billion hours per year. If one assumes that the average hourly wage is $10, that time is worth *$2.5 trillion.* If we could collect just $1 per hour we could wipe out the yearly federal budget deficit.

Figuring out who is actually watching the tube and when he or she is doing so is tricky. Nielsen's method shows when a set is on and what channel it is tuned to, but many studies have found that during much of the time the TV is on, no one is watching. Researchers have developed People Meters to try to determine who is watching, but these gadgets rely on viewers to "punch in" when they sit down in front of the set and "punch out" when they leave—hardly a foolproof method. As best as researchers can determine, the average person "watches" about four hours per day, varying by season (more in winter, less in summer), age (kids and senior citizens view the most), and race (African Americans and Hispanics watch more than whites).[1] When are the most Americans watching? Prime time (8 to 11 P.M., Eastern Standard Time) on Sunday nights in the depths of winter.

TV is one of the things that bring us together as a nation. Thanks to television, the Super Bowl has become our greatest national spectacle, watched in at least 40 million homes. (By contrast, 1992 presidential candidate Ross Perot's first "town meeting," which was wildly successful compared to other political broadcasts, was watched in only 11 million homes.) Such peak moments generate mind-boggling revenues. Advertisements during the 1993 Super Bowl, which NBC sold out a month before kickoff, cost in the neighborhood of $28,000 per second. Nevertheless, because virtually the entire nation assembles to watch this single game in January, advertisers such as Pepsi, Budweiser, and Gillette gladly ante up, and others have found it a perfect showcase for major new products. It was during Super Bowl XVIII in January 1984 that Apple introduced the world to the Macintosh personal computer. (The Los Angeles Raiders beat the Washington Redskins, 38 to 9.)

TV is a multibillion-dollar business. Sales of new sets alone come to about $7 billion per year. Advertising revenues amount to more than $30 billion, still collected in large part by the major broadcast networks—ABC, NBC, CBS, and, since 1986, Fox. Prime-time ads generate some $4 billion, and billions more come from morning, soap opera, news, and late-night offerings. Cable TV in 1992 received ad revenues in excess of $3 billion, and another $2 billion came from subscribers who paid for the privilege of watching its millions of advertisements.

Buying and selling television shows was a $25-billion business in 1992, principally done by the major Hollywood studios. TV shows, from the latest episodes of *Baywatch* to 1960s-vintage series such as *Bewitched,* are also one of the nation's biggest exports. If once it was said that the sun never set on the British Empire, now it never sets on *I Love Lucy.* The U.S. trade in sitcoms and soap operas shaves some $4 billion per year off America's chronic trade deficit, a contribution exceeded only by that of the aerospace industry.

The TV industry itself is split in two. As a result of antitrust policy decisions during the Nixon administration, the networks were barred from owning Hollywood studios, and the studios are barred from owning networks—with one famous exception. To promote the development of a fourth network, the FCC in 1986 allowed Fox to create a limited TV network while owning a major Hollywood studio, Twentieth Century Fox. As a rule, the networks can only show (not own) TV's valuable series. These complex rules are now being phased out and should be gone by the end of the century. Then we are likely to see a spate of mergers joining Hollywood studios and the TV networks.

Despite all the hype and hoopla that attend its doings, TV is a mouse among industries, a relatively small collection of enterprises whose earnings, even if lumped together, are still smaller than those of either Exxon or General Motors alone. TV's cultural influence likewise tends to be exaggerated. The medium is so pervasive that whenever critics confront a vexing social problem, they blame TV. Crime on the rise? It must be TV's fault. Scholastic Aptitude Test scores dropping? Blame the Boob Tube. Now it is said that TV-induced passivity is literally killing us: a study in the *American Journal of Health Promotion* concluded that couch potatoes are twice as likely to develop high levels of serum cholesterol as those who rarely watch television.

Our anxiety about TV increases as the nation changes. More and more children in this divorce-ridden society watch TV unsupervised. "Behold every parent's worst nightmare: the six-year-old TV addict," says *Time* magazine—who takes Bart Simpson as a role model, one might add.

Violence on television is probably the public's main concern. A Times-Mirror survey found that 80 percent of adults think that television violence is harmful to society. More than a thousand studies have been carried out to search for links between TV viewing and violent behavior. Under pressure from Congress, the networks have agreed to provide warnings before their most violent offerings. One mother declared in the *Washington Post:* "I find myself curiously unmoved by television producers covering themselves with a First Amendment flag. As far as I'm concerned, they have abrogated their rights to freedom of speech by being so resolutely unconcerned about the impact of what they put on television. That includes the 100,000 acts of violence . . . that the average child will have watched by the end of elementary school."

In 1992 the American Psychological Association concluded that televised violence can sometimes stir aggressive behavior in certain kinds of disturbed viewers. Most researchers probably would concur. But this is a narrow case. Whether video violence has a significant impact on the general public is quite another matter, and the pile of studies published so far has not produced a consensus. It is clear that heavy viewers of televised violence are more likely to engage in aggressive behavior than are light viewers, all other things being equal. But it may be that people with a predisposition toward violence are more likely to watch action-adventure programming to begin with, not that watching makes them become violent.

To regard some of the more extreme claims about the impact of TV skeptically is not to dismiss the challenge posed by the medium. By the time an average American child enters the first grade, she or he has seen at least five thousand hours of TV and by all accounts has fallen in love with the medium. New video diversions soon appear, such as Nintendo (which has sold an astonishing 25 million machines in the United States). According to a 1991 National Assessment of Educational Progress study, nearly three of every four fourth graders admit to watching more than three hours of TV every day. By the end of high school, teens have seen some 19,000 hours of TV—and an equal number of televised homicides. We do not need hundreds of studies to know that the time children spend spaced out in front of the tube is time they are not devoting to homework or baseball or daydreaming or any number of other more worthwhile activities.

There are legitimate fears about the effects of TV on young children. But once children learn how to use TV—how to pick acceptable shows to watch, for example, or to substitute videotapes when nothing good is on—only excess seems to prove harmful. Putting a positive spin on this, critics such as Ellen Wartella, dean of the College of Communication at the University of Texas, argue that the accumulated "effects research" suggests that classes in "visual literacy" for the young are a better bet than more radical measures to control what is aired.

Technology, meanwhile, is rapidly changing the very nature of the television challenge. It has already proffered a partial solution—a technological fix—to the problem of children's excessive TV watching. Consumers can now purchase digital TV sets that can be selectively "deprogrammed," allowing adults to block certain programs from their children's eyes and ears.

For 30 years after the FCC's landmark Sixth Report and Order, TV changed very little. During the last ten years, however, it has been transformed. Roughly two of three households are now connected to cable television, and that proportion is steadily growing. Cable households have access, on average, to 30 networks rather than the traditional three. A generation ago, five of six viewers tuned into one of the Big Three networks; today only three of six do. The medium, in other words, is now more diverse. And we have changed not only what we watch but the way we watch it. Armed with remote controls, another relatively new piece of technology, viewers now "graze" or "surf" across cable's never-ending channels, from all-documentary formats (Discovery) to channels aimed at African Americans (Black Entertainment Television), from an alphabet soup of movie channels (AMC, TNT, TBS, and HBO) to all-weather and all-consumer news. We are promised all-crime, fashion, military, book, and (horror of horrors!) game-show channels in the near future. We can even shop by cable TV—and we do so to the tune of $2.2 billion annually. Soon, in all likelihood, we will do our banking and pay our bills through TV as well.

It was not only cable that overthrew the Big Three and transformed the TV experience. During the 1980s, the VCR took America by storm, occupying only one of every five households in 1985 but four of five today. Last year Americans rented an amazing 3.5 billion videos, which works out to an average of one a week for each household. Videotape rentals are now a $12-billion industry.

Impossible as it may seem, more technological change is coming. By the end of the century we will have digital high-definition television with movie-quality images, and in the next century, if not sooner, we will acquire the ability to summon (for a fee) an electronic newspaper on our screens and search through the biggest libraries in the world for information.

Already, these far-reaching changes have injected an undemocratic element into what was once in many ways a most democratic medium. Everybody could watch Neil Armstrong walk on the moon or Richard Nixon tender his resignation. That was because a TV set by the early 1970s cost only a third as much as the first '50s sets had. Cable TV offers no such bargains. The average monthly bill is $30 and climbing, despite recent congressional attempts to roll back prices. As a result, poor Americans subscribe to cable at half the rate of their wealthier counterparts, going without a whole slew of information and entertainment, from C-SPAN to local-access TV to ESPN. Many also go without VCRs. Add in the cost of videotape rentals and new gadgets and watching TV can suddenly become a $1,000-per-year habit.

It is typical of the American attitude toward TV that, much as we may criticize the medium, we are also troubled by the fact that some Americans do not have equal access to it. Television has become the greatest entertainment and information machine of all time. Love it or leave it, we all—rich and poor, the powerful and the underclass—use it to educate ourselves in various ways and to define a common culture. Nielsen's Top 10 tells us what is "in." *Murphy Brown* elicits the wrath of former vice president Dan Quayle. *Monday Night Football* defines the quintessential male-bonding night at the bar. *Jeopardy* teases PhD candidates away from their dissertations to see if they are really smart. *Sixty Minutes,* the single show virtually everyone agrees is entertaining and enlightening, has become as a consequence the most popular program in TV's history—and surely the one we all hope never to be caught on.

Television is like the fabled uncle who came to dinner and never left: it is difficult finally to decide how we feel about it. In one recent survey people were asked how much money it would take to convince them to give up TV for a year. Almost half refused for anything less than $1 million! After a half-century-long love-hate relationship, we are just not sure if the story of TV in America will have a happy ending. But we do know that TV—probably in some advanced version we have yet to imagine, and surely not as all-consuming or as controlling as its current critics believe it to be—will be forever with us.

NOTES

1. African Americans and Hispanics watch more TV than whites because they have lower incomes, on average. TV is, after all, just about the cheapest form of entertainment available. Only as one gets richer can one afford the luxury of fancy meals, nights at the theater, and other forms of diversion.

TODD GITLIN

Today, there is no getting away from the electronic hearthland. Commentators may routinely misinterpret one of the more widely circulated statistics about television—that the average household has a set *on* more than seven hours per day—to mean that the average person *watches* that amount. (It is no mere pedantic detail to note that a set being *on* does not mean that it is being *watched.*) But even the correct figure of four hours a day is nothing to trifle with. Television watching is second only to work as the primary activity, or inactivity, that Americans undertake during their waking hours. One sign of how thoroughly television has been assimilated, even among the more literate, is that it has become a sign of inverse snobbery to proclaim affection for a pet series. Whole generations of popular-culture scholars now unashamedly rhapsodize about the stellar qualities of their favored habits.

The nation has assimilated television. Has it, then, been assimilated *to* television? More to the point, is television now a dominant force in shaping the character of Americans? Many analysts have argued the affirmative, even though they disagree on whether this is for the good. Television, it seems, has served as an instrument for the nationalization of American culture, furthering tolerance while eroding ethnocentrism and other forms of parochialism. For good reason did Edward R. Murrow choose to inaugurate the first coast-to-coast broadcast, on November 18, 1951, with a split screen showing the Statue of Liberty and the Golden Gate Bridge simultaneously.

It was no small blow against white supremacy, during the 1950s and 1960s, to bring into the living rooms of white America images of the brutal treatment

---

Reprinted from the autumn 1993 issue of *The Wilson Quarterly.*

of blacks, nor for that matter, during the 1980s, to convey to a white audience that professional-class blacks such as Bill Cosby were effectively identical to their white counterparts. In *No Sense of Place* (1985), Joshua Meyrowitz argues that television has brought to public view the "backstage" of American social life, educating the public to see through appearances and cultivating a knowledgeable skepticism even while contributing to the spread of egalitarian sentiments. On the other hand, conservative critics such as Michael Medved and Richard Grenier suggest that television promotes adversarial attitudes, incites mindless rebellion, and cultivates a corrosive attitude toward social responsibility. The interesting thing is that both viewpoints presume that the impact of television is considerable, rather uniform, and, on balance, subversive of established authority.

The presumption in all these arguments is that television operates in a space left vacant by the demise of traditional authority. Some, such as George Gerbner, former dean of the Annenberg School of Communication, go so far as to call television a "religion." Others, more subtly, see television purveying identities, especially for the young, in a fluid, unsettled society where neither work, religion, nor family is stable or compelling enough to do the traditional job. Has an entire culture become, in the words of novelist William Gass, "nothing more than the darkening cross-hatch where the media intersect"? The smothering hypothesis, anticipated by novelist Aldous Huxley's *Brave New World* (1932), has a dire appeal. It is easy to see why. Television not only looms large and loud in every private domain, its pervasiveness transcends that of all previous systems of communication.

Indeed, to call television a medium of communication misses much of the point. It is somewhat like calling a family a system of communication. Family therapists do so, but their descriptive power falls short of Tolstoy's. It might carry us somewhat further to say that television is a medium of cultural power. What happens on, or through, television—the images, topics, and styles that circulate through living rooms—does proceed from headquarters outward to take up a space in the national circuitry. But to speak of television as if it were nothing but a sequence of images is to miss a crucial feature of the machinery, namely *how much of it there is and how easily it enters the house.*

To think of American life today without television taxes the imagination. One extraordinary social fact about television is that it is both ubiquitous and, on the scale of social goods, disappointing. Television has the virtues of being cheap and accessible, and does not require much engagement—it is therefore most popular among children, the old, the poor, and the less educated. Society's most powerless receive television as a consolation prize. Even many of these, and most other people most of the time, think watching it an activity not so much valuable in itself as preferable, perhaps, to other choices near at hand. Yet, in several social experiments, many people have refused large sums of money for volunteering to do without television for one month. But even these diehards, like most people, rank television low among their pleasures. It is an enjoyment that turns out to be not so enjoyable after all. *What are you doing? Nothing, just watching television. How was the program? OK.* Watching television is something to do, but it is also and always *just* watching television.

The low status of TV watching obscures, however, a deep truth about the peculiar place of television in American life. Consider that in most households the television set itself has prestige. True enough, as the price of low-end televisions came down and households acquired more than one, the large-screen console television lost some of its majesty. Still, especially in the households of the working class, and probably in the majority of American homes, the set remains a centerpiece of the living room—to judge from the framed photos, trophies, and other esteemed objects surveying the room from the top of the set—something of a conspicuous secular shrine. It takes up, one might say, prime space. In this respect, the TV is an extension of the piano that was, in earlier decades, a virtually mandatory certificate of status in the parlor of actual or aspiring middle-class families. Members of the working class buy console sets and display them proudly in their living rooms, while members of the professional class buy high-tech large screens for their living rooms, keeping their smaller, simpler sets sequestered, for private use, in their bedrooms.

In all these households television is, I suggest, more than an amusement bank, a national bulletin board, a repertory of images, an engine for ideas, a classification index, or a tranquilizer. It is all of these, in some measure. But television's largest impact is probably as a school for manners, mores, and styles—for repertories of speech and feeling, even for the externals and experiences of self-presentation that we call personality. This is not simply because television is powerful but also, and crucially, because other institutions are less so.

As work, family, and religion lose their capacity to adumbrate how a person is expected to behave, television takes up much of the slack. In the working world, for instance, the focus of employment has shifted during the twentieth century from the craft itself ("I am a tailor") to the paycheck and the status ("I am an Assistant Grade II" or alternately "I am a working stiff"). Religious belief, while prevalent, is awkwardly coupled with the roles that most people act out in their daily lives, so that, even for most believers, "I am a Christian" is no longer a very clear badge of identity. Moreover, divorces, remarriages, stepparents, and live-in arrangements increasingly characterize family life, so that one (or one's subself) belongs to more than one family at a time. In this setting, where primary identities have slackened and people are members of many "clubs" at once, Americans look to popular culture for ways of identifying themselves. Consider, for example, the personal ads in local newspapers or magazines. Fifteen years ago you might have read, "Woody Allen seeks his Annie Hall"; today it will more likely be, "L.A. Law type looking for Vanna White."

It is reasonable to suspect that, at the least, television teaches people how they should talk, look, and behave—which means, in some measure, that it teaches them how they should think, how they should feel, and how, perchance, they should dream. Ideologically minded critics from the Right (those writing for the editorial page of the *Wall Street Journal*, for example) or from the Left (Noam Chomsky, for example), obsessed with the power of ideas over benighted citizens, have distracted us from recognizing the deepest workings of television because their own rational bias impoverishes their social imagination. They cannot imagine that there might be any other reason for wrong-headed policies than the misinformation of influential publics.

In speaking of the cultural power of television, I am referring not simply to its impact on knowledge. For decades, researchers have published literally thousands of studies of the effects of watching television. As a result, many things can be said to be "known" about "the effects of television." But all the hard-nosed studies qualify as hard-nosed—and therefore receive funding—only insofar as their scope is limited to specific, measurable effects on distinct behaviors and conditions such as buying, voting, aggression, and sexual arousal; or, more ambitiously, on ideas, attitudes, perceptions, and the salience of particular concerns in people's minds. Indeed, the very notion of "effects" suggests the sort of before-and-after controlled experiment that can be done, or simulated, only when the effect under scrutiny is demarcated precisely.

What interests me are more elusive and arguably more important matters: the tone and temper of American culture. Intuitively, one senses that the transformations of television in the past half-century are deeply implicated in the way Americans feel. Of course, all cultures change, none more than America's. (If we think of technological innovations alone, and make a rough estimate of the cultural changes that followed, it is hard to imagine any decade to compare with 1895–1905, which brought the automobile, the airplane, the motion picture, and radio.) But the forms of cultural change in recent decades are remarkable. Distinctions that were formerly sacrosanct—urban/suburban, northern/southern, public/private, national/local, naughty/nice—have blurred. To borrow Joshua Meyrowitz's terms, themselves borrowed from the late sociologist Erving Goffman, the frontstage world of formal American life is more tolerant—there is a growing degree of routine sexual and racial acceptance. Gay figures pass across the evening news without scandal; Oprah Winfrey, Arsenio Hall, and Whoopi Goldberg have their talk-show billings; suburban white teens thrill to African-American rappers. Meanwhile, the backstage world of ordinary relationships is nastier. From domestic battering to automatic cursing and the rudeness of motorists—note the decline in directional signaling over the last few decades—a harshness has settled into the texture of everyday life. It seems to me that television has furthered these changes—without having, all by itself, devised or caused them.

I am struck, in particular, by the growth of "knowingness," a quality of self-conscious savvy that often passes for sophistication. Knowingness is not simply access to or a result of knowledge; knowingness is a state of mind in which any particular knowledge is less important than the feeling *that* one knows and the pleasure taken in the display of this feeling. Knowingness is the conviction that it is possible to be in the know; it is the demonstration that one hasn't been left behind, that one is hip, with it, cool. It is a mastery of techniques by which to reveal that one has left the sideshow and made it into the big tent. The opposite of knowingness is unabashed provincialism, naiveté, complacent straightforwardness. This provincialism and straightforwardness have been eroded within the American culture of recent decades—with the help of television.

Two generations ago, "simple people," morally straightforward types along with rural and other uneducated types, were amply represented on network television. There were the staunch, steady, plainspoken Western figures of *Gunsmoke* and *Have Gun, Will Travel.* There were the rural butts enacted endearingly by Red Skelton and the apparently artless working-class heroes of *The Honeymooners.* There were the unself-conscious rubes who served as Groucho Marx's foils on *You Bet Your Life* as well as their offensive racist equivalents on *Amos 'n' Andy.* On all these shows, sophisticates got to show off by distinguishing themselves from buffoons. The conflict between the two often drove the plot.

As late as the 1960s, despite the decline of the Western, rural settings and folksy types were still on display in *The Beverly Hillbillies, Green Acres,* and *The Andy Griffith Show.* As I explain in my book *Inside Prime Time* (1983), these shows were canceled in the early 1970s, despite their commercial success, when the incoming president of CBS made the decision to seek younger, more urban, more affluent viewers with "sophisticated" series such as *All in the Family, The Mary Tyler Moore Show,* and *M*A*S*H.* Later in the 1970s, a few rural revivals succeeded: *The Waltons, Little House on the Prairie,* and *The Dukes of Hazzard.* One running theme in many of these programs was that deviousness got its comeuppance at the hands of moral earnestness—though of course the comeuppance was never final, deviousness getting a new lease in the next installment.

But television's most affectionate renditions of plain folks in small-town America were delivered to the West Virginia hollows and Nebraska farms just as the hollows and farms were emptying out. The volunteers who troop onto the contest shows, quiz shows, and dating games today are vastly more media-savvy than the bumpkins who took their chances with Groucho on *You Bet Your Life* two generations ago. Today's hopeful contestants still submit to teasing, but unlike Groucho's foils, they can also tease back. They know how to banter without skipping a beat. They may still be shocked by Oprah's transsexual priest, Sally Jessy's teary molester, or Donahue's tortured immigrant, but boy, do they have a story for you, too. In the talk-show studios as well, spectators in the live audience wear appraising looks. Ordinary fans may be thrilled by the presence, the sheer aura, of their stars, but they are also—as Yale sociologist Joshua Gamson shows in his *Claims to Fame*—able to stand back and chat knowingly about the techniques with which publicists go about the business of manufacturing glamour and fame.

I do not want to suggest that television has merely replaced the plainspoken down-home characters and bucolic settings of the older shows. Literary critics, preoccupied with "text," have led cultural analysts to concentrate on representation—on the content of the programs. Many who criticize television criticize it because they take its representations as categorical and dislike the way various categories are represented. Thus conservatives have argued that when businessmen are treated as "crooks, conmen, and clowns" (to quote the title of a pro-business pamphlet of the 1980s), they inspire public contempt for business; likewise feminists have argued that when a woman character is victimized by violent crime, the representation teaches women that their role is to play the victim. Such critics tend to assume of television the principle, *Monkey see, monkey do*, and they also assume, rather as in Stalinist Russia, that characters must be exemplary in the manner prescribed by the critic. But if television exercised influence simply by spurring emulation, the popular rural comedies of the early 1970s should have led to rural resettlement.

The content of television is not simply one story after another. In fact, to think of television as nothing more than a sum of stories is like thinking of a lawn as nothing more than a sum of blades. The very significance of the units derives from their membership in the ensemble. As the British critic Raymond Williams pointed out, one remarkable thing about television is the sheer profusion of stories it delivers. No previous generation of human beings has been exposed to the multitude of narratives we have come to take for granted in our everyday lives. The impact of each one may be negligible, but it hardly follows that the impact of the totality is negligible. Moreover, the profusion of stories changes each component story. The stories exist in multiplicity; their significance bleeds from one story into another.

Most people watch *television,* not discrete narrative units. The flow of television is both *rapid* and *interrupted*. A story begins with credits. A few minutes of story take place. The story is interrupted for commercials—probably more than one per commercial break. There may be previews of news bulletins, promotions, previews of other shows. The story resumes. There are more commercials, more announcements. The story resumes. And so on. At the hourly or half-hourly station break, there may be trailers for the following week's episode, trailers for shows later that night, announcements of coming events. As the remote control–equipped viewer "zaps" or "grazes" through dozens of cable channels at the touch of a button—to the delight of postmodernist theorists celebrating the recombinant culture of juxtaposition as an exercise of freedom—cacophony is in the nature of the pastiche. In the wonderful world of television, anything is compatible with anything else. The one continuity is discontinuity. The flow resembles that of a mountain stream, complete with white water, more than a slow, steady passage. Indeed, rapidity and interruption are central to the sensory impression television leaves.

The question then arises: What kind of social education, what type of character formation, occurs when there are so many stories and each one is constantly interrupted, is soon over, and flows immediately into an unrelated story that, in turn, is swallowed up by the next? In an earlier America, even the uneducated could know well, and reflect upon, a small stock of stories—in particular, the Bible and Shakespeare. Lincoln, largely unschooled, read Shakespeare deeply enough in his youth to be able to rank one soliloquy over another in a letter written two years before he died. By contrast, every evening television tells a Scheherazade's 1,001 Nights–worth of stories, and the meaning of any particular show has a shelf life of, usually, minutes. A viewer engages less with the content of one program than masters an attitude of superiority to them all. Rather than learn one subject well, he or she acquires a sophisticated repartee and light banter good for discussing anything and everything that comes up—a style in which, as noted before, to seem quick and knowing is more important than what one knows.

Obviously rapidity and interruption are not brand-new features of Western civilization. Television is a caricature of what, before television, was already a way of life. The ideals and sins it depicts are those of America's formulaic modernity. The picture may be sepia but the frame glitters. Thanks to slick visuals (known in Hollywood as "high production values") and crisp movement, glibness rules. Like the Sears catalogue performing its service in the outhouse, the commercials and network IDs and promos and news flashes emanate from the cosmopolis. Willy-nilly, the slick wrapping carries the tumult and velocity of a commercial version of urban life, the cornucopia of desire, the lure of consumable things and "lifestyles." Commercials don't simply announce the wonders of goods and the lives they promise, they also bring energy and novelty—news of what passes for fun, freedom, and security these days.

Television and its spin-offs have thus furthered what psychologist Martha Wolfenstein called in the 1940s America's "fun culture." The motto is Hey, No Problem! A bright happiness is more the equilibrium state on television than in any other cultural form at any other time in history. In commercials problems are easily surmounted or minimized—as in a child's world where difficulties can be left behind. It is no coincidence that in almost all family sitcoms the parents, especially fathers, are typically shown as slightly stuffy, misguided, or well-meaning bunglers who are set straight, at the end of 30 minutes, by their sons and daughters. Children Know Best.

On TV both children and adults speak with an unprecedented glibness. Thanks to the wonders of editing, no one on television is ever at a loss for words or photogenic signs of emotion. Not even the bereaved parent asked "How do you feel?" about the death of a child is seen to hesitate. Hesitancy, silence, awkwardness are absent from TV's repertory of behaviors, except in sitcoms or made-for-TV movies where boy meets girl. Yet outside TV, awkwardness and hesitancy often characterize the beginning, and each further development, of interiority, of a person's internal life. On TV, however, speech is stripped down, designed to *move*. The one-liner, developed for ads, is the premium style. TV's common currency consists of slogans and mockery. Situation comedies and morning shows are in particular obsessed with the jokey comeback. The put-down is the universal linkage among television's cast of live and recorded characters. A free-floating hostility mirrors, and also inspires, the equivalent conversational style among the young who grow up in this habitat.

As critic Mark Crispin Miller has observed, the knowingly snide attitude is so widespread and automatic that it deserves to be called "the hipness unto death." The promotion of David Letterman to CBS's 11:30 P.M. talk-show slot signals the ascendancy of this style. Relentless if superficial self-disclosure is one of the conventions of television today. The audience is simultaneously alerted to the contrivance, transported behind the scenes, and pleased by both—and by the possibility of enjoying both. It is obvious how this plays in *Saturday Night Live,* but more surprising to see how it plays in "straight"commercials and programs designed for people one would not commonly think of as sophisticates. In one commercial of the 1980s a man in a white coat looks you in the eye and says, "I'm not a doctor, but I play one on TV." The audience is expected to recognize him as a soap-opera actor. (He goes on to say that other people also think they can "play doctor" and as a result may take the wrong medicine. He has come to sell the right one.) There followed the "Joe Isuzu" series, in which a huckster makes outrageous claims about Isuzu automobiles: They get 100 miles per gallon, they cost $99.98, and so on, while subtitles provide the truth. Consider further the business news and gossip of *Entertainment Tonight,* along with its knockoffs on CNN, MTV, and the local news, and the canny entertainment sections of today's newspapers, making the audience privy to Hollywood marketing calculations, casting tactics, career moves, and box-office figures. We are invited to understand Hollywood not only as a machine for dreams but as a game through which we, the spectators, are dreamed of—a game whose success or failure we are also invited to inspect.

Through this relentless inspection, character is dissected, torn apart. Indeed, character—based upon self-mastery, moral resolve, learning or understanding, and quiet or heroic action—is reduced to personality, impression management, the attractions of body and mannerism. Here again, television is not inventing but perfecting already long-standing trends in our social life. In *Within the Context of No Context* (1981), George Trow traces the changing nature of American magazine covers to show how character has been supplanted by personality. The typical faces on the cover of *Time* and *Life* through the 1930s and '40s—faces of people such as Roosevelt and Churchill and Hitler, who were famous, for better or worse, for what they achieved or brought about in public life—eventually gave way to personalities (Madonna would be a contemporary example) who are famous mainly for being famous.

The equivalent process operates in our thinking (and feeling) about politics. Coverage and conversation are dominated, first, by a focus on personality, and second, by the inside analysis of the stratagems of campaigns and governance. Politicians concluded that the arts of governance are less fateful than acts of spin control—and as television observes the spin, reporting thus feeds cynicism. The audience is flattered that it is superior to the corruption, dishonesty, and hypocrisy of public servants. The viewer has been brought into the know. He or she is treated as an inside-dopester, savvy to spin doctors, speechwriters, electorate-pleasing "positioning," and all manner of practical calculations. In one sense, what is going on is democratic unmasking: Let the politicians be put on notice that they are hired hands! In another sense, at least under present circumstances, the cynicism that has become so widespread in politics is more likely to generate withdrawal than political engagement. The increased voter turnout in the 1992 general election, in which Ross Perot served as a third-party sideshow attraction, may only have been an interruption in the otherwise long-term decline in the size of the electorate.

The glibness, relentless pace, sloganeering, and shrinking attention spans of private life filter into television, via the selective antennae of the television-industrial complexes of Hollywood and New York, only to be reinforced there, like a rocket that accelerates by swinging close to Earth, using its gravitational pull to swing free of that same gravitational pull. The free-floating nastiness of sitcom existence may well be cultivating an equivalent show of popular sentiment, so that the endless put-downs of popular comedy penetrate the rest of everyday life.

Take your own brief survey of bumper stickers (Florida's "We don't care how you do it up North"), of slang (e.g., *drop-dead* as an adjective meaning "stunning," as in "She has a drop-dead body" or "Our paints are available in 36 drop-dead colors"), and of T-shirts ("I'M NOT DEAF, I'M JUST IGNORING YOU"; "OUT OF MY WAY, BITCH"), which then recycle, especially via the Fox network's youth-oriented shows, into the popular domain.

In summary: *Television has nationalized American culture and made it more knowing.* This conclusion may seem to fly in the face of predictions that television's homogenizing days are waning. On the surfaces of culture, distinctions do multiply. Basic cable service now enters 62 percent of American homes, bringing an average of 30 channels. What the postnetwork cable channels offering popular music, home shopping, evangelical Christianity, African-American music, and Spanish-language soap operas have in common is that they thrive on undiminished enthusiasm for breathless, slick entertainment. Advances in interactive technology will probably not divert from these main tendencies; they will render more efficient the services that people already use—banking, video games, commercial movies, quiz shows. Pride in the national cornucopia will become a cornerstore of the orthodox American identity. White bread has already ceased to be the symbol of national unity. It has been supplanted by the new standard supermarket shelf of 72 different loaves, each bland in its own way. TV programs that would truly widen the spectrum—as far as character types and kinds of approved behaviors presented—are nearly as unlikely in the postcable cornucopia as they were on the Big Three networks. For a series about, say, a gay couple disturbed about restrictions on military service or a devout Catholic family worried about the increasing materialism of daily life, a viewer, remote control in hand, will zap through his or her 30 channels in vain.

Make no mistake. The uniformities in present-day American style are not simply the creatures of television or of corporate culture more generally. They build, in turn, on cultural uniformities already observed in the early 1830s by Alexis de Tocqueville, who pointed out, long before Stallone, Schwarzenegger, Roseanne, or MTV, that America's cultural products

> substitute the representation of motion and sensation for that of sentiment and thought. . . . Style will frequently be fantastic, incorrect, overburdened, and loose, almost always vehement and bold. . . . There will be more wit than erudition, more imagination than profundity; and literary performances will bear marks of an untutored and rude vigor of thought, frequently of great variety and singular fecundity.

In such passages where Tocqueville describes the arts in America, and where he predicts that surface and motion will replace the exploration of the soul, he appears almost to be anticipating the development of a democratic "art" like television. Tocqueville often speculated about what could hold together a country of such disparate regions and so many varieties of people. Not even he could have dreamed, however, of this slick and all-knowing personality—this glib persona fostered by television, which undermines all authority and is adaptable to every class and ethnicity—that would become, as it were, *the* American citizen, the glue that in its peculiar way unites the country.

One hardly needs to read Tocqueville to surmise that, regardless of the channel or brand name, the odds are that the rule of the slick, the glib, and the cute will prevail. The once-over-lightly glibness of American culture prevails not only on television but in the movies and magazines, among sports announcers and talk-show hosts, in the jargons of politics and psychotherapy alike. It is difficult to resist the conclusion that America's culture of comfort and convenience, of the quick fix and fast relief, of mass-manufactured labels of individuality, has acquired in television a useful technology to reduce the range of colors in the spectrum of life to a bleached center glittering with sequins in many drop-dead colors.

SEEING THROUGH THE TUBE

FRANK D. MCCONNELL

I begin with a true story. In 1974 I was having coffee in the English department lounge at Northwestern University when two of my colleagues—a younger, untenured man and an older, tenured woman—entered in mid-conversation.

"Oh, no," the woman was saying, "I just won't have a television in my apartment. I know there are *some* good things on it, especially on public broadcasting. But so much of it is just garbage!"

My younger friend laughed. "Joke's on you, then," he said. "It's got an off button."

For years I've thought that a brilliant riposte: If you don't like it, you don't have to do it. It certainly has all the bracing moral simplicity of our former first lady's insouciant slogan, "Just Say No." But now, having immersed myself in as many anti-TV jeremiads as anyone can digest, I wonder. The vast majority of media studies over the last 30 years, both anti-TV and, in a few heroic or quixotic cases, pro-TV, are unanimous on one point and one point only: that TV is not just a new medium but a revolutionary and cataclysmic alteration in the way humans perceive and process their world, destined to change forever the nature of consciousness and society itself. The consensus, in other words, is that, though "it's got an off button," the button doesn't really work. We are all creatures—or prisoners—of the Tube.

Now this is a fairly apocalyptic tonnage of significance to load on what is, after all, an entertainment or advertising or information medium barely 40 years old. Developed in the 1930s but largely dormant during World War II, TV blossomed only in the early years of the atomic bomb and the cold war. As Robert C. Toll reports in *The Entertainment Machine* (1982), although in 1950 there

---

Reprinted from the autumn 1993 issue of *The Wilson Quarterly*.

were only about 3 million sets in the country, by 1953 the number had grown exponentially to 21 million. Today it is the rare American household that possesses only one set, and the atypical American who watches less than four hours of TV a day.

This much is statistical fact—a crucial *psychic* fact of late-twentieth-century life. But the facts do not prepare one for the Druidic solemnity with which writers, many brilliant, have attacked TV as a kind of cultural succubus, seducing the Republic and draining it of its vitality.

In the 1976 film *Network*, Paddy Chayefsky, himself one of the great early TV writers, created a nightmare vision in which TV "news," driven by the ratings race, becomes a tawdry, debased, debasing, and ultimately murderous form of entertainment, pandering to the most prurient appetites of its audience. Recent, popular "reconstructed reality" shows such as *Hard Copy* and *A Current Affair*, in which actors re-create tabloid "true stories," can seem a chilling fulfillment of Chayefsky's fantasy—as does the recent admission by NBC that, in a report on the safety failures of GMC trucks, the producers had "enhanced" the explosion of a truck by planting what were in effect bombs under the chassis. Novelists such as Don DeLillo (*White Noise*, 1985) and Thomas Pynchon (*Vineland*, 1990) use TV as a central metaphor for what they see as the Novocainized, universal moral stupor of present-day America. And media critics, from the populist to the high-culture mandarin, have argued that TV, *by its very nature*, reduces culture to the lowest common denominator, provides a false, substitute reality from which the viewer cannot escape, and is in fact little less than mind control.

But not only do intellectuals hate TV; TV seems to hate itself. A number of highly popular series since the 1960s—*The Dick Van Dyke Show, The Mary Tyler Moore Show,* and *Murphy Brown,* to name a few—have orbited around the idea of writing for, producing, or selling a TV show. In each case, the assumption has been that the industry itself is well short of the respectable or the grown-up. In the vast range of the family sitcom—surely one of TV's staple crops—I cannot call to mind a single instance in which the image of a family watching TV together is presented as in any way a good thing. One example will serve. (And I note in passing that few of TV's most vituperative critics ever deign to discuss the specific details of a given show.) In *The Simpsons*—the widely praised cartoon sitcom about a preternaturally dense family that is itself a parody of the archetypal TV-sitcom household—each episode begins with the father leaving work, the mother coming home from the supermarket, and the kids returning from school, all of them arriving simultaneously and throwing themselves on the sofa, their glazed-over eyes fixed on the TV set.

Plato, notoriously, attacked the art of writing as an unworthy vehicle for wisdom—in, of course, some of the greatest writing the world has known. And

Jonathan Swift and Voltaire, among others, satirized the dangerous side effects of the proliferation of printed books—in, naturally, printed books of their own. We can even fantasize that, at the dawn of language itself, some anxious shaman delivered an eloquent speech to the effect that this newfangled thing, speech, would lead to no good.

Nevertheless, the salient fact about the birth of TV is the complexity of its historical moment. I have said that the industry began to burgeon in the late 1940s and early '50s, the age in which it first became thinkable that humanity, in possession now of the atomic bomb, could commit global suicide. The planet itself, again for the first time, began to align itself in two mutually hostile tribes—the "Free World" and the "Communist Conspiracy," to use the phrases that now almost elicit nostalgia. But that was not all. The moment of TV's birth was also the moment at which information itself began to be perceived as the only truly valuable commodity for the future. World War II, more than any previous conflict, had been a battle of and for information. The breaking of the Japanese code "Purple" and the German code "Enigma," and the instantly legendary Manhattan Project, whose secrecy was soon after revealed to have been penetrated by the Soviets—all of these information struggles were as crucial as any "real-world" military engagement in securing victory for the Allies. As much as TV, in other words, it was the war itself that guaranteed that ours would be a period obsessed with info-tech as its prime tool for survival.

In 1948—the year, by the way, that Milton Berle became the first TV superstar—Claude Shannon published his seminal book *The Mathematical Theory of Communication*. Shannon, a cryptographer during the war, was then working for Bell Laboratories, trying to devise a more efficient, static-free system of telephonic exchange. His monograph does not make for chair-gripping excitement, yet it may be one of the defining works of this century. For what Shannon, the sublime technologue, did was reassign the priorities: The *content* of the message sent, he argued, is less important than the *means* by which it is sent. Shannon could not have known in 1948 that his theories were mapping a phenomenon—TV—that would come to be seen as the third pivotal revolution, after writing and printing, in the history of communication. It would require Marshall McLuhan, in *Understanding Media* (1964), to translate Shannon's argument into what is certainly the slogan of the info-tech age: "The medium is the message." It was McLuhan who single-handedly raised the "question of media" to a level of philosophical and moral urgency it has not yet lost. And it is McLuhan who is perceived as the Great Adversary by virtually every later, anti-TV writer.

McLuhan, a professor of English at the University of Toronto, discovered the new world of media not through information theory but through his discipleship to a very remarkable man, Harold A. Innis. A historian and a humanist,

Innis was concerned with the ways writing and printing technologies, "monopolies of information," influenced the growth of empires. In his 1951 book, *The
Bias of Communication,* he argued that the print revolution, by making "texts"
available to a hitherto ignored class of readers and by encouraging a new sense
of *privacy* in the act of reading, contributed to the formation of modern, indi-
vidualist, and democratic man. His argument has, by now, become all but
dogma.

What McLuhan did was extend Innis's idea to include the technology of
speed-of-light, audiovisual information: radio, and above all, TV. His two definitive books, *The Gutenberg Galaxy* (1962) and *Understanding Media,* contain his
major argument, and they turned the man himself into something of a media
celebrity—rare and heady for an academic! The conclusion of *The Gutenberg
Galaxy* reveals McLuhan's prophetic fervor:

> The new electric galaxy of events has already moved deeply into the Gutenberg galaxy.
> Even without collision, such coexistence of technologies and awareness brings trauma
> and tension to every living person. Our most ordinary and conventional attitudes
> seem suddenly twisted into gargoyles and grotesques. Familiar institutions and associa-
> tions seem at times menacing and malignant.

There is something vaguely Nietzschean in the urgency of "new electric
galaxy"—in its paradoxically apocalyptic optimism. McLuhan was unquestion-
ingly sanguine about the effects of the revolutionary TV on human consciousness and culture. If oral society had been a media extension of hearing, he
argued, and manuscript and print culture an extension of sight, then the new
"electric galaxy" was, or would become, an extension of the central nervous system itself. TV would usher in a postliterate, immediate linkage of all peoples
with all peoples, a hot line from self to self that would deliver us all from the
bondage of literacy and establish us as a "global village"—humankind's long
dream of one world, at last accomplished by the infinite crisscrossing of electromagnetic waves around the world.

It is easy for anti-TV critics to read McLuhan's great expectations as yet
another excrescence of the solipsistic 1960s, like tie-dyed T-shirts and macrobi-
otic cuisine. The TV set, around whose glow we gather in our darkened living
rooms, becomes an avatar of the primal campfire around which the tribe would
collect to share its grievances, its gossip, and its gospel. Does the phrase
"Woodstock Nation" call up an embarrassing ghost here?

And yet, in ways McLuhan could not have predicted, we have become, thanks
to TV, a global—or at least a continental—village. To take two obvious
instances, it was indisputably TV coverage of the war in Vietnam that generated

a massive public revulsion against that particular adventure, and it was obviously Ronald Reagan's superbly telegenic presence, more so than his policies, that made him the first two-term president in 30 years. More recently, in the 1992 presidential campaign, Bill Clinton and H. Ross Perot simultaneously contrived the "TV town meeting," an electronic question-and-answer session that gives the illusion, at least, of coast-to-coast intimacy with the candidate. This phenomenon, certain to be a feature of all future campaigns, is itself modeled on a genre that didn't even exist when McLuhan wrote: the "talk show," in which Phil Donahue, Oprah Winfrey, or Geraldo Rivera, guests, and audience all share a conversational space at once glaringly public and deeply private, one part group therapy to two parts tribal council. To give a final example, it is now a very real challenge in heavily covered court cases (the Rodney King beating trial, the William Kennedy Smith rape trial, the Amy Fisher assault trial) to find jurors fit to serve. If they have seen the TV coverage of the alleged crimes, how impartial can they be? But given the ubiquitousness of TV in our lives, if they haven't seen any coverage, how *awake* can they be? The global village, in other words, turns out to be a reality. The question is whether the secret name of the village is Salem.

McLuhan's enthusiasm was for TV as a technology, a new way of perceiving, a new connectedness. What he did not take into account is that TV is also a *business*. Until very recently, three major networks held and enforced a crushing monopoly on what could be shown and what could be said, reducing the viewer to the passive status of a chooser-among-sames. Could the electromagnetic Eden of the TV tube be a return not to the primal garden but to the state of enslavement?

Jerry Mander's *Four Arguments for the Elimination of Television* (1977) makes this case. Mander is a former advertising executive who used his first book to recant his sins. Sometimes *Four Arguments* reads almost like an auto-da-fé. The common theme of his four arguments is an almost exact inversion of the Innis-McLuhan approach to media. Yes, TV is a new and startling way of perceiving reality, but it is a false, engineered "reality" thrust upon its passive victims in such a way as to isolate them from the reality of their own lives. Yes, TV is a unifying force, but it is a unifying force only insofar as it turns us all into eager consumers of the products it exists, above all, to convince us we need. TV, for Mander, is more than anything else a sales medium, its other functions (news, entertainment, etc.) serving only as a kind of narcotic foreplay for the Big Sell:

Whenever we buy a product [advertised through TV] we are paying for the recovery of our own feelings. We have thereby turned into creatures who are the commodities we buy. We are the product we pay for and all life is reduced to serving this cycle.

This is a powerful indictment. Part of the enduring charm of Mander's book, in fact, is his brave sense of himself as a lone voice crying out in the wilderness against the final closure of the TV-addicted mind. Few, if any, later anti-TV tracts catch quite his pitch of anger or risk his uncompromising solution to the problem of TV, which is, to quote Voltaire on Christianity, "Crush the infamous thing!" Mander is a man on fire with a vision of a great wrong, and we cannot expect such men to speak always with complete realism. The conclusion of his book is ringing and poignant:

> How to achieve the elimination of television? I certainly cannot answer that question.
> It is obvious, however, that the first step is for all of us to purge from our minds the
> idea that just because television exists, we cannot get rid of it.

Between McLuhan's enthusiasm and Mander's apocalypticism, later discussions of TV occupy a moderate, perhaps more habitable space. The Mander final solution to the TV problem is "Luddite," as Neil Postman calls it in his 1985 book, *Amusing Ourselves to Death: Public Discourse in the Age of Show Business*. And Postman sensibly observes that this recourse is impossible. To date at least, the single indisputable fact about technology—any technology—is that it is not reversible. You cannot uninvent TV any more than you can uninvent the alphabet, the printing press, the wheel, the smelting of iron, or nuclear fission. As a species, just as individuals, our fate is to learn to live with what we have imagined.

Postman accepts, as Mander does not, the inevitability of the TV revolution, but he analyzes the negative effects of that revolution. Postman is not a disaffiliated adman but a distinguished professor of communication and rhetoric. And the debasement of mature public discourse caused by the "televising" of reality is the gravamen of his argument. Whereas Mander accuses TV of being primarily a narcotic, Postman's perhaps more damning position is that it is lethally trivializing.

What Postman claims here is not that television is entertaining but that it has made entertainment itself the natural format for the representation of all experience. Our television set keeps us in constant communion with the world, but it does so with a face whose smiling countenance is unalterable. The problem is not that television presents us with entertaining subject matter but that all subject matter is presented as entertaining, which is another issue altogether.

Television then not only abstracts and etiolates experience, it compartmentalizes it—within the single compartment of entertainment. In a universe of discourse in which everything from tragedy to farce is presented simply as spectacle, both tragedy and farce and everything between become impossibly confused. Postman uses the example of the evening news. No one seems to notice, he remarks, the irony that the evening news on every channel in America is introduced with urgent-sounding signature theme music. The implication is that the events of the day, whether a plane crash in California or an international crisis, are all contents of a "show." A serious-looking anchorman or anchorwoman narrates, with video, the more ominous or violent events of the last 12 hours. After a break to advertise completely irrelevant products, a usually jocund weatherperson discusses what the weather might be like tomorrow. (In California, especially, this is virtually null information.) After another ad break someone appears to talk about sports; then, with perhaps a few local news items, the serious person with whom we began "wraps it all up," more often than not urging that one stay tuned for the sitcom or movie of the week that is to follow. The real and the fictional, the serious and the trivial, become hopelessly blurred, until only the uninterrupted, zombifying carrier wave itself is the "real" meaning of the transmission. The medium is not the message but, in McLuhan's best pun, the massage.

The political implications are ominous. Postman compares TV culture to the smilingly mindless dystopia of Aldous Huxley's *Brave New World* (1932). In Huxley's novel the people are kept in happy servitude by the drug "Soma," which reduces all stress and makes the world look just perfectly all right. "Better a gramme than a damme," as they are fond of saying. TV, Postman argues, *is* Huxley's Soma: an infallibly relaxing drug that reconciles the individual to his or her own tyrannization.

Social critic Jonathan Kozol hailed Postman's book as a "prophetic vision." In his own book published the same year, *Illiterate America,* Kozol makes his case with at least equal earnestness. Kozol's own "prophetic" credentials as a passionate advocate of public education are impeccable. And while *Illiterate America* has relatively little to say about TV, what it does say is damning. On the much-touted use of TV as an educational tool, he writes,

> The television learner is entirely passive. The television mode is intellectual disjunction. The consequence of televised instruction is a deeper balkanization of the human consciousness than anything that academic fragmentation has engendered up to now. The mechanistic dangers are no longer metaphoric but specific when we learn from a machine. The separation of a skill from a reflective understanding of its ethical or anti-human implications is enhanced (and it is often virtually assured) by televised indoctrination.

Kozol, even more than Postman, understood that the ultimate extension of TV technology would be not the simple passive-receptive viewer entranced by whatever happened to be "on" at the time, but the burgeoning—now triumphant—technology of *interactive* TV: the video game, the computer-enhanced curriculum, and the soon-to-be-perfected "virtual reality." Kozol suggests that this particular brave new world is even more Huxleyan than its immediate ancestor:

> The learner manipulates the terminal that sits beside her television console; yet it is she who is manipulated by the button she selects. Her only option is to choose at which specific moment she will plug into the sequence of accredited information which has been approved by those who know what is best for her, and for themselves, and who have planned the literacy curriculum with sensitive anticipation of its probable results.

For Kozol, TV is a disease of republicanism. At the opposite pole from a cordial "global village," we face the specter of a semi- or largely illiterate population, TV junkies all, voting, reacting, feeling, and desiring precisely as the "virtual" or, better, *ersatz* reality of the Tube tells them to. Marxist cultural critics such as Herbert Marcuse (*One-Dimensional Man*, 1962), Jacques Ellul (*The Technological System*, 1978), and Jean Baudrillard (*For a Critique of the Political Economy of the Sign*, 1981) have argued along similar lines. They charge that the salient feature of "mass culture" in advanced capitalist society is that it infinitely forestalls revolution by making the concept of *revolution* just another form of show business. How to form an underground movement when the "underground" is immediately taken up and celebrated on *The Tonight Show?*

Not surprisingly, the major anti-TV arguments begin, after a while, to sound the same. All are aimed, after all, at the same target. But we can say, at the risk of caricature, that Mander's main objection is that the medium, as primarily an advertising tool, narrows the scope of experience to artificially implanted needs and wants; and that, as a corollary, the experience of TV watching is, neurophysiologically, a trancelike or comalike state that short-circuits rational thought. Postman's concern is directed more to the body politic than to the awareness of the individual watcher. To him, TV's worst effect is that it cheapens the quality of public discourse by reducing it to the sensationalism of the sound bite, giving us the illusion of sophistication without the reality of experience. And Kozol is alarmed at the implications of all this for a public-education system that is manifestly in crisis. An illiterate underclass, dependent solely upon the Tube for its information, is perfect prey for totalitarianism. You need not be so crude as to burn dangerous books if you can simply render them unreadable.

What all these arguments have in common, even Mander's call for a jihad, is that they are written, as it were, by "metaphysicians" of television. These authors are not objecting (only) to this or that show, or to a particular kind of programming, or to a specific network. When they write about TV, the sum of the parts has almost nothing to do with the parts. They attack TV *as a medium,* almost as though it were a destructive metaphysical force. Or, put another way, in the land of television the important point is not that the individual citizens are bad or good but that the country itself is so corrupting and polluted that it scarcely matters who or what the individuals are.

In the various exchanges about television *as medium,* two arguments furnish the subtext for almost every discussion. The first argument is that TV is the next phase of communication, supplanting print. The second is that television creates an artificial reality—the world as advertisement, or entertainment, or passively viewed spectacle—that distances us from our real or "natural" surroundings. To attack TV in either of these two ways is to fault the medium not for how it works but for what it is.

Alvin B. Kernan is a distinguished literary critic and historian at Princeton University. In *The Death of Literature* (1990), he articulates the academic humanist charge against TV that has been uttered, though less authoritatively, ever since TV came to be: that it is evil *just because it is not literature.* Kernan is too thorough a thinker to be a rhetorician. Book reading and watching TV, he concedes, both involve a distinctively human act of decoding some kind of signal to create a meaning. (Cats do not read; nor do they watch TV.) And yet he wants to insist that the reader, as opposed to the watcher, is "intensely active mentally," involved in something that is somehow *serious,* since reading is—again, somehow—more complex than watching.

But to say this is to make what can only be called a leap of faith, faith in the sacramentalism of the printed as opposed to the electromagnetic Word. Are we, indeed, becoming significantly more doltish than our print-oriented ancestors? Are we increasingly submissive hostages to the light show of the Tube—like the chained prisoners in Plato's allegory of the cave in *The Republic,* condemned to watch only the shadows of the real world?

We do not know. More important, we cannot know. And we cannot because TV is part of our reality. Kernan assumes that we can judge the new medium from the perspective of a "pre-TV" sensibility. That is as impossible for us as it would have been for, say, Shakespeare to imagine a universe without printed books. The eye, as Wittgenstein says, can see everything except itself. Indeed, it is far from clear that literature is "dying" in the TV age any more than painting "died" with the evolution of photography or concert performance "died" when Edison recorded sound.

Perhaps more serious than the charge that TV is bad because it is not literature is the charge that TV is bad because it is not the real world, or that TV somehow occludes our participation in the real or natural world. That, at any rate, is the charge registered in Bill McKibben's remarkable book, *The Age of Missing Information* (1992). McKibben is a naturalist with a brilliant prose style.

In *The Age of Missing Information* he produced a book that, whatever else it may be, is a work of belles-lettres. It is a book about two "days." McKibben enlisted his friends to tape an entire TV "day" of all the shows on all 93 cable channels in Fairfax, Virginia, and he watched *every show that was on that day.* Then, on another day, he climbed a hill in the Adirondacks, took a swim, had some lunch, and slept under the stars. The book narrates these parallel days in alternating chapters. The chapters about the "TV day," timed precisely (e.g., "2:00 P.M.") describe the welter of shows, from sitcoms to televangelism to infomercials, that were on at the named time. The chapters about his day on the mountain are ruminative, Thoreauvian in tone, and given comfortable, cuddly titles like "Twilight" and "Deeper Twilight Still." McKibben's conclusion is that by becoming TV addicts we deny ourselves the real "information" of what it means to hike up a mountain, take a solitary swim, and simply be one with nature.

It is a gorgeously written, elegantly planned, and deeply unfair book. McKibben assumes that the only alternatives are total deliverance to or total liberation from the beast of commercialism. In fact his conclusion is implicit in the very terms of his experiment. And that is bad science.

No one watches TV the way McKibben did on his extended "day" in front of the set. I can inject a lab rat with large quantities of virtually anything—caffeine, beer, or vitamin X—three times a day for a week, and I will very likely find that by Sunday the rat is having some problems. Have I proved anything—except that the SPCA should tap my phone?

It should be obvious that I am still thrashing over the problem of the off button. If it really works—that is, *if we can use it*—then it seems the new medium is no more, or less, dangerous to civilization than any of its predecessors. (Who, after all, has not let the coffee boil over while engrossed in a book? Is this "enslavement to print"?)

In *The Five Myths of Television Power* (1993), Douglas Davis asserts that the ominous warnings about TV as mind control, substitute reality, and insidious counterliteracy drug are all, not to put too fine a point on it, nonsense. His subtitle is *Why the Medium Is Not the Message.* And his claim is that the cataclysmic alteration in consciousness assumed by both pro- and anti-TV writers is, after all, not much of an alteration at all and surely not very cataclysmic. The TV watcher, he says, "knows precisely what is wrong, as well as what is right, with the drug that only appears to enslave him."

Nothing, perhaps, is as truly shocking or scandalous as common sense. Could it be that we always do know that we are just watching TV, just as we always knew we were just reading books? And that we still manage to get on with our lives much as we always have? Davis is, if nothing else, a threat to most of the writers who have built their careers as "media analysts" since he assumes that people, however they communicate, tend to remain sane. And this is a very alarming thing for him to say, because it is *not* alarmist.

So what, finally, are we to make of all this moral anxiety over a technological *fact?* I said earlier that technology is irreversible. For all the cautions and caveats about its deleterious effect on human society, one thing is as certain about TV as about the wheel: it will not go away. Our relationship to the Tube, as both Davis and Postman observe, is a matter of dealing with the way the world is for us. A Bill McKibben may want to insist that TV is not natural, but I find it hard to imagine "nature" as anything other than the total surround of experience as it is given to me in this time and place.

There is perhaps something better to compare TV to than nature. Running through all the anti-TV jeremiads is the metaphor of TV as drug: TV hooks viewers, saps their will, and makes them demand increasingly higher dosages. This is, rhetorically, an attractive image, since America in the 1980s and '90s substituted the idea of "addiction" for what used to be called moral choice. People write books and appear on TV explaining that they are "addicted" not just to drugs or alcohol but to gambling, shopping, TV itself, or even sex (an especially curious addiction, one must observe).

If TV is "addictive," let us then compare it to the other addictive substance which is not only legal in our society but subtly promoted by it, in ads, mythologies, and general behavioral standards: alcohol.

There *are* alcoholics. There are men and women whose lives are defined and circumscribed by an organic compound without which they find that they simply cannot function. For these people the substance is a living death, and the only escape is total abstinence.

But there is a far greater number of people for whom alcohol is a palliative and perhaps a not destructive enhancement of life. As my wife observes, there is a vast difference between someone who wakes up and thinks, "I want *alcohol!*" and someone who at 5 P.M. thinks, "A martini would be nice." (Did any of McKibben's neighbors, one wonders, wake up thinking, "God, I get to watch and tape *television* all day!"?)

And there are people for whom the drug—and alcohol *is* a drug—is, more than an enhancement, a perceptual tool. Some people can use the booze—knowing its dangers and side effects—to make their internal and social lives richer and more productive. The only necessary ingredients for them are self-consciousness and control.

The same hierarchy, I suggest, obtains among TV watchers. It is surely possible to become a "Simpson"-style couch potato, imprisoned by the endless wash of images, immobilized, imbecilic, impotent. But most people are probably not quite so addicted: They know how to use the off button and they watch only those shows that give them some sort of pleasure. Our anti-TV pundits notwithstanding, they have lives of their own beyond the glow of the set.

There are even those for whom TV is a cultural experience no less nor more rich than poetry, music, or drama. The "complexity" of an art has to depend, after all, upon the complexity of the observer's intelligence. If you can watch *Hamlet* stupidly—and a number of very distinguished people have—then possibly you can watch *Gilligan's Island* intelligently, perhaps even notice that *Gilligan's Island* is actually a version of the pastoral romance of *As You Like It* or *The Tempest.*

In fact, when considering *individual* television viewers, one can be quite optimistic. Anybody with a little intelligence, self-awareness, or irony can manipulate TV rather than be manipulated by it. But if you consider the "sociology" of TV viewing, that optimism may be strained. There do seem to be groups of TV watchers caught in a typology as inflexible and harsh as the old class system was once thought to be. Certain types of viewers *are* particularly vulnerable to the Tube—children, illiterate or semiliterate people, poor people. TV provides their major source of information, and they have fewer alternative resources by which to measure its distortions. Certainly the three major networks, during their long domination of the airways, showed a crass cynicism in marketing programs that targeted these groups even while reinforcing their marginalized self-image. Detective series, for example, from *I Spy* and *Hawk* in the 1960s to *Matlock* and *Miami Vice* in the '80s, attracted African-American audiences by featuring a black detective who was invariably a sidekick of or lesser partner to the white detective. Today, MTV addresses an adolescent audience to whom it presents a picture of teenage life dominated by fashions and consumerism, fast in body and shallow in thought. The demagogic possibilities here are exactly Kozol's burning concern.

The avuncular Federal Communications Commission (FCC) has belatedly recognized the dangers of TV: it has prohibited cigarette commercials on television and, more recently, required stations to post "warning labels" on programs featuring excessive violence. It is a bit unrealistic, however, to expect the FCC to protect the more vulnerable groups of TV viewers from themselves. I would rather place my hopes on cable TV, which has grown explosively during the last 20 years. Today there are nonnetwork channels that are not merely aimed *at* but are actually produced *by* and *for* nonmass audiences—Spanish-language channels, channels with African-American news, channels for gays, and channels for senior citizens—which break the networks' old dominance and, as it were, democratize TV. When such "marginal" groups speak to themselves about their own concerns, paradoxically they cease to be marginal and enter into the public discourse. And let me disagree with Jonathan Kozol one last time: The coming developments of "interactive TV" can only enhance this democratization, as the technology grows beyond the clumsily "authoritarian" mechanisms of its early stages.

I conclude with a true story. In 1992, HBO ran a series of sleazy documentaries called *America Undercover*. In one episode, "The Best Hotel on Skid Row," a young, heroin-addicted prostitute was interviewed sitting on the bed in her flophouse room with her boyfriend, an older wino. She wanted to get off junk and into a methadone clinic, but at the time there was no room available. In the middle of the interview she broke down crying. Her boyfriend looked at the camera and said, "Will you turn that thing off?" But the camera came back on, obscenely, a moment later, over their shoulders, while the broken little guy hugged his friend and tried to console her for the—what?—terribleness of existence.

Never mind that the cameraman and the director filmed these unhappy people against their will. That little fellow—like the young man who stood before the tanks in Tiananmen Square—is a model of ethics in the age of mass, TV culture. He knew where to find the off button, and how to use it, even against itself. More than any of the critics we have discussed, he understood that TV neither saps our humanity—nor allows us to give that humanity up.

19 IN SEARCH OF THE CYBERMARKET

DOUGLAS GOMERY

That crashing noise you keep hearing in the distance is the sound of Big Deals collapsing on top of Big Hype about the information superhighway. In 1993 regional telephone company Bell Atlantic and cable giant Tele-Communications Incorporated (TCI) announced their $15 billion marriage, the largest corporate merger in history, and promised us all the moon and the stars—a new era of faster and better communication, international interactive bridges, more high-tech jobs, and an information-fueled economic expansion lasting into the next century. This was only the biggest and fanciest of a string of shotgun weddings that were announced as corporations scrambled to get in on the imminent arrival of the superhighway. The deals included a $4.9 billion union of Southwestern Bell and the Cox Enterprises cable company, and a $12.6 billion AT&T takeover of McCaw Cellular Communications.

The hype approached the dimensions of hysteria. Several months before the Bell Atlantic–TCI merger was announced, John H. Gibbons, a science adviser to President Bill Clinton, declared, "Information highways will revolutionize the way Americans work, learn, shop, and live." Alan Kessler, head of 3Com Corporation, predicted that the infohighway "will collapse time and space, erase cultural boundaries and move continents and people closer together." In January 1994, Vice President Al Gore promised that the National Information Infrastructure, as he calls it, will "educate, promote democracy, and save lives."

Now many of the deals have come undone, the fragility of the dreams—and especially the economics—underscored by the fact that the big Bell Atlantic–TCI deal was wrecked in part by federal regulators' decision to trim

Reprinted from the summer 1994 issue of *The Wilson Quarterly.*

cable TV rates slightly. Some sort of information superhighway will certainly be built, skeptical dismissals of the "superhypeway" notwithstanding. But it now seems clear that a certain modesty about our expectations for when it will be built and what it will accomplish is in order.

A generation ago, futurists heralded the coming of cable TV in terms very similar to those being heard today. In 1971, the foundation-backed Sloan Commission on Cable Communications predicted that "Cable technology, in concert with other allied technologies, seems to promise a communications revolution. . . . The potential of cable television in the service of formal education— that is, as part of the school and higher educational system from kindergarten onwards—has been universally acclaimed." Our metaphors are as old as our hype. In 1972, writer Ralph Lee Smith published a book called *The Wired Nation,* arguing that the United States should use cable TV as an "electronic communications highway." By the 1980s, Smith was predicting that Americans would be learning at home, corresponding by electronic mail (E-mail), and scanning far-off libraries in search of information.

Cable TV has arrived, but it is not very close to what was imagined or hoped for. A tiny minority of Americans are now doing the sorts of things that Smith and others talked about, but not through cable TV. Smith's wired nation is basically a one-way televised street, with plenty of mass entertainment, some new information, and little in the way of formal pedagogy. The big networks still dominate. Despite a few success stories (CNN and C-SPAN), there has been no flowering of "serious" TV programming. All-opera and all-ballet cable channels have come and gone, and the state of public-access TV, which was supposed to have given us a new electronic commonwealth, is summed up by *Wayne's World,* the fictional public-access show hosted by two teenage heavy-metal music freaks in the hit film of the same name. Perhaps the biggest surprise on cable is the success of QVC and other home-shopping networks, which ring up $3 billion in annual sales. After 20 years, cable TV is a lot less like an information superhighway than an entertainment supermarket, or, if the highway metaphor must be maintained, the traffic-clogged road down by the local mall.

The lesson ought to be plain: Technology alone does not a communications revolution make. Economics trumps technology every time. People must be offered things they want at prices they are willing to pay, and in the information arena, as in other realms of human life, people tend to want things that are not supposed to be good for them. Many of the futurists who see a new day dawning are going to be disappointed by what they find at dawn's early light. The notion that people who spend dozens of hours watching sitcoms every week and never read a newspaper will somehow be transformed into Renaissance men and women by the availability of new information services in the home seems overly hopeful, to say the least.

At the same time, to make at least a few dreams come true, it is important to lay down in the near future a general political and regulatory framework for the new system. The choices range from a more or less laissez-faire approach, favored by many in industry, to something like the regulated monopoly model that governed the nation's telephone system until the breakup of the Bell system in 1984. The first possibility would likely get the infohighway built somewhat more quickly; the second would give regulators a stronger voice on such matters as ensuring access for all. All of the competing bills now actively under consideration in Washington represent efforts to strike some sort of middle ground between these extremes. Uncertainty over what the federal government will do is one of the big imponderables forcing a readjustment of corporate timetables.

The technological force driving many of today's developments is *convergence.* Television, movies, radio, newspapers, books, and data have all in the past been composed in different media—on paper or film or magnetic tape. Today, however, all can be reduced to a single form of "information," the common language of the computer's binary code, an endless string of ones and zeroes. No longer is it necessary (technically at least) to print a newspaper on paper or to distribute a movie on film. Everything can be reduced to the same simple form and transmitted directly to—and in some cases from—consumers by wire, or, for that matter, on floppy disk or compact disc. And if film, print, and music are similar forms of "information," then the traditional divisions among industries that produce them begin to make less sense. This partly accounts for the frenzy of business mergers and ventures. "Our vision is: all forms of information, any place, any time," Michael Braun, an IBM executive, told the *Washington Post.*

The technology needed to reduce sound, pictures, and words to a common form of information already exists and is being rapidly improved. The real economic, political, and technological question is how best to deliver all this information to Americans in their homes. What makes the delivery question so confusing is that some very basic questions have yet to be settled. Will there be one "wire" to the average household or two—one from a telephone company, another from a cable TV company? What kinds of wires will they be? Fiber-optic cables can carry massive amounts of information, but wiring the nation with fiber optics would be very expensive. Since technologies exist to get more out of both the coaxial cable already strung by cable TV companies and the copper wires run by phone companies, it may turn out that the average household will have no fiber-optic connection in the near future. Or one fiber-optic and one copper connection. In theory, there are at least nine possible combinations that may answer the simple question, How will the average household be wired in the years ahead? And this is without mentioning various wireless technologies, such as direct broadcasting from satellites or by microwave technology, that have lately received reams of publicity. (Technically and financially, the odds are against these wireless alternatives.)

There is much to be said for some of the cheaper wire alternatives, but clearly the future will not have arrived until fiber connects all homes and businesses with the network. Fiber carries at least 150,000 times as much information as copper wire. Forty fiber-optic strands, each as thin as a human hair, together can carry 1.3 million telephone conversations or nearly 2,000 cable TV channels. (Parts of a fiber-optic highway already exist. Between 1985 and '92, for example, telephone companies laid some 95,000 miles of cable between cities, in new communities, and in a variety of other places.) Only with the wide bandwidth of fiber optics will the system reach its full potential to carry vast quantities of complex information.

The basic device serving consumers at home will almost certainly be some sort of hybrid telecomputer that marries a computer processor and a television screen. It will display wide-screen images, easily accommodating all of Hollywood's CinemaScope-like images without lopping off the sides. Since sound and pictures will be recorded in digital code rather than as analog magnetic waves, as they are today, they will be crisp, clear, and distortion-free. A CD-ROM component will allow consumers to store and later retrieve data, from train timetables to family photographs. The telecomputer will have a keyboard, but its interactive heart will be a semiconductor chip.

All of this will be enormously expensive. Even allowing for the fact that competition can be counted on to drive down costs, telecomputers of the sort described here will cost thousands of dollars each. When they finally become widely available, for example, digital high-definition television (HDTV) sets are likely to cost in the neighborhood of $5,000. To wire the nation with fiber-optic cable, add at least $1,000 per household, or a cool $100 billion for the whole country. That is not to mention the cost of wiring businesses, government offices, and nonprofit institutions. Sums of this size serve as reminders that, much as we like to think of the infohighway as the centerpiece of a "postindustrial" era, building it will be a very old-fashioned, capital-intensive undertaking. It will take a long time, and it will be very expensive.

Since, unlike the actual highway system, the infohighway is being built by private industry rather than government (and is likely to remain a private venture), the question of how to ensure access for all is central. The Clinton administration provides a somewhat contradictory answer. Vice President Gore told the *Wall Street Journal*, "As the National Information Infrastructure develops, President Clinton and I believe strongly that we must choose competition and protect it against both suffocating regulation on the one hand and unfettered monopolies on the other. . . . President Clinton and I are committed to making the benefits of the communications revolution available to all Americans across all sectors of society. It is a priority for this administration that every classroom, library, hospital, and clinic be connected to the National Information Infrastructure by the year 2000."

Clinton and Gore envision corporations developing the information super-highway with modest government encouragement and regulatory nudging. The administration anticipates a bimodal world. On one side, cable TV companies will begin to offer voice and data services. On the other side will be the Baby Bells (the seven regional telephone companies) and long-distance carriers such as MCI and AT&T, which will begin to offer entertainment services. There will be two (probably fiber-optic) wires into homes and businesses, provided by com-peting companies.

Clinton and Gore want the best of both worlds: the advantages of competi-tion and those of monopoly. They call for a classic cross-subsidy, similar to what the Bell system provided in the days before its breakup. Money will be trans-ferred from well-off users to underwrite services for nonprofit institutions and poor people. In this very spirit, Bell Atlantic has already announced that it will give 26,000 public schools free access to the information superhighway, paid for by profits it will make from mainstream users. But Bell Atlantic's free wire does have a catch: it will run only to the schoolhouse door. Local school systems will still be responsible for wiring inside the building, buying necessary equipment, and providing training, not inconsequential expenses in this age when poorer school districts are unable to afford new library books.

Finally, Gore insists on a "switched" system. Today's telephone system is a switched network: it allows one user to connect directly with any other user. By contrast, traditional cable TV systems are nonswitched: the same message goes to everyone who tunes in. For financial reasons, some cable providers prefer a future highway with limited two-way communication capabilities. Their experi-ence as providers of mass entertainment rather than communications further impels them toward that option. The telephone companies and infohighway enthusiasts favor a switched system. The Electronic Frontier Foundation, a self-styled public-interest group founded by software multimillionaire Mitchell Kapor, points out that a nonswitched system restricts access because there must be a fixed number of channels. With a switched network, "anyone with content to distribute—whether to one, 100, or 100,000 users—can do so without the permission or advance approval of the carrier." Such a system is essential to Kapor's "Jeffersonian vision" of the electronic future, in which every American is a potential creator (of videos, software, political tracts, etc.) and every home is a de facto broadcast studio. The unanswered question, however, is whether there will be enough demand for such active uses of the new technology to justify universal service of this kind. The Jeffersonian road could, alas, lead us to a gold-plated version of today's public-access TV.

Once all the wires and other hardware are in place, what will they bring to America's homes, schools, and offices? And who will pay for it? These are questions that, apart from a number of agreeable generalities, have not been widely examined. If you build it, they will come, seems to be the attitude of Gore and many of his fellow enthusiasts. One formulation of Say's Law, a controversial hypothesis of eighteenth-century economics, holds that supply creates its own demand. But Say probably could not have imagined a market already overwired with 80 or so cable channels per household and about to move up to hundreds of channels. Research shows that as things stand now most cable viewers simply tune out the vast majority of their choices and repeatedly view only five or six channels. (Another item from the annals of survey research that does not augur well for a high-tech future is the finding that more than half of all VCR owners have not even managed to program the time on their machines, apparently preferring to stare at an eternally flashing "12:00.")

What will Americans want from their wired world? One embarrassing truth is that plain old TV programming will almost certainly be a mainstay during the early days of the highway, and possibly for quite a long time. Only one entirely new service seems obvious to all: video on demand. It is easier to order up movies from the comfort of one's couch than to hop in the car and drive to a video store, where inevitably every copy of the latest Arnold Schwarzenegger epic has already been signed out. The video rental trade is now a $12 billion business, and the high-tech info entrepreneurs are intent on capturing a slice of the humble home-video pie. Time Warner's chief executive officer Gerald M. Levin is blunt: "People clearly want [these movies] and they are already paying for them now. All we need is a fraction of that demand."

Some other possibilities for interactive systems include home shopping, video conferencing, education at home, town meetings, video games, and home banking. Some of these are bound to fail. Michael Noll, dean of the University of Southern California's Annenberg School of Communication, observes, "[Home banking] has gone through generations of failure and failure and failure. Until we invent a home terminal that dispenses cash, home banking won't get far, except for people who want to do extra work." When *Wired* magazine asked four experts to predict when interactive TV would be widely available, two said never. (The other two said the turn of the century or later.) Yet entrepreneurs will certainly invent entirely new and as yet unimaginable kinds of products. For example, Carol Peters, one of Silicon Valley's most respected computer designers, has formed DaVinci Time and Space to develop an interactive video network for children. Blending the lure of a Disneyland-style electronic theme park with the pedagogy of *Sesame Street,* DaVinci Time and Space seeks to go beyond video on demand to provide a computerized "space" in which kids can play games, watch videos, or simply hang out on-line. Since someone has to pay, the plan is to sell advertising and provide the service free. In that respect, Da Vinci Time and Space is like old-fashioned TV; interactivity is what makes it radically new.

Leaving aside such experiments, the basic economic principle best suited to an understanding of the technofuture is simple (and uninspiring) enough: the substitution effect. If one technology is currently being used, can an interactive on-line video version do a better job? Can catalogues now printed on paper and delivered by the U.S. mail be displaced by interactive TV sales that allow customers to enter an electronic showroom? Economic logic says that business elicited by printed catalogues will go down as sales generated by TV technology increase. The big players already recognize this. The substitution effect target list, when added up, is staggering. In 1993, shopping ($160 billion), telecommunications ($150 billion), information services ($35 billion), and entertainment ($28 billion) totaled well over a quarter-trillion dollars. Yet "obvious" substitutions do not always work and experiments frequently backfire. In suburban Denver, where TCI is running a market test offering its customers movies on demand, it has found that customers like the service, but also that those who sign up simply cancel HBO and the Movie Channel, making the experiment essentially a wash for the company.

Some futurists see the germ of the twenty-first century in today's nascent "on-line" services, such as America Online, Prodigy, and CompuServe. Pay a membership fee and dial up one of these services using a modem attached to your personal computer, and you can catch up on the news, check your mutual fund investments, and chat with like-minded folks on bulletin boards devoted to such specialized topics as your hometown hockey team, office etiquette, opera, or nuclear proliferation. But so far the services have attracted only a specialized clientele of affluent, highly educated, gadget-oriented users. The total subscriber base of these three top on-line services stands at less than three million, smaller than the subscriber base of *Newsweek.* At America Online, the hottest of the services, the largest number of pioneers actually traveling in cyberspace at any one time is only about 8,000.

One sticking point is money. After a burst of keystrokes, sticker shock sobers up even the selected sample of on-line users, and thereafter those who remain on-line—the dropout rate is high—rarely again exceed their minimum monthly charge of $10–$15. It would cost hundreds of dollars per month to make full use of these services. And even at these prices, providers are not having an easy time making a go of it. Prodigy, jointly owned by Sears and IBM, has failed to turn a profit in six years.

To see what consumers want, telephone, cable, and other technology companies are testing other combinations of services in a variety of places around the
United States and Canada. Experiment after experiment so far has proved incon-
clusive at best. In June 1993, Bell Atlantic began offering movies on demand
over existing telephone lines to a selected set of employee-customers in a suburb
of Washington, D.C., with plans to extend the test to two New Jersey sites.
Results will be coming from other tests in Seattle, Omaha, Denver, Salt Lake
City, West Hartford, and various sites in California and Ontario throughout
1994 and '95. The biggest experiment is scheduled to commence at the end of
1994 with Time Warner's trial offering to 4,000 Orlando, Florida, consumers of
the world's first true "full-service network": switched, digitized, fiber-optic, multimedia, and interactive. The lucky few will be able to see any movie they want
at any time, view all current and any new TV services, shop, play video games,
telecommute, and read E-mail.

Interactivity is the heart of this million-dollar experiment. "Our new electronic superhighway will change the way people use television," declared Time
Warner's Gerald M. Levin when he announced the plan in January 1993. "By
having the consumer access unlimited services, the Full Service Network will
render irrelevant the notion of sequential channels on a TV set." In other words,
out go NBC, CBS, ABC, and Fox, and in comes Time Warner.

Yet all has not gone well. For the moment Levin has quietly placed his full-
service network test on hold; his two major software and converter suppliers cannot meet the deadline. It is one thing to display the power of 500 or so channels in a laboratory, quite another to make the future work in 4,000 homes.
William Weiss, the chief executive officer of Ameritech, one of the regional Bell
telephone companies, deserves a prize for realistic punditry for telling the trade
publication *Electronic Media,* "There are about five quantum steps between the
prototype and what the customer will eventually pay for its use."

Apart from the commercial on-line systems and the experiments by Time
Warner and other corporations, there are two other models that in interesting
ways mark out some future possibilities for the information superhighway.

To see true popular interactivity of the kind envisioned by some futurists actually working today—albeit in a crude, simplistic way—one must turn to, of all
places, France. The Minitel system links 6.5 million French households, using a
simple video screen and keyboard combination that allows users to play chess,
scan lists for bargain vacations, and chat with new friends by means of typed
messages. When Minitel was introduced ten years ago, teenagers made it a fad.
The yellow pages became passé; it was more fun to type in the requested name
and see the phone number appear magically on the screen. Punching in "3615

arts" provides newspaperlike lists of the latest movies. To order a pizza, a hip French teen no longer calls, but types "Zapizza."

Minitel works with an unassuming little box and a relatively primitive computer system. The device costs about $4 per month to rent from the national telephone company and is attached to the copper-wire (not fiber) French telephone system. This is a highway based on early-1980s technology. An American telephone company, US West, is conducting tests in San Jose and Minneapolis of a version of Minitel that links parents and schools. Minitel has the great virtue of being practical and workable, but its decade-old technology is a severe limitation.

A better-known model is the Internet. "The future will look and work like the Internet today," Vice President Gore declared recently. Started during the 1960s by the Pentagon for scientists in universities and other research institutions, the Internet has expanded rapidly in recent years. It has gone beyond the exchange of scientific studies and academic data to become a vast international network whose users enjoy such things as E-mail, databases, and specialized bulletin boards and lists where Chaucer scholars, foot fetishists, rock 'n' roll junkies, and particle physicists can converse in text. At least 15 million people in more than 100 countries are hooked up—there is no central authority, and the system's unofficial demographers have lost count.

There is much to admire about the Internet. It promotes diversity; it is truly interactive; it encourages commentary by one and all. But the Internet will not work as a mass medium in the future. There is no revenue stream (it is underwritten by the federal government, universities, and other institutions), and it requires too much time and expertise to learn and use. Indeed, in the next few years there will be a struggle for the soul of the Internet as advertisers seek to use its reach to send messages to its millions of users.

The future will not look like America Online, Minitel, or the Internet. If the information superhighway is to be for all, then it cannot (and should not) be limited by price, technological crudity, or scientific configuration. The new infohighway ought to be as advanced as possible and available to all who might like to use it. But here is the central contradiction: cost of access will be high if corporate combatants expect to rake in millions of dollars in fees. But such access fees will limit use and growth. Michael Schrage, a columnist for the *Los Angeles Times,* calculated the real cost of the new technoworld by adding up a mock monthly bill for the wired consumer of the future. His "United Multimedia's First Consolidated Monthly Statement" for two dozen on-line connections, setups, entertainment and news services, home-shopping purchases, and assorted extras came to $2,467.48—a bit of exaggeration that makes an important point. The fear that the information superhighway may be only for the well-to-do, even if every household in America is wired, is not entirely unrealistic.

Building the infohighway is the most immediate challenge, and the phone and cable companies are justified in complaining that it is difficult to figure out how to invest when no rules and regulations are in place. Congress has moved very slowly. The Energy and Commerce Committee of the U.S. House of Representatives has approved two sweeping telecommunications bills that allow cable and telephone companies to compete on a limited basis. The House Judiciary Committee has approved a conflicting version of permissible bimodal competition. Fights on the House floor, actions by the Senate, compromises, the signature of the president, and reviews by the courts await.

In the meantime, new regulatory schemes continue to be floated to satisfy the major corporate players (who desire deregulation) or consumer advocates (who call for regulations requiring universal access and affordable rates). Some sort of requirement for universal access probably will be written into law, but legislating a requirement is one thing and devising definitions of terms such as "universal" and the regulations to implement them is another. Accustomed to free access to information—television, radio, public libraries—we are perplexed by the prospect of pay-as-you-go information.

With significant technical, economic, and regulatory impediments to overcome, our multimedia future will remain unsettled for some time to come. When there is risk involved, conservative corporate America treads ever so carefully and ever so slowly. Alexander Graham Bell invented the telephone in the 1870s, but as late as 1940 most Americans did not have a phone at home and the vast majority had never made a single long-distance call. Everything about the information superhighway will continue to be the subject of vigorous debate. Hype and hysteria will continue, as will mergers and megadeals. But because of the uncertainties that remain, it will be a long time before somebody peddling access to the information future knocks on your front door and makes an offer you cannot refuse.

EDWARD TENNER

The end is NII. That's the National Information Infrastructure, of course, the amorphous web-to-be that has become an inkblot test of the national psyche. Some proponents dream of a 24-hour global symposium combining the best of Madame de Staël and Mortimer Adler, while skeptics fear a future of conference calls with the likes of John Wayne Gacy and Joseph Goebbels. Some fear a surveillance machine of the Federal Bureau of Investigation and Internal Revenue Service, others a witches' Sabbath of hackers and virus artists. And while dreamers await a fiber-optic fountain of packet-switched wisdom, naysayers expect an overflowing bathtub brew of banalities, recycled programming, and junk messages. Glimmerings of all of these things are already visible.

What will the NII really be, whatever its ultimate name? The central problem of electronic futurism is that even the most gifted pioneers miss essential features of systems to come. That is inevitable. How can we know what is to be discovered and invented without discovering or inventing it? Paul Valéry pointed this out when he wrote in 1944 that "unpredictability in every field is the result of the conquest of the whole of the present world by scientific power." Even the legendary John von Neumann, one of the fathers of the computer, did not foresee small, personal machines. As a colleague of his has pointed out, von Neumann was interested mainly in developing machines for weather prediction. Yet many of the issues that will concern us for at least the next ten years can already be seen in the operation of networks today. Much of this experience suggests that a National Information Infrastructure may be depressingly like real life.

Reprinted from the summer 1994 issue of *The Wilson Quarterly.*

The NII's promoters use a highway metaphor to describe it not only because the NII will allow individuals to travel hither and yon electronically but because the metaphor powerfully suggests other possibilities as well. Americans believe that an Infrastructure grows a Superstructure. Look what the interstate highways did. Americans are still willing to contemplate the prospect of immense wealth generated by something that has yet to be described or explained. We are all aware that hype is our birthright, that most of us are here because our ancestors believed equally extravagant promises. The fact that nobody knows how the NII will work or be financed is no great concern. Few people can describe all the workings of the Internet, but it works.

The real problems with the NII are in the Superstructure we expect. As to that, no one can safely say that an open, competitive order by itself will create the electronic promised land we hope to find. To the contrary, the benefits created so far by the Internet have come not from market-oriented firms but from enlightened monopolies and oligopolies, and these seem increasingly endangered just as the Internet is making their value clearer. Moreover, experience with the Internet today suggests that no matter what is done to promote access, electronic networking will promote elitism and secessionism as much as it does collegiality and community. The issues are, respectively, "depth" and "breadth." But first a few words about what today's Internet is.

In computer networking as in real life, results often do not have much to do with intentions. The free-spirited, cosmopolitan, decentralized Net was hatched under the wing of the cold war eagle. It depends on a technique called packet switching: cutting up data into discrete, labeled units, sending them over high-speed lines by various routes, and reconstructing them for the recipient shortly before they reach their destination. If it is a highway, it is one in which vehicles and contents are dismembered, the pieces carefully labeled for reassembly, and each sent independently to be joined again in a single unit at the destination. The packet-switching idea was put into practice three decades ago by the Air Force–funded RAND Corporation as a safeguard against the collapse of defense-related communications in a nuclear attack or other emergency. There was no master switchboard; if one node went down, data could be routed around it. The first organization to use this system was the Pentagon's Defense Advanced Research Projects Agency (DARPA), which sponsored "Arpanet" at the University of California at Los Angeles in 1969 and expanded it through the 1970s. The network soon assumed a life of its own. In the early 1980s, Arpanet split into military and civilian networks, and the U.S. National Science Foundation (NSF) began to administer the Arpanet backbone. The NSF still contracts out the maintenance of lines and equipment to a variety of telephone, hardware, software, and service concerns.

During the 1980s three developments helped networking expand. First, the NSF insisted that all faculty and students at member institutions, not just those receiving NSF or Pentagon funds, have access to the network. Second, the adoption of the Transmission Control Protocol (TCP) and Internet Protocol (IP), already embraced by the Department of Defense in 1974, gave all Internet members a common method of sending and receiving data. Third, the organizations and committees in charge of the Net allowed new members—chiefly universities and other institutions—to join at flat fees related to the number of users rather than the volume of traffic. Commercial information services such as CompuServe and Dialog can readily track the amount of time individual users spend on-line (and bill them accordingly). This is not done on the Net. Knowledge, the system implies, is good for you. Because most owners of copyrighted information are reluctant to release it in this freebooting realm, the Net may provide a very spotty view of human knowledge. But the Net is also available for extended use at a cost trifling compared to that of the commercial databases. The commercial sector is hard on browsers. The Net loves them—perhaps more than it loves readers—and that is one reason for its explosive growth.

The best thing of all about the structure of the Net is that a user need know almost nothing about who runs it, who pays for it, or how it works. When I log on to something on a faraway computer on the Net, let's say to a service called Gopher at the University of Minnesota, I am doing a number of things. From my home personal computer, connected by a modem to telephone lines, I am operating a sophisticated Sun computer in a nearby Princeton University building. (A dozen or more other users may be on-line at the same time, but each appears to have exclusive control.) That machine is linked to the university's high-speed Ethernet ring, one of two networks that circle the campus. Another Princeton computer then forwards my request to one of 19 regional centers around the country. Here the request, broken up into packets or units the size of a typed page of text, passes through dedicated fiber-optic lines to the regional center for Minneapolis, and from there to the right computer on the University of Minnesota system. Data flowing back to me from that computer follows a similar course in reverse.

The Minnesota Gopher can be imagined as a branching burrow offering the user a series of new menus. Each menu may offer from one to dozens of choices, or more. Each item may be as practical as a campus telephone book, as broad as a nationwide list of research library catalogues, or as cute as a mock dictionary of electronic smiley faces. Gopher—named after the university's mascot—is only a few years old, and it illustrates the fact that the wider and more powerful the Net becomes, the easier it is to use.

Convenience has made Net connections contagious. According to *Computerworld,* by 1994, 15 million users around the world were connected to the Net. The system's size doubles every year. And as graphics, sound, and animation supplement plain old text, the size of files transmitted is growing rapidly as well. (A digitized image for a book jacket can easily require more disk space—perhaps a megabyte of information—than the whole text.) The Net seems destined to become the main way corporations exchange data internally and externally. This is unsettling news for most of the people who have been regular users of the Net. While industrial laboratories have been members since the beginning, the Net is most uncorporate. Suits are not its strong suit. Users revel in individualism. They are proud of the absence of a central authority and, in many cases, of their ability to overcome whatever local authority or obstructions exist. Of course, that means investing a small amount of time, and often the result is that one simply finds more things to waste time on in the Net. But value is not the point. Freedom is.

The system works as well as it does for two reasons. First, at a cost of about $11 million annually the federal government modestly subsidizes the Internet backbone, the leased lines that connect regional centers, branching out to cover the entire country. Second, each Internet "site" is a network of its own, often with multiple servers (computers that supply end users' machines with programs and data), which are accessed by individuals using personal computers or work stations. Such decentralization has advantages. It allows academic departments, computer administrators, and others to make their own decisions about software and other matters, yet keeps the whole Net working together.

Behind the Net's usability and expansion is a paradox. Its agreeable anarchy rests on an efficient and unobtrusive (and largely informal) bureaucracy, just as the individualism of the American suburb and the romance of the open road require billions in tax and public works subsidies. The spirit of the Net may be self-realization through exploration of infinite possibilities and sources of knowledge. But the soaring fantasies of its users require untold subsidized person-hours. Holding up the Net is a corps of professionals paid by universities, government laboratories, and businesses, yet often doing work that benefits users elsewhere. The Internet would be useless to me and most other Princeton users, for example, if people in the university's academic computing and telecommunications departments did not troubleshoot the cables, upgrade the software, keep out the rogues (usually), and otherwise make the world safe for individualism. Other people at Princeton and other institutions develop and support the software that even proficient users need. Still others provide, free of charge, the amazing multifaceted contents of the Net: the endless supply of bibliographies and texts and data files and images. They need salaries, grants, and contracts. In other words, they need to be part of a well-funded organization.

The software commonly used on the Net comes not from entrepreneurs but from big technological corporations and academia. Unix, the Net's basic operating software—the equivalent of the personal computer's DOS or Windows—is an industrial-strength operating system written for programmers, not end users. ("User" and "user friendly" have long been disparaging words in some programmer circles.) Unix is uncompromising and unforgiving to the novice. On-line help consists of a stark, laconic glossary of commands mastered by trial, error, peer advice, and a growing number of third-party handbooks. But Unix is fast and effective once the user learns it. It should be. Bell Telephone Laboratories originally developed it for the operation of long-distance telephone switching. Barred by regulators from marketing it—these were Bell's monopoly days—the company gave the program away to educational users.

More recently, universities have developed Net programs on their own. From Columbia University comes the nearly indispensable Kermit communication software. From the University of Minnesota comes Gopher, the almost foolproof menu system for navigating the Net. The World Wide Web (WWW) is an even more flexible and powerful system for doing the same thing. A click on a computer's mouse can point a user from one document to another source containing related information—possibly on computers thousands of miles away from the one containing the original document. The Web was developed for research at the European Particle Physics Laboratory (CERN) in Geneva, big science at its biggest and best. The Mosaic software that lets me access the WWW comes from the National Center for Supercomputing Applications (NCSA) at the University of Illinois at Urbana, another elite, government-funded program.

What makes the Net so accessible, in other words, is research the public has funded in one way or another: not only through taxes but through ordinary payments for products and services, especially tuition and long-distance phone service. The cost of this research was always hidden in the prices of other things. It all seemed part of overhead, like new scales and postal meters for the mail room. Up to a point, it was. But by the early 1990s, it had become clear that the whole Net had become much more than the sum of the parts.

Now that the Net appears about to go public, the depth that helped create it is increasingly seen by captains of industry and finance as a luxury and "curiosity-driven research" as a profanity. In real dollars, industrial research and development spending has stagnated since the late 1980s, according to one estimate. A few miles from my Princeton home, one of the country's greatest research organizations, RCA's Sarnoff Laboratory, was devastated during the early 1980s when its main project, the videodisc, floundered. Other corporate laboratories are shadows of their former selves. More than ever, universities are the deep organizations of last resort for established researchers. But they have few career positions to offer young PhDs.

In the new age of the lean, "re-engineered" corporation, depth no longer counts for much. We once resented the arrogance of big science, big government, big education, and big medicine. But we respected their competence and above all their commitment to planning and standard setting. Even today, a battered IBM maintains specialized laboratories to test computers for interference with other electronic devices so that airplane passengers, for example, can use their portable computers without endangering aircraft navigation systems. The second-tier suppliers and clonesmiths of the world cannot afford such high-mindedness. It is true that for all their contributions, big, proud, securely financed organizations are not always fun to work with. They offer few bargains. But they do have the luxury of assigning people to worry about standards, systems, and details. With secure market share, they can help out weaker firms and niche producers. They also can impose private and semipublic taxation systems in the public interest. Stiff rates for long-distance calls helped the Bell system keep local residential service cheap and reliable before its 1984 breakup. The British Broadcasting Corporation's license fees supported in-house symphony orchestras. The Ivy League's stratospheric tuition permits guaranteed financial support for low-income students. These attitudes and practices are what IBM, DuPont, Merck, and others have, at least in the past, shared with the British Museum, the former Soviet Academy of Sciences, the great universities, and at different times the Benedictines and Jesuits.

The fate of deep organizations may also have a powerful affect on the content that will travel on the NII—and, for that matter, via conventional media. Thin is a polite term to describe much of what is now produced. Creating innovative, exciting projects to feed the NII will be an immense challenge. Editors and producers already struggle to find good work in conventional form. Commercial media depend not only on the marketplace but on deep organizations, with their academic salaries, libraries, and computer centers. Even so, more and more high-quality books and documentary films have shifted from the commercial economy to more or less deep, subsidized, nonprofit institutions, such as university presses and public television. And these, too, are under financial pressure that new technology will not relieve. Somehow people have to be paid to produce new knowledge.

Financiers, journalists, and even customers once respected depth, even if they did not always like the haughtiness and conservatism that often accompany it. But depth seems to be waning, and nobody knows whether institutional leanness will turn out to be technological anorexia.

Can we substitute new broad structures for depth? Can a network take the place of deep organizations? Using programs like Gopher and Mosaic, can the newly empowered masses navigate their way to new knowledge and connections? Once more, the Net is all too much like real life.

For people who belong to an existing community, whether it is a corporation or a research project involving a dozen or more universities, the Net can be a powerful tool for collaboration. Yet as communication specialist Phil Agre has pointed out in a document widely circulated on the Net, the system does not alter certain fundamental human truths. Behind electronic communications there are still the same three-dimensional people, occupying the same points in space and time, and having the same power. The Net mirrors their social structure. An "alias group" of 6, 12, 50, or more researchers or administrators seems to form a key social unit of the Net. They are another expression of what the sociologist Diana Crane has called "invisible colleges"—communities of researchers intensely concerned with the same problems, such as earthquakes in southern California. In general, the more prominent a person, the more likely that most of his or her time on the Net will be spent with these close electronic collaborators, not chatting with casual inquirers.

The reticence and indifference of much of the elite makes space for the rest of us, allowing the bright graduate students, postdoctoral fellows, and some assistant professors to shine. It encourages people from related fields to join discussions. But the silence of the Establishment also creates problems. On a science-studies mailing list (an automated bulletin board for subscribers, sometimes open to all and sometimes not) I once saw a call for action against the Acoustic Thermometry of Ocean Climate (ATOC) for using sound waves to measure possible effects of global warming in the oceans. The author predicted ear injuries fatal to thousands of whales and other marine mammals. Disturbed, I consulted a colleague and through the Net he was able to search the resources of the Scripps Institution of Oceanography in La Jolla, California, and retrieve page after page of description and environmental defense of the project. Nobody at Scripps or elsewhere had posted a rebuttal to the original item on the list—they may not even have seen it. Somebody who relied only on the list would not have enough evidence. ATOC *might* still be hazardous to marine life, but the Scripps people had a good case that it would not be. Unfortunately, the case was not made when and where it should have been.

There are excellent, balanced discussions on Net lists as well as dreadful ones. The expertly moderated Risks Digest (available as *comp.risks* on most systems offering news groups), one of the best, is an invaluable chronicle of cautionary tales and informed opinion on the hazards of computing. But in most lists, lacking participation by the best and most active minds in the field, exchanges may be irregular and turnover rapid. Flaming—the practice of sending scorching reproofs and rejoinders via E-mail—is less common than I had expected, but what might be called fading (just dropping out) is endemic. So are drift and fatigue. Where the Net excels is less in evaluating ideas than in pooling factual intelligence. It is a great place to get suggestions for a reading list on almost any subject. If one needs a reference on the origin of left- and right-hand driving rules, on the location of a nineteenth-century French artist's papers, on the refraction of light through water, or on Aristotle's rhetorical terminology, the Net is superb. But it is an impractical substitute for any other form of learning, and is likely to stay that way.

The real test of breadth, though, is not the experience of academics, writers, scientists, and technical people in discussion groups. Most of these people are connected in some way with a deep organization, even if they are independent professionals or entrepreneurs. Nor is it the medical use of networks. What the Clinton administration wants is much broader: access for all citizens and connections for all primary and secondary schools. If the old AT&T was the ultimate deep organization, the American public schools are the consummate broad organizations, curiously like the Net in their loose coordination and grouping in autonomous districts.

Americans are proud of depth but not always convinced it pays. They are even prouder of breadth, though, and the political support for the NII shows it. In a December 1993 speech, Vice President Al Gore declared that "broadcasts, telephones, and public education were all designed to diminish the gap between haves and have nots" (a debatable assertion), that the NII should do the same, and that "schools and our children are paramount." He went on to call for giving "every child access to the educational riches we have in such abundance."

Admirable as the idea of wiring all schools sounds, it is financially not a simple thing. As the vice president himself noted, only one-quarter of all schools possess even a single modem, even though one can be had for about $100. And wiring and hardware are only a small part of the true cost of computerizing. Far greater costs accrue in the time specialists spend installing, maintaining, and debugging equipment and software. Computer prices may be dropping, but these hidden costs of computing are not. Indeed, some have been rising sharply as hardware and software manufacturers discontinue free telephone support services for customers.

Setting aside such difficulties, the real challenge to breadth is the character of the educational software on the future NII. Vice President Gore seems to assume that this material already exists in "abundance." But does it? True, vast amounts of literary, scientific, artistic, and musical material can now be transmitted electronically, and more will certainly become available. Even at today's prices, a book can be scanned and digitized for under $10; a library of ten million volumes could be scanned for a price modest by Washington standards. In the near future, students presumably will be able to download great books, hear symphonies, visit the great art galleries of the world, and so forth. But the vice president may be missing the point.

Using any resource demands what social scientists call "tacit knowledge": skills and ideas that may not be recorded in written form but that arise from person-to-person learning and experience. One of the functions of computer networking at the highest professional levels is to draw on just this kind of experience. An expert radiologist, for example, may see patterns in a nuclear magnetic resonance scan sent over the Net that most other physicians would probably overlook. My colleagues in structural geology and geophysics can see things in plots of seismic data that elude even many experienced petroleum geologists. The Net lets people with a high degree of tacit knowledge share it with others at similar levels.

The anthropologist and computer writer Bryan Pfaffenberger shows in *Democratizing Information* (1989) that even for adults, using on-line information depends on tacit knowledge acquired through personal interaction, information and skills that may not be documented anywhere. Someone beginning to study a subject, whether as a schoolchild or an adult, needs these hard-to-define abilities. Learning any game or skill requires immersion in a group of people who already have the skill. Weight training can improve an athlete's game, and a flight simulator can sharpen a pilot's abilities, but machines cannot develop a skill that is not already there.

Networked information can develop and extend skills that have already been taught by schools. And many computer operations are becoming important skills in their own right. It is another thing, however, to expect networked software to replace the social world of the school as a social order of teachers and learners. We do not really know what learning is, and we do not understand why some people are so much better at teaching and learning than others. We certainly do not know how to teach a computer to teach. By brute force, today's dedicated chess computers can defeat even grandmasters in the speed game. What programs alone still cannot do is tutor an average beginner to expert level. Even if the same material is available free to all schools, students without a strong basis in tacit knowledge will benefit far less than those who have it. If the haves and have-nots are treated equally, then the gap between them will probably grow, not shrink.

When it comes to building better software for a future Net, educators are likely to find another unpleasant surprise. The better and more powerful the hardware and the greater the network bandwidth, the more expensive software may be to produce. As the historian Steven J. Ross has pointed out, the improved production values of motion pictures after World War I increased costs and helped concentrate power in major studios. Labor unions and political dissenters had far fewer opportunities to get their views into national distribution. While improving the medium, technology had helped multiply producers' expenses. In the 1990s, movies with spectacular electronic special effects, such as *Terminator 2* and *Jurassic Park,* have had the biggest budgets. Educational animation and sound are unlikely to reach the same stratosphere of cost, but software development remains both labor intensive and risky; some of today's acclaimed educational CD-ROMs have sold only a few thousand copies. The outlook for high-quality products is good, but they will not be cheap, and in one way or another they will need heavy public financing, especially if equity is a concern. How will schools that can barely afford almanacs pay for on-line multimedia software?

If the deep organizations that developed the Net are in trouble and the broad organizations do not yet provide the base that can take advantage of it, what can the future of an NII be? We already have multiplied our ability to communicate and to collaborate. Our problem, and the challenge of any future network, is that we have multiplied it all too well. Communication is the only thing in society that risks self-destruction as it is multiplied. Imagine an Infotopia in which any person or organization could send a multimedia file of any size to anyone else, at almost no charge. Infotopia would collapse almost instantly. Many people already resent junk E-mail and incipient advertising on the Internet. News groups, the discussion forums that are probably the best-known feature of the Net, are already dangerously unwieldy just because of the growing volume of traffic. That does not mean the Net itself is going to collapse, but only that selection and self-selection are going to grow.

It might be time to think again about the overused but unavoidable super-highway metaphor. Roads and networks do have something important in common. Both make it easier to work with people dozens, hundreds, or even thousands of miles away. And both thereby give you an alternative to getting along with the people next door. You can get out of uncomfortable situations. You can limit your visits to people who share your interests, biases, and outlook. And if your new space becomes unpleasant, why, you can move again. Building suburbs and exurbs is not so different from building networks.

Yes, networks can help people strengthen neighborhoods and communities. But they also encourage people to find ways out. Unhappy with your schools? Join the parents who have turned to home schooling. Teaching materials and mutual support are already available on-line, and home educators have been using electronic mail effectively to organize and lobby for their rights. Their children may learn all they need to, but the economist Albert O. Hirschman has pointed out that when the most quality-conscious users are free to leave a troubled system, whether railroads or schools, the system suffers further by losing its most vocal critics. Any future information network will help unhappy people secede, at least mentally, from institutions they do not like, much as the inter-state highway system allowed the affluent to flee the cities for the suburbs and exurbs. Prescribing mobility, whether automotive or electronic, as an antidote to society's fragmentation is like recommending champagne as a hangover remedy.

Equality, like community, can also be elusive. We have seen that much of the real business of the Net is invisible to most of the people on it, not through elitist conspiracy but through operational necessity. It turns out to be not an alternative world but an extension of the conventional world and its hierarchies. For example, the Net in its majesty grants to the faculties of rich and poor universities equal electronic means for filing grant applications, but if government panels include affiliation snobs (as they often do), all the equal access in the world will not help the first-rate applicant from the second-rate school. Electronic networks, like highways, may bring you to the door but won't necessarily let you in, or upstairs.

Why are so many people ill at ease with the administration's proposals for telecommunications law reform? It's because of the assumption that more flexible regulation will unleash investments that will open a cornucopia of knowledge. It's because of the claims that a system can assure universal affordable access *and* respect copyright as we know it. But above all, it's because of the tendency of communication to divide people as effectively as it unites them. What desperately needs attention is not tomorrow's infrastructure but the knowledge base, in depth and breadth, on which it will depend.

THE CULTURAL CONSEQUENCES OF THE INFORMATION SUPERHIGHWAY

TOM MADDOX

The coming of the information superhighway, or, more modestly, the National Information Infrastructure (NII), has reanimated America's running debate about the vices and virtues of technology. It has also reshuffled the ideological deck in interesting ways. Latter-day counterculturalists who have joined the ranks of the technological optimists, such as Howard Rheingold of the *Whole Earth Review,* find themselves encamped alongside the likes of George Gilder, the onetime apostle of Reaganomics. Even as Theodore Roszak, one of the popular prophets of the 1960s, assails the emerging "cult of information," staid members of the academic Establishment scramble to log on to the Internet. In truth, these new ideological divides are little more helpful than the old, for it is as right to be hopeful about the future unfolding before us as it is to fear it.

As technophobes are fond of pointing out, technology's effects are generally unpredictable, often negative, and almost always produced at the expense of traditional ways of life. From the technophobe's point of view, therefore, a moral, sensible response to the NII is to reject it in principle and fight against it with whatever means are at hand—to sabotage it intellectually and combat the policies that would bring it into being.

Persuasive as some of its concerns may be, such a neo-Luddite view of the NII seems beyond the pale of serious consideration. As a people we are wont to explore the paths along which our desire leads us, and it seems virtually foreordained that our desire will lead us to build and use the NII. Even after one sets aside the reflex reactions of the technophobe, however, there is much reason to feel uncertainty and anxiety over the NII. The history of electronic media, espe-

Reprinted from the summer 1994 issue of *The Wilson Quarterly.*

cially television, is a powerful reminder that new information technologies can easily be turned to malign ends. Through advertising and other means, they have been used not only to exploit our hearts' desires but to manufacture new ones. Along with the specter of greater government control over citizens' lives that becomes possible with the new information technologies, this "commodification of desire" must be considered one of the darker prospects of the NII. Add to it the inescapable unease one feels in contemplating a wired world, an almost subliminal fear of the accession of what historian Manuel de Landa, in *War in the Age of Intelligent Machines* (1991), calls the "machinic phylum"—the set of things that operate according to the machine's laws of rationality and order. To put these fears more succinctly, with the NII, it seems likely that the machines will grow stronger, as will marketers and governments.

It is possible that another, less defined group, at once the weakest and least organized and also the most numerous, subtle, and relentless, can wrest control of the NII. That is the group of each of us, insofar as we represent ourselves and not the need to consume, on the one hand, or to behave obediently, on the other—each of us as we represent what the philosopher Michel Foucault called "a certain decisive will not to be governed."

Certainly, in many situations this group has virtually no voice and no power. Against it, Foucault insisted in books such as *Madness and Civilization* (1961) and *Discipline and Punish* (1975), is the power of the modern state. And there is as well the vast array of businesses and organizations that exist primarily to sell us images of our wants and needs, to ply us with our own fantasies. Their most effective and characteristic medium is commercial television, where the advertising surrounds and overwhelms a content that, as MTV videos and elaborate "infomercials" illustrate, increasingly becomes indistinguishable from it.

The same groups can be seen working, along with others, to create the NII. Government spokespersons and telecommunications industry flacks ply the media promising manifold blessings, at least to citizens of the United States. "All Americans have a stake in the construction of an advanced National Information Infrastructure," according to a U.S. government "Agenda for Action." "Development of the NII can help unleash an information revolution that will change forever the way people live, work, and interact with each other." In *Business Week,* an MCI Telecommunications ad fantastically asserts, "The space-time continuum is being challenged. The notion of communication is changed forever. All the information in the universe will soon be accessible to everyone at every moment." All because of a dream known as the information superhighway and a vision known as network MCI. The pitchman's hyperbole and the government's bland assurances alike should tell us that we are being hustled, worked—like a crowd standing in front of the ring-toss stand at a traveling carnival.

Note the two passages' common theme of changing things forever: "communication," according to MCI; "the way people live, work, and interact," according to the government. Oddly, just here, where the hyperbole appears to be at its worst, both advertising agency and government are telling the simplest of truths: Should the NII come to pass, it will change things forever. Like the magician's showy gesture or the pitchman's barked promise, these declaiming voices serve to distract our attention from something else: in this case, the subtler, more disturbing truth that no one—neither the White House nor MCI nor anyone else—can predict the nature of the changes that will be brought about by the NII.

Consider some of the characteristic technologies of the last 100 years: the telephone, the automobile, the radio, the television, and the computer. At the time of their inception and for many years afterward, no one understood the implications of their invention and use. Sociologist Colin Cherry, writing about the history of telephone systems, says, "The new invention can first be seen by society only in terms of the liberties of action it currently possesses. We say society is 'not ready,' meaning that it is bound by its present customs and habits to think only in terms of its existing institutions. Realizations of new liberties, and creation of new institutions means social change, new thought, and new feelings. The invention alters the society, and eventually is used in ways that were at first quite unthinkable." That the automobile would become such a common killer of adolescents, for example, or the telephone a powerful instrument for the gratification of a distinctive brand of aural sexual pleasures that did not exist as such before its invention—who could have predicted these and a myriad other such things?

"Mechanical properties do not predestine the development and employment of an innovation," social historian Claude Fischer notes in his study of the social consequences of the telephone, *America Calling* (1992). "Instead, struggles and negotiations among interested parties shape that history. Inventors, investors, competitors, organized customers, agencies of government, the media, and others conflict over how an innovation will develop. The outcome is a particular definition and a structure for the new technology, perhaps even a 'reinvention' of the device."

One could write the history of the broadcast media in the United States in very similar terms. When radio stations began broadcasting in the 1920s, they sprang up almost at random and did pretty much what they wanted. "Radio" was still up for grabs; the nature of the medium was undefined. Advertisements, for example, were extremely controversial in the early days, many people (including Secretary of Commerce Herbert Hoover) holding that the airwaves should be employed for the public good, not for commercial purposes. In 1927, motivated in part by the need to keep stations on separate wavelengths, Congress created the Federal Radio Commission (FRC), directing it to regulate the radio waves according to "public interest, convenience, and necessity." This remains the standard for the regulation of broadcast media today by the FRC's successor, the Federal Communications Commission, the justification for de facto censorship of radio and television and other regulation of program content.

There were dissenters, of course. Radio preacher Aimee Semple McPherson, who in fact trampled all over other stations' wavelengths, telegraphed Washington:

PLEASE ORDER YOUR MINIONS OF SATAN TO LEAVE MY STATION ALONE STOP YOU CANNOT EXPECT THE ALMIGHTY TO ABIDE BY YOUR WAVE-LENGTH NONSENSE STOP WHEN I OFFER PRAYERS TO HIM I MUST FIT INTO HIS WAVE RECEPTION STOP

Despite her plea, the situation was becoming clear: If the Almighty wanted to go on radio, he would have to play by the U.S. government's rules. Anybody who has listened to much radio or watched much television can draw his or her own conclusions about how well those rules have served the public interest, the public convenience, or the public necessity. Whatever defects unregulated radio and television might possess theoretically, it is difficult to imagine that they would be more numerous and thoroughgoing than those of the existing regulated varieties.

The NII today is in a condition much like that of radio during the 1920s. The stakes, however, are much greater. Through the NII, it may become possible for businesses and arms of the government to acquire an intimate knowledge of every citizen—what we love and hate, what compels us and what we ignore— and with it perhaps the ability to manipulate our needs and our behavior. Every choice we make could be recorded, as could every moment of consumer bliss or image consumption. We could be profiled in terrifying detail, almost casually, as a kind of side effect of the network software. Viewed this way, the NII becomes the Panopticon triumphant, to borrow Michel Foucault's notion of a machine for constraining our desire within socially acceptable limits, on the one hand, and commercially viable ones, on the other.

The experience of the Internet suggests how this can be prevented. It shows that the individual users of telecommunications and computer technology can sometimes achieve a kind of victory by wresting control of the technology. Originally created by the Pentagon to keep defense-related computers connected even in the aftermath of a nuclear war, the Internet has become one of the prime sites of many kinds of individual and collective activity. Almost from the beginning, the Internet has served the individual's purposes with enormous flexibility—as much as, if not more so, than it has served the institutions that brought it into being. As personal computers became nearly ubiquitous during the 1980s and Internet connections commonplace, they unlocked possibilities entirely unforeseen by the technicians or the managers who oversaw the system. Defense Department bureaus found their employees swapping recipes; staid and reputable organizations of all sorts found their members or employees engaging in unlicensed and uncontrolled debate, discussing the theory and practice of sadomasochism or chatting about whatever they wished with people from all over the world. In short, while the technology (of computers and networks) made such things possible, it neither anticipated nor encouraged them, nor could it stop them.

Perhaps we can expect more of the same from the NII. If, as seems likely, there emerges out of today's struggles and negotiations over the new medium considerable freedom for individuals in their use of the NII, people will exploit it in currently unimagined and unsanctioned ways. To many people, some of what occurs will seem wasteful, disgusting, obscene, sexist, racist, even criminal; to others, merely vulgar and depressing. Some already lament the waste of network resources—or "bandwidth"—resulting from the storage and transmission of binary files of explicit sexual images or from "antisocial" modes of behavior such as "flaming" (i.e., sending abusive E-mail to an individual one finds annoying). Such practices stand as honorable evidence of that "certain decisive will not to be governed," and so we must protect them above all, as we must protect the speech that most offends us and the religious beliefs we find most stupid and repulsive.

In fact, because the new information technology we are creating seems to lend itself more readily to improvisation and freedom than to rigid planning and control, it is not unreasonable to hope for triumph. Still, the possibility remains that the NII could turn into a largely one-way street, one where "consumers" receive information but will not have freedom to retransmit or alter it. This is the "500 channels of TV" model, the worst scenario for the future because it implies an audience composed of inert consumers and passive paracitizens, easily manipulated by any technically adept spin doctors with access to the profiles. Many of today's cable television providers are eager to offer just this sort of service.

The history of American broadcast media is not greatly encouraging. Network and local programming alike have proceeded according to unspoken canons of propriety that defy adult standards of free speech and journalistic practice. As a result, we have a national standard of infantilized media, which allow necessary human chaos only as it sneaks through in the form of eroticized violence and violent eroticism, both typically subtextual, subliminal, and dishonest. If we wish the NII to escape such a malign fate, we should work toward an opaque and open NII, one that, for instance, allows universal and near-anonymous access, guarantees the individual the right (which the government does not currently do) and means to encrypt information, and provides individual control over content, both outgoing and incoming. Taken together, these technical attributes would combine to create an NII that might actually serve us without entangling us even more in the embrace of commercial and governmental forces.

Telecommunications and computer technologies are themselves also forces to contend with. Building the NII, we create a vast and productive niche for the enlargement of de Landa's "machinic phylum," worlds in which machines can grow and evolve, and this eventually may have profound implications for human consciousness. Even in the relatively primitive forms it takes today, information technology seems to encourage a fixation on virtual rather than real experience—on technologically mediated perception, not direct apprehension. It can also saturate us in a hypnotic image-repertoire that works to render us passive and dream-struck no matter who, if anyone, controls it.

Marvin Minsky, the dark knight of the information age, generally considered, along with John McCarthy, one of the founding fathers of the field of artificial intelligence, said in a speech a few years ago that he preferred virtual sunsets to real ones because the virtual sunset could be constructed so as to be perfectly enjoyable. Provocative lunacy, I thought at the time, not realizing how many people agree with him.

The virtual can seduce us because it offers the promise of being completely shaped to our wishes, while the material world remains refractory—there we suffer and die and live out fates that cannot be edited or replayed to render them more beautiful, more charming, less disastrous. The virtual worlds we can master, the material world we cannot. Even the most open model of the NII—one that does not lock individuals into passive roles as consumers and citizens—forces us to contend with this dialectic of virtual and real, and especially with the ethical dimensions of an allegiance to the virtual.

As the electronic media make us more aware of conditions around the world—or, at least, of images of such conditions—we realize how much horror exists and how connected we are to it. Thus, despite our prosperity and plenty, we find ourselves intolerably affronted by images of disease and destruction. We do not wish to see starving children or piled-up bodies as we wait for our evening meal. However, through the virtual worlds we master the horrors, discovering ways to prevent them from deeply disturbing our composure. And virtuality has a wide domain. The Holocaust becomes a museum and a Spielberg movie, a spectacle, as the Situationists say, and we watch and weep yet are strangely exultant at the end of it all, and why not? We are alive and have our technology to instruct and amuse us. Today the corpses pile up in Bosnia (or was that Croatia?) and Rwanda, and the day's bald television images and puerile narrations haunt us, but tomorrow they will have become elements of an aesthetically rewarding film.

The NII will serve us efficiently in this regard. In Wim Wenders's film, *Until the End of the World* (1992), characters become addicted to image technology, lost in reliving memories of their infancy through a device that turns their thoughts into pictures. The NII would not grant us this power, but it would put rich, complex sets of images at our command—"All the information in the universe will soon be accessible to everyone at every moment"—and thus generate the potential for its own kinds of addictions: to beautiful images and to virtuality itself.

Ultimately, the NII finds us being ourselves in the late twentieth century: caught in the web of our own fantasies, governed by forces that inscribe their orders into our being, fighting nonetheless, through a stubborn will, to manifest something like authentic individual desire. The sharp-edged technology of the NII can cut a number of ways: it can enlarge the domain of the commodifiers and controllers; it can serve the resistance to these forces; it can saturate us all, controlled and controllers alike, in a virtual alternative to the real world.

Meanwhile, most of humanity will live and die deprived of the wonders of the NII, or indeed of the joys of adequate nutrition, medical care, and housing. We would do well to regulate our enthusiasms accordingly—that is, to remember where love and mercy have their natural homes, in that same material world. Otherwise we will have built yet another pharaonic monument to wealth, avarice, and indifference. We will have proved the technophobes right. More to the point, we will have collaborated to neglect the suffering of the damned of the earth—our other selves—in order to entertain ourselves.

Yet as William Gibson says in *Neuromancer* (1984), the canonical work of cyberpunk science fiction, "The Street finds its own uses for things," the Street referring to the unauthorized, unsanctioned play of human desire. Thus, we can approach the NII in a properly skeptical or suspicious frame of mind and yet remain open to its possibilities. After all, the Internet has shown that even a technology designed to enable the military to fight on after a nuclear holocaust can be made to serve the unfettered human imagination. With this experience to guide us, it is possible, perhaps even likely, that the same can be accomplished with the NII.

FURTHER READING
TELEVISION AND NEW TECHNOLOGIES

Orson Welles allegedly once noted, "I hate television. I hate it as much as peanuts. But I can't stop eating peanuts." Like it or not, most of us are like the great actor and filmmaker—hooked.

TV comes in many forms, none more important than the news. John P. Robinson and Mark Levy's *The Main Source* (Sage,1986) takes a comprehensive look at how TV journalists communicate and how viewers respond to what they see on the small screen. "The good news . . . is that the public is far better informed about the news than most previous studies have suggested," Robinson and Levy conclude. "The bad news is that public information levels are far lower than most news workers may assume as they prepare their stories."

Shanto Iyengar and Donald R. Kinderin, in their *News That Matters: Television and American Opinion* (University of Chicago Press, 1987), find that network news influences its audience in two fundamental ways. First, it helps set the political agenda: "Those problems that receive prominent attention on the national news become the problems the viewing public regards as the nation's most important." Second, TV news "primes" its audience, setting up "the standards that people use to make political evaluations."

Television journalism began in the late 1940s and its relatively short history is lovingly summarized in Edward Bliss, Jr.'s *Now the News: The Story of Broadcast Journalism* (Columbia University Press, 1991). Bliss also chronicles the history of radio journalism in the United States, from its beginnings in the 1920s to the fabled coverage during the Second World War. An unexpected hero in *Now the News* is Dwight D. Eisenhower, a skilled self-promoter on radio, and the first "television president." Craig Allen's *Eisenhower and the Mass Media: Peace, Prosperity, and Prime-Time TV* (University of North Carolina Press, 1993) convincingly argues that Ike's tremendous popularity and grandfatherly image were all carefully crafted as he broadcast his accomplishments to the American public under the skilled direction of Hollywood actor Robert Montgomery. Although John F. Kennedy often is heralded as the first television president, Bliss and Allen tell us that Eisenhower really deserves the title, for his televised "fireside chats," stately press conferences, and dignified Cabinet meetings.

Many critics believe that TV news would be improved if practitioners more generally represented the full range of the socio-economic characteristics of their audience. In other words they want to see more women and blacks on screen as reporters and anchors. Marlene Sanders and Marcia Rock, in *Waiting for Prime Time: The Women of Television News* (University of Illinois Press, 1988), offer a curious combination of a first-person memoir by Sanders, a veteran correspondent for ABC, and third-person analysis by Rock, of New York University's School of Journalism. The result is a disturbing look at glacial change. A proper companion is Daniel Paisner's *The Imperfect Mirror: Insider Stories of Television Newswomen* (Morrow, 1989). The author compiled interviews with such noted reporters as Jane Pauley, Connie Chung, Lesley Stahl, and Mary Alice Williams, and all conclude the same sad state of female underrepresentation in the business as do Sanders and Rock: men only reluctantly give away their turf.

To viewers the most important symbols of TV news are its highly paid "anchors," stars who have increasingly come to assume the aura of moral and intellectual authority so vital to success in the ratings. Barbara Matusow's *The Evening Stars: The Making of the Network News Anchor* (Houghton Mifflin, 1983) offers a comprehensive survey of the history of the species. Robert and Gerald Goldberg's *Anchors: Brokaw, Jennings, Rather and the Evening News* (Birch Lane, 1990) is a behind-the-scenes look at the three stars of the evening-news business of the 1980s and 1990s. Their immense power, wealth, and fame, both books argue, leave anchors dangerously isolated from the real world they seek to describe and interpret.

One network—CBS—has garnered all the attention as the pioneer of today's TV news. For an insider's view, one of the best of a score of available memoirs, read David Schoenbrun's *On and Off the Air: An Informal History of CBS News* (Dutton, 1989). Based on a 17-year career, Schoenbrun lovingly details his 20 years as the CBS man in Paris. As one of "Murrow's boys," he helped make CBS the top news network. He laments that in the 1980s no correspondent covers any beat long enough to learn the ropes. The rules of current network economics prohibit anyone from remaining 20 years in Paris; indeed, by 1989 all three networks had closed their Paris bureaus.

Les Midgley, author of *How Many Words Do You Want? An Insider's Stories of Print and Television Journalism* (Birch Lane, 1989) and also one of the founders of *CBS Evening News,* offers not just a memoir, but a vivid description of the process of news making, television-style. The enormous pressure of deadlines, he says, offers those who labor in TV news no time to dig out complex stories or to reflect on the significance of events. Peter McCabe in *Bad News at Black Rock* (Arbor House, 1987), Bill Leonard's *In the Storm of the Eye* (Putnam, 1987), and Ed Joyce in *Prime Times, Bad Times* (Doubleday, 1988) simply provide more detail, defending their own roles as the "good guys" in a process gone bad.

The legend of CBS from the glory days of the 1950s, of course, begins with the fabled career of Edward R. Murrow. There have been two major biographies of Murrow in recent years: Ann M. Sperber, *Murrow: His Life and Times* (Freundlich, 1986), and Joseph E. Persico, *Edward R. Murrow* (McGraw-Hill, 1988). Both are filled with dazzling details, but Persico's book is better organized. Peter J. Boyer's *Who Killed CBS? The Undoing of America's Number One News Network* (Random House, 1988) is the best-researched single-volume account of the colossus founded by Murrow and company. Boyer, who covered TV for the *New York Times,* seems to have talked to everyone involved, past and present. Central to Boyer's story is the role of Van Gordon Sauter, the CBS veteran who held a series of important positions, landing in the early 1980s as head of news. Boyer lays out in detail how Sauter destroyed TV's most important news organization before departing for Hollywood.

The glory days of CBS news came to an end when the network was taken over in 1986 by Wall Street financier Laurence Tisch. His reign of terror—characterized by selling everything not nailed down—is well covered in Christopher Winans's *The King of Cash* (Wiley, 1995). Yet before Tisch CBS had its share of controversies. *Fair Play: CBS, General Westmoreland, and How a Television Documentary Went Wrong* (Harper & Row, 1988) by Burton Benjamin, a former vice president and producer at CBS, is the result of a request by CBS management to do an internal investigation of a documentary about Vietnam that caused William Westmoreland to file a $120 million libel suit. Benjamin found the CBS broadcast to be unbalanced but argued that critics should focus on the truth of the documentary's assertions rather than on the extent to which the producers did not meet standards of fairness and accuracy.

The most popular news show in the history of CBS, indeed in the history of television in general, has been *60 Minutes*. This newsmagazine skillfully enveloped the detective story within a shortened documentary form to examine the news behind today's headlines. Richard Campbell, in his *60 Minutes and the News: A Mythology for Middle America* (University of Illinois Press, 1991), explains the basic journalistic techniques now known as the "60 Minutes method." Campbell seems in awe of their storytelling abilities and portrays the news show as a series of mysteries, therapies, adventures, and arbitrations—all solved and resolved by the noted hosts/stars within one hour.

NBC and ABC have long-standing TV news organizations as well, although books about their operations are comparatively scarce. Reuven Frank's *While It Lasted* (Simon & Schuster, 1991) deals with NBC News, while longtime ABC network CEO Leonard Goldenson's autobiography, *Beating the Odds* (Scribner's, 1991) contains a fascinating chapter on the rise of news broadcasting at ABC. In the end, whatever account one reads of any of the three major networks, one soon realizes that TV news is just one part of a multifaceted business in which there is relentless pressure to secure top ratings and generate and sustain steady profits.

Drives for profit surely explain why TV news can craft stories out of the strangest events. Tom Rose, in *Freeing the Whales: How the Media Created the World's Greatest Non-Event* (Birch Lane, 1989), shows how even in October 1988, as a presidential campaign was in full swing and Ronald Reagan was glowing in the final hours of his presidency, the nation was fixated on the rescue of two whales trapped in the ice in Alaska. Then, "network news producers loved animal stories," says Rose. "They gave the network anchors a chance to display their warm, human side." This was a perfect made-for-television story, with little real effect on public understanding of the complexities of an ever-changing world.

TV news, on whatever network, is just one division of a corporate colossus. Thus it is not surprising that we have biographies of the great figures who created NBC, CBS, and ABC. *The General: David Sarnoff and the Rise of the Communications Industry* (Harper & Row, 1986), by Kenneth Bilby, offers a typical example of seeing history though the life of a "founding father"; Sarnoff's creation—the National Broadcasting Company—is still a leading TV channel. Sarnoff's counterpart William S. Paley of CBS tried to be more secretive and operate behind the scenes, and so has spawned a small industry trying to figure out how a Jewish American turned out so many WASPy television programs. Lewis Paper's *Empire: William S. Paley and the Making of CBS* (St. Martin's, 1987), and Sally Bedell Smith's *In All His Glory: The Life of William S. Paley, the Legendary Tycoon and His Brilliant Circle* (Simon & Schuster, 1990) offer partial answers. Paley promised a couple of memoirs but delivered only the ironically titled *As It Happened* (Doubleday, 1979). In it he proudly touted CBS-TV as "the largest advertising medium in the world" and largely ignored the TV shows millions watched on a daily basis.

But his network creation, and all that have come after, surely have influenced our lives in countless ways. Thousands of scholars have tried to divine how this impact has worked. *Television and Human Behavior* (Columbia University Press, 1978) by George Comstock and others summarizes the literature as of the mid-1970s. *Big World, Small Screen: The Role of Television in American Society* (University of Nebraska Press, 1992) by Alethea C. Huston and eight other authors does the same thing a decade or so later. Begun as a report for an

American Psychological Association task force seeking to finally settle the psychological impacts of TV viewing, Huston worked in collaboration with noted authorities Edward Donnerstein, Phyllis Katz, John P. Murray, and Eli Rubinstein. But their conclusions will leave many frustrated: TV can be both good and bad, and so we all ought to use it carefully.

Jib Fowles in his *Why Viewers Watch: A Reappraisal of Television's Effects* (Sage, 1992) is alone in trying, in a refreshingly candid manner, to assess the staggering pile of studies that claim harm to all who watch TV. Fowles's point is that most of us, whether we admit it or not, watch hours and hours of TV each month and go about our daily lives more informed and well entertained, hardly deformed or deranged. Following up on Fowles any reader can begin to gain a further handle on TV's impact by carefully examining its audiences. Ronald T. Bower's *The Changing Television Audience in America* (Columbia University Press, 1985) is a sequel to the author's 1973 study and Gary Steiner's classic early analysis *The People Look at Television* (Knopf, 1973). Using a national sample for the 1980 census (as the other two books did for the 1960 and 1970 censuses, respectively), Bower evaluates audience reactions to TV. He concluded that the public's all-embracing love affair with the tube was over. He was wrong. With cable television, people are watching more TV, suggesting it is wiser to examine what people do, not what they say.

One group that has had little place in making television, but a large place in the audience, has been African Americans. The shameful history of racism behind the camera is told by J. Fred McDonald in his *Black and White TV: Afro-Americans in Television since 1948* (Nelson-Hall, 1983). The tale is brought up to date by Jannette L. Dates and William Barlow in their edited volume, *Split Image: African Americans in the Mass Media* (2d ed., Howard University Press, 1993). Both books surely challenge the claims by conservatives that TV is a liberal industry. African Americans understand that television executives and producers may pay lip service to acting progressively, but rarely act on any liberal agenda.

The overall impact of television in society is best covered by Leo Bogart in his *Commercial Culture: The Media System and the Public Interest* (Oxford University Press, 1995). Bogart tellingly writes, "Society as a whole has a stake in every form of media expression, inasmuch as this helps to shape the outlook and behavior with which all its members must coexist. The profit-centered rules of the marketplace are not necessarily the only ones, or even the most appropriate ones, that should apply to an institution that shapes national values and character." But profit maximizing, regulated only at the margins by the Federal Communications Commission, is what we have. Lucas A. Powe, Jr.'s *American Broadcasting and the First Amendment* (University of California Press, 1987) clearly examines the FCC and makes the classic conservative argument for eliminating all government regulation and letting industries and individuals "speak" unfettered. These two studies follow a generation of deregulation, arguing that unless there is a compelling case for the failure of the marketplace, then the government (in this case represented by the FCC) has no business regulating anything.

Critics would say that with greater concentration of ownership, reduced spending on news, and complete domination of children's TV by toy companies there is a "market failure," and the FCC should continue to play a major role in television regulation. Kathryn Montgomery's *Target Prime Time* (Oxford University Press, 1990) looks at how advocacy groups influence what is shown and reported on television, with only limited success. The record in the 1990s is better as discussed in Brian R. Clifford's *Television and Children* (Lawrence Erlbaum Associates, 1995).

Although radio and television advertising has been the biggest budget item in presidential campaigns since 1928, only since George Bush's 1988 use of Willie Horton ads has the daily press taken a keen interest. *Packaging the Presidency: A History and Criticism of Presidential Campaign Advertising* (rev. ed., Oxford University Press, 1992) by Kathleen Hall Jamieson offers a good history prior to the Bush innovations. Robert E. Denton's *The Primetime Presidency of Ronald Reagan: The Era of the Television Presidency* (Praeger, 1988) deals with the political effects of television in its broadest political dimensions. Denton, like Jamieson, is no optimist. Indeed, it is difficult to find an analyst who thinks that coverage of politics and government does not need reform; fundamental is an assumption that TV, not newspapers, plays the most powerful role in American elections—*too* powerful a role.

To see how all forms of television programming have changed over the years— as interpreted by historians and communication scholars—dip into the 14-essay anthology *American History—American Television: Interpreting the Video Past* (Ungar, 1983), edited by John E. O'Connor. We can learn much about race relations in the U.S. by examining *Amos 'n' Andy* and *Brian's Song,* and much about failed radicalism from close examinations of the controversial documentaries of the 1960s such as *The Selling of the Pentagon.* O'Connor and company find that Hollywood has been the center of the production of prime-time television programming since the mid-1950s. Hollywood's history as the leading TV entertainment producer in the world is told by Tino Balio and others in *Hollywood in the Age of Television* (Unwin Hyman, 1990). How Hollywood got involved— and how New York lost out as a center of making TV—is told in scholarly detail by William Boddy in his *Fifties Television* (University of Illinois Press, 1990). One genre that has made millions for Hollywood producers—from *Dr. Kildare* to *E.R.*—has been the medical drama; this TV evergreen is skillfully dissected by

Joseph Turow in his *Playing Doctor: Television, Storytelling, and Medical Power* (Oxford University Press, 1989).

There had been literally millions of programs presented by the time TV passed its 50th birthday in 1995. But who, save the most committed fan, can even name the shows that were on five years ago, that have since faded to rerun obscurity? Fortunately, we have a regularly updated source to help us: *The Complete Dictionary of Prime Time Network Television Shows, 1946 to the Present* (Ballantine), compiled and updated every couple of years by Tim Brooks and Earle Marsh.

But by the 1990s it had become obvious that television of the past—three networks plus PBS—had ended. Cable TV opened up dozens of channels; entrepreneurs promised even more—maybe 500! There is a definite irony in trying to recommend books about the new TV technologies, but some fine tomes have appeared. One profitably starts with Anthony Smith's monumentally edited volume *Television: An International History* (Oxford University Press, 1995) which tries to situate TV in the 1990s and discern where it might be headed. Case studies abound and offer lessons for the future. No one, when it began, expected CNN to change the world of news, but it surely has. The story of how the former "Chicken Noodle Network" became the mighty CNN is told in Hank Whittemore's *CNN: The Inside Story* (Little, Brown, 1990). The man behind CNN is the subject of so much myth that it is best to get the facts straight with Porter Bibb's *It's Ain't as Easy as It Looks: Ted Turner's Amazing Story* (Crown, 1993).

We can also learn a great deal from the emergence of the videocassette recorder (VCR), which during the 1980s made movie watching at home a multibillion-dollar industry. The penetration of the VCR into American life is deftly told by James Lardner in his *Fast Forward: Hollywood, the Japanese, and the VCR Wars* (Norton, 1987). The VCR's impact, according to a distinguished group of sociologists, has been profound, as noted throughout Mark R. Levy's edited collection *The VCR Age* (Sage, 1989).

No new technology has changed modern communications more than the space satellite. Circling the globe at 22,300 miles above us are a plethora of "birds" that transmit TV signals from China to the United States to Liberia—in an instant. We are still not sure of all the implications of what they have done to our video age, but Heather Hudson has tried to figure it out in her *Communications Satellites: Their Development and Impact* (Free Press, 1990). Hudson is right to claim that satellites have changed communication as profoundly as the telegraph did a century ago.

Another key technology that has also changed TV watching is the remote control. James R. Walker and Robert V. Bellamy, Jr., gathered 16 essays about the impact of this ubiquitous device in *The Remote Control in the New Age of Television* (Greenwood, 1993).

We can also learn from failures in the past. No better example has been studied than *The Business of Research: RCA and the Videodisc* by Margaret B. W. Graham (Cambridge University Press, 1986). There were few more powerful communications corporations in the 1960s when RCA began seriously to try to create a new consumer electronics industry based on disc recordings of video images. No one would have bet that a generation later RCA would be out of the consumer electronics industry (as a brand label) and that most households in the United States would have a VCR beside their TV.

The work of an important group of scientists and futurologists trying to figure out TV's impact in the twenty-first century is detailed by Stewart Brand in *The Media Lab: Inventing the Future at MIT* (Viking, 1987). My hat goes off to Rob Shields for his *Cultures of the Internet: Toward a Social Theory of Cyberspace and Virtual Realities* (Sage, 1995), to G. F. Jankowski and D. C. Fuchs for their *Television Today and Tomorrow* (Oxford University Press, 1995), and to Steven G. Jones and his fellow contributors for their *Cybersociety: Computer-Mediated Communication and Community* (Sage, 1995). Yet they cannot all be right, and are surely not.

MARTHA BAYLES is former literary editor of *The Wilson Quarterly,* former *Wall Street Journal* reporter, and author of *Hole in Our Soul: The Loss of Beauty and Meaning in American Popular Music* (1994).

LEO BOGART is former executive vice president of the Newspaper Advertising Bureau and author of numerous books including *The Age of Television* (1956, 1958, 1973), *Preserving the Press: How Daily Newspapers Mobilized to Keep Their Readers* (1991), and *Commercial Culture: The Media System and the Public Interest* (1995).

JAMES BOYLAN is professor emeritus of journalism at the University of Massachusetts, Amherst, and founding editor of the *Columbia Journalism Review.* His books include *The New Deal Coalition and the Election of 1946* (1987), and *Mass Media: Systems and Effects* (1982).

MICHAEL CORNFIELD, a former guest scholar at the Woodrow Wilson International Center for Scholars Media Studies Project, is visiting professor of political management at George Washington University.

ROBERT DARNTON is Shelby Cullom Davis Professor of European History at Princeton University and author of *The Literary Underground of the Old Regime* (1982), *Berlin Journal* (1991), and *The Corpus of Clandestine Literature in France* (1995).

ROBERT J. DONOVAN, a former guest scholar at the Woodrow Wilson International Center for Scholars Media Studies Project, was chief of the Washington bureaus of the *New York Herald Tribune* and the *Los Angeles Times* and is author of a noted biography of Harry Truman. He is also the author of

P.T. 109 (1961) and (with Ray Scherer) *Unsilent Revolution: Television News and American Public Life* (1992).

TODD GITLIN is professor of journalism at New York University and author of *The Whole World Is Watching* (1980), *Inside Prime Time* (1983), and *The Twilight of Common Dreams: Why America Is Wracked by Culture Wars* (1995).

DOUGLAS GOMERY is professor in the College of Journalism at the University of Maryland, College Park, and a columnist for *American Journalism Review.* His books include *The Hollywood Studio System* (1986), *The Future of News* (1992), and *Shared Pleasures: The History of Movie Presentation in the United States* (1992).

ANTHONY J. LA VOPA, a former fellow of the Woodrow Wilson International Center for Scholars, is professor of history at North Carolina State University and author of *Prussian Schoolmasters: Profession and Office, 1763–1848* (1980), and *Grace, Talent, and Merit: Poor Students, Clerical Careers, and Professional Ideology in Eighteenth-Century Germany* (1988).

T. J. JACKSON LEARS, a former fellow of the Woodrow Wilson International Center for Scholars, is professor of history at Rutgers University and author of *Culture of Consumption* (1983) and *Fables of Abundance: A Cultural History of Advertising in America* (1994).

LAWRENCE W. LICHTY is professor of radio, television, film at Northwestern University and former director of the Media Studies Project at the Woodrow Wilson International Center for Scholars. He has been a director of audience research at National Public Radio, and his books include *The Future of News* and *Ratings Analysis: Theory and Practice.*

FRANK D. MCCONNELL, a former fellow of the Woodrow Wilson International Center for Scholars, is professor of English at the University of California, Santa Barbara, and the television critic for *Commonweal.* He is author of, among other works, *The Spoken Seen: Film and the Romantic Imagination* (1975) and *The Bible and the Narrative Tradition* (1986).

TOM MADDOX is writing coordinator at Evergreen State College, author of *Halo* (1991) and a science-fiction novel, and a columnist for *Lotus* magazine.

NATHAN REINGOLD is senior historian at the National Museum of American History and author of *Scientific Colonialism* (1987) and *Science, American Style* (1991).

A. H. SAXON is author of *P. T. Barnum: The Legend and the Man* (1989).

RAY SCHERER, a former guest scholar at the Woodrow Wilson International Center for Scholars Media Studies Project, was NBC's White House correspondent during the Truman, Eisenhower, Kennedy, and Johnson administrations, and is author (with Robert J. Donovan) of *Unsilent Revolution: Television News and American Public Life* (1992).

EDWARD TENNER, a former fellow of the Woodrow Wilson International Center for Scholars, is author of *Why Things Bite Back* (1996).

BOOKS SUPPORTED BY THE MEDIA STUDIES PROJECT

Cook, Philip S., ed., *Liberty of Expression*. Washington, D.C.: Woodrow Wilson Center Press, 1990.

Cook, Philip S., Douglas Gomery, and Lawrence W. Lichty, eds., *The Future of News: Television-Newspapers-Wire Services-Newsmagazines*. Washington, D.C., and Baltimore: Woodrow Wilson Center Press and Johns Hopkins University Press, 1992.

Donovan, Robert J., and Ray Scherer, *Unsilent Revolution: Television News and American Public Life*. Washington, D.C., and Cambridge, Eng.: Woodrow Wilson Center Press and Cambridge University Press, 1992.

Fialka, John J., *Hotel Warriors: Covering the Gulf War*. Washington, D.C.: Woodrow Wilson Center Press, 1992.

Gordon, Michael R., and Bernard E. Trainor, *The Generals' War: The Inside Story of the Conflict in the Gulf*. Boston: Little, Brown, 1995.

Gruley, Bryan. *Paper Losses: A Modern Epic of Greed and Betrayal at America's Two Largest Newspaper Companies*. New York: Grove, 1993.

Jamieson, Kathleen Hall, *Dirty Politics: Deception, Distraction, and Democracy*. New York: Oxford University Press, 1992.

Kimball, Penn, *Downsizing the News: Network Cutbacks in the Nation's Capital*. Washington, D.C., and Baltimore: Woodrow Wilson Center Press and Johns Hopkins University Press, 1994.

Rowan, Bonnie G., and Cynthia J. Wood, *Scholars' Guide to Washington, D.C., Media Collections*. Washington, D.C., and Baltimore: Woodrow Wilson Center Press and Johns Hopkins University Press, 1994.

Skidmore, Thomas E., *Television, Politics, and the Transition to Democracy in Latin America*. Washington, D.C., and Baltimore: Woodrow Wilson Center Press and Johns Hopkins University Press, 1993.

INDEX